IDIOT'S
GUIDES.
AS EASY AS IT GETS!

Creative Writing

by Casey Clabough, PhD

ALPHA
A member of Penguin Group (USA) Inc.

ALPHA BOOKS

Published by Penguin Group (USA) Inc.

Penguin Group (USA) Inc., 375 Hudson Street, New York, New York 10014, USA • Penguin Group (Canada), 90 Eglinton Avenue East, Suite 700, Toronto, Ontario M4P 2Y3, Canada (a division of Pearson Penguin Canada Inc.) • Penguin Books Ltd., 80 Strand, London WC2R 0RL, England • Penguin Ireland, 25 St. Stephen's Green, Dublin 2, Ireland (a division of Penguin Books Ltd.) • Penguin Group (Australia), 250 Camberwell Road, Camberwell, Victoria 3124, Australia (a division of Pearson Australia Group Pty. Ltd.) • Penguin Books India Pvt. Ltd., 11 Community Centre, Panchsheel Park, New Delhi—110 017, India • Penguin Group (NZ), 67 Apollo Drive, Rosedale, North Shore, Auckland 1311, New Zealand (a division of Pearson New Zealand Ltd.) • Penguin Books (South Africa) (Pty.) Ltd., 24 Sturdee Avenue, Rosebank, Johannesburg 2196, South Africa • Penguin Books Ltd., Registered Offices: 80 Strand, London WC2R 0RL, England

International Standard Book Number: 978-1-61564-501-5
Library of Congress Catalog Card Number: 2013957747

16 15 14   10 9 8 7 6 5 4 3 2 1

Interpretation of the printing code: The rightmost number of the first series of numbers is the year of the book's printing; the rightmost number of the second series of numbers is the number of the book's printing. For example, a printing code of 14-1 shows that the first printing occurred in 2014.

Printed in the United States of America

Note: This publication contains the opinions and ideas of its author. It is intended to provide helpful and informative material on the subject matter covered. It is sold with the understanding that the author and publisher are not engaged in rendering professional services in the book. If the reader requires personal assistance or advice, a competent professional should be consulted. The author and publisher specifically disclaim any responsibility for any liability, loss, or risk, personal or otherwise, which is incurred as a consequence, directly or indirectly, of the use and application of any of the contents of this book.

Most Alpha books are available at special quantity discounts for bulk purchases for sales promotions, premiums, fundraising, or educational use. Special books, or book excerpts, can also be created to fit specific needs. For details, write: Special Markets, Alpha Books, 375 Hudson Street, New York, NY 10014.

Publisher: *Mike Sanders*
Executive Managing Editor: *Billy Fields*
Executive Acquisitions Editor: *Lori Cates Hand*
Development Editorial Supervisor: *Christy Wagner*
Senior Production Editor: *Janette Lynn*

Cover Designer: *Laura Merriman*
Book Designer: *William Thomas*
Indexer: *Brad Herriman*
Layout: *Ayanna Lacey*
Proofreader: *Gene Redding*

Contents

Appendixes

Introduction

Creative writing is generally understood to be writing that comes from the imagination, or writing that isn't factual. It's the very fine art of making things up, in the most attractive, apt, and convincing way possible. It's the telling of lies in order to reveal illuminating and dark truths about the world and our place in it.

Some creative writing is partly inspired by real events or based on biographies or autobiographies, such as Jack Kerouac's *On the Road* or Sylvia Plath's *The Bell Jar,* and the extent to which real life and real people can sometimes directly or indirectly inform creative work. "Write about what you know" is the writer's maxim that has long since fallen into a crashing cliché—but it's a cliché for a good reason. Many writers do precisely that. Nonetheless, such creative writing remains in essence a fiction and makes no actual claim to the facts.

Creative writing came late to the educational realm as something that's written about and taught. The first textbooks did not appear until the early 1900s, and the first educational programs were developed in the 1950s. Before those years, the great writers you've heard of learned primarily by reading extensively, copying other writers, and regularly writing on their own. Today, however, creative writing is a popular area of study in high schools and colleges, and publishing it can be very competitive. At the same time, electronic media has made it possible for people to self-publish their own work. You might say we're in the midst of a transitional era between book-based creative writing and that which is published only in electronic format.

Creative writing itself has continued to evolve as well. In the 1970s, the term *creative nonfiction* came to describe a type of factual writing in which the narrator's personal involvement with his or her subject or subject matter is a common element. Likewise, events are rarely recounted in the objective way, which we tend to associate with journalism or other types of factual writing.

Who knows how creative writing will evolve over the next several decades. It's an exciting time to be a writer and to watch it all unfold.

How This Book Is Organized

The book is divided into seven parts, designed to build your basic knowledge of writing technique, the different kinds of writing, and how to go about conducting research and publishing. Ideally, all portions of the book are to be used in concert with each other in order to give you the best possible introduction to and tools for creative writing.

Part 1, You, the Writer, introduces you to the practice of and most essential elements of writing. It covers the most basic characteristics of what writing is and how to conduct it in a manner that is convincing—and that will relate to readers.

Part 2, Speech, Voice, and Point of View, discusses the importance of where the speaker is in your writing and the best ways to say things and convey your information.

Building on this knowledge, **Part 3, Character, Setting, and Types of Stories,** focuses on the people in your writing and where your action takes place, along with descriptions of the kinds of stories you can choose from when creating your own.

Shifting from craft to genre, **Part 4, Short-Form Genres,** covers the shorter types of writing you can try, such as the essay or the short story.

Part 5, Long-Form Genres, shows you ways to develop these shorter forms into book-length undertakings such as an autobiography or a novel.

Part 6, Drafting, Researching, and Editing, moves on to pragmatic matters, including various methods of composition and research.

Part 7, Getting Published, tackles the complexities of the publishing world and what techniques will serve you best in getting your work produced and read by others.

In the back of the book, I've included a glossary, resources for additional information, and a compendium of the writing samples used throughout this book.

Extras

Throughout the text, regardless of what comes under discussion, sidebars frequently appear as means of emphasizing aspects of the topic under analysis, while also offering new information, tricks of the trade, exercises to try, and things to avoid. You might think of them as a running commentary on the main text, continually offering additional aid. Here's what to look for:

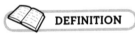 **DEFINITION**

These sidebars present explanations of what terms or phrases mean.

 IDEAS AND INSPIRATION

Look to these sidebars for pointers on overcoming a problem or improving your writing.

 WATCH OUT!

Be sure to heed these sidebars that contain warnings regarding common pitfalls.

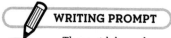 **WRITING PROMPT**

These sidebars share exercises or assignments to apply a creative writing technique.

Acknowledgments

Many thanks to Lori Hand and Christy Wagner for their invaluable editorial expertise in improving the book.

I would also like to thank the publishers who first published my writings, which serve as examples in the following chapters.

Trademarks

All terms mentioned in this book that are known to be or are suspected of being trademarks or service marks have been appropriately capitalized. Alpha Books and Penguin Group (USA) Inc. cannot attest to the accuracy of this information. Use of a term in this book should not be regarded as affecting the validity of any trademark or service mark.

You, the Writer

In Part 1, you get an introduction to the practice of and most essential elements of writing, including craft and details. It covers the basic characteristics of what writing is and how to conduct it in a manner that's convincing and will relate to as many readers as possible.

The most central of principles is that all writing is both autobiographical and invented. Although you can imagine other people and places when you sit down to write, you cannot escape yourself. You draw on your own knowledge and experiences that are particular to you. Simultaneously, everything you write is an invention. Even the most faithful account of an event is made up in the sense that it's filtered through the eyes, feelings, beliefs, and memories of one person.

Before writing courses came to exist in higher education during the 1960s, writers learned to write predominantly by reading other writers and then trying out the techniques they noticed. Because the point of this book is to maximize your writing ability without necessarily having the benefit of a class or mentor, it underscores the importance of reading widely and deeply on your own. It is also a book about doing, about educating yourself and generating good writing on your own through the use of a journal. Chapters 2 and 3 cover the use of craft and details, respectively, in helping you to create and judge your writing.

Part 1 puts you firmly on course to begin your promising writing adventure.

Reading and Writing

Creative writing is an art, and a living one at that. Language constantly is changing, and creative writers are participants in that change, whether we realize it or not, by virtue of what we write. Creative writing, therefore, can serve as a means of improvement, both for yourself and your culture.

In this chapter, you learn about the fundamental nature of creative writing and reading, what they can teach you, and how best to begin the practice of creative writing. In doing so, you, the writer, not only improve yourself, but also participate in the expression and recording of collective human existence. That's kind of a big deal.

In This Chapter

* You write from your life
* Everything you write is made up
* Learning from reading
* The "doing" of writing
* Retaining ideas with journals
* The benefits of habitual journaling

All Writing Is Autobiographical

Think of any story, novel, or movie you've read or seen. Some may have been set in other universes and incorporated highly eccentric characters. However, unless they were co-written, they emerged from the mind of a single creative writer.

You and I are shaped by the backgrounds and socialization that make us the ever-changing people we are. Your writing reflects your distinctive personality and is somewhat *autobiographical*, even if you as a writer remain unaware of it.

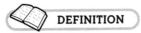 **DEFINITION**

> An **autobiographical** piece of writing is created by the writer and is about her or his own life.

The wonderful and exciting aspect of this fact is that although many individuals may share certain experiences from your life, no one else on the planet is precisely like you. Thus, even with a minimal reading background, you possess a deep well of unique knowledge to draw from in your writing that others have yet to articulate.

All Writing Is Invented

In what might seem like an opposing fact to the autobiographical background of creative writing, all writing also is invented. Actually, these two facts complement each other. Even when writing about a true event from your life, it's important to remember that it's filtered through your individual mind, set of senses, and memories, all of which are solely yours. Thus, even the truest event you might recount is still an invention in the sense that it's shaped by your unique perspective and subjective interpretation.

Invention is a fun and liberating force in writing. It means you can do virtually anything you want. Other time periods, mysterious people, and alien civilizations are all fair game. The way you choose to portray them—the nature of the writing itself—also is subject to your inventive choices and decisions.

Literally combining autobiography and invention is a key way to engage a reader because they'll realize you're doing your best to invent the circumstances of an event from your life that actually occurred. The following example, from the beginning of a book-length *memoir* titled *SCHOOLED*, attempts this approach:

I count myself among the luckiest of creatures. By nature and profession I have had the good fortune to have been a teacher and a learner for nearly my entire life. It is the best occupation I could ever hope for. I am surrounded by brilliant young people and coworkers who constantly teach me new things, and who also seem to believe there are things I can teach them. Though I have not always been so, I have become grateful in retrospect for the other jobs I've had—farm hand, trail guide, manual laborer, park ranger, bus driver, writer of semi-important speeches and unimportant manuals, among many others—and have come to love them all in different ways for the things they taught me. In the end, however, my collective experience in these employments has only served to make me treasure even more my current occupation, which I happen to consider my true calling.

 **DEFINITION**

A **memoir** is a record of events written by a person having intimate knowledge of them and based on his or her personal observation.

The autobiographical element of this example is self-evident, but the inventive quality lies in the way the author choose to frame his life and occupations. Indeed, his positive tone and the energy with which he relates his wide-ranging jobs promise to draw in the reader. This person is thankful for the nature of his life and the many different types of employment he has experienced. Why? In order to discover the answer to that question, the reader must continue reading the book.

 WRITING PROMPT

Think of an actual event from your own life. Try to inventively portray it from a number of perspectives: happy, nostalgic, remorseful. Note how the event changes as it takes shape through these different filters of invention.

Reading Educates Writers

One of the truths I have learned as someone who both teaches books to others and also writes them is that the more extensive your acquaintance becomes with the works of writers who have excelled, the more extensive your own powers of invention, your own ability to make something new and original, will be.

That might seem like a paradox on the surface, and many creative writers do view it as such. For example, I know many southern authors who refuse to read the books of William Faulkner for fear of having their own work resemble his to the point they're overwhelmed by his example and, thus, appear imitative.

On the contrary, when you read good writers—especially those whose work is close to your own in terms of content or style (or both)—your writing stands to improve a great deal as you take note of how those writers successfully wrestled with challenges that resemble your own.

 IDEAS AND INSPIRATION

When it comes to selecting what to read, try to pick out the best writers in the genre you are attempting to write. (Check online for lists of classic writers, or look at anthologies.) If you want to write short stories, for example, read the best short story writers. Take note of memorable scenes, characters, and settings. Even if you don't consciously understand why something moves you or seems to function successfully, there's a reason it resonates, which might well reveal itself to you as you work on your own material.

"Doing" Writing

Having established that creative writing is autobiographical, it's invented, and that you benefit from reading it, the most fundamental issue—and the primary purpose of this book—comes to the fore: how do you actually do it? Following are some proven fundamental approaches for producing creative writing, regardless of genre.

Perform short writing exercises. If you have trouble generating ideas or getting started, the trick is to write anyway. You'll find many writing prompts in this book, and many more are available in books and on the web. As you perform exercises prescribed by other writers, you'll find that your own ability for written expression will grow and develop. If possible, try to write every day, even if it's just for 5 minutes, and even if it's *free writing*.

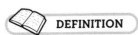 **DEFINITION**

Free writing is the practice of writing nonstop about whatever enters your mind for a set period of time without making corrections or censoring anything. Free writing helps you become more comfortable with the act of writing, makes you aware of unconscious writing ideas and potential self-censorship, and improves your formal writing.

Don't worry about lack of clarity, grammar, and general sloppiness. Even the very best writers have to revise and edit their work. After you've completed a free writing piece, leave it alone for several days. Then pick it up again, read over what you wrote, and pluck out the ideas and phrases you believe may be potentially useful in the future.

Also determine the time of day or night when you're at your most creative. For many writers, this is first thing in the morning, before all the other demands of life set in. Others write well late at night, when the rest of the day's business has been put to rest. Pay attention to when you feel most creative and alert while writing and are producing the best—not necessarily the most—work.

Finally, don't forget to have fun. Remember that creative writing is a limitless art form rather than a conventional rule-laden job or chore. You have the freedom to write whatever you want. The only boundaries are those of your own imagination.

The Importance of Journals

If you're having trouble developing ideas, and organized free writing exercises aren't proving as productive as you'd like, carry a notebook with you everywhere and write down your ideas and observations as they come. You'll discover you hear lines of *dialogue,* that may have never occurred to you, in the most unlikely of places. Moreover, a smell or something you taste could trigger a memory or observation worth pursuing at greater length. Take out your journal and jot down these observations.

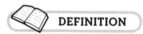 **DEFINITION**

Dialogue is a conversation between characters in a narrative.

You can also use your journal to record relevant ideas as you read other books. The inspiration you receive from other creative writers can manifest itself unconsciously in your own work. For example, here is an excerpt from a section of a writer's journal that consists mostly of quotations from other people:

> "This country is an unknown place suffering the invasion of a people whose minds have never touched the earth."
>
> —Wendell Berry, *A Continuous Harmony*

> "We all have to participate in some form of marriage in this life, and mine has been to farming and writing. ... I have made the land wait for its harvest while I have finished a book. ... To be happy on the farm the writer will need to know how to content himself in isolation."
>
> —Byron Herbert Reece, "I Grow Books and Potatoes" (*Chattahoochee Review* 27.3–4, Spring/Summer 2007: 9–12)

"The first farmer was the first man. All historic nobility rests on the possession and use of land."

—Ralph Waldo Emerson, "Farming"

"If an average person was stuck out in the thick of a forest, more times than not they are probably going to perceive the area around them as dull or even irritatingly isolated, all because of the lack of human existence. Nature is simply the 'middle of nowhere' for a lot of people. In actuality it is somewhere, and it is a very significant somewhere at that."

—student paper

"I knew what I willed to do I could do."

—Stonewall Jackson

What can you tell from the quotes this writer has recorded in his journal? Obviously he has a pronounced interest in nature and agriculture. His reading also is broad and varied. Ralph Waldo Emerson is a classic American writer, and Wendell Berry has won many contemporary humanities awards and advocated for agricultural sustainability and environmental protection half a century before it became popular to do so. The quotes of these two writers celebrate the person who knows the land—the farmer—and laments those who do not.

Then there are lesser-known quotation entries: ideas on farming and writing from regional writer Byron Herbert Reece published in a literary journal and a passage on the identity and importance of nature from a student paper. These quotes, while focusing on similar material, reveal that this writer reads academic literary journals and also peruses the papers of students. Likely he is a professor as well as a writer.

Lastly in this writer's journal excerpt come what we might call a wild-card quote: a statement on the importance of willpower by the Civil War general Thomas "Stonewall" Jackson. This is perhaps something the writer jotted down in as an inspirational or motivational reminder to keep writing.

Following this speculation regarding the meaning of this journal excerpt, let's have a look at the first three paragraphs of the published essay it eventually aided in forming. Here's the first:

A Writer's Harvest

It is often the case my farm seems to me the only sane place in this country. I take it this is because, other than my wife and some animals, no one else inhabits it. Madman, bore, or perhaps something in between, I am the primary possessor of the human agricultural perspective on a bit of earth American law recognizes as mine, but which, in reality, possesses me as one of its minor living inhabitants.

I have tried to do right by it within my significant limits, but, alas, have made enough agricultural mistakes in my life to forget most of them and curse myself in remembrance of those I do recall with a silent condemnation. Since my school days, truth be told, I have not ceased to marvel each year at the fool I have been the year before. Yet, on the extreme other side of these many active mistakes there dwells an attitude of complacency reflected in the way I sometimes idly watch the fields from my rocker, contemplating them all the while—particularly if a jug is handy. The agricultural problems and attributes of the landscape are laid out before me—the solutions to which, if any ever present themselves, destined eventually, in retrospect, to be reckoned ignorant and those of a fool. The former version of me, the doer, is something of an innovator (however meager his rate of success); the latter, the muser, a leisurely pragmatist with a practical, rather than idealistic, penchant for strategizing an approach to something that may never occur. I will be the first to admit my perspicacity often is suspect and misspent, but then trial and error are part of the farmer's (as well as the writer's) trade.

Both in the title and first paragraph you can see how this writer's published essay was shaped by elements of the quotes in his journal. The use of *writer* and *harvest* in the title summons the journal's general thematic focus on writing, nature, and agriculture. Moreover, at the end of the first paragraph he comes full circle and likens the practice of trial and error to both agriculture and writing.

Now for the second paragraph:

I have chosen to write briefly on my agricultural identity for a number of reasons, not least of which is to combat ongoing negative stereotypes of farms and farmers. In popular culture farm life frequently continues to be characterized as stagnant, dull, parochial, stupid, and backward, largely on account of its hard remitting toil. As with all stereotypes, each of these qualities may prove true depending on a given farm. Yet I also find each one of them problematic with regard to my own agricultural background and observations. As one who has traveled a bit, I would take special exception to the first pejorative word—"stagnant"—by noting simply that all excursions are relative and carry with them their own inherent limitations: life remains life wherever one idealizes and experiences it, even in transit or within the space of a few square miles. Moreover, I would assert the other characterizations primarily arrive from the observations of those who either suffered tragically in their agricultural upbringings or who failed, sometimes willfully, to discern the value of a farm's many underlying nuances.

This paragraph provides the writer's motivation for penning his essay and again, the journal gives you clues by identifying other writers (Berry, Breece, Emerson) who strongly believed agriculture was worth defending.

WATCH OUT!

If you are drawing on quotes from your journal that come from the published writings of others, be sure to use them as inspiration—applying their value in your own words—or to give credit to the writer who came up with the quote. In the second paragraph of "A Writer's Harvest," the author abstracts the earlier ideas on agriculture to the twenty-first century. If he were to simply use them verbatim, without crediting the earlier writers, he would be guilty of plagiarism and subject to potential legal prosecution.

Now for paragraph three:

> One simple fact is that the labor farm life demands of an individual usually is to the purpose of the betterment of the self, literal and artistic. "Work is the law," wrote the painter da Vinci. "Like iron that lying idle degenerates into a mass of useless rust, like water that is an unruffled pool sickens into a stagnant and corrupt state, so without action the spirit of men turns to a dead thing, loses its force, ceases prompting us to leave some trace of ourselves on this earth." Work delivers people from evil, or at the least lessens the evil they would do, in most any vocation. In farming, seasonal changes, the almost imperceptible lengthening and shortening of light hours, and variable weather make its undertaking a constant and rigorous exercise in observation, planning, and critical thinking. There is always something different to do, and it may demand to be done very quickly—as during harvest—or at a more leisurely rate (the mending of fences in winter comes to mind).

Here, the essay transitions into the idea of work—or *doing*. (There's that word again.) Although writing is not mentioned explicitly, it remains implicitly present in the essay because a powerful association between writing and farming already has been established.

In addition, a quote from the well-known painter Leonardo da Vinci is employed to help strengthen the writer's perspective on personal labor. Interestingly, however, it did not appear in the writer's journal, meaning he must have encountered it or sought it out at a later juncture. What does come from the journal, though, is the Stonewall Jackson sentiment: that possessing the gift of willing yourself to do something, whether you feel like it or not, is an enviable advantage in farming, writing, and most any pursuit.

Making Journal Writing a Habit

We creative writers must write: freely, openly, and without regard for future implications. And you, as a writer, must keep what you write, however *hyperbolic*, outrageous, or sloppy it might seem at the outset. Your journal is the primary reservoir for your ideas and observations—some eventually useful and others perhaps not. Time and the context of what you're working on will reveal which of these categories a given entry eventually falls into.

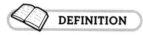 **DEFINITION**

> If something is **hyperbolic,** it has been exaggerated or enlarged beyond what's reasonable.

Similar to free writing, journal entries need not concern something you're working on. On the contrary, they can articulate your feelings about the overall endeavor of writing or perhaps your reactions to what others have written about work you've presented in a workshop or published someplace.

By way of example, here are a few entries from my own writing journal. I no longer advocate these thoughts, but they were necessary for me to write at the time:

> The opinions of other people, including academics, seldom matter to serious writers. I know English professors who haven't and likely never will produce a book, yet pompously spout off on how others should go about their writing. Who would ever take such a person's ideas on writing seriously? No-count critics and academics always will be envious of a serious writer's production. That is because they believe they understand the writer's work and fancy they somehow could fix its perceived shortcomings, and make it better by applying their past training and the various highly structured systems of thought they champion. Ironically though, for all their knowledge, it is simply not within their means to generate successful creative work. If it were, then they would do so rather than sitting around nit-picking and attacking what a more talented person developed using the powers of their mind and soul.

That passage lays it on heavy and pummels the literary intelligentsia, and you know what? That's totally fine. Journals are great mediums for airing frustrations with rejection or the areas of the creative writing undertaking you find personally unpalatable. I no longer agree with this sentiment, but at the time, it was both necessary and cathartic to write. Moreover, things in the writing profession, as in life, have a funny way of coming full circle, so who knows when it may become relevant again and find its way into a publication.

You'll find that your own work occasionally gets attacked in a writing workshop or, if published, by a reader or reviewer. Your journal is a good way to express your reactions in a healthy manner without responding to your critic(s) publicly. Here's another somewhat hot-blooded journal entry I once wrote in defense of two of my books that I no longer feel strongly about:

> Believe it or not, there actually are people out there who can't stand the fact that I created *The Warrior's Path* and *Confederado,* and thus bitterly take issue with aspects of those books. It baffles me that some people seem to want to live in a fantasy world where my work exists in the public domain and I should do as they say regarding the direction my writing and career take. My response to their delusion is simple: if you don't enjoy my artistic vision, then don't read the books. You have

that right, but you don't have the right to control my artistic vision. The great thing about producing creative work in this country is that you can do whatever you want without having to answer to others. Your only limits are the limits of your mind and spirit. Who could ask for a better gift or vocation?

Here, the journal entry takes on a more constructive response to criticism, as opposed to the earlier one, which might seem haughty or aggressive. It abstracts my books and the people who have taken time to criticize both them and my career to the universal purpose of creative writing. Regardless of what happens or how readers react, you remain free to express yourself as long as you're alive and possess the drive to write. In this sense, even the most negative criticism a writer can receive remains a by-product of the gift of free expression via creative writing.

This observation on the limitless freedom of writing extends itself, in another entry, to an idea about fundamental existence and the way in which our planet currently is organized:

> It is important for Americans to realize that the end of our finite little society is not the end of the world. The so-called western nations could all disappear suddenly and the impact would be negligible on the rest of humanity. In fact, in some ways the world would be better off. It is true that an apocalyptic end could arrive for us at any moment, but those who believe abstract powers like magical entities, extraterrestrials, or other deity-like beings are going to save them are clinging to a mass delusion.

This entry constitutes an existential declaration to live for now in light of the uncertainness inherent in our lives. Many of you may disagree with these expressed sentiments—in fact, there are parts of this entry I no longer agree with—but the point is that they were on my mind at the time and I felt compelled to record them.

Likely, this entry never will be extracted into a published work, but it serves as an example that, even for published writers, not all journal entries are going to prove useful or even helpful. Yet that only should encourage you to write in your journal *more* because the more you record, the greater your chance of generating material that's useful to you at some point.

 **WRITING PROMPT**

Having perused my journal entries on responding to writing criticism and contemplating how to live in the world, begin keeping your own journal. Write anything you like, but if you find yourself stuck, perhaps begin with responses to my last two entries.

I have every confidence that as you continue to keep your journal, both writing in it and working on your more formal pieces will become increasing easier. Even when you're at your best, writing is rarely effortless. In fact, even with several books to my credit, I still have days when the terror of the blank page gets the best of me or what I record proves utterly useless in the long run.

However, as I have continued reading and writing over the years, those days have become fewer and fewer. True, it can be frustrating, but the key is to stick with your writing and keep doing it. The best writers I know possess greater quantities of relentless determination than raw literary talent.

The Least You Need to Know

- Your own life is the genesis of your writing.
- Made up material exists in all writing.
- Writers are educated by the things they choose to read.
- It's essential that you "do" or perform the act of writing.
- Make it a habit to use a journal to record quotes, ideas, and observations.

Compelling Craft

Creative writing is the art of using words. That statement might seem simple, but it's actually a truth so profound, many writers never get down to it. And it's so subtle, many other writers who think they see it never, in fact, really comprehend it.

As an author, your business is with words. The practitioners of other arts, such as music and painting, deal with ideas and emotions, but only creative writers have to deal with them purely by means of words. Words are your raw material—your tools and instruments—to afford your ideas and emotions expression. Yet they remain limited to the extent of their expression, and their expression is limited to the extent of your skill in the use of words.

Skill—or what creative writers refer to as *craft*—counts and is always worth its cost in time and labor. Many beginning creative writers have an erroneous notion of the significance of the phrase *literary craft*. Many imagine it necessarily includes the idea of pomp, stateliness, magnificence, lyricism, richness, elaboration; that it's something beyond, and in addition to, accurate, lucid description. It's true, these elements sometimes may be present in good craft, but they're by no means essential. When you express the mood you want to

In This Chapter

- Utilizing your senses
- The danger of unfocused writing
- The peril of summarizing too much
- The importance of determining

convey with accuracy, lucidity, and sincerity, then—consciously or unconsciously—you have practiced good craft. Craft is the result of self-expression, of being your genuine self for the reader via the appropriate use of words.

In this chapter, I show you methods of improving your *craft* by attempting to capture in words what your senses convey to you, by learning to recognize the dangers of generalizing and summarizing too much in your writing, and by knowing how to judge when your craft has been applied appropriately. Many beginning creative writers overlook the importance of craft in the interests of getting on to what they conceive of as the bright promise of their narratives. Here you learn that craft is not only crucial in generating your writing but also in reading it—that is, appreciating when it's truly good or perhaps needs some improvement.

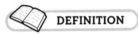 **DEFINITION**

In this book, **craft** refers to a proficient skill in the art of making something. Here, it's creative writing.

Using the Five Senses

How often do you use your five senses in everyday life? Most all the time. How often do most creative writers use them when writing? Probably not enough.

The senses are the most amazing craft tool available to a writer, yet they're also the most underused. I believe this is due mostly to simple forgetfulness. Writers tend to overlook some of the senses when they render descriptions. However, frequently including them enriches your writing and makes it more vivid and lifelike.

Arguably the most important tool in creative writing is observation. When you want to convey anything, you must highlight the colors, people, situations, and everything else around you by bringing your written world to life. More importantly, you use your five senses to convey to your reader a sense of *belonging* within your writing.

Observation brings in the five senses:

- What can you hear?

- What can you taste?

- What can you touch?

- What can you smell?

- What can you see?

Using your senses is important to enable your reader to vividly experience your writing. Readers want to see and feel the world you envision—the background, the people, and the places. Readers want to smell the scene—what odors are there? Can you describe what the hint of a newly bloomed lilac is like or fecund garden greens simmering in a pressure cooker? Can your reader hear what you're evoking—a dump truck depositing a load of gravel, a young woman angrily yelling at her lover, or the gentle stirrings of a Chopin melody drifting down from a second-story window? Do your characters speak in individualized voices and tones?

Can your reader taste what you have in mind? For instance, if your character is walking along a beach, can your reader taste the salt in the air? If your protagonist is in a pub, can your reader taste the subtle flavor of milk in the character's pint of stout?

Lastly, can the reader feel the various elements of your writing? Touch can convey powerful emotion and accomplish much without the aid of dialogue. What about the softness behind a cat's ear or the smooth quality of a lover's skin? Touch heightens feeling in ways other senses cannot.

As we examine how each of the senses can be useful to your writing, keep in mind that it's possible for your work to become overly sensual—to the point that it bogs down the *pacing* of your writing. If, for example, a character has just had a shouting match with her boss and proceeds to run down some stairs and out of a building, it's best not to dwell on the polished mahogany railing or the staircase's stained and frayed yellow carpeting. Given the circumstances, a simple "she rushed down the stairs and out of the building" will do.

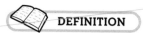 **DEFINITION**

Pacing is the speed at which action takes place in writing.

The Sense of Sight

Because you normally see action within your mind when you write, observation is perhaps the most used of the five senses. Of course, for you, the challenge is to express what you see mentally, to translate the images to the page.

Remember that what your character sees is what your reader sees, and if you fail to describe very much, your reader won't fully appreciate what you're trying to describe. What does the character see? What's in the background? What's in the foreground? What surrounds them?

Here's an example from the beginning of a novel titled *Confederado,* which casts the reader into the action primarily by way of observation:

> Every time the hell bent little mare took a curve of the narrow wagon rutted woods road, Alvis Benjamin Stevens felt as though the animal was a splinter's breadth from losing her footing and sending both of them sliding and tumbling into the mud and puddles of brown water passing beneath. It had been hard riding for what he figured the better part of seven miles. But as the trail straightened out and firmed in the midst of ascending a bald rise, Alvis took a chance to wheel and consider his pursuers.
>
> It was a graceful maneuver, man and horse wheeling as one, the man as much the animal as the horse the man. All the more remarkable since Alvis Stevens was tall and rode high in the saddle. He had the look of the countryside about him: sun-browned skin and tangled hair that stirred in the wind like stalks of wheat. Hunted as he was, there was no panic in him and, indeed, one might remark that he moved with the natural ease of a hunter himself—that he likely had been a hunter of many things over the course of his young life, men not least among them.

In this passage, the reader receives quite a few vivid observations, despite the fact that the character is fleeing and the pacing is brisk. Despite the galloping, the reader is able to see brown mud passing beneath, and—when the horse wheels (a pause of sorts)—that the character is an accomplished rider, has been outdoors a great deal, and possesses hair the color of wheat—that is, it is blond. Such details lend depth to what's occurring and offers clues about the character without getting in the way of the fundamental action.

 IDEAS AND INSPIRATION

One way many creative writers negotiate pacing and observation is to focus on one before the other and then determine which works best. Does a narrative in which action is established before the visual details are added work better, or is the reverse true? In my experience, the answer depends less on the kind of writer you are and more on the material you happen to be working with.

The Sense of Smell

The sense of smell can invoke powerful memories: a certain perfume might remind you of a former love, or perhaps it's a lingering trace of Lucky Strikes cigarette tobacco or the strong odor of freshly mown grass. Smell often is an overlooked sense, but it contains the power to provide potent detail to your writing.

Here's an example from a creative nonfiction piece titled "Satyr" that demonstrates how smell can be employed:

> The first time I ever took notice of her was in a class—the subject of which now escapes me—in which the discussion had drifted fancifully off topic toward the question of whether there was more grass covering the planet or more sand. Though I was dozing in the back, as was my custom, I remember one of the serious, scientifically-inclined boys asserting there most certainly was more sand on account of the size of the world's oceans and that most all their deep dark floors were covered with it. But to this Emily—that was the girl's name—responded with something to the effect that those same deep recesses might instead lie covered in a dark waving grass that required almost no light: a grass that no one probably had ever even seen but that likely was as tall as trees and stood in stands that rendered miniscule the earth's greatest prairies. Miles beneath the undulating surface, she maintained, it moved like corn in the wind.
>
> The class had laughed at her when she had finished conveying her deep ocean vision and though I believed their opinions meant almost nothing to her, she had blushed nonetheless. I myself said nothing, did not move even from my drowsy reclining position, but in that moment Emily had won me as a devoted admirer and friend.
>
> And we did become friends, our bond sustained by the most unlikely of variables and exchanges. I admired, for instance, how she smoked in the bathroom between classes, yet was never actually caught doing so even though everyone—teachers, janitors, students—knew her as the culprit. I liked the way in which the rancid tobacco odor would drift across the room to me in the one class I had with her. A student or two sitting close to her occasionally would wrinkle their noses in disgust at the smell, but for me, assigned to a seat on the far side of the room near the back, the wandering smell was a way for her to reach me. When it wafted my way and entered my nostrils it was as though she was sitting beside me so that we might witness the farce of yet another high school class session together.

Although this excerpt begins with seeing (both Emily and the underwater vision she describes), it's the odor of her cigarettes that intimately defines Emily for the speaker. When the smell of the tobacco reaches him, it's as if Emily herself inhabits a special proximity to him. Moreover, the smell of the cigarettes is used to augment her difference. Just as her unique oceanic vision is met with scorn by her classmates, so her singular smoking garners disgust from those sitting near her. For the speaker, however, Emily's imagination and smoking are linked and define, in part, his deepening affection for her.

The Sense of Hearing

Most of what your reader hears comes from your dialogue, but that's just one aspect of hearing. How many sounds other than talk can you hear within a given scene? What sounds can you conjure? Is there a distant train whistle? Perhaps a cacophony of car horns to represent the chaos of a bustling city. How about the irregular lapping of water against a boat? All these sounds have the capacity to deepen the realism of a given scene.

In the following example—the beginning of a creative nonfiction piece called "The Skeleton Woman"—the sound of a sports car engine arguably plays as important a role as the dialogue:

> "Tell them I am going to show them what they are." This from my mother while dropping me off at primary school.
>
> She'd agreed to come to Parent Show and Tell Day but we had to report to the teacher what our visiting parent would be talking about. I leaned forward to hug her and she kissed me on the forehead. I always looked up at her, reluctant to go.
>
> "Go on now," she'd say after a moment.
>
> But once I was out of the car I'd always turn around and wave, as if the hug and the kiss hadn't been enough. She would smile a warm, slow smile and then shoo me on with a flick of her wrist.
>
> I'd walk away slowly so long as I could feel her eyes on my back. But when I sensed them move and heard the car pull away, I would stop and walk back, watching as she pulled out onto the road in front of the school. Her car was very loud and rumbled like a faraway storm. Unless a teacher made me move, I would wait listening until it reached the place half a mile away where the speed changed from 25 to 55. Then I would hear the sudden burst of sound that came when Mama stomped the floor. She didn't know it, but that was her real daily goodbye to me.
>
> "Go Mama!" I would say in my mind and wonder if she heard me.
>
> Her car was an old Mercury Cougar she'd bought years ago, before she quit her job. It had an engine called a V8, like the drink I liked.
>
> "It's getting old, like me," she'd say sometimes, "but it's still got plenty of power. More than three hundred horses' worth."

Not unlike the way in which the smell of cigarettes forms a connection between the speaker and Emily in "Satyr," the sound of the Mercury Cougar functions as a basis of attachment between the boy narrator and his mother.

Yet the significance of the sound does not end there. The engine is very powerful, and the mother likes to drive fast, suggesting the car and the sound it makes may be a reflection of her personality. Moreover, the V8's sound is compared to faraway thunder, which suggests *foreshadowing:* it's possible something stormlike may occur later on in the narrative.

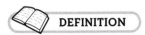 **DEFINITION**

Foreshadowing is a usually subtle advance hint of an action that will occur later in a narrative.

The Sense of Taste

Taste is perhaps the most neglected sense in writing. Eating can be a shared, sensual pastime. If your characters are eating, some of your readers will want to be involved and have their taste buds aroused, too.

The next time you write a scene with characters eating, hint at what they taste and how it might affect them. What do you liken Chilean cabernet to as your character sloshes it about his mouth? How about Colt 45 malt liquor? What does the vegetarian character taste when she bites into a sausage-filled quiche prepared by her prankster host? Are the brownies overcooked and rough against the top of a character's mouth, or are they warm and gooey?

Keep in mind that taste isn't just about food. During a passionate kiss, what do a character's lips taste like? Are they sweet, bitter, or fruity? Even something seemingly mundane like licking an envelope before sealing it can deepen overall narrative realism.

In the following passage, drawn from a creative nonfiction book titled *The End of the Mountains,* a man is on the run in the Smoky Mountains. As you read, take note of the roles food and taste play in the excerpt:

> The shadows were growing long when Columbus forsook the game trail and ascended the nearest ridge, where he knew the air would be warmer. He had been on the lookout for rock outcroppings in the hopes of discovering an overhang or cave. He had seen none, but he had discovered a bed of early ramp shoots near the game trail where a spring faintly welled up—one of those small natural pockets in the Smokys where the ground keeps moist and warm year round. The ramps he could eat, though they would intensify his odor.
>
> In a stand of towering hemlocks he ignited his fire with rock, dried leaves, and brittle pine needles. The rising smoke, meager as it was, was thinned by the thick heavy boughs above. He had been fortunate to come across a roughly bowl-shaped rock and this he had filled with water where the ramps grew. When the flames were strong enough he sat the rock atop them and waited for the ramp leaves to soften, setting his boots and socks near the fire and scooting forward so that his feet and lower legs were closest to the heat.
>
> A meal solely consisting of ramps most often would be deemed wanting, but after weeks of the terrible cavern soup, they seemed to melt in his mouth and revive him with their powerful freshness and warmth.

In addition to the freshness, warmth, and boiled softness of the ramps, the taste of the food described here is important for educating the reader about a unique regional dish. Ramps are leafy wild onions with a strong, garliclike odor. Seldom consumed in other parts of eastern North America, they constituted a common food item for poor mountain people. In the excerpt, a dish that would taste repugnant to most twenty-first-century readers comes across as a delicious meal for this hard-pressed mountain man.

The Sense of Touch

Touch is another neglected sense. Unless you can describe the feel of something within a scene, you aren't involving all the readers' senses. Can you describe the feel of a character's thin cotton dress, the grittiness of sand, or the sting of salt against the skin? Or what about the feel of cool water around your ankles as you walk through the surf in early October? If a character is touching something, don't be afraid to describe it.

The following example, drawn from a creation nonfiction piece titled "Home Court Advantage," demonstrates how something as mundane as a gym floor can amaze a person who comes into contact with it—especially eighth-grade boys from a poverty-stricken school system about to play a basketball game:

> Arrival. Off the bus and through heavy school doors into a lobby-like area, cheerleaders ahead of us, peeling off in search of a place to practice their hops and yells.
>
> Then through another set of heavy doors and into a ...
>
> And here language fails us, the dim tangerine venue before us unlike any athletic facility we ever have encountered. A basketball court to be sure yet covered end to end by an orange carpet, made to appear even oranger by the weak sunburst light in which it is cast, emanating in conical shafts from bizarre hanging ceiling lights resembling black suspended jet engines. The wanting illumination also conspires to irregularly shroud sections of the bleachers and walls in darkness, affording the peculiar impression that in certain places this place spans indefinitely into some black dimension, elsewhere and forever.
>
> Coach, speaking as we gape, looking back from yet another door he's shoved open. "Stay here, fellas. I'm gonna see what locker room they want us in."
>
> Tye, first to recover, gaze dropping to the floor, kicking at it. "What the f--- is this?" Then looking up, eyes wide, lips parted in wonder. "It a f---in rug, man!"
>
> And Lonnie, crouched on bended knee, prying and hacking at the surface with his white, deer-bone-handle knife. "It's some tough s--- for sure, fellas. My blade can't do nothin with it."
>
> Tye, yanking the ball bag away from the little benchwarmer whose duty it is to tote it, tilting it so that a basketball spills forth. We watch as it bounces on the floor—not so high as it would on a normal court and accompanied by a curious sound: heavy, muffled, and hollow all at once.
>
> Lonnie, addressing us all. "This is some weird s--- right here, fellas. It ain't even their school colors. Who puts a big 'ol orange rug on a basketball court?"

Scooby. "Maybe their principal's some kinda f--."

Meanwhile Tye, bouncing the ball slowly, head bobbing as he follows it, face cast in a rare studious expression. Then looking up in wonder. "Check it out yall. My dribble be soundin all funny and s---."

Lonnie, flick of the wrist, knife rotating end over end toward the floor, striking the carpet, bouncing once, then abruptly going motionless and dead. He bends over, swooping it up irritably. "Man, this court is stupid. I ain't never seen the like."

And Me, silent through it all, peering around: noting the placement of the wall outlets, the barely discernible lumpy weld patterns on the big steel frames above the goals, the low hum of the orange lights shaped like jet engines, and the gentle billowing of the raggedy old cobwebs hanging here and there from the ceiling girders like tiny ghostly banners.

Then, kneeling down, gently tracing the rough irregular bristles with a forefinger, deciding I like it.

For these youngsters, the texture of this gym floor—the fact that it's inexplicably covered by a carpet—is made all the stranger by their delinquent educational status and adolescent age. In the wake of one student bouncing a ball on the carpet and the other ineffectually hacking at it with a knife, the speaker, running his finger over it, concludes that he likes it for the very reason his teammates are uncomfortable with it: because of its novelty. It's the sense of touch that leads him at last to this opinion.

IDEAS AND INSPIRATION

Keeping all five senses in mind as you write is something of a tall order, especially for beginning creative writers. So one of the best ways to remind yourself of them is to keep a writing-prompt note on your desk or computer that asks: What can I see? What can I hear? What can I taste? What can I touch? What can I smell? You don't have to overload your narrative with all the senses, but employing some of them, especially in key scenes, is important. Poor description gives the reader nothing, but great description necessarily involves successfully conveying the senses.

The Power of Abstractions

As demonstrated by studying the uses of the senses in craft, good creative writing relies on detail. Yet that's not all it depends on.

Description has many types. *Abstractions* are broad forms of description that provide an overall idea of what's being described. They should be used sparingly in your writing because they don't usually paint a strong enough image for readers. They also often rely on *telling* as opposed to *showing*.

 **DEFINITION**

Abstractions are condensed, general ideas or concepts in a piece of writing.

Consider, for example, the sentence, "He was nervous as he approached her door." Notice that instead of actually showing how this fellow feels through action and detail, abstraction simply tells you. Yet it's still a description, and not always an inappropriate one.

It's true your writing should mostly contain concrete detail if you want to create vivid images for your readers. However, when you use concrete detail, you draw attention to something. Therefore, you don't want to use particular detail when describing something of little significance. In those instances, you're better off using abstractions.

Consider this brief excerpt from the creative nonfiction piece "Coaches":

> Coaches: those curious beings of authority, both of the academic places where they practice their art and yet also, simultaneously, somehow apart from and beyond them. Teachers and professors tend to view them—sometimes rightfully so—as muscle-heads and clods. If they glimpse them at all, it is usually stalking across some field or ducking into an office or locker room. There is perhaps something unsettling, even threatening, in the ability of coaches to cultivate desire and exert power over their charges in a way mere teachers cannot. And if they are winning coaches they are much better known to the community and the world at large than an institution's finest teachers and deans, even its president. Yes, more profitable to retire to your books and papers, teacher, than ponder the irrational power and influence of a skilled coach.

In this passage, details are neglected in favor of establishing the concept of coaches, as opposed to teachers, in scholastic settings. Later the piece summons specific coaches in great detail, but first it establishes the abstract idea of them for readers who may not be familiar with coaches.

The Function of Generalizations

You might think of *generalizations* as siblings or cousins to abstractions. Like abstractions, generalizations tend to ignore detail in favor of broad ideas. Moreover, they apply to many examples. For instance, the statement, "Creative writers spend many hours working with words" lends itself to a host of ways in which writers conduct their craft. In other words, a generalization is formed from a number of examples or facts and what they have in common.

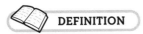 **DEFINITION**

Generalizations are broad statements that apply to many examples.

Readers recognize and evaluate generalizations made by an author; they make and support their own generalizations based on reading a particular selection. Certain clue words support instruction for generalizations: *all, none, most, many, always, everyone, never, sometimes, some, usually, seldom, few, generally, in general,* and *overall*. Attentive readers are able to evaluate if a generalization is adequately supported by specific facts.

Here's an example from the opening of a short story titled "The Succubus and I":

> It has been noted that supernatural events are not so much uncommon as irregular in their incidence. There may be, for instance, not one marvel to speak of in a century, and then there arrives a plentiful crop of them: monsters of all sorts swarm suddenly upon the earth, comets of curious color and trajectory blaze in the night sky, while shadowy mermaids and sirens beguile, shapeless *sea creatures* engulf passing ships, and terrible cataclysms beset humanity as a whole. The event I am about to recount, however, was not one in a great host, nor was it apocalyptic in its implications. Yet the very fact that it arrived in a most quiet time of enlightened scientific assurance and affected but one man may prove what makes its telling worthwhile.

Although no clue words appear in this passage, a phrase that performs a similar function—*a plentiful crop of them*—does. It's followed by a gathering of assertions designed to sway the reader to accept the generalization that strange occurrences often arrive in waves. Yet the reader must decide if the author's assertions are convincing enough to justify the generalization.

The Importance of Judgment

The reader's decision mentioned in the preceding sentence leads to the important question of *judgment*. Like abstractions and generalizations, judgments neglect details in favor of overarching concepts. Judgments usually focus on evaluating what your writing is and what it should be. This can be quite tricky because it's often based more on a writer's or reader's personal opinions and biases than on verifiable evidence. At its worst, if judgment does not accept what a piece of writing is, it cannot see how the work may be improved.

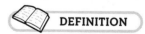 **DEFINITION**

A **judgment** is the act of evaluating if your writing is achieving its potential.

Outright negative judgments consist of sweeping generalizations: "The entire thing is crap; it's hopeless, pointless and irrelevant; the characters are flat and uninteresting; the plot is unbelievable and trite; the language is hackneyed and cliché." Criticism of the work often slides to scathing indictments of the writer: "I'll never be able to do this right; I don't have what it takes; s/he is a hack." To top it off, negative judgment assumes that what's wrong is so wrong, it cannot possibly be made right.

Positive judgments, while often more helpful and certainly more pleasant, have the capacity to be detrimental as well. Sometimes they make sweeping generalizations that the writing is perfect just the way it is. There's no need to revise or improve because the work has magically achieved perfection on the first attempt. Whereas negative judgments deny the possibility of improvement, positive judgments can dissuade any need for improvement.

The challenge, then, to make your judgments useful is to focus on observations that open possibilities—that free you to explore and expand your repertoire. Ideal judgments allow you to improve your current work and develop the craft skills you need to keep growing as a creative writer.

Short-sighted judgments offer mere preliminary evaluation and then reject (as bad) or inflate (as good) based on that incomplete evaluation without ever fully seeing, understanding, and accepting what is. Useful judgments, on the other hand, simultaneously accept the work as it is and appreciate what it can be—that is, how it can be improved. This acceptance allows a discerning person to evaluate writing honestly and make effective changes.

It's a tricky balance, but you need to find it within yourself to be both critical and accepting at the same time. It's from such a perspective that the best improvements emerge.

The Least You Need to Know

- Employ your senses in your writing so your reader can, too.
- Abstract writing favors concepts over details.
- Generalizations in writing can be bad, unless they're backed up.
- Judging your writing should involve both acceptance and critique.

Dynamic Details

As the cliché maintains, "The devil is in the details." The right mix of them can be the difference between a scene nearly diabolical in how unforgettable it is and one that might be found in any number of hundreds of long-obscure, out-of-print books—bland, vague, forgotten.

Details ground the reader in a scene—in an era, a locale, a tone or feel. They create instant identifiers and evoke memories and feelings in the reader that then connect the reader to the narrative. One or two well-chosen words of detail can do more for a scene than long phrases of description or yet another exchange of dialogue. The details can create an instant image in the reader's mind. And with that image comes one or more emotions: anxiety, hope, lust, well-being. Writers can take advantage of this instant identification to create powerful scenes by employing just a few mere words. However, they need to be the *right* words.

This chapter shows you how to go about rendering your details effectively. It covers the differences and uses of them that are "concrete" and those referred to as "significant." As in the previous chapter, I again address the importance of judgment because a writer can easily become overly detailed. Lastly, I offer techniques for how to make your writing seem more real and lifelike through the use of details.

In This Chapter

- Writing concrete details
- Creating significant details
- Judging the quality of your details
- Ways to make your writing seem lifelike

WATCH OUT!

Details can be overdone. Too much detail means nothing stands out. Instead of defining every little object, highlight what's important and let the reader imagine the rest based on what you've already supplied. Including detail does not mean you need to identify every item with a description or brand name. Be specific, yes, but don't overdo. Naming brands for every object in a scene is unrealistic and quickly distracts the reader from your work.

A Concrete Core

Concrete details are specific details that form the core of a piece of writing. If you think about it, most people don't use enough concrete details in everyday speech to really tell you anything that's especially particular. They have the specifics in their mind, but they either don't want to take the time to relate them or they don't know what's important to tell.

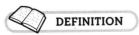

DEFINITION

Concrete details are the factual, descriptive details that form the foundation of a piece of writing.

The creative writer has to be the opposite of the everyday person. You have to describe almost everything: an object, its shadow, a person's slightest gesture, the temperature of the breeze, the scents in the air. You can always cut back if it's too much, but you can't make that decision until you have the details down on the page. And cutting is almost always easier than adding.

Concrete details invite the reader into the world you're creating and let them see what you see, taste what you taste, hear what you hear, smell what you smell, and touch what you touch. Remember the importance of evoking the senses (see Chapter 2)?

Of course, a writer has to be selective, too. You can't put in *everything* or the pace of your piece will grind to a near halt and the reader's expression will shift from one of wonderment to a deep yawn. If you describe the bark of a tree, the shape and shine of the leaves, the root structure, or the scent of its blossoms or needles or leaves, you've given the reader a picture of a whole forest. However, if you fail to use the most provocative words in doing so, your writing will be greeted by that readerly yawn and the sentiment that it's "just a tree."

The art of choosing the concrete details to build your images is one that takes practice. The best way of testing whether you've got the proper balance is to read your written details out loud to someone and watch to see if they lean forward in their chair to absorb more or they begin to nod off, head drooping. If you look up from your pages or laptop to discern an open-mouthed snore, it's time to delete some details.

The following example from the novel *Confederado* recounts the protagonist of the book's first experience of combat:

> As news of the impending attack spread along the line, the men, the majority of them as green and raw as Alvis, looked at each other uncertainly, as if asking the same question and then gleaning a common answer, which arrived to them all in a sinking, empty feeling that some horrible end had been foreordained and lay in the nature of all things. Their eyes, shifting from the uneasy glances they exchanged with comrades, fixed themselves upon the line of the wood below them.
>
> When movement came, however, it was not charging, blue-clad figures but rather a scattering of rabbits and fluttering birds, even a doe, bursting forth from the edge of the trees and hurtling toward them, only to veer aside, left or right, once they apprehended the peculiar, unnatural line of men along the hilltop. Following the eruption of forest creatures occurred a strange, heavy stillness. Alvis's heart jumped involuntarily and then momentarily seemed to cease. A chill passed along his spine and through his hair. He felt as though, even if he wanted to, he could not cry out or utter even a whisper. The only sound was that of his own pulse, steady in his head like the loud ticking of the grandfather clock in the hallway outside the parlor when he napped on the horsehair sofa after Sunday dinner.
>
> "May God give us victory," someone muttered, the men pressed so close together it was impossible to determine who.
>
> "And may all glory go to Him, and none to man," Alvis rejoined, thinking of his mother, his voice sounding stronger than he felt. A soft chorus of Amens followed and those whose heads had bent briefly now raised them back to their rifles, a single hope housed within many wills.

The details in this excerpt are numerous and rich. They have to be because they're describing a life-altering event: a young soldier's first time preparing for live combat. It's true that the amount of detail here slows the pacing, but that's acceptable given that fast-paced violent action will shortly follow. Indeed, the slow pacing actually helps build the reader's anticipation for what's to come.

Also notable in this sequence is the fact that the reader is given access to the interior consciousness of one young soldier while also receiving a more general impression of those around him. The details of his feelings are shared but remain his own. As a result, the reader is able to experience the singular chill that passes through the protagonist but also the collective idea of "a single hope housed within many wills."

 WRITING PROMPT

Using concrete details, describe the consciousness of a single character and use it to reflect the feelings of the characters around them. Your character might be a woman at an opera, a man at a football game, or an animal of some kind experiencing a natural disaster.

Making It Significant

In order for you, the creative writer, to make your reader believe in your narrative, you "show" the reader what happens. To accomplish this, you narrate the story using *significant details*. In short, you attempt to create a dream inside your reader's mind, convincing them the story is plausible—perhaps even true—by showing, not telling. Details become significant when they articulate more regarding a person or milieu.

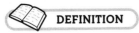 **DEFINITION**

Significant details are those that suggest something greater about a character or setting, making a narrative more plausible.

Telling statements are often far too vague for their own literary good. For example, "She was angry when she arrived home from work" gives you little significant information. We know the female in question is angry, and you can assume her anger probably stems from something that happened at her place of employment. A reader might empathize with her situation, but they can't really see or feel her anger with so few details.

You need to show how she expresses her wrath without having her "stamp her foot," which would constitute a cliché. In real life, most people demonstrate their anger by throwing and kicking things, slamming doors, cursing, crying out, and the like. They often take their anger out on inanimate objects, other people, and—if they are particularly loathsome individuals—children or pets.

I'll endeavor to make the above character appear extremely angry by supplying a few significant details for her:

> She gouged the nineteenth-century mahogany dining room table with her new BMW's trunk key; shattered the colonial-era corner cupboard's blown glass with her Pineider Milano briefcase; kicked ineffectually at her registered Siamese cat, Todd; and launched herself onto her Marshall and Stewart Cullinan bed, where she thrashed about, ripping and tearing at her favorite pillow until its goose feathers burst forth and began swirling about the room, many of them drifting up toward the ceiling fan.

While this description is over the top with details, it gives readers a vivid snapshot of this woman's wrath. More importantly, it shows readers both her anger and the degree of her wealth without telling readers, "She was both furious and rich."

IDEAS AND INSPIRATION

Just like when you employ concrete details, use significant details in conjunction with pacing. For example, the angry woman's actions constitute a brisk action scene. Even though the reader is told the exact kinds of things she punishes, her physical movements unfold quickly from one sentence to the next.

As with all details, it's vitally important to describe scenes with enough significant details to make it easy for your readers to see them. Yet it's equally important not to give them too many. Pick and choose your significant details carefully, and place them exactly where they belong, always keeping the action moving.

You might think describing a house as "beautiful" and "classy" is enough to satisfy readers. But what exactly makes it beautiful? What *specifically* makes it classy? Add enough significant details to these vague descriptions, and the house will become much more than a house. Here's an example of a distinguished home from the novel *Confederado:*

> One of the finest houses in Piedmont Virginia, Wildway was built of deep red brick and stood two stories high, though it appeared much larger on account of the fourteen-foot ceilings which defined its spaciousness both upstairs and down. The home was lent additional grandeur by its situation atop a gentle rise of ground with the foundation set in such a way that any individual peering out through a front window looked full upon Piney Mountain, a small shapely peak resting some three or four miles to the southwest. Across Wildway's front stretched a beautiful portico formed by four massive Doric columns, supporting a heavy roof of Arvonia slate. Opening upon this portico and facing the marble steps was the front entrance, over the door of which spread an ornate fanlight, and on either side of which glimmered curious broad lights, formed by numerous small diamond shaped panels. The brass knocker represented the family coat of arms while the door's massive brass knob spoke of another time. Inside, a spacious hall promised comfort to the newly-arrived guest; a long stairway ascending, on the side of which hung several skillfully wrought portraits of family personages, some of them bearing more than a slight resemblance to Alvis. The great room lay beyond a wide open entrance to the right, its mantle framed fireplace flanked by inviting mahogany chairs, upholstered in black horsehair. Yet the piece of furniture that most attracted Alvis's attention on that day as he was ushered into the room by Bocock's favorite house servant, Perkins, was a large, marble-topped table upon which stood a considerable candle stand, distinctive for its richly figured globe and cut glass pendants. As Alvis took his place in one of the chairs, a gentle methodical sound drew his gaze away from the candle stand and toward a corner of the great room where stood the large, dark-polished grandfather clock from England, whose quiet constant tick and melodious periodic chimes measured out the lives of all the Bococks and their people.

Once you've used significant details to welcome the reader into a scene, transition from describing to significant action and drama. If, for example, your main setting is a house such as Wildway, describe it once in detail but don't describe it in detail again, unless it meaningfully changes in some way. In the case of Wildway, for instance, the ravages of war destroy its splendor and transform it into a defunct shell of its former grandeur. In a later chapter, readers receive a much different set of specific details that describe the now-rundown home.

Crucial Judgments

Even in the action-adventure genre of writing, some authors (the late Tom Clancy comes to mind) tend to overdo the technical specifications of items such as weaponry—sometimes for pages at a time. Do most readers really care what the size, color, speed, shape, manufacturer, history, trajectory, and payload of a particular missile is when it's fired from an altitude of 4,800 feet with 10-mile-per-hour crosswinds pressing from the northeast? Generally, no. Most readers would rather know about the damage such a weapon renders or threatens to incur.

If you find that your writing has too many significant details, delete what isn't absolutely necessary to keep the action going. If you compare Tom Clancy's earliest books to his later ones, for instance, you find that the pacing is much swifter and works in conjunction with his details in his initial novels. However, once he developed that expectation in readers, people were still willing to purchase his later books, even if they were flooded with long sequences of significant details.

 WRITING PROMPT

Think of a place you know well, and employ as many concrete and significant details as you can in describing it. Then go back and delete the ones that seem extraneous or threaten to slow down the overall narrative pacing.

It's worth reminding yourself that, as in Chapter 2, useful judgments that pertain to details simultaneously accept the work as it is and appreciate what it can be—that is, how it can be improved. This acceptance allows a discerning person to evaluate writing honestly and make effective changes.

Making It Seem Real

Now that you've applied judgments to your use of craft and details—both of which usually are located on the more formulaic side of the creative writing spectrum—it's significant to keep in mind the general maxim that creative writing is not truth. It is an illusion; it is a lie that makes us realize truth.

When you read an excellent work of fiction or poetry, you become aware of something new about the human condition. Life, as the cliché tells you, often is stranger than fiction. Events in real life occur at random; you function every day in the midst of a million chaotic forces that conspire to shape your existence. On the other hand, events in fiction and poetry are engineered to resemble life, but they rely on craft and description to come anywhere near embodying it. For creative writing to work effectively, you must insert a dream inside your reader's mind, which enables them to suspend disbelief and believe the fictional story is plausible.

This concept brings me to the notion of *verisimilitude,* or how much truth is in a creative work. The idea has its roots in the ancient Greeks' theory of mimesis: the imitation or representation of nature. They generally believed that for a piece of art to hold significance or persuasion for an audience, it must have grounding in reality. This idea laid the foundation for the evolution of mimesis into verisimilitude via the Italian heroic poetry of the Middle Ages. No matter how fictionalized the language of a poem might be, through verisimilitude, poets had the ability to present their works in a way that could still be believed in the real world.

 **DEFINITION**

Verisimilitude is the degree of lifelike reality present in a creative work.

With the development of the novel, these elder notions of verisimilitude gave way to instruction and a pleasurable experience. A novel, although fictional in nature and fact, had to facilitate the reader's willingness to suspend his or her disbelief. Verisimilitude became the means to accomplish this mind-set. To promote the willing suspension of disbelief, a fictional text needed to have credibility. Anything physically possible in the worldview of the reader or humanity's experience was defined as credible. Through verisimilitude, then, the reader was able to glean truth, even in fiction, because it reflected realistic aspects of human life.

Applying this notion to all the genres of contemporary creative writing in a simplified way might sound something like this: the way people and events are structured are going to have to be believable, or else readers are going to call shenanigans on your work.

To underscore the importance of verisimilitude and how creative writers grope for it, here's an example from the book *SCHOOLED*. Note how the writer tells, shows, switches writing genres, and employs quotes in an effort to "get at" the verisimilitude of the material in question:

> B— died alone one spring mid-morning in a single vehicle highway wreck two weeks after I kissed her, running off the road without any cause or reason anyone could determine. Several months later, A— dove head first through an upper floor dormitory window, was withdrawn from school by her parents, and sent away, circumstances equally unfathomable, causes unknown.

*

Sitting at my writing desk, morning sun on the back of my neck, dwelling upon those occasions in my life when events have occurred that seemed already familiar—that I already somehow knew. Thinking too that my way of writing is not unlike those occasions: that I am only discovering what I already know. And that I was meant to know it all before. I am a time traveler: my past becomes my destiny in the symbols I set now to paper.

Yet another morning, at my desk, sun on my neck, forming characters slowly, gently, as a calligrapher might, with a black felt-tip pen, careful to afford them their slight leans and rounded curves, attempting to infuse them with warmth.

*

"None of the acceleration options has been shown to do psychosocial damage to gifted students as a group; when effects are noted, they are usually (but not invariably) in a positive direction."

—Nancy Robinson

*

In my waking mind, I hold their images to me.
Then I set them down in grass, push away the clouds, and summon the wind to curve round their brows like kisses.
If I were a better writer, I would breathe life into these girls.
They would play out their lost lives with my words.
If I were a better writer, I would summon them from their oblivion and give them to the world.

*

Poem given to me by B— (Spring 1992)

For all her learning, the meaning of this eludes her.
Oak leaves blown across endless fields.
The succession of lovers who have held her,
possessed of hands as soft as hers,
watching as she sleeps with eyes grown weak
from endless paper trails.

In dream she wanders empty, lonely places,
A wayward blizzard of unstable molecules,
Until a shadow being arrives to gather her,
Felt more than seen: rough, dirt-stained hands,
As gentle and as warm as the upturned ground in May.

Let's consider briefly the progression of this writer's struggle for verisimilitude. It begins with telling: mere reportage of dire events that have befallen two female schoolmates. In the next section, the reader joins the writer at his writing desk, as if the writer is inviting the reader to appreciate his challenge and help him make sense of what he has told.

The writer offers his own particular philosophy of writing, but when he forms his words, the reader discovers in the next section that they merely constitute a quote about how well adjusted gifted youngsters tend to be. Moreover, they quote is made to appear ironic when, in the next section, the writer laments the girls' adversity in a short poem and shares with the reader how he would do them justice if he were a better writer. Yet because he is not, he offers another quote in the final section: a poem given to him by one of the girls prior to her death. And indeed, this is the best verisimilitude the writer can offer, because he feels he lacks the requisite writing tools to render either of the girls himself.

Now let's consider another description of a female character in which the writer seems confident enough to present her circumstances. In the following passage from the novel *Confederado*, the protagonist encounters his eventual love interest for the first time:

> Glancing down at the old men, Alvis followed their shared gaze across the room to a circle of youths among whom stood a slender figure in a black bombazine, cut low in the neck and possessed of long angel sleeves which fell away from her arms, above the elbow to the hem of her dress. Her naturally curling tresses were raven black and glossy, and around her neck was a band of black velvet with a black onyx cross. The conspiracy between her dark beauty and unusual attire afforded her an otherworldly quality which captured Alvis's attention in a way that forced him to stare longer and harder than he intended, so that when she suddenly turned her eyes full upon him, it was apparent she had sensed his watchful look for some time.

> Having been discovered in his staring, there was nothing for it now but to approach her and make his introduction. She had turned back to her circle of friends, but when Alvis came to stand at her side she cast her frank, disconcerting gaze upon him once more. Up close she was beautiful to be sure, yet it was her eyes, her grey-green eyes, that chiefly denied Alvis attention to everything else. Their expression, though soft, blunted all inquiry or analysis. Cleopatra might have had such eyes, he thought to himself.

> "Alvis Stevens," he said, bowing slightly. "May I have the honor of the next dance?"

> "I do not make it my habit to dance with men I do not know," she replied coolly.

> "Then, by all means, let us dance and come to know one another," countered Alvis with a smile.

> "Poor, poor provincial," she mocked, but her own slight smile was inviting. "Is this what passes for cleverness among your acquaintances?"

> "I confess I have little cultivated imagination or wit," said Alvis. "I am only a plain, simple fellow, but one who can see to the end of his nose with extreme clearness."

> At this she laughed warmly and placed her hand upon his offered arm as the next song began. She moved gracefully and, in the middle of the room, danced upon feet so light as to make her appear to drift at times. Alvis, for his part, though a passable dancer, was made to feel not unlike a clumsy draft horse by comparison. The concentration her dancing exacted of him foiled all conversation, and when the song concluded he had gotten no further than her name.

She declined to dance with him a second time though she smiled at him warmly. When pressed as to her reason she grinned mischievously and replied, "Caprice de femme enceinte!" before turning from his uncomprehending face to take up the arm of a red haired confidante whom she addressed as Arabella. Walking across the busy room, heads leaned together, they giggled suddenly and looked back at him before continuing on into another part of the house. He shrugged and made for the nearest tray to collect a glass of bourbon.

To feel nervous in a potentially romantic situation is a natural human reaction, and the writer plays off that *archetype* here by turning the tables on his forward male protagonist and having him both outwitted and out-danced by the young woman.

Simultaneously, however, a certain connection is established in the way the two converse and make light of each other and themselves. This tension is something to which most all readers can relate, and the touch of humor at the end—the protagonist's inability to understand French and his decision to resort to bourbon—bring the scene's verisimilitude home with a flourish.

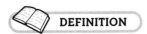 **DEFINITION**

> An **archetype** is a recurring pattern or model from which similar patterns or models are drawn. Characters, action, and even writing itself can be archetypal.

To sum up verisimilitude, remember that you need to remember your written characters and events almost as if they really exist. The reader needs to see, hear, touch, taste, and smell them. But more than that, the reader needs to "feel" that they're real, that somewhere in the universe, what you've written conceivably happened.

This form of total immersion in a piece of writing can have curious side effects. It leads to a certain level of divorce from reality, involving spending large amounts of time living in your imagination. You might even find yourself talking to your characters in your head, holding conversations with them. This might feel odd, but it's actually a phenomenon many of the best creative writers regularly experience. And if it's the price of extraordinary creative writing, it's a rather small price to pay.

The Least You Need to Know

- Be sure many of your details are concrete.
- Be sure many of your details are significant.
- Employ proper judgment when weighing pacing against the number of details you employ.
- Endeavor to have your details create a written reality that seems lifelike.

Speech, Voice, and Point of View

In Part 2, you delve deeper into the essentials of good writing, focusing particularly on the underpinnings of a writer's expression and vision. Chapter 4 tackles the types of speech you can use to create different effects in your writing. *Metonymy, synecdoche, personification, metaphor,* and *simile* may collectively sound like a dizzying array of options, but you learn how each functions and where and when they're best employed.

Strongly connected to the speech aspects of Chapter 4, Chapter 5 explores the various methods of rendering character voice. These include concepts you use in your own verbal communication, consciously or unconsciously, every day: mimicry, contrast, irony, and conflict. As with Chapter 4's speech elements, there are times and places in which the different aspects of character voice work best, and you learn what those are.

Chapter 6 focuses on point of view. This concept will be very familiar to you because *first, second,* and *third person* are among the first terms you learn in grammar class. What's different here, however, is the challenge of employing them in your writing and deciding when each is most appropriate. The essential question of distance sums up both Chapter 6 and Part 2. It's a fitting concluding concept considering how close or how far away you place your writing from the reader affects how they respond to it.

Energetic Figures of Speech

Lock and load, friends!

Why did you throw her under the bus like that?

No one's holding a gun to your head.

When read literally, these expressions are significantly violent and disturbing—especially since two of them reference firearms use. However, when interpreted as *figures of speech* (and fairly common ones at that), they lose their threatening aspects and assume the function of indirect avenues for commenting on a situation.

"Lock and load" becomes "let's get ready"; throwing someone under a bus means placing a person in a tough situation; and holding a gun to one's head refers to pressuring someone to do something, usually a disagreeable and reluctant task.

Figures of speech can be used to mean several things or even imply deeper meanings. Rather than being straightforward, they help create a different emphasis or indirect connotation. Done well, such a configuration of words makes your writing "sing" (a one-word figure of speech because words can't literally sing). Some books are full of figures of speech and can be a joy to read … as long as the author is skilled in employing them.

In This Chapter

- Making substitutions with metonymy
- Substituting with synecdoche
- Bringing objects to life with personification
- Making comparisons with metaphors
- Showing simile comparisons with *like* or *as*

DEFINITION

A **figure of speech** is the opposite of a literal expression: a word or phrase that means something more or something other than it seems to say and departs from conventional order or significance.

Many creative writers, especially poets, enjoy playing around with words. It's not surprising to discover that a great number of them read various old dictionaries for fun or play *Scrabble* rather than spend a night out on the town. In truth, whether playful or serious in nature, creative writers are performing important word usage exercises by engaging in such pastimes. Twisting words into new meanings takes the form of a game or compulsion—or both. Indeed, I find myself doing it without thinking, often while performing a repetitive physical task such as hoeing weeds in my garden or splitting firewood deep in the forest.

In this chapter, you learn about the different kinds of figures of speech—metonymy, synecdoche, personification, and metaphor—and how you can employ each to make both your content and wordplay more lively. These terms might not sound that exciting now, but what they do to your work is among the most provocative events in all of creative writing.

WATCH OUT!

As you write, you might find yourself unconsciously using a figure of speech repeatedly. There's nothing wrong with that if it fits your piece's overall style, but be cautious not to overdo it. In an attempt to make their work fresh, writers tend to enjoy creating phrases with unusual meanings. Instead of clarifying themselves, though, they may end up muddying the waters. Employ figures of speech carefully, or risk confusing your readers. Too many can make a piece of writing tedious to read and difficult to decipher.

Making Replacements with Metonymy

The pen is mightier than the sword!

Although unfortunately erroneous much of the time (and nearly always if interpreted literally), this oft-used expression is a favorite of creative writers because it empowers the act of writing and exalts the writer. Sometimes it's accurate, such as on those occasions when the words of a statesmen or political activist help bring about social change or conclude wars. But what does the statement mean figuratively? It posits that the ideas expressed through writing ultimately possess greater power than the visceral act of warfare. See? Sometimes accurate, sometimes not, but certainly catchy and clever.

Ultimately, it's less important that such an expression always turns out true and more significant that its meaning is such that readers can grasp it and admire it for the freshness it affords your writing. A thing's drab common name is colorfully replaced by its meaning or the characteristics it possesses. When creative writers perform this action, they're employing *metonymy*.

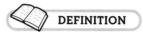 **DEFINITION**

> **Metonymy** is the act of substituting something's meaning and/or attribute for its common name.

The primary word used in metonymic expressions often is referred to as a *metonym*. Here are some common metonyms:

"The bottle" for any alcoholic drink

"The press" for journalism and journalists

"Chopin" for music by Chopin, or "Poe" for writing by Poe

"The Oval Office" for the U.S. presidency

Metonymy enables creative writers to refer to concepts or large groups of people with a single word. Although it often comes across as hip and is always at the forefront of change in the English language, it is, in fact, a very old device. Consider, for example, this passage from the first book of the Bible: "By the sweat of thy brow thou shalt eat thy bread." (Genesis 3:19) In other words, hard work (or the lack thereof) leads to sustenance (or its lack). In fact, a book of the Bible like Proverbs is in some ways a collection of metonymy at its best.

Yet metonymy also functions frequently in the most secular and nonintellectual of contemporary walks of life. A common athletic example is "That pitcher [or that quarterback] has a really good arm," meaning the athlete in question can throw the ball both hard and accurately.

Not to be left out, modern intellectuals do care about metonymy, as witnessed by literary theorists employing it to designate the process of association by which metonymies are produced and understood. This involves establishing relationships of contiguity between two things—that is, how they rely on each other.

However, because you and I are creative writers rather than scholars, our task is to happily invent metonymies or select the preexisting ones that afford our writing energy and wit, though—as the pen and the sword demonstrate—not necessarily truth.

Synecdoche Substitutions

An important kind of metonymy is *synecdoche,* in which the name of a part is substituted for that of a whole, or vice versa. An example of this relationship is *farmhand* and *worker.* The entire entity, the whole group of laborers, is represented by way of a faction of it (the single *hand* stands in for the larger group of *workers*) or a faction of the object is symbolized by the full (the larger group of *workers* stands in for the single h*and*).

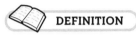 **DEFINITION**

> A **synecdoche** is **a** type of metonymy in which the name of a part is substituted for that of a whole, or vice versa.

Synecdoche also can be useful in designing memorable proper names of characters. Think of the pirate Bluebeard or the Marvel superhero Cyclops. Each name employs a distinguishing feature of the character (the former's beard, the latter's eyes) to capture the visual and conceptual essence of who they are.

The following constitute some examples of synecdoche, which you might want to employ in your writing or use as catalysts for the creation of your own combinations.

Part of something used to represent the whole sentence:

> After the wreck, Jimmy got a new set of wheels. [a new car]
>
> Nina has many mouths to feed. [many others to look after]
>
> White-collar criminals. [upper-class villains]
>
> Give us our daily bread. [a daily supply of food]
>
> Another day, another dollar. [a daily supply of money]

Whole sentence used to deliver a part of something:

> "At midnight I went on deck, and to my mate's great surprise put the ship round on the other tack. His terrible whiskers flitted round me in silent criticism."
> —Joseph Conrad, "The Secret Sharer"
>
> "Friends, Romans, countrymen, lend me your ears …."
> —William Shakespeare, *Julius Caesar*

> "Tell that its sculptor well those passions read
> Which yet survive, stamped on these lifeless things,
> The hand that mocked them …."
> —Percy Bysshe Shelley, "Ozymandias"

> "I should have been a pair of ragged claws.
> Scuttling across the floors of silent seas."
> —T. S. Eliot, "The Love Song of J. Alfred Prufrock"

As with metonymy, synecdoche easily can be overused in a piece of creative writing to the point of readerly distraction. Given that warning, try to focus on employing it at points where it seems consistent with the narrative voice and doesn't threaten to disrupt pacing.

Giving Life with Personification

Be careful what you say around here. The walls have ears.

Personification is the act of assigning human qualities to something that isn't human or, in some cases, to something that isn't even alive. Personification can be used as a method of describing something so others can understand or to emphasize a point. In fact, it's such a commonly favored literary tool, you might find yourself using it without even realizing it.

 **DEFINITION**

Personification is a figure of speech in which human characteristics are attributed to an abstract quality, animal, or inanimate object.

Personification shares much with metonymy and synecdoche insofar as it provides another way you can make a comparison and give deeper meaning to a concept. It's an effective writing tool because readers intuitively understand human traits and qualities and, therefore, can easily grasp the concept you're conveying. Because it relies on universal meanings and understanding, you can find personification in jingles, advertising, and cartoons, as well as in poetry and prose.

Here are some lively examples of personification to get your own creative juices flowing and perhaps elicit a chuckle or two:

The clock seemed to laugh at me.

My razor bit me today while I was shaving.

The peaceful and fun-loving village on the coast was swallowed by an angry tsunami.

The bed groaned in pain and protest beneath the immense weight of my extravagantly obese houseguest.

Writing is a jealous mistress.

My life came screeching to a halt.

When I saw those cowboy boots in the store they screamed, "Buy us!"

Assigning human qualities to nonhuman objects changes the way readers think and feel about them and provides them with emotions, personalities, and occasionally a certain measure of charm.

As with the other figures of speech, excessive use blunts the effect of personification. Yet sprinkled throughout your narrative, it gives your writing energy.

Comparing with Metaphors

"Joshua's vocabulary was so bad … I mean it really was … I don't know, like, you know, whatever."

Why use *metaphors?* Because, just like the other figures of speech, they enliven ordinary language. We get so accustomed to using the same words and phrases over and over, in the same ways, we sometimes forget what they really mean. Creative writers have the power to make the ordinary strange (or funny, or different) and make the strange (or funny, or different) ordinary, making life, and reading, interesting again.

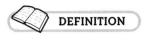 **DEFINITION**

A **metaphor** is **a** comparison between two things, based on resemblance or similarity, without using the words *like* or *as*.

Metaphors are generous to readers (and listeners); they encourage interpretation. When readers encounter a phrase or word that cannot be interpreted literally, they have to think—or rather, they're given the pleasure of interpretation. If you write "I am frustrated" or "The air was cold," you give your readers nothing to do. They'll think to themselves, *So what?* On the other hand, if you write, "My ambition was Hiroshima, after the bombing," your readers can think about and choose from many possible meanings.

Metaphors also are more efficient and economical than ordinary language; they afford maximum meaning with a minimum of words. By writing "My job is a prison," you suggest to your readers that you feel like you're locked in solitary confinement, fed lousy food, deprived of all of life's great pleasures, made to endure a poorly lit and cramped work area—and a hundred other things, that, if you tried to say them all, would probably take several pages.

Like the other figures of speech, metaphors can be fun to experiment and play with. Here are some examples to get you thinking of your own:

> The little boat gently drifted across the pond exactly the way a bowling ball wouldn't.
>
> It hurt, the way your tongue hurts after you accidentally staple it to the wall.
>
> It will take a big tractor to plow the fertile fields of Karen's mind.
>
> Wendy's face was a perfect oval as though two sides of a circle had been violently compressed by a ThighMaster.
>
> Even in his golden years, Granddaddy David had a steel-trap mind, only one that had been left outside too long, so it had rusted shut.

 WRITING PROMPT

Think of your current occupation or a hobby or pastime you know extremely well. Using your specialized knowledge, write as many metaphors as you can. Then show them to a trusted friend, taking note of their favorites and reasons for liking them.

Humorous though these examples may seem, they attest to the fact that there are many gaps in language. When a child looks at the sky and sees a star but doesn't know the word *star,* she might say something like, "Mommy, look at the lamp in the sky!" Similarly, when computer software developers created boxes on the screen as a user interface, they needed a new language; the result was *Windows.*

In your poems, you'll often be trying to write about subjects and feelings so complex, you have no choice but to employ metaphors. They're often the best devices for attempting to say what initially might seem unsayable.

In his *Poetics,* Aristotle asserted that metaphors actually are indicators of genius in a person. They are "a sign of genius," he explained, "since a good metaphor implies an intuitive perception of the similarity in dissimilars." Whether you agree with this or not, it's true enough that writers should take the requisite time to practice creative ways of using metaphors. Doing so might not make you a genius, but it will certainly improve the documents you pen—perhaps even to the point readers will believe they must have been written by a genius.

Comparing with Similes

> Mr. Burke plunged 23 stories, hitting the pavement like a garbage bag filled with vegetable soup.

Splat! This example constitutes a disagreeable description, but that's its purpose: thinking about the plummeting man's impact in terms of chunky, red-colored soup and a squishy plastic bag is so vivid, it will leave many readers squirming in their seats.

As you've witnessed throughout this chapter, you can use any variety of figures of speech to hold your reader's attention. A *simile* is perhaps the easiest and most vivid to employ. They make your writing more creative and help readers generate powerful mental images.

 **DEFINITION**

> A **simile** is a figure of speech that uses the words *like* or *as* when making a comparison. A simile usually compares two quite different things in a way that helps the reader form a mental picture.

Here are some examples—funny, disturbing, or perhaps both—that demonstrate how easily similes can perk up your written descriptions:

> The ballerina rose gracefully *en pointe* and extended one slender leg behind her like a dog at a fire hydrant.
>
> Hailstones leapt from the pavement like maggots being fried in hot grease.
>
> The plan was simple-minded, like my friend Laura. But unlike Laura, the plan might just turn out okay.
>
> Criticism rolls off me like a duck.
>
> Daura's lips were red and full, like tubes of blood drawn by an inattentive phlebotomist.

Using similes attracts attention and appeals directly to your reader's senses (remember the importance placed on using the five senses in Chapter 2?), encouraging their imaginations to embrace what's being communicated. In addition, similes inspire lifelike quality in daily talk and in the characters of a work of creative writing. Perhaps most significantly, they allow readers to relate your feelings to their own personal experiences. Therefore, the use of similes makes it easier for your readers to understand the subject matter of what you've written, which may have been otherwise too demanding to be comprehended. Like metaphors, similes also offer variety in ways of thinking and provide new perspectives for viewing the world.

As a way of relating similes to the other figures of speech as tools in your writing, remember that fresh, original figures of speech enliven a text, whereas dull, overused ones weigh down the text. An excerpt from the creative nonfiction piece "The Skeleton Woman" illustrates this maxim in action. In it, the boy narrator (a primary school student) describes how his retired scientist mother stores the human skeleton she used in her research:

> She kept the skeleton in a corner of the upstairs cedar closet. It was easy to miss on account of all the various things clinging to different parts of it: winter caps stacked upon its smooth head; heavy old shirts and frayed coats flung over its shoulders; an assortment of Christmas ornaments hanging from its lower ribs; and a child-sized basketball resting in its pelvis. The piled hats leaned slightly to one side, affording the skull a jaunty aspect, while the rough clothing drooping from the shoulders hung irregularly—not unlike rock-hewn prehistoric furs from some distant cold-climate predecessor of us. The basketball resting in the midsection suggested an impossible pregnancy, and the bone-suspended ornaments could not help but appear festive, speaking, it seemed to me, of some secret grisly truth yet to be celebrated. A big steel rod rose out of a metal base resting on rollers and ran upward through the spinal column before terminating in the skull, creating the illusion of a body somehow hovering in air of its own volition, feet dangling three or four inches above the floor.
>
> Despite the novelty of the thing's presence, the skeleton really was just another item in storage—something put away, half-forgotten. Sometimes when I was helping Mama in the closet, she would address the occupant with "And how are we today, my good man?" or "Excuse us, sir" or "Don't mind us, old friend." She always seemed happy to see him—an acquaintance from another time; a fondly remembered ally from a war long over.
>
> I would visit him sometimes when I was upstairs alone, rush of cedar as I swung forth the door and flipped on the light. Carefully I would place my little hand against his, studying the contrast, and then pressing each of my fingers against a corresponding fleshless digit.
>
> Even at that age I did not need my mother to tell me this was what I would be some day. That it was what lay in store. Some fundamental cognition knew. And it was comforting in a way, a privilege, to have this visual testament available day or night, close at hand and always the same, which seemed to say, "Beneath all the motion and coating of life, here is what you are."
>
> I have no recollection of the truth of this ever troubling me. Perhaps it had something to do with the fact he did not seem to mind it so much himself. Whenever I opened the door, his expression was the same. He was always smiling.

 WRITING PROMPT

Make a list of the different figures of speech that appear in this excerpt. Then go back and place asterisks next to those you believe give the most energy to the narrative's pacing.

In the interests of not foiling your writing prompt, I'll refrain from elaborating on the figures of speech in this excerpt. Instead, I will point out one of the larger meanings they help fuel. For instance, you likely know the expression "skeletons in the closet" and that it refers to secrets from one's past. As it turns out, the narrative's skeleton is a metaphor for the mother's secrets concerning her child—only she also literally has a skeleton in her closet. This may be interpreted as a symbolic and macabre form of ironic humor, which is confirmed at the conclusion of the excerpt by the skeleton's perpetual smile. (All human skulls appear to smile when they're not covered by the flesh, muscle, and tissue that conspire to cover the mouth and jaw.) Hence, the boy narrator is reassured by the skeleton's smile, even though it's not actually smiling, in the living human sense of the word, at all.

If your creative work lends itself to the occasional use of a figure of speech, go for it. Just try to be creative when you use language in this way. One of my favorite uses of such wording—as witnessed in my utilization of the skeleton—is to say something and then insist I meant the literal, not the figurative, interpretation. A writer friend does this to me all the time. If I say of a manuscript page, "Let's toss it," she will crumple up the page and hurl it somewhere, often at me, rather than deleting some of the manuscript's writing, which is what I really meant.

I have often thought such a reaction could prove a wonderful inspiration for a character who is forever taking things literally and causing problems (or just laughter for readers) over it. None of this has to be difficult. Just think about how you say everyday things (like the preceding example) and then have fun goofing around with it.

However you choose to employ figures of speech in your writing, enjoy the process of creating new ways to say the same old things.

The Least You Need to Know

- In metonymy, a thing's drab common name is colorfully replaced by its meaning or the characteristics it possesses.
- Synechdoches are a type of metonymy in which the name of a part is substituted for that of a whole, or vice versa.
- Personification attributes human characteristics to an abstract quality, animal, or inanimate object.
- A metaphor is a comparison between two things, based on resemblance or similarity, without using *like* or *as*.
- A simile uses the words *like* or *as* to compare two quite different things in a way that helps the reader form a mental picture.

Convincing Character Voice

It's one of those undefinable, hard-to-give-five-easy-steps sort of concepts in writing: voice. Not author voice, but *character voice*. You know, that thing everybody says they want in a book but no one can say exactly what it is. However, having just concluded a chapter on figures of speech, let's wade through the ambiguity and tackle the evasive notion of character voice. Along the way, I share a few tips on the best ways to go about using it.

For many creative writers, voice is a given character's worldview as expressed through his or her language. Think of it this way: everyone has a unique take on the world. Your experiences and inborn traits shape your perception of everything around you. Voice is how a character expresses his or her own unique view.

You can reveal character voice as you write through subtle things like word choice and sentence structure, although ultimately it's about more than words and tone. True, those subtleties are important parts of it, and sometimes I do a full draft just tweaking those things for my characters' voices. But equally important, if not more, is your character's thought process. When something happens, how does your character process it? What do they think about it? What do they connect it to? Something in their past? Something else in the world around them? Someone in the world around them? This a tough concept because we're talking about a character's mind, which—if the character is lifelike and believable—needs to be as complex as your own.

DEFINITION

Character voice is the primary speech, thought patterns, and attitude of a figure in a piece of creative writing.

Because a character's voice is shaped so much by his or her traits and history, it's important to know those things about your character. This can involve different things for different writers. For some, it means creating an extensive character worksheet, while others spend a great deal of prewriting time trying to view the world from their character's mind-set. It also means discovering your characters through your narrative, meaning you need to be willing to let their voice change in subsequent drafts.

You need to ask yourself the questions of *Why?* and *How?* with regard to your characters. Why is this character sarcastic/sweet/bubbly? How does her love of X, Y, or Z affect the way she sees the world? How do certain character traits (optimism/pessimism, dry sense of humor, impatience, etc.) come out in her voice? This helps you place a particular character's voice into a more concrete and definable realm so you can stay consistent with the voice instead of running the risk of letting it run all over the place.

To facilitate the best ways to employ character voice, in this chapter, you consider how your writing can copy other voices, employ opposite voices from those of your characters, make use of ironic voices, and heat up your narrative with contentious voices. Together, these types of character voice give you plenty to choose from when it's time to convey what the people who populate your writing world are thinking and saying.

Employing Mimicry

Learning and copying from the works of others—that is, *mimicry*—is one of the best ways to establish character voice in your writing. Taking inspiration (and words) from the best who have gone before increases your chances of your own writing working out well. It's a well-known cliché that "every poet is a thief," but, like many clichés, it's largely true. If you've ever wondered if your creative writing is too alike another author's—whether that has been an unwitting accident or intentional—this section may help you figure that out.

DEFINITION

Mimicry is the activity or art of copying the thoughts and speech of other character voices in creative writing.

Consider for a moment why so many children (and not a few adults) want to be the superhero Batman. He has a cool voice, ingenious and unconventional weapons, and a great ride in the Bat-mobile. Also, unlike most other superheroes, he has an altogether human—albeit spectacularly trained—body. The dream of Batman and the desire to copy him stems from the fact that he's human like you and me. The dream follows that, with the right amount of wealth and training, you, too, could be Batman and make noble sacrifices for the lesser humans around you.

Yet Batman has countless precursors, stretching back into antiquity. Consider the Greek warrior Achilles: although half-god, half-man, he possesses human vulnerability but also extraordinary equipment and finely honed skills. Like Batman, he is plagued by doubt, frailty, and mistakes, but in the end, he sacrifices himself for his countrymen.

Whether you realize it or not, your character voices will strongly resemble many who came before them. That's in part what makes you want to copy from the works of other authors. When you're aware of it, it constitutes both a safety net and a learning process—if you didn't copy from someone else, how would you learn how to write? A legendary anecdote among southern writers is that an impoverished young aspiring author named Harry Crews copied many of William Faulkner's novels (some more than once), word for word, by hand in an effort to educate himself. (He wound up penning nearly 20 books and enjoying a successful career.) Imitation, then, is often the first stage of a writer's cycle but then you must learn when and how to break free and make your own character voices sound as distinctive as possible.

There are ways to copy respectfully. After all, copying someone else's writing is a form of respect. As another cliché states, "Imitation is the highest form of flattery." Yet when it comes to actually doing it, there are some important things to keep in mind. One of them is don't copy anyone; copy everyone. As John Milton famously noted, "Copy from one, it's plagiarism; copy from two, it's research." If you want to learn how to write, read the works of many authors who resonate with you, and study all of them in equal parts. If you spend too much time with any one author, reaching into his or her inner voice and borrowing phrases from their vocabulary, you run the risk of walking a tightrope of copyright laws (that is, unless you're Harry Crews).

Another way to imitate respectfully and responsibly is to keep a copy. If you copy anything from anyone, even if it's just writing down a good catchphrase you heard on TV, be sure you keep a note of it. When you're flipping through an old writing journal, it's very easy to come across something scrawled in the corner and think of it as your own. However, if you could turn back the clock, quite often you'd find that it was actually someone else's. That doesn't prevent you from taking it for yourself and putting a new spin on it, modifying it to your own purposes, but you need to know it was someone else's originally. You need to be aware of how much you've taken from others so you can judge if it's too much.

So how much is too much? If your writing only takes ideas from a single author, if it contains the full character or plot scenario or location of another author's, you've gone too far.

WRITING PROMPT

Select a favorite prose or poetic passage and, using content of your own, mimic it to the best of your ability. Then go back and attempt to determine at which point mimicry proved most helpful to your writing without coming across as simple copying.

Finding Similarities and Differences with Contrast

A compare-and-*contrast* sequence in a piece of creative writing might, in fact, end up reflecting only similarities or only differences, although more often than not, both comparison and contrast are used. When writing a piece that contrasts your ideas, you have to determine the items that are at odds in some way. It's impossible for you to try differentiating two diverse things altogether.

After you've determined your contrasting ideas, it might be useful for you—as it does for many creative writers—to take time to map out a rough outline to assist with organization and demonstrate how your ideas duel. This also helps you have a strong picture of your ideas and when and where they're most relevant in the overall narrative.

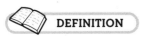

DEFINITION

Contrast is the use of opposing elements, such as colors, forms, or lines, in proximity to produce an intensified effect in a work of creative writing.

It's often remarked that some of the best movies are so-called "emotional roller coasters." People also often praise books that contain dramatic ups and downs—those that make readers laugh and cry. In short, readers love narratives with contrast, and most often the ideas behind that contrast is executed through dialogue.

Here's an example of dialogue contrast from the creative nonfiction piece "Home Court Advantage." As you read the characters' voices, try doing so aloud and see if you can determine what they reveal about other aspects of their personality:

> Faded old pale yellow school bus, cast off of a wealthier school system, scion of Michigan and another decade, engine knocking, no shocks to speak of, rocking and shuddering along the highway, carrying uniformed middle schoolers westward, raggedy ill-fitting outfits not unlike the seen-better-days bus that bears them: hand-me-downs of classes long since graduated, of teams past—of people grown now into their full bodies.

Boys gathered about the middle of the bus, eyes focused on two of their number seated and facing each other across the aisle, extending their fists so that they almost touch, one of them clutching a tan plastic comb.

"Hold up, fellas," says a skinny little greasy-haired boy named Lonnie. "Yall haven't said yet what you're playin for?"

The contestants, myself one of them, withdraw their fists and peer up at him.

Tye, the boy across from me, responds. "If I win, I gets his lunch money for next week."

Me, glancing away toward the front of the bus, then beyond it, through the glass, at a distant blue line of ridges on the horizon. I look at Tye and smile a slow smile. "If I win, you have to walk to the top of a hill I point out."

Questioning look from him as Lonnie assumes again his self-appointed role of referee. "Yall's bets have been staked," he says, solemn voice brimming with ridiculous pomp. "Now we got to see who gets first go. I'm thinking of a number between one and a hundred. Fella comes nearest gets dibs at grabbing U's comb."

"Easy for me," I say, chest-thumping the digits on my jersey with the fist that clutches the comb. "Number, name, game. Always the same."

Tye, confused, squinting at the floor in thought for a moment, then brightening. "Fifty be half-a-hundred and that be what Jordan scored the other night. Put me down for fifty, man."

Lonnie, solemn again, guiding the proceedings, enjoying his rare authority. "Tye the 2-guard gets it cause the number on my mind, fellas, is sixty-nine. Sixty-nine."

"Hell yeah!" someone says.

Laughter from everyone, self included.

"Alright now, gentleman," says Lonnie expectantly, and the smiles on the surrounding faces deepen even as the ones on Tye's face and mine fade and disappear.

I extend my right fist, Tye's coming forth to mirror it. Then with my left hand I set the comb down flat just behind the ridge of my knuckles, jagged, uneven teeth facing outward, toward Tye. If an onlooker happened to guess the crude teeth of the comb had been inexpertly sharpened with a pocketknife, breaking off a few in the process, he would be guessing right.

Even as my left hand comes away, Tye's—fist unclenched, thought and action almost as one—has the comb, ripping it hard to the right. I jerk my hand back and down, but not fast enough to avoid having the skin on the outer three knuckles raked open: a scratch more than a cut, but enough to etch into the flesh a bright crimson line and heap little white curling mounds of flesh on either side of the narrow wound.

Tye laughing and tossing the comb back to me. "This gon be easy money."

This excerpt, violent as it is, illustrates well the voice contrast among the three main speakers. The narrator, U, seems to use a rather conventional form of English, while Lonnie speaks in a white southern or Appalachian dialect, and Tye employs ebonic language. The fact that U speaks a more conventional type of English makes him the best candidate for narrator in terms of the highest number of readers being able to understand everything he says. Although Lonnie and Tye speak colorfully, albeit differently, readers might struggle with some of the cultural references attached to their socio-cultural backgrounds. The numbers the pair select, for instance— Lonnie's 69 as a sexual connotation and Tye's 50 as a reference to the number of points Michael Jordan scored (Tye is wearing Jordan's number 23 jersey)—won't be obvious to all readers, yet they also add a sense of realness to the character personalities.

In conclusion, contrast is an element of creative writing that's not often discussed, but it is key to layered, interesting narratives. It helps you emphasize strong emotion (Tye's sense of humor), lets you highlight characters (Lonnie's role as master of ceremonies in bloody knuckles), and can even be worked into symbol and theme (this violent coming-of-age ritual among poor athletic teenage males while en route to a game).

Understanding Irony

> "Isn't it ironic?"

Often I have heard this rhetorical question employed as a form of catch-all commentary on something that's been said or overheard in a classroom or at a cocktail party. Usually the individual who utters the question has found what they've heard amusing in some way and want to sound somewhat sophisticated when commenting on it. Yet just as often, what they've overheard isn't ironic at all. This isn't to say the person who misused *ironic* is a simpleton; irony is one of the most misapplied terms in the English language and journalists, politicians, and even college professors regularly take it out of context.

Let's start by considering what makes an effective shock in writing. It's very similar to what makes a joke funny: the shock when the punch line is unexpected. You generally don't laugh at jokes you know because you already know what's coming. Humor usually follows this basic formula: set pattern, reinforce pattern, break pattern. Now you shouldn't start trying to perform your creative writing in the same manner you deliver jokes, but shock can prove a very powerful compositional tool. When your story subverts your reader's expectations, your story shocks, which is usually a memorable moment in the text.

Irony can only be used effectively when used with intent, so it's important to understand what irony is. As you've seen, people often mistake the meaning of irony. What they usually mean is really an *oxymoron*.

 **DEFINITION**

Irony is a literary device that presents a conflict between appearance and reality. An **oxymoron** is when seemingly contradictory terms appear side by side.

Given that irony can cause interpretive problems for writers and nonwriters alike, I'll try to clarify it for you by illustrating the three kinds of irony: verbal, dramatic, and situational.

Verbal Irony

Verbal irony, or when what's said is the opposite of what's meant, is the kind of irony you're probably most familiar with. Also referred to as sarcasm, verbal irony occurs when a character says one thing but means another.

Here's an example of verbal irony that's also sarcastic:

> "You're really wasting away to nothing," Lesley commented to the obese man who was consuming his second dessert.

It's very easy, and very tempting, to use verbal irony in your writing, but there are two points to be aware of. First, creative writing often tries to re-create the impact of a situation. Saying something untrue to mean something else can accidentally remove the suspension of disbelief. Employing verbal irony creates a mental barrier the reader has to get past in order to understand the situation. The reader has to "get it" to understand the scene correctly. Using irony poorly can mean you confuse your reader, so be careful.

Also, watch out for characters who are frequently sarcastic. This isn't sympathetic, and if your character routinely uses sarcasm to belittle others, you've got to be very careful. Overdo it, and your character ends up being a jerk and your reader stops liking him. Now, there's nothing wrong with unsympathetic characters, but if you want a sympathetic character, you'd better watch the sarcasm.

Dramatic Irony

Next is dramatic irony, or the difference between what a character says or does and what the reader knows to be true. This type of irony occurs when we know something the characters don't. The classic example is *Romeo and Juliet*. We all expected Juliet to reawaken, but to Romeo, it appeared she was dead, so he took the poison. Appearance differs from reality, and we are aware of it, creating the dramatic irony in the play.

Dramatic irony is most often employed to create tragedy or comedy. In fact, it was employed much earlier in the Greek play *Oedipus the King.* The audience knows Oedipus is the murderer he seeks, but he doesn't. This dramatic irony creates suspense, as the reader tries to anticipate when he will finally learn the truth of the matter.

The following example illustrates a more contemporary use of dramatic irony at work:

> The gunner finished spray-painting the big pink peace sign on the left side of the tank before climbing back inside to inventory the ammunition belts.

Situational Irony

Situational irony is the difference between how things look and how they really are—between what happens and what should have happened. It's the subversion of our expectations to produce a result with a troublingly accurate quality.

Some other short examples of situational irony include the spectacle of a tow truck being towed, a fire station burning down, and a man leaping to avoid a revolving water sprinkler and falling into a mud puddle.

Situational irony is also present in O. Henry's "The Gift of the Magi," in which a girl cuts off her hair to buy her boyfriend a watch chain, and the boyfriend sells his watch to buy the girl a set of combs for her hair.

The following example demonstrates situational irony at work using limited materials and a short sentence:

> At the end of the police investigation, the authorities finally arrested the guilty party: Special Investigator Burke.

Remember that however much or how little of it you use, irony should be a tool employed to create drama and interest in your story. And remember that sarcasm used as a tool to belittle others should be included with caution to avoid potentially alienating readers.

Creating and Using Conflict

Most all creative writing needs *conflict* of some kind. Without any conflict, narratives wilt, stagnate, and noticeably tread water—not exciting to read, to say the least.

The good news is that conflict can come from nearly anywhere, from anyone, and at any time in your writing, but you need to have at least a little conflict early on. Varied sizes and intensities of conflict can come all throughout a narrative and exert power over readers as much as any other writing device.

DEFINITION

Conflict is the heart of any narrative. Conflict can be between the protagonist and another character, the antagonist; between the protagonist and nature; or between the protagonist and society. The conflict can also be internal or psychological.

The type of genre you're writing in plays a role in deciding the types of conflict available to you. Military and romance fiction have expected types of conflict: warring nations or factions, rival suitors or desires. The writing and action reflect the conflicts as well: hands attempting to choke each other and hands removing clothes. So a good place to start is by familiarizing yourself with the types of conflict that typically appear in your genre.

In terms of your own narrative, you should begin with a problem located as close as possible to the overall main conflict, but don't jump in so quickly your reader will feel lost. Too much confusion too early won't engage most readers, but using too much background information too soon can make interest wane.

WATCH OUT!

Conflict can exhaust a story—and your readers, if there's no let-up or humor mixed in. So schedule the magnitude and force of the conflict at the correct places in your story. This can help you avoid the dreaded contrived conflict.

Conflict should have strong purpose—it should move your narrative along. Argumentative banter just for the sake of conflict appears contrived and even meaningless. Most importantly, your readers will notice this.

To combat that danger and to get you going, here are some of the archetypal conflicts that repeat across many narratives:

Man against man   The ancient man versus man is one of the oldest conflicts. Cain and Abel both wanted approval; Achilles and Hector wanted Troy; in Swift's *Gulliver's Travels,* war broke out over how to crack an egg. Even in the last ridiculous example, a natural conflict arises from personal desires usually involving characters with powerful personalities.

Character against the world   This approach involves placing your protagonist against high odds. Let the literary snobs and intellectuals say what they will, but nothing adds more conflict to a story than sheer survival. From *The Swiss Family Robinson* to *Robinson Crusoe* to *Tarzan,* survival of man against his world is epic. Even if you change the world for your character, as in *1984* or *The Hunger Games,* survival remains the basic driving force.

Unsweetened romance   Sweet romances, often in the young adult (YA) genre, tend to be more on the less-conflicted side, but they should still have at least minor conflicts, such as multiple suitors. Romances with stronger, more mature themes have more choices for conflict. Try to stagger and strengthen these conflicts between characters, keeping their pining and yearning unfulfilled for as long as possible.

Throw rocks   Chucking rocks at your characters is another way to afford your narrative liveliness. Conflict can arise from goals, other characters, time constraints, and environment. Run your protagonist up a tree or corner him and then let the rocks fly. And don't be afraid of injuring or even killing characters; vengeance can serve as a most powerful form of conflict, and you can always work on further character development while a weakened character heals.

Of course, these types of conflict can be mixed together and applied to various characters. It's also okay for more than one character to have the same goals and desires, as long as they pursue them differently. Maybe two men are in love with the same woman, two nations want the same strip of land, or two teens want the same spot on a cheerleading squad. Let clashes the happen, and use them to nudge each character and the narrative itself.

Inevitably in conflict, there are also going to be failures and setbacks for some of the characters. These reversals actually help keep conflict alive and the story moving. Think of all those successful romantic comedies that conclude with a wedding but then tally up all the adverse situations that occur along the way. Don't let your characters ever get too stable, too comfortable. Keep them on edge, even if it's an internal emotional edge, until the end.

Lastly, as in all writing, keep your ideal readers in mind when you create conflict. What might work for a sultry romance won't be welcome in a YA novel, and what a younger reader sees as conflict might not be a challenge for a veteran reader. Know your intended readership and its general expectations. Otherwise, you're going to have a conflict on your hands—one you'll lose as a writer!

The Least You Need to Know

- Mimicry is a useful tool for both learning to write better and for making your characters authentic.
- Contrast makes for more dramatic writing as a result of employing opposites.
- Ironic writing can generate both humor and deeper meanings.
- Conflict is very useful in moving along a narrative and holding reader interest.

Influential Point of View

The discussion of *point of view* is one of the touchiest craft debates among creative writers and their editors. Yet choosing your point or points of view is one of the most important things you'll do as you plan your narrative. And to do it well, you must be aware of the intricacies of viewpoint and consider how it will impact your overall piece.

Artists generally don't like rules, and so writers usually balk when advised not to write in first person present tense because it's too hard to sell—or when they're told they shouldn't use the omniscient viewpoint because it simply isn't done very often these days. I'm that way myself. I want to stretch my abilities and try different styles and forms. In fact, if I happen to be confronted with too many rules, I've been known to rebel and break a few.

On the other hand, as the editor of a small literary magazine (that often breaks rules, by the way), I recognize the value of the other side of the coin as well. Editors have seen omniscient viewpoint executed poorly more often than not. It's true that omniscient is very hard to do well. Yet there's no denying the mastery of Joseph Conrad, who wrote books in which the point of view might change with each sentence—sometimes five times in one paragraph! In most instances, the

In This Chapter

* Telling a story from first person point of view (POV)
* Employing second person storytelling
* Writing in the third person
* Achieving remoteness with POV

effect would be dizzying, but Conrad could pull it off so that you always knew who was talking and it felt perfectly natural.

Rules are made to assist creative writers, but if you feel confident enough to pull a Conrad, go ahead and break the rules. Just be sure your choice of POV makes the most of narrative, and never forget that narrative drive is everything to the reader. Readers are not interested in the writer's angst or cleverness if they don't fit well within the narrative.

It's time to learn how the key to successful choice of viewpoint is understanding thoroughly how your choice of *point of view* (*POV*) will impact your narrative. You probably already have heard point of view referred to by the pronouns we use to tell our story, and that's how you're going to be learning about its best functions and uses: by considering POV in terms of first person, second person, third person, and distance. My aim is to show you who should render the action in different situations and why.

DEFINITION

Point of view (POV) is a way the events of a story are conveyed to the reader. It's the vantage point from which the narrative is passed from author to the reader.

I Am the First Person

When you construct a narrative through a viewpoint character using *I* or *we*, you're using *first person* point of view. Every detail of your narrative must be filtered through the teller. This impacts your choice of narrator, although it might be—and most often is—your main character. If your main character cannot see, hear, touch, smell, taste, think, know, or feel it, you can't include it. Therefore, if you want to introduce something outside the range of your main character, you have to use the words or observed actions of some other character who is in a position to see/know the events and convey the information you want the reader to have. Remember that unless they are the clairvoyant, the POV character cannot know the thoughts or unspoken feelings of another character.

DEFINITION

First person is a point of view in which an *I* or *we* serves as the narrator of a piece of fiction.

Despite the limitations of what a character can know when you use first person, it often succeeds in making the reader feel like the character's best friend or closest confidant. In fact, the viewpoint character often confides in the reader things he or she wouldn't tell his closest friend.

This can be a comfortable point of view because it allows the writer to get right into the character's head. However, beginning creative writers often find first person POV challenging because you really need to completely understand your character in every conceivable way to write well from this POV. For example, you can't use language your character wouldn't use or describe things your character wouldn't notice.

 WATCH OUT!

The most common problem when using first person POV is that it's difficult to resist the urge to tell the reader everything rather than show it. It also can be frustrating to be trapped in one character's head for the length of a book. This forced closeness can breed boredom, if not contempt, which is particularly problematic if your character is a thinly disguised version of yourself.

Even if I ultimately choose another point of view, I always find it helpful to write a couple scenes in first person as an exercise to really get into my main character's head. In fact, many authors suggest it's helpful to write your first chapter from several points of view before you settle on the POV that's most comfortable for you as a writer and also most effective for the narrative you're working on.

Here are some things to keep in mind to maintain the POV character's voice throughout:

Consistency   The voice of the narration should be consistent with the character's cultural, social, educational, and regional background.

Voice   The voice itself is important as well. There's a fine line between unique and annoying—not to mention the current obsession with political correctness. How easy, for instance, would it be to read an entire novel written in heavy dialect valley girl or hipster-speak?

Language   Word choice can reveal a lot about a character, so if you have a professional wrestler in your narrative, be sure he or she employs the buzzwords of that sport.

Character   Character is developed not only through dialogue, but also through narration. You need to be careful that the reactions and personality of the viewpoint character don't disappear or lose consistency during emotional moments in the story. The character needs to be involved—to react to events physically and verbally—not just describe the reactions of others. The professional wrestler, for example, is going to have feelings and opinions about other wrestlers. What are they?

So why would anyone choose first person point of view? Most notably, because it generates an intimate perspective. The reader's vicarious experience is heightened by the tightly focused perspective created when everything is being filtered through the viewpoint character. This is particularly attractive to young readers who can easily see themselves in the story. It also can open some interesting plot possibilities because the narrow viewpoint can hint that things aren't what they seem, allowing for narrative twists later on. Finally, first person POV can be a lot of fun to write because the author gets to "live" the story through another set of eyes. By the end, you feel as though you've come to know another person intimately, even though that person is only a character you've invented.

You Are the Second Person

Writing a narrative employing *you* is called *second person* point of view. Using this viewpoint, you control all the information, and you give the reader whatever you want.

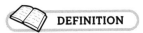

DEFINITION

Second person is a point of view in which the narrator tells the story to another character using you. The story is told through the addressee's point of view.

Very little creative writing is written in second person, with the exception of choose-your-own-adventure types of books, or poems and prose that usually involve psychosis in some way. Yet it is a popular vehicle for many nonfiction self-help books (such as this one!) as well as tourism ads.

Second person POV can be a bit jarring in creative writing and, thus, it's the least popular viewpoint. Your reader picks up a book to escape into another character for a while, and using *you* disintegrates this illusion. Moreover, depending on the writer, it can simply feel weird, as though you're being bossed around and programmed with someone always telling you what you're doing and feeling.

As a result of these considerations, second person point of view is certainly the most rare viewpoint, and the most difficult to use, but there are instances when you might find it beneficial to your narrative.

Often writers use second person to address the audience directly, and especially unexpectedly, in the middle of a narrative. Here's an example in which a creative nonfiction piece (which might seem first person at the beginning) that's narrated by a younger version of the writer is interrupted by an older version of himself who eventually comes to identify with his fellow inhabitants, addressing the reader (and all outsiders as *you*, in contrast to *us*):

> Here I feel the necessity of pausing, a bit intrusively perhaps, and unveiling my older voice for an interval in the interests of context, for wanting as my behavior may have been during the prideful adolescent time I have just evoked (and rest assured I wince to record it as faithfully as I have on account of the doubtful light it places me in), it was not without its broader causes, most of which stemmed from that particular place and time.

By that point in my high school career I had long known Appomattox County—its disparate people and geography: the different sorts of white and black inhabitants and the manner in which the scenic hilly northern part of the county bumped up against the foothills of the Blue Ridge and the serpentine curve of the James River, while the rolling tobacco fields of the district's most southern reaches crossed unbroken over into Charlotte County and onward toward the Carolina border, the ground becoming ever flatter, its soil ever redder. The county seat in those days was a provincial settlement of no great size clinging to a largely defunct stretch of railroad, and remains so today. As there is little to do or see in the county, it is a pleasant enough place to linger—a fitting spot to hole up if your accommodations and traveling companion are attractive enough. It is also a place where you can lose yourself. There remain bridgeless gravel backroads in the remotest areas on which one is forced to ford creeks and where you can spend the better part of a day parked along the shady, tree-lined shoulder without glimpsing a single passerby.

As is the case in most sections and villages of the American South, the county is defined largely by its many Protestant churches. The largest of them naturally is Baptist and, to this day, remains perhaps the ugliest of all churches I have encountered. It is a long graceless brick structure which parallels a well-traveled street in the town, the walls rising abruptly just before the road as though the church would have liked to have continued on across the thoroughfare but instead was forced to halt as if the street's makeup constituted some magical barrier the building lacked the power to breach. The abruptness of the structure's architecture in conjunction with the nearby road affords one the impression the building has been struck on its side and flattened with a great board, pancaked backward as it were, so as to observe the necessary distance from the road's nearmost shoulder. Yet the church's most heinous ugliness stems from the parapets pretentiously mounted atop its unnaturally steep sudden walls. When I was a boy I was quite fond of these faux battlements and liked to envision archers launching storm clouds of arrows from them at some vast marauding siege army approaching from below. But as such gentle fancies of boyhood melted away, these parapets came merely to look out of place— like the gaudy points of a crown sitting atop some sad, unattractive, flat-faced despot who long ago realized the narrow, wanting confines of his kingdom.

Though rising no more than three stories all told, the church is massive by the architectural standards of the sleepy southern village in which it dwells. The building is reckoned magnificent by some inhabitants on account of its size alone, but its extreme ugliness again comes to the fore when one compares it to the town's more venerable eighteenth century colonial homes or those meticulously maintained in accordance with their mid-nineteenth century architecture by the employees of the county's Civil War park. It is difficult for me to believe that a religious construction anywhere has sunk much lower than it has in the form of this particular church and that the deity in whose honor it was erected did not long ago level it via natural disaster, as the old desert legends of the Good Book might lead us to expect, or by other, more modern, means. Perhaps it is a testament to his infinite patience and love for even the most misguided and unbecoming of his creatures that he has not … yet.

The dominating power of religion in the county notwithstanding, I must here confess to the reader I am making no attempt to afford an exhaustive perspective of the nature and appearance of Virginia's Appomattox County. As quiet and provincial as the place may appear, such an undertaking would require a greater erudition than I possess and demand a life's exhausting dedication on the order of what Yoknapatawpha County exacted of Faulkner. Yet I do not feel as though I can deal properly with my "hero's"—that is, my petulant younger self's—peregrinations and conflicts without having provided some sketch, however rough and incomplete, of the culture in which he/I was functioning. And that culture ultimately was evident not in the place's more hallowed buildings (however wanting they may have been) or its almost nonexistent arts (an impromptu musical "picking" or an assortment of student compositions hung along the walls of the public library accounting for the high water mark in that regard), but in its people, who were not overly given to art or thought; often bigoted; fiscally and politically conservative; passionately religious; more or less dutiful in and defined by their work; generally lazy, conventional, and given to routine in their personal lives; kind to strangers almost without fail (even if they privately thought ill of them); and intimately attached to and involved with their families (whether in the interests of love or abuse or both). And mark well that I render these descriptions myself with love rather than abuse, disgust, or disownment, for these people were and are, after all, my people and I remain loyal to them even now, despite their—despite our—many faults and shortcomings.

Consider then these broad descriptive strokes, inadequate as they admittedly are, against the faithful juvenile academic tale offered to this point with its petty teacher (who was unhappy and probably felt herself destined for a better job in a better school system somewhere far away), its brainy student characters (their intellectualism rendered all the more freakish to most everyone else by the poor public school system and decidedly anti-intellectual classmates and county surrounding them), the absent heroine (whose name in truth was not Bree but has been altered so as to echo Briseis from the old Greek tale), and the arrogant protagonist (who likely constitutes myself at my self-important, adolescent worst).

One thing more before I abandon my mature voice and deliver us back to those events of an earlier time which I have left temporarily incomplete. I should like to admit to the reader that in writing this piece I have come to be a little afraid of this earlier version of myself. He was, after all, quicker in mind and possessed of a body finely-tuned to inflict pain upon or run away from the bodies of others. Everything was in working order for him/me in those days, and work well it did—sometimes not for the best of purposes. The mature me might give him a run for his money in a scrap on account of a trick or two I have learned via hard-earned experience, but I have little doubt he would get the better of me in the end, and probably not without some smug pleasure and taunting words at having bested his elder, fading self.

It may interest readers as well to know that as a writer I am very wary of what he stands for. Such beings of vivid personality and action have a tendency to overpower their authors, bearing us along paths we have no wish to tread. And perhaps this obnoxious younger version of me has done so already in this narrative, stiff-arming me aside as he might some opponent on a football field. Such fellows, I have observed (and recall firsthand with significant shame), dare do as they wish and take what they want. And perhaps already he has done so here to the detriment of us all, including this weaker, older self grasping nonetheless and perhaps in vain for the greater meaning of ourselves.

Depending on the reader, this use of second person will either prove helpful in understanding the overall narrative or feel disingenuous for butting in and allowing the elder author to have his say. Perhaps it achieves a little of both.

Some creative writing teachers maintain you should never use second person. So if it is risky, unpopular, and rare, why would anyone want to write in second person point of view? My answer, as a writer who has used it, is that instances do arise when you need to make a certain impression on the reader for which second person is the best technique. A writer friend of mine used it in the opening chapter of her book to forcefully place the reader in the protagonist's shoes. It resulted in significant drama and narrative power.

I certainly would urge you to be careful with second person POV as a beginning creative writer, but if you feel your narrative calling for it, don't *you* hesitate to use it.

We Are the Third Person

Chandler went to the shops and bought the most expensive champagne he could find. He used his ex-wife's credit card.

When using *third person* point of view, you're writing *about* someone, yet there are a variety of subtleties to doing so. The following distinctions help you recognize and employ the nuances of writing that call for its specialized pronouns.

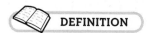 **DEFINITION**

> **Third person** is a point of view in which the narrator relates all action using pronouns such as *he* or *she*.

Third Person Subjective, Limited

A limited third person viewpoint means the reader sees the events through just a single character's perspective rather than all the characters'. It's written in the third person—*he, she*—but the reader only views proceedings through one pair of eyes. This means the reader only knows what that particular character knows. Any information hidden from that character is also be hidden from the reader and must be revealed through plot and/or dialogue.

Third Person Objective

Third person objective—also called third person *dramatic*—is a style of writing in which the narrator does not reveal the thoughts, feelings, and emotions of the characters. Instead, the author objectively relates the events without offering opinions or emotional reactions.

This style of writing is often used for newspaper articles or scientific journals. The aim is to present the facts and allow the reader to make up his or her own mind. This version of third person is not very often used in fiction.

Third Person Omniscient

Also known as "universal omniscient," this point of view is that of a narrator who takes no part in the story but knows all the facts and all characters' innermost thoughts and feelings. It is a general overview, good for sweeping sagas such as J. R. R. Tolkien's *The Lord of the Rings*. The narrator can move inside different characters' minds at will, relating thoughts and feelings of all them. (Note this is different from third person subjective, which has to stay with just the main character.)

The omniscience of this point of view allows the reader to know everything about every character and event in the story. It is by far the most popular form of writing in modern fiction.

Third Person Descriptive

One of the main advantages to the third person point of view is the scope for description. Unlimited to person, place, or time, an omniscient narrator can describe events to which there are no characters as witness. It can fill in details of which characters are unaware, allowing the reader to know things about characters they don't know themselves. This serves to increase drama and tension in writing; readers want to know what will happen when characters discover things about themselves or other characters.

Description can include analogies the characters themselves would never use, rich, atmospheric metaphors to heighten drama or make a reader fall in love with a place, person, or time.

When the storyteller is not inside a character's head, he or she can see more and hear more and, therefore, relate more to the reader. This can cause readers to feel they're a little distant from their characters. To remedy this, you must balance this with a proportionate amount of time directly inside characters' lives and thoughts.

Understanding and Establishing Distance

It's important to determine the *authorial distance* you'll use in a story. For instance, the narrator can be very much involved in the point of view, offering opinions about the character, his life-style, the culture or community he belongs to, or not be involved at all and have the narration told completely from the character's perspective.

 **DEFINITION**

Authorial distance is how much the narrator intrudes on the story and the character's point of view.

Authorial distance can be as close as the narrator revealing the character's actual thoughts ("He thought, *What in the hell do I do now?*") or be completely distant from the character, as a journalist might be while writing a newspaper article ("On June 14, 1979, the Morgans departed LAX at precisely 3:15 P.M.").

Depending on the type of story you're telling, decide how much or how little authorial distance is needed for your story. If you begin writing from a distant authorial distance, such as the previous example, the next sentence should continue to move toward the individual character, his thoughts, and his feelings. You might not want to be so close that you reveal his actual thoughts, but you do want to establish the third person POV for your protagonist. Once you've established point of view, maintain the level of authorial distance you've chosen.

Remember, don't slip from third person once you've established it. If you've chosen third person limited omniscient POV, don't slip into omniscient POV by revealing the thoughts and feelings of other characters who are not your protagonist.

After you've written the story, put it away. When you return to it to review it again, you'll be able to look at it with fresh eyes. With a pen, mark moments in the story where you've slipped from third person or switched authorial distance without justifiable cause. Be aware of this happening in your fiction, and make whatever corrections you need.

If you've noticed many slips in your story, you might want to determine whether the point of view or level of authorial distance you've chosen needs to be re-evaluated or even modified to fit your narrative goals.

The Least You Need to Know

- Point of view is the way the events of a story are conveyed to the reader; it's the vantage point from which the narrative is passed from author to the reader.
- First person point of view uses *I* or *we*.
- In second person point of view, the narrator tells a story to another character using *you*.
- Third person point of view uses pronouns such as *he* or *she*.
- Whatever authorial distance you choose to employ, be consistent with that distance.

Character, Setting, and Types of Stories

In Parts 1 and 2, you've been introduced to some generalities about writing and a number of its most minute details. Part 3 is about assembling all those components—along with some new ones—into coherent works of creative writing that stand on their own, in their entirety. What might have seemed overwhelming without the content in this book's first two parts is now fully possible. You are ready.

Part 3's chapters address the three fundamental things that make a narrative: character, setting, and action. Chapter 7 focuses on characterization through the avenues of dialogue and authorial design. The idea of design also informs Chapter 8 and its information on rendering setting. As you'll discover, setting can function as everything from a kind of camera to action itself. Settings can even be characters, as witnessed in all the horror movies that have been made in which a house possesses is a nefarious personality. As you know, characters do things; they make things happen. Chapter 8 covers the kinds of things that can happen: the patterns of plot that endlessly repeat themselves in creative writing.

Believe it or not, by the end of Part 3, you'll have knowledge of all the requisite tools to generate creative writing of your own.

Magnetic Characterization

Characters are the most important component of any narrative. Without them, there wouldn't be much of a story. *Characterization* is an essential skill to master, therefore, because characters are vital parts of any creative writing, from books and short stories, biographies and autobiographies, to poetry.

The development of a character is a very detailed process and one that requires a lot of thought. In fact, creative writers often describe it as "living with their characters," because for some writers, their characters come to be as vivid as real people—perhaps more so. Fully realized characters can be as complex as real people, so you need to consider many factors when introducing a character to your readers. Among them are physical details, the other characters surrounding the primary one, things the character does, and what the character says or thinks.

So where do you begin? Usually with a lot of written notes and background that's never going to appear in your completed piece of writing. Indeed, some creative writers create entire life stories on their characters before they even start to write. They know where they were born, whom they first kissed, when they were arrested, and how many fillings they have in their teeth. I don't happen to work like that, but I do

In This Chapter

- Dialogue that's direct
- Dialogue that's indirect
- The writer's interpretation
- Recurring characters

believe you need to know more about your character than what appears on the page. If you don't really know who your character is and how he or she might react in a certain situation, you'll never be able to create believable 3-D people.

As you should know by now, characterization is more effective when the author reveals traits about the character through the afore-mentioned ways and allows the reader to make his or her own judgments, rather than stating character traits directly. Once again, showing rather than telling usually is the way to go. With that in mind, in this chapter, I focus on character dialogue and various types of characters, along with the writer's challenge of interpreting characters correctly so they perform the way you want them to.

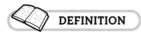 **DEFINITION**

> **Characterization** is the act of describing the qualities of someone or something in attempt to make them or it seem real.

Employing Direct Dialogue

You probably can recall, many of the memorable moments in books and film are those in which a character addresses someone else. Here are some favorites:

> "You are about to begin reading Italo Calvino's new novel, *If on a winter's night a traveler.*"
>
> —Italo Calvino, *If on a winter's night a traveler*

> "Play it, Sam. Play 'As Time Goes By.'"
>
> —*Casablanca*

> "Mrs. Robinson, you're trying to seduce me. Aren't you?"
>
> —*The Graduate*

> "Yo, Adrian!"
>
> —*Rocky*

"You've got to ask yourself one question: 'Do I feel lucky?' Well, do ya, punk?"

—*Dirty Harry*

"Nice to meet you, Karen. My name is Doug. That's God spelled backward with a little bit of you wrapped up in it."

—Anonymous

First, a quick grammar reminder: direct dialogue almost always is set off by commas, whether they come in the middle, at the beginning, or at the end. Some creative writers employ neither commas nor quotation marks in their direct discourse, but for most readers, these novelties prove distractions rather than conveying an artistic point.

The punctuation is the easy part. It's not a difficult rule to follow or to understand. What gets me when I sit down to edit my own creative prose is that I usually have too much direct address in my dialogue. Even after three or four passes through a draft, I still find instances of direct address I need to change because they follow too closely upon each other. They're too clumped together, and that's as distracting as improper punctuation or any other kind of compositional redundancy.

Of course, the issue isn't that direct address is wrong or ungrammatical (providing you use your commas the right way). In fact, direct address can be the simplest and most logical way to let your readers know who a character is talking to when multiple people are present. The problem with overdoing direct address is that your dialogue starts to feel stilted. It doesn't flow. It feels forced and dry. Fake. And that's definitely not something you want your readers to feel.

Pay attention to direct address in your edits. Try to take out every instance of direct address you think your piece can do without. I feel as though I never remove enough, but it's something to shoot for.

 **WRITING PROMPT**

In the accompanying excerpt, chart every instance of direct discourse. Then go back and determine which can be effectively cut or revised to make the excerpt collectively read better.

When not at school we often frequented cemeteries. Why? "Because a lot of them are beautiful and no one's usually around," she said, "and sometimes the tombstones are flat so you can lay down on them and watch the sky." There was more to this, of course, though I did not realize it until much later. Part of what had attracted me to Emily was her fascination with death: with physical being and its lack. Her mother, she said, had bore many children, some of them afflicted or dead on arrival, and one of Emily's favorite and most entertaining pastimes was musing upon alternative scenarios involving these doomed or damaged siblings.

"If that one hadn't died," she'd lament, "I'd have had a playmate almost just my age."

"What if he were right in the head?" she'd say, another time, of a younger brother who wasn't. "Wouldn't all the girls think he was handsome?"

Despite this sad family history, however, or perhaps because of it, Emily was not very sympathetic toward the shortcomings of other people and, in fact, took great pleasure in criticizing their flaws.

"Have you ever noticed how ugly most people are?" she asked me once. "You'd think they'd try to make up for it by being more agreeable."

Her fascination with death and critiques of others had led her to a profound fondness for the carnal aspects of existence: slumber, food, and—especially—sex. Indeed, as if vaulting beyond any ordinary natural impulse, Emily seemed determined to couple with as much frequency as circumstance and her impressive resourcefulness allowed. And so there would be a cold, hard tombstone beneath my back, bouncing breasts and blushing, grunting face above, while a blue sky, stars, or the clouds of night or day wheeled above.

"Emily, I don't want you just for this," I would say, believing I meant it, even as my bobbing cock nodded otherwise.

On one such occasion some lines came to me from the Jove and Europa story translated in my Latin class a week earlier: "Dignity and love are seldom known to go to bed together." I wondered then and know now I did not love her. She was the first girl I had sex with, which for a fourteen-year-old boy seems like love, and we enjoyed some of the offbeat-young-couples-fun that made me think we might could be a couple. But for the most part I found myself shrugging off too much contemplation or misgiving and, as they say, simply enjoying the ride. Walking on jelly legs, surroundings a confusion, head and body reluctant to process them in the wake of what they had just experienced, I would absently consider her in retrospect.

"So this is having your brains f---ed out," I would remark in my mind.

Though it disappointed me at the time, I have grown to be glad that she was the one who ended it. Of course, many of the clichés one expects of a terminating teenage relationship came into play, including the moment when she said, "We can still be friends."

Employing Indirect Dialogue

I've cited the dangers of using too much direct dialogue and urged you to revise or cut as much of it as you can. Yet what exactly might you revise it to? The problem persists: what do you do if there is no escaping a long and potentially boring speech in, say, a novel?

I can virtually guarantee that in every extended creative prose piece you write, this problem will arise somewhere. A character will have something to say—something necessary that will take several pages to write—but it's neither exciting enough nor emotional enough to particularly hold the reader's interest. Simultaneously, it's not inconsequential enough to leave out. The solution is writing the dialogue *indirectly*.

In essence, *indirect dialogue* is the term I use for dialogue that is told, not shown. A speech that's shown is reproduced in full, word for word, with quotation marks around it. On the other hand, a speech that's told is summarized in a few sentences of prose. What would take many pages to cover if you were writing dialogue word for word can be neatly reduced to a brief paragraph.

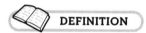 **DEFINITION**

Indirect dialogue is the act of summarizing dialogue.

When the final paragraph of summary is over, simply return to the "real time" of the scene at hand and continue as normal—as though the preceding 10 minutes of conversation had not been condensed into 30 seconds of narrative summary.

Note that you do not have to summarize an entire long speech using indirect dialogue. In fact, the process might proceed something like this:

1. You, as the writer, can have the character start to tell his or her tale by writing the dialogue word for word.

2. You then slip into narrative summary (i.e., indirect dialogue) for the middle section.

3. You return to writing dialogue word for word again toward the end.

Similarly, you can use this technique to summarize part or all of a lengthy conversation between two or more characters. You could summarize the uninteresting small talk at the start of a conversation, for example, but render the meatier or more profound second part of the conversation in proper dialogue.

Whenever you have a long speech given by a character in your novel, or a lengthy exchange of dialogue between two characters, just remember that you don't have to reproduce the dialogue at length. Sometimes writing dialogue indirectly is a much better choice.

WRITING PROMPT

Go back to excerpt, and identify every instance of indirect dialogue. Then go back again and determine which can be effectively cut or revised into direct dialogue.

Understanding Authorial Interpretation

Authorial interpretation sounds a little complex, and it is. But like many complicated things, it's important and worth learning about.

DEFINITION

Authorial interpretation is the act of the author writing with an intent that can be identified within his or her work.

For a while now, people who write about literature, called critical theorists, have argued that the author's particular interpretation is irrelevant to understanding a piece of literature. In other words, for the purposes of discussion, who is right about how the text ought to be interpreted and what subtexts are engaged within the story: the reader or the author?

That's a tough question and one for which there might not be a definitive answer. But just as an example, I'll give you take on it: I happen to believe I am the authority on my experience of writing the novel and what my intentions were during the writing process. However, I am not a unique authority on how a reader reads and interprets the text.

Every reader has his or her specialized experience of reading and thereby interacting with the text. If I hear that experience described, I might believe it profound and sophisticated, wrong-headed and simplistic, or something in between. But I'm not in control of the reading experience.

Beyond actual factual errors, I can't "correct" a reading experience, nor would I want to. A book, like a child, has its own life after it leaves my hands. For me, that's one of the great charms of writing: that people interact with my books unmediated by me. However, I do remain the authority about my experience of writing my books.

Over the years, I've seen many discussions dealing with potential differences between the author's view of his or her own work, and the reader's reading of it. And unfortunately, I've dealt with it firsthand.

When my historical novel *Confederado* was published, it was met by many positive reviews and only one negative assessment. However, the negative account was so damning and dismissive of the novel that the editor of the magazine in which it appeared actually contacted me to write a response. The very person who was publishing the review felt it was unfair enough to merit input from the author.

Now, out of legal concerns, I won't include the negative review or reviewer's name here, but I will include my response, which combats his points based on what I knew about my book as its author.

Upon receiving the recently published review of *Confederado,* the editor of *SLR,* indicating that aspects of the novel may have been overlooked or misinterpreted, contacted me with a request to compose a response. I was happy to do so. However, I would preface my remarks with the general assertion that, having authored a number of reviews myself, the art of reviewing is a deceptively difficult genre of writing. The reviewer brings with her or him, unconsciously or not, her or his own tastes, agendas, and pet-peeves, which—depending on the reviewer—conspire, a little or a lot, to alter the undertaking less into a consideration of the presented fictional world and more into a looking glass which offers back the reviewer's own predispositions. This review of *Confederado* constitutes an example of such a phenomenon.

The review begins with a complimentary formal analysis not unlike what one might encounter in a creative writing workshop. Yet the reviewer proceeds to assert that the "power" of the writing, reminiscent of Faulkner, comes at the price of fully-realized characterization. Already, then, we have encountered a fundamental interpretive problem: one cannot generally compare the writing to that of Faulkner—a novelist lauded for his rich characterizations—while also asserting that it suffers from a lack of characterization

The review then performs an additional remove from the southern modernist Faulkner, speculating that the novel is based on nineteenth-century southern romances which make it "overly didactic." Yet, before doing so, the review establishes the book's concerns as connected to the "Global South, an approach to southern literature that tries to develop a broader sense of what regional difference might mean in the U.S. and beyond." It is as if, instead of composing a coherent argument regarding the novel, the reviewer is more interested in advertising, in fragmented bits and pieces, his knowledge of southern literature. By the review's third paragraph, it has been asserted the book simultaneously possesses modernist Faulknerian writing, qualities of didactic nineteenth-century romance novels, and a shared conceptual concern with contemporary southern literary criticism. However, any relationships between these tropes remain unarticulated.

Things get worse. The reviewer proceeds to identify the former slave who treats the protagonist upon his return from the war as a "loyal black mammy" and criticizes her "elevated syntax and diction." As the back cover of the novel states, the book is based on a true family story. The author did not make up the fact that this former slave stayed with the protagonist's family, aided in his convalescence, and was made literate with the assistance of the family. Yet the reviewer seems to prefer and insist upon an uneducated "mammy," dismissing her speech as "improbable" and appropriating her presence as a symbolic opportunity for the narrator to offer an "apologist" position on slavery. It seems a sad state of affairs that almost half a century after the publication of Styron's *The Confessions of Nat Turner* a white author may not offer a characterization of a former slave—and a laudable one at that—without inviting tired, worn-out arguments and criticism from backward-looking individuals.

The reviewer continues to find fault with the narrative once it moves to Brazil, the chief objections being wanting characterization (again), comparisons of Brazilian people and culture to those of the American South, and the protagonist's killing of an anaconda as a symbol of his general superiority to his Brazilian peers. While the characterization issue already has been discussed, the comparison dynamic seems altogether unavoidable. After all, how is the protagonist supposed to interpret his new surroundings other than against his previous background, regardless of what and where that might have been? As for the killing of the anaconda, the reviewer might simply consider background again: while the hunting party is made up almost entirely of the local sons of civilian farmers, the protagonist is a four-year war veteran nonplussed by physical violence and very adept at, well, killing. The reviewer goes on to compare the protagonist's hunting success to "St. George slays the dragon," and here it is worth pointing out that throughout the review all of the reviewer's comparisons are to western and white American literature: Faulkner, Virgil, St. George. In a novel which contains not so subtle references to several well-known African-American and Brazilian works, the reviewer's inability to detect any of them demonstrates a pronounced lack of multicultural reading background, a general Eurocentric literary sensibility, and a willful determination to have the book fit a predetermined conservative white southern framework.

In the concluding paragraph, the reviewer muses, "Were this novel about the thorny moral question surrounding Reconstruction policy or even a realistic attempt to understand the psychological position of those southerners who chose to emigrate, it would be fair to ask readers to suspend certain disbeliefs." On the contrary, that the disbeliefs of this reviewer are largely self-manufactured rather than gleaned from the book at hand constitutes the prime reason for the review's almost complete failure as a useful document. Gazing into the mirror of the novel, the reviewer has offered up his own means and bases for interpretation. And it is not a pretty picture.

Admittedly, the mirror association and last sentence are pretty hard-hitting, but then this reviewer essentially was trying to label me a racist and Confederate apologist. I believe my own position was validated by the fact that the reviewer never responded to my points; that was the end of it.

A good reader and reviewer who is evaluating work they did not create often deploys words like *seems* or *appears* in order to make it clear they're only speculating, whether they're lauding the work or pointing out problems that arise because of the imperfection of the craft. In other words, a good critic never imputes motive where he can't actually know. Unfortunately, though, it happens quite a bit, often with an attitude of mocking cleverness and/or snide superiority.

Often I read interpretations of books that have little to do with the book and more to do with the filter the individual critic is reading through. Indeed, many professional critics build their reputations on such grounds. This doesn't mean the reader cannot or should not find such interpretations in a text; I think texts are mutable things within the framework of reading. But it also doesn't mean that any given reader is always more right than the writer, or more right than another reader who sees something different in the text. Just as writers might bring unexamined assumptions and defaults to a text, so might readers.

So if I say X was my intent in writing Y, then X was my intent. If the reader doesn't see X, or sees Z instead, that doesn't change my intent, although it might call into question my craft, or my ability to bring across to readers what my intentions were. But what if Reader 1 sees X while Reader 2 sees Z? Is one reader right and the other wrong? Who decides?

Ultimately, as a creative writer, you have to pursue your vision, not one mediated through the reactions of others. Yet at the same time, you have to be able to hear and listen to voices that challenge your understanding of received wisdom. Sometimes they can help you. The goal, after all, is to bring as clear, extensive, and undistorted a view as you can to the thing you want to tell.

Writing Stock Characters

One of the main reasons—and there are many—my first, unpublished novel doesn't work is that most of the characters in it are *stock characters*. Populate your narrative with enough of them, and you're going to end up with melodrama.

 **DEFINITION**

A **stock character** is a figure drawn from widely acknowledged cultural types for their characteristics and mannerisms.

Consider the following character types: the noble and selfless warrior; the rich, pretty young woman who feels trapped by her sheltered life; the evil, scheming rich guy; the poor girl in love with the warrior who's too blind to see it. Throw these characters together, and you can see all the probable possibilities of what's going to transpire. That's the problem with stock characters: there's no wondering about who they are or what they'll do. Readers already know. Although it's usually best to avoid them, there are ways you can make stock characters work.

One maxim is that if you use a stock character, make him or her as minor a character as possible. Consider the warrior mentioned in the preceding paragraph. What if he is made to be something of a fish out of water? That is, other warriors who are more prominent in the narrative seem hypocritical when compared to him. This makes him a subtle foil and catalyst for the work's more major players. He's not the reader's focus of attention—and he shouldn't be—but he has an impact on events simply by virtue of his presence. As this example illustrates, you need to know why a stock character is in your work and limit them to scenes in which you can clearly name the way they help the overall purpose.

Another valuable—and fun—way to use stock characters is to turn their qualities inside out. This is a great way to be creative and do something new with an old, familiar, and boring type. Why not make the warrior very selfish and something of a coward? Make the poor young woman scheme and rebel instead of casting her as an economically challenged damsel in distress? Maybe instead of the warrior rescuing her, *she* has to wipe out his enemies for *him*. Every little difference from the classic type makes your stock character less typical and more of an individual—which also makes them more believable.

 WRITING PROMPT

In your journal, make a list of stock characters in a content area that interests you. Then try to reverse their characteristics and put an asterisk next to the combinations that interest you. This exercise might prove helpful when the time arrives to get to work on a particular creative writing project.

Remember that great characterization is the opposite of what makes up a stock character. Inverting stereotypical characters and drawing on real people and areas of experience you know gives you figures that seem to leap off the page. They'll feel real to your readers if you succeed in conveying how real they are to you.

The Least You Need to Know

- Direct dialogue is a powerful tool, but use it sparingly.
- Indirect dialogue helps summarize action, but too much of it becomes an exercise in excessive showing.
- Authorial interpretation is important in weighing your intentions versus what others might have to say about your work.
- Avoid stock characters unless you can make them minor figures or invert their qualities for more interest.

Potent Setting

In previous eras of literature, long descriptions of *setting* were often admired and respected, but most modern audiences want their stories to get to the action sooner. The same transition has taken place more quickly over the past few decades in mainstream film. However, don't let these trends convince you to sell setting short or abandon it altogether. In fact, if you don't use it wisely, you risk alienating or even losing your readers.

It helps if you think of setting as more of an exciting opportunity rather than a duty. Just as some plays can get away with almost no stage design or props, some narratives can get away with minimal setting. Yet consider how much information you glean from settings in your everyday life.

Imagine, for example, you're going to a party at a house you've never visited before, given by people you don't know well. You aren't sure what to expect, and you're a bit nervous. As you walk toward the house, you might look at the front lawn as you approach the house. Is there a fancy birdbath, a plastic kiddie pool, or pink flamingos? You'll probably look at the house itself. Is it large or small? How many lights are on? Do you hear music and if so, what kind? By the time you ring the doorbell and/or saunter in, you already have a much better idea of what to expect, just from a fairly unconscious assessment of the setting. It makes you a bit more comfortable having some idea of where you're going and what you're walking into.

Setting does the same thing for readers of a narrative. The question is, how?

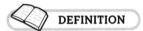 **DEFINITION**

The location, or locations, in which a narrative takes place is called the **setting.**

Thankfully, concrete base elements of setting exist:

- **Location**   Are we on a football field or in a prison cell? In Berlin or in Tokyo? On Earth or in outer space?

- **Time**   When is your narrative taking place?

- **Historical time**   Is it the modern day, the seventeenth century, or some imagined past or future time?

- **Seasonal time**   Is it autumn or spring?

- **Daily time**   Is it morning or evening?

- **Weather**   What's the temperature like? Is it humid or arid? Is it raining, or is there only distant thunder?

You needn't give your readers information about all these things in every narrative. Just include the ones that are most relevant—the ones that will communicate something useful and interesting (and perhaps symbolic) to your audience.

 WATCH OUT!

Setting provides writers with a sometimes-overwhelming desire to describe things. So watch out for runaway adjectives and adverbs because too many of them will weaken your writing. You needn't avoid them completely, but try to use strong, specific nouns and verbs whenever possible.

Constructing Your Story's World

If you're not going to set your story in the present time and in real-world locations, it's usually best to come up with the basics of your own world before you move on to a narrative. Your environment affects your life, so your created world plays a crucial role in it. Simple.

Now for the hard part. Where does your setting begin? You might have a fantasy Earth, or an Earth-based world. You might decide your story takes place on another planet, on a spaceship, or under water. That's the beginning.

What follows is deciding what the physical world is like: what do people build with, warm themselves with, wear for clothing? The type of world affects these things. You can't easily get away with bonfires underwater, for example, so it's not very likely that your characters use them in spiritual ceremonies—that is, unless you explain how your created world possesses different physical laws.

When you have a good idea what kind of world your narrative is takes place in, you can start looking at what inhabits the world. If yours is a slightly alternate version of Earth, are your animals the same ones found here? Or could they be mythological, something completely new, or a combination?

Keep in mind that realistic consideration plays into the most fantastic worlds. If, for example, you have three dozen kinds of fanged, claw-wielding monsters, be sure they plenty of prey. They opposite can be true, too. Think of all the deer that inhabit U.S. cities and suburbs. This is because humans hunted wolves to extinction in many areas, so the deer have no natural predators.

Just as important is the society that whatever advanced inhabitants have: government, law, the arts, recreation, education, religion, types of jobs, the economy, etc. Don't worry, though. You won't need to go into detail and explain all these things, but you will need to know the answer if the narrative calls for it.

To decide on the society, you'll also have to determine the "when" of your world. Is it based on the Dark Ages? A far-distant super technological future?

I realize all these world-building variables I'm throwing at you can seem overwhelming. What many writers do is sit down with good 'ol pen and paper and draw a map of their world. How many continents are there? Or are there any? It's not something that works for everyone, but it has proven useful for many published writers.

It's amazing how much the layout of a map can inspire more story ideas than a single person could ever write in a lifetime—and how a map provides a lot of rules, too. If your characters are living on the coldest, highest peak of the most treacherous mountain range in the land, you can readily imagine the hardy folk you're dealing with. Then, you can research societies in our own world to support them. Do your hardy, snow-dwelling people resemble the Norse, or are they more like Inuit? Note all the options and details you have.

IDEAS AND INSPIRATION

Don't make your created world more complicated than necessary; stick with what you're comfortable with. A lot of science fiction fans, for instance, know a lot about science, technology, and space, and they will take delight in pointing out your mistakes. The same is true of Civil War buffs and all manner of enthusiasts. So although you're creating your own world, you can't toss away all the rules. Stick to your own areas of knowledge, or conduct the necessary research to be sure knowledgeable readers will buy into the world you've created.

So go be creative, but remember that your readers are Earth dwellers like you who know the rules of this world better than any other. They'll feel insulted if you try to throw out all the rules they're used to without sufficient justification or explanation.

Through a Camera's Lens

Most people lead rather busy lives, which cause them to miss out on the story ideas constantly unfolding around them. Often, if you don't write down an idea, you'll forget it. (Hence the aforementioned importance of keeping a journal on hand.)

Some of you might find yourselves stuck for writing ideas because, instead of looking to the world you live in for inspiration, you only see the rushed, unromantic, day-to-day duties you're forced to perform. However, a little imagination and mental discipline can change that. Try looking at your life through the lens of a camera, and suddenly things will appear quite different.

Have you ever gone on a journey to a new place and been amazed by the beauty of your surroundings? Do you wish you still had the sharp imagination you had when you were little? Do you wish you could better keep track of the story ideas you get when you're on trips or visiting new places? You can dig deep into your childlike imagination to establish setting through photography.

One way to be sure you remember the narrative ideas you get from nature, or the things around you, is by taking pictures with an actual camera or your phone's camera. Then, you could use your pictures to create an electronic or print story photo journal. Alongside the pictures, write about how the place made you feel, along with setting, characters, histories, and narrative ideas.

When you come across areas that inspire a work in progress, get detail shots. If you're in a forest that inspires you to write about glow fairies, be sure to get up close and personal with the blades of grass, toadstools, and tree bark. Those detail shots will help you word things better when you write.

Of course, if you're able to go wherever your story is set, do so.

WRITING PROMPT

Arrange printed photos on the ground around you or on a table. Or create a set of photographs in a notebook. Go through your photos and pick out eight to start with, and add as you go. Then put together a narrative with your photos. Remember, you can interpret the photos in any way to make your piece more interesting. This is an exciting way to find new ideas because you're using the tools of creative writing in conjunction with visual stimuli.

Establishing Atmosphere

As opposed to photos, *atmosphere* is abstract and describes the overall feeling of a place—romantic, threatening, welcoming, etc. It depends largely on your word choice, as a room with "oppressive low ceilings and blood-red curtains" feels much different to a reader than a room with "cozy low ceilings and cheerful red curtains."

DEFINITION

Atmosphere is the impression or vibe a given setting gives off to other characters and the reader.

To be successful, almost any piece of writing needs to develop a strong sense of atmosphere. It draws your readers into your piece so they can vividly imagine the world you're creating. It also sets up expectations and sometimes gives them information about any characters they're likely to encounter.

Given their similarities, it's important to note setting isn't the same as atmosphere, although atmosphere is a big part of the setting and can help shape the mood of a narrative. A piece set in an old, rundown, river-bottom warehouse immediately evokes a sense of eeriness and isolation; of neglect and dreariness.

Be sure to choose a setting that suits the type of narrative you're writing. Different settings create different atmospheres. In a ghost story, for example, you want the atmosphere to be creepy and one of trepidation. An ideal setting is an old theater or graveyard. A setting on a crowded nude beach in Brazil, on the other hand, calls for a very different atmosphere. Keep in mind, though, that having the aforementioned glow fairies on hand in either of these settings would seem rather odd. You would really have to stretch your narrative to make that work.

As with setting, you can't create atmosphere without description. But this doesn't mean you need paragraphs and paragraphs of clinical observation to ensure your readers can picture the scene. A few powerful adjectives and adverbs will effectively make your readers feel part of the story. Say you've chosen a warehouse as your setting; using different words can dramatically vary the atmosphere created. For example, look at the following description from the story "The Shadow Over Lynchburg":

> Though the Lynchburg downtown had been privy to a measured, years-long movement toward revitalization and improvement, there remained whole corners and blocks that were as dark and rundown as they had been three or four decades previous. The rectangular quarter-mile expanse of the Felwealth warehouse complex constituted one such stretch. Built along the Richmond-Roanoke railroad, which roughly paralleled the James River between those disparate municipalities, the complex rested almost upon the water and during periods of flooding it was not unusual for the westernmost building to have brown river muck standing as much as a foot-deep on its ground floor. In the early 1980s Reverend Felwealth had decreed that a flood wall be constructed to protect the complex, but the James had other ideas and, during a week-long period of heavy rains, washed away the preliminary building materials, wrenching them from their platforms and moorings or soaking them into uselessness, before they could ever be utilized.

This passage affords images of darkness and dilapidation, coupled with floods and watery space and a pleasant place. From this piece, your readers can also imagine the type of people a protagonist would meet here, such as working-class laborers and homeless individuals.

The following describes a contrasting view of the city and produces a very different mood:

> Early one summer morning Isaac stood naked at the kitchen bay window in Lyra's townhouse, gazing out—as had become his habit during such clear dawns—at the extraordinary view of the city's southern mountains. Construction projects had been initiated on three of the ridges, but it still pleased him to dwell upon the range of hills in the early morning light.

Here, although construction is underway, the collective vista before the protagonist is one of pastoral beauty. Your readers might picture bulldozers and loggers among the hills but also deer, bear, and other forms of wildlife.

You've already learned about the importance of the five senses, and they should not be neglected in atmosphere. However, something related I haven't mentioned yet—weather—can be just as important. A gloriously sunny day, for example, immediately conjures feelings of warmth and joy—perhaps even a premonition that something happy is about to happen. This might be the atmosphere you want to create for an occasion such as a wedding. On the other hand, perhaps it's a wedding doomed not to take place or a marriage destined for dysfunction. Again, you can use the weather to change the mood of the narrative and build a mounting sense of tension, such as when the wind gathers momentum and thick, dark clouds begin swirling slowly overhead.

Like weather, the time of day can make a difference to the type of atmosphere your readers feel as they read. For example, you can darken and intensify a story by setting it at night. There's always an extra sense of menace, of threat and uncertainty, in a narrative in which most of one's senses are blunted.

Writing Setting as Action

As noted earlier, in eras past, it used to be the norm for writers to use several pages to describe setting. The rises and falls of multiple families and estates seemingly had to be disclosed before a reader could finally reach the action at hand. And that was okay at the time. Readers were more patient then. In fact, it was what they wanted.

Yet readers change along with everything else, and today, anything you publish must compete for attention not only with TV and movies, but also with video games, the internet, and myriad other distractions. Readers want to get on with the story, and the younger the readership, the less patience you're going to get. As a writer, therefore, you need to invest the reader in the world you've created not only with descriptions of the landscape, but also with interesting characters as they move through that setting. In other words, you need your setting to become part of the action of your characters.

Let me show you what I mean. Here's the opening of a creative nonfiction piece called "'Reunification by Bayonet'?":

> "A reliable scout has informed me Generals Lee and Grant would like to join us." These words, spoken aloud in a clear welcoming voice on an overcast morning, came neither from a soldier nor politician of the Civil War era, but rather served as the first lines uttered by site President S. Waite Rawls III at the grand opening of the Museum of the Confederacy's new state-of-the-art satellite facility in Appomattox County, Virginia on March 31, 2012.
>
> Members of the audience cast their heads in every direction, albeit in vain. The legendary leaders Mr. Rawls announced did not appear directly or, as a famous Civil War battle account once related, rise "like demons out of the earth." No such luck. However there did occur a ruckus of some sort off in the distance behind the couple hundred or so of us gathered on the comfortable grassy area outside the museum to witness its dedication. The noise grew louder, a shuffling of feet, and a line of men, marching shoulder to shoulder, swung into view on the asphalt road leading up to the building.

In fewer than 200 words, you know where and when you are, the state of the weather, some of the people in attendance, and the purpose of the occasion. The announcement of the historical generals is an effective lead, only it turns out they are Civil War reenactors. The cloudiness of the weather metaphorically mirrors the ongoing problematic politics accompanying that war and a storm of sorts that breaks open overhead later in the piece. Thus, setting and action are woven together in such a way that they afford readers an idea of place while also giving them notions of who's on hand and what's transpiring.

Identifying Types of Setting

Now that I've led you through the different manifestations of setting as the world, camera, atmosphere, and action, consider the excerpt from the creative nonfiction piece "Satyr." As your writing prompt, identify which types of setting are employed. Then try to determine if they're the right ones. In other words, what would happen if different forms of setting were employed at various points in the essay?

"Satyr"

"Marvellous!" a character once exclaimed—a British character to be exact, hence the double-L spelling of the word. "The marvellous beauty and fascination of all wild things! The horror of man's unnatural life, his heaped-up civilization!" As it is the magical essence of the former exclamation I wish to get at, I shall say again something of my own relationship with nature, for I have written on it more than once but never seem to get it exactly right. Too often I fear I dwell on its darker, wilder manifestations—the storms, the predation, the ahumanism—since it is they which have left the deepest marks on body and mind alike, shaping them in the process. Yet in truth I have loved just as well and been molded by a great host of harmless, benign representatives of the natural world, having always possessed, for instance, a pronounced fondness for flowers: whether admiring the uniform arrangements of rare varieties in gardens or watching the wild natural sort sway and bob on a windswept field. Even the manmade manifestations have proven attractive and moving to me on occasion, in particular those which grew beneath Grandmother's needle as I sat at her feet holding the quilt and watching.

Though it was home to three separate fenced-off pastures—the wire of which I had spent many a weekend and summer day running tree to tree or post to post, or some mixture of the two—my family's farm was covered mostly in woods. I am well aware I am not alone in having always felt there is something about a forest, any forest, when considered as an entity of its own, that remains primal, enigmatic, and majestic. It resembles a vast dark sea in the mysteries it conceals and the manner in which it envelops you. One may judge by its sounds how it senses and greets your approach—the scattering and silencing of wildlife, the modulations in bird song, the give of the ground and the old decaying matter beneath your feet. Though I have always found that greeting reassuring, as though returning to a beloved homeland or other sacred place, it is a response which nonetheless forces you to sense your insignificance. You do not matter to a forest. Yet the knowledge is comforting to the extent that it also renders your modern trials—paying a bill say, or quarreling with a coworker over some forgettable trifle—into their proper places of insignificance. In a forest the synthetic human communities and accompanying rules which modern life forces us to function within and observe are made to appear ridiculous. Stay there long enough and your concerns give way, consciously or no, to the old animal verities of food, shelter, water. Your shoes and clothes begin to look and feel increasingly out of place, ridiculous even. Our bodies make themselves known to us again and, in doing so, move us a little closer to the stripped down essence of ourselves.

I have found it a great joy and privilege in the woods merely to sit and listen. Doing so over the course of your youth develops within you certain gifts: the ability, for example, to close your eyes and tell what time of year it is solely by the manner in which the leaves rustle. So precious were the woods to me during my own youth that I went through periods during which I loathed to leave them at all and would spend the entire weekend, day and night, within their confines. In preparation for a night's slumber in the forest I would always try to find the thickest bed of bracken to lie down on—often set on the north face of a hillside beneath a dense stand of mountain laurel or rhododendron. If I had heard tell of rain or knew of its coming by other means, I would choose a spot where the leaves on the overhanging branches were thickest so that they might shield me. Otherwise, I slept beneath an opening in the canopy where I might contemplate the moon's cataract or the slow sweep of the stars. Then I would fall into an untroubled yet attuned slumber known only to hunters and other forest folk. Sometimes it seemed to me as though the ragged brittle leaves and sharp pine needles I had heaped about and upon my body were the forest's version of the protective wings of some great loving bird which sought to enclose me in a downy safety. And I loved how the pale white sycamore branches, rising from the low watery places and visible sometimes even in a moonless dark, called to mind bone or silk depending on my mood. They came to be a second home to me, those woods, though a full understanding of them would always evade me. I never felt fearful or restless there, but rather loved that long silence which has been likened to death but in truth was merely the life of the place.

For all their subtle teeming life, it remains forests are places which know death constantly, that rely on it in fact for the ongoing promulgation of their life systems. The most notable human participation in death's function in a wood or grove nowadays presents itself via the mostly lamentable pastimes of logging and hunting. The former most often takes the form of outright annihilation—the severe alteration of the environment into a non-forest: something unrecognizable, or even just "not"—while the latter, though distasteful to many forest lovers, visits a far more negligible impact. Yet the endgame of both actions is "caused death," which is really a form of murder. I continue to count a number of hunters and loggers among my friends, despite the fact I consider them death dealers by virtue of their craft. And I myself—having grown up on a farm and cut short the life of many a tree and creature—would be remiss not to acknowledge my complicity in such actions. But then we might say something similar of undertakers and doctors who specialize in terminal maladies. There is, after all, an art in the way a being chooses to render death; there is too an art of dying. And at least one of those blank canvases will be set before each of us, ready or not, at a certain time, appropriate or not, during the course of one's life.

Remember that setting predominantly is important in a narrative because it draws the reader into your written world. Setting can also be like another character in your story; it can make things happen.

Keep in mind, too, that setting should be a pleasurable creative exercise rather than a chore. It can be quite fun developing a world consisting largely of your own whims and preferences.

Lastly, remember that the story of your world—of your own particular setting—often is a wonderful and inspiring place to start your story.

The Least You Need to Know

- Setting is its own functioning world and should appear lifelike.
- Photos can help you order and detail your setting.
- Settings should emit a sense of atmosphere that gives readers feelings and impressions about what they're reading.
- Settings should be intertwined with action to help propel your narrative.

Plot/Story, Struggle, and Connections

Many creative writing teachers are fond of maintaining there are only two types of stories: "someone went on a journey" or "a stranger arrived in town." Regardless of the particulars— in this case, the journey and the town—stories must contain conflicts and at least a little reconciliation. When various phenomena (cultures, generations, genders, hoods) encounter each other, conflict is bound to occur. Likewise, when human beings make connections, some form of love and understanding occurs.

A character, like you and me, is someone capable of change. Story is the process of that change. The transition may be alive to dead, ugly to beautiful, ignorant to wise, callous to compassionate, certain to uncertain—or the reverse of all these things. The important thing is that the change occurs because the character confronts a situation that will change his or her assumptions and somehow shake up their beliefs.

In This Chapter

* Your hero's journey
* Creating power struggles
* Making character connections
* Dealing with disconnections

If a story succeeds, we as readers will have our capacity for empathy enlarged by having lived in a character's skin for the duration. And typically, it hinges on these questions:

- Where does the protagonist want to go? What does he or she desire?

- What are the obstacles encountered? What discoveries are made, and what conflicts arise?

- What does he or she do to overcome these obstacles? What decisions does he or she make?

- Is the goal reached? Is it expected?

Now it's time to have a closer look at how these questions get woven or built into a story.

The All-Important Journey

Heroes have challenges to overcome, and often those challenges take the form of journeys. You can see this form in an old legend like *Beowulf*, all the way up to the most recent blockbuster Hollywood action film. In fact, it's not surprising that heroic epics like *Beowulf* and *The Iliad* have been made into twenty-first-century movies because their stories still resonate with viewers.

What exactly is it that resonates from such stories across centuries? A professor named Joseph Campbell spent much of his life studying and explaining the life principles embedded in the structure of ancient stories. What he discovered after researching hero myths from hundreds of cultures is that they're all basically the same story told in infinitely different ways—that is, they involve a hero or protagonist and a journey.

How does this relate to creative writing? It enables you to write stories that make sense and are satisfying to your reader. However, it's important to remember that the hero's journey is a guideline only. Like grammar, once you know and understand the rules, you can break them. Nobody likes a rigid formula—at least creative writers usually don't. And the hero's journey is not a formula. It gives you the understanding you need to take familiar expectations and then turn them on their heads in creative defiance. The values of the hero's journey are what's key: they are symbols of universal life experience.

It's important to realize that the journey can be outward to an actual place (think *The Wizard of Oz*) or inward to the mind, the heart, the spirit. Sometimes the journey of the story ends in fulfillment, sometimes not. Sometimes the goal is reached and proves not worth the trip; sometimes a detour leads to a paradise or a kind of hell. As the writer, you get to decide where your protagonist's journey leads.

Here's an example of a journey the begins a creative nonfiction piece titled "Coaches":

Did I hear you asking about the old man? I thought so. He has become a regular feature and, I dare say, something of a conversation piece along this desolate stretch of Outer Banks national seashore where one may still ride out onto the beach in a 4-wheel drive truck or jeep and churn through treacherous red sands until, like some sportsman's mirage, that whimsical portion of land and water presents itself where it is the fisherman's hope that current, tide, wind, and a dramatically sloping sandbar will have conspired to create a place where the tastiest of blues, croakers, spot, drum, and sea trout will have gathered together in eager anticipation of his hook. There he will park, bait, and cast out his lines. Then the waiting, short or long, as the sun arcs and swings high above the Atlantic, passing east to south and then sinking low behind him to the west, playing tag as it were with the horizon and marking by cloud-interrupted degrees the unfolding of another day at the beach.

It is probable the careful observer will divine something of the curious quality of the old man in question before he ever steps forth from his vehicle—before it even rolls to a stop on the shell-littered prominence he has chosen for it—for following his rusty black pickup, hovering above it, will be the scores of shore birds that have learned to recognize the truck and its treats—the innards, heads, and tails of fish, as well as the unwanted sandwich crusts—that fly forth from its tailgate, hurled by the old man, when he has cut away or consumed that which he desires for himself. I hope you will appreciate, then—will see, as I do—that when the old man drives toward us down the beach, assortment of sea fowl in tow, the collective image of motion is less suggestive of a land-loving black truck grinding its way, axle dragging, through deep heavy sands and more the quaint impression of a miniature galleon cutting through a heavy sea, holding its course true, gulls and albatrosses flapping about its masts.

When at last the old man finds his place in the sun, a chief requisite of which must be that he can discern no other vehicle along the shore in either direction, he will cast anchor by way of emergency brake and disembark, squinting at the water's morning glare as he does so. Studying him closely, as he studies the rolling tide, you will note that though wanting in height, he presents a physique unusually broad and strong for a person of his seventy-odd years. Indeed, a dormant, hunched power seems to lurk disguised behind those tanned shoulders that slope gently forward from decades of bending at hoe, plow, work bench and—in a much different arena of experience—absorbed both the punishing physical blows of tacklers and the gut-wrenching emotional lows of narrow losses in the course of enduring the heavy mantle of great athlete and, later, great coach.

Yes, there is still much of the coach and athlete about him: in the careful way he manages both his fishing lines and the menagerie of animals that dwell on his inland farm, as well as in the games he plays on the beach to ward off idleness when the fish are not biting. Chief among these diversions is a variation of golf he has created for himself which involves the ocean, the dunes, and even the sporadic holes of the fiddler crabs. Rusty eight- or nine-iron in hand, up and down the beach he goes, keeping score for himself and his imaginary opponent, who might be an acquaintance, sports celebrity, or relative. Though I was never exposed to any country club sports and possess no affinity for golf, the old man insists I am one of his most difficult imaginary opponents, having taken him into overtime, pressed him to the point of defeat, many times.

As he plays, his eyes never wander far from his lines and when there is a hit—when short vigorous tugs bend the top of one of his poles—he drops his iron and rushes to take up one sport in place of the other. Athlete and coach he may be no longer, yet he cannot give up his games. They remain his great passion.

Indeed there is no happier time for him on the beach than when the fish are running and he is pulling them in as fast as he can pry them off his hooks, rebait, and cast again. And that happiness extends into evening when, back at his little cottage, beer close at hand, the cooler is flung open and the day's catch spills forth onto the cutting board.

"Clean 'em and eat 'em, by George!" he will declare if someone is present, or even if someone is not, and commence to chopping and gutting the fish with a rusty old steak knife, taking periodic sips from his Budweiser, greasy fingers sliding around the aluminum. Perhaps he will hum one of the mountain songs of his youth or elect to cut in silence. He requires no audience to savor his victory.

Although it sticks mostly to a seaside setting, this piece manages to afford the reader a panorama in space and time—as well as details that particularize both the setting and the manner of protagonist they're getting to know. Do any changes take place in the character during this opening journey? What does the final line of the passage say about the character as a person?

 WRITING PROMPT

Write about a time you started out on a trip but failed to arrive at your destination. Make yourself the hero or central consciousness in this telling. What was the obstacle—weather, accident, mechanical failure, human failure, human conflict? Characterize both the people involved and the setting through significant detail; give a sense of the trip itself. What changed from your beginning expectations? How did you change?

Protagonist Versus Antagonist

Narratives, whether they're journeys or not, contain their own substructures. In ancient times, Greek philosopher Aristotle identified the portions as a beginning, a middle, and an end. More recently, creative writers have begun looking at story structure in terms of conflict, crisis, and resolution.

Think about your day-to-day existence. Life offers periods of comfortable communication, peaceful pleasure, and productive work, all of which are extremely interesting to those involved. But in a narrative, passages about such times make for dull reading; they cannot be used as plot. In life, people seek peace and posterity. In creative writing, only trouble is interesting.

That "trouble" often takes the form of a power struggle between two nearly equal forces: a *protagonist* and *antagonist*.

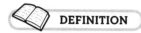 **DEFINITION**

> The **protagonist** is the central character of a narrative. The **antagonist** is a representation of the obstacles to the protagonist's desires. It may be another human being or some other force.

If the antagonist is some abstract force, like the character's desire, it will also have a very specific manifestation: not "nature" but "seven miles of water rapids in northeast Georgia"; not "the supernatural" but "a mutant reptile embryo capable of hatching in a mammal's ear."

Narratives typically begin with a situation in which the power is with the protagonist or the antagonist. Something happens and the power shifts to the other—think of the Trojan War in which power switches back and forth repeatedly, depending on which side the gods favor. Ideally, each time the power shifts, the stakes are raised and the tension increases. Each conflict is bigger and more intense than the last, until—at last—one of the two opposing forces manifests its power in a way the other cannot match.

The following visceral example from the novel *Confederado* pits two characters—who are more or less physically equal but possess very different backgrounds and motives—against each other:

> The better part of half an hour passed and then, as if answering some cue of fortune, Emilio appeared from around the curve of the hill, guiding Heliodoro carefully over the rocks. As man and horse approached, Alvis discerned the animal was nearly lame, his legs working unevenly as he stumbled on the broken terrain. When they drew closer still, he observed Heliodoro's swaying gait and noted the whip marks, resembling crimson brush strokes, about his flanks and rear.
>
> "You are a fool, foreign trash," said Emilio by way of greeting, coming to a halt not twenty feet from his nemesis, "to have come back here. But this beaten old nag deserves a beaten rider, though I promise you that when we are finished today you will never ride again."
>
> Alvis eyed Emilio's contemptuous countenance for a moment before gazing beyond it, letting his eyes wander up and down the barren hillside and then farther, across the span of lonely hills. A light breeze filtered through the draw, raising miniature dust devils out of the earth as if some sorcerer were seeking to summon his demons. When Alvis's glance at last returned to Emilio he slowly shook his head.

"No, Ferreira bastard," he replied at last. "I fear it is you who are the fool for having come here with those poor outlaws, bearing your customary words but aided no longer by the customary allies you depend upon to realize their intent. There is an old saying in Paraguay: that when two devils come together, hell is to pay. Yet I have grown weary of killing and will spare you even now if you give me my horse and walk back down that draw."

Emilio spat at Alvis in contempt and, with a curse, drew out his knife and dismounted.

"Get down off that horse!" he yelled, voice hoarse with malice, "or I'll cut its neck open and drag you from it!"

Alvis stared at the raving bastard as he shouted anew and brandished his knife.

When at last Alvis dismounted and loosed his gun belt, wrapping it about the pommel of the saddle, Emilio let loose a string of filth, punctuated with a sneer. Yet for all the bastard's high bravado, Alvis noted that his knife hand trembled.

Then the Confederado drew out his own knife—a jewel-hilted razor of a blade lifted from the headless corpse of a Paraguayan brigadier in the wake of Piribebuy. It was a cruel looking, curved weapon, the nicks of which boasted it had drunk the blood of many men before finding its way into the possession of this North American whom so many had sought to kill.

Slowly Alvis walked toward Emilio, eyes locked on the wild orbs of his nemesis.

"Let these few moments," he said, raising the knife familiarly, "decide our fates forever."

Emilio's trembling increased but he gritted his teeth and spat. Alvis's mind was cool. It harkened back to days of his youth when he and Silvanus Stenson had stabbed at each other with harmless wooden sticks, the little woodsman teaching him the Monocan way of handling a knife mixed in with the rough tutelage he had received from the mountain men who had reared him. The instruction had proven useful on occasions in both wars when, while fighting at close quarters, both pistols spent, he had stabbed and hacked his way out of danger with the foot-long blade he carried in his waistband.

Alvis had possessed no knife on the last occasion the Ferreira bastard had attacked him. He knew Emilio's knifesmanship to be considerable, but he believed he had the advantage in that the bastard knew nothing of his own foreign skill.

He recalled from the last confrontation that Emilio's reach was greater than his, so that when his nemesis sprang forward with a shout and a sweeping right to left cut, Alvis sidestepped to the left. Emilio's wicked slash cut only air where Alvis had been, while the Confederado's backward cut tore cloth, scratching the skin above Emilio's hip bone, drawing blood.

Howling, the bastard turned and slashed empty air again before the two lapsed into circling each other warily, stones crunching beneath their feet. Emilio struck suddenly at Alvis's face, lunging with the agility of a cat, and the Confederado's head shifted only just in time. His knife hand out of position to strike, Alvis delivered a jab to the bastard's stomach with his left fist. Emilio stumbled back, gasping, nearly falling, dropping a hand to the ground to steady himself.

When the hand came up, Alvis failed to assess what was in it until the dirt and rocks were hurled into his face. A stone rolled under his foot as he retreated, blinking to regain his vision, and he tumbled to the ground.

When Emilio charged forward Alvis thrust upward with a leg, catching him in the pit of his stomach. Growling in rage as he recovered himself, Emilio lunged again and their knives clashed, but Alvis let his slide off to the side and, gripping the wrist of the bastard's knife hand, plunged the curved Paraguayan blade deep into the bastard's torso.

Emilio staggered back, inspecting the wound incredulously, unable to accept it, as Alvis rolled to his feet. Then he came on anew like a wild man, cutting and slashing. Though he gasped for air like a drowning man, in his fury he did not even seem to feel his wound. Bleeding as badly as he was, he seemed as intent as ever on killing the hated foreigner.

Emilio lunged, but this time slower, his breath ragged, and Alvis, holding his knife low, sidestepped the blow, then brought his blade up hard, driving with all the force in his powerful legs and thighs. It drove in to the hilt and for a moment the combatants were eye to eye.

"You could have walked away," Alvis said quietly before withdrawing his knife with a sudden jerk.

Emilio tottered to one side like a drunken man before falling to his knees. Dull eyes fixed on Alvis; he struggled to rise but instead fell flat on his face and moved no more.

Let's contemplate a few questions in the wake of this example. Why do you think the author chose to relate this fight in this manner? Does the back and forth of the battle complement the back and forth of the dialogue, or vice versa?

What does the protagonist want? He seems reluctant to fight, so why do you think he does it?

Is the victory worth it? You know the protagonist is a reluctant combatant, so do you think killing the adversary will gnaw at him and undermine him in the future?

With regard to the last question, it's not unusual in twenty-first-century creative writing that the more powerful crisis is depicted as occurring in the mind of the narrator and that the resolution does not offer a solution. The completion of the action changes the characters not by a dramatic reversal, but by moving them deeper into their personal struggles. After all, in "real life," closure never quite happens unless death occurs. Think of all the happy endings you can recall from books that involve developments such as marriage and birth. The book might conclude with these events, but in "real life," domesticity, childrearing, and the cooling of romance have to be dealt with.

On the other hand, tragic endings, such as separation and death, leave trauma and bereavement in their wake. Narratives absolve us of these variables because whether or not the lives of the characters end, the narrative does, and we are left with a sense of completion and the freedom to cheerfully move on to our next book. We know in advance that all narratives are going to be over eventually.

WRITING PROMPT

Write an entry in your journal that places two characters in a dangerous setting. Each has half of something that's no good without the other half. Neither wants to give up his or her half. What happens?

Connections Between Characters

As you've seen, nearly every story presents some sort of journey—literal or psychological or both—that results in a change in the central character. Every narrative shows a pattern of conflict between approximately equal forces, which leads to a crisis and a resolution (even if that resolution also poses more questions). These dynamics turn on the fact that a pattern of connection and disconnection exists between human beings, which is the primary source of meaning and significance in most any narrative.

Although they could be considered in tandem, let's examine connection first. While connecting carries a positive connotation, even something negative like conflict proves sterile unless it's given human dimension through the connections between characters.

In narratives where connection is front and center, there's usually an element of comedy that informs the connection following a conflict. Take, for example, the creative nonfiction piece "Home Court Advantage," in which two young basketball players have been ejected from a game and sent to the locker room:

> Banished derelict pair, the two of us, slumped on a bench in the locker room, listening to the faint sounds of the game which has degenerated into a route.
>
> Tye, looking over at me. "U, don't take me wrong, you cool and all, but I don't think you should be captain no more. You don't even give a damn if we win or lose."
>
> Me, shrugging, not wanting to explain, changing the subject. "Do you ever remember your dreams, Tye?"
>
> Tye, stumped, uncertain, then forming a sly grin. "Yea, I dream of pom-pom b----es doin pyramids on top of me."
>
> Answering smile from me. "Who doesn't? I mean other dreams."

Tye, thinking hard. Then, "Naw."

"Well imagine you did dream and that you remembered your dreams, and that what you dreamed about were people and places that you knew, except that they might appear very old or very new sometimes."

Tye. "That what you dream about?"

"It is."

"What happens in them dreams?"

"It depends on the people and the places, but sometimes they tell me things about people and places. When I wake up, I know more about them and it's true."

Tye, quiet, thinking. "Ever seen me in one of them dreams?"

Then it is my turn to think, to try and remember. "I did one time, but you were far away—very hard to see."

"What was I doin?"

"Nothing. Nothing at all. I think you must have been waiting or something."

"Chillin, huh? But I was OK and all."

Me, lying. "Yea, you were OK." Then, trying to explain. "Stuff happens in life that pulls people away, Tye—like you and me waiting in here now, apart from the team. Life is very powerful—I can feel it all around us—and it can be very sad because it pushes people apart."

Tye. "Man, don't nobody push me and get away with it."

"That's right. Just because life's so strong doesn't mean we should give up—that we have to lose everything."

Tye, growing irritated. "Man, talkin to you gives me a headache. What be the point, U?"

"Life is going to push us apart."

Tye, silent.

I look at his torn up hand and feel the soreness in my own. "But memory will keep us friends."

Tye, squinting as though thinking hard, as if about to say something profound, but then laughing instead, head thrown back. "S---, what the f--- you talkin bout? You crazy, U. A crazy motherf----er. There ain't nobody like you."

And Me laughing with him, thinking he may be right, voices echoing off the ceramic tile and steel lockers of this empty place where girls our age we'll never meet change clothes every day, mirth drowning out the faint whisper of the final buzzer sounding.

As the content of the dialogue demonstrates, these characters are very different from each other yet are attempting to connect across a rather large educational and cultural chasm. Near the end, they come close to making a profound connection—an *epiphany*—yet ultimately fail to do so. However, because this form of connection proves impossible, they're left with laughter instead— a form of fellowship that does not require the intellectual understanding of what they'd been discussing.

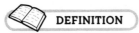 **DEFINITION**

An **epiphany** is a sudden realization in which someone or something is seen in a new light.

Writing Disconnections

Given the dynamics of connection, it shouldn't surprise you that a narrative ending in disconnection, especially death, tends toward tragedy. The most casual conversation includes anecdotes of destination (including death) and detour. Yes, it's a sad fact to contemplate, but slowly our bodies and minds unravel and fall apart until they can no longer function.

Let's move on to an example that illustrates disconnection at work. It's the conclusion of a creative nonfiction piece in which a beloved horse succumbs on a farm:

> In the last few weeks which remained to him of that, his last, season of life, I saw the stallion but little. The trials of my own life kept me away.
>
> When at last the day came upon which that beautiful strength settled itself to earth, it did so gently as though relaxing into a comfortable state of repose. The expression in his eyes I will never forget. The old labyrinth of stern, cruel memories—the wild blur of darkness—was gone and in its place was something contemplative, yet all its own: like if you threw a stone up in the air and it didn't come down, but rather just stayed there. Perhaps he died marveling at the strange beauty of such a sight.
>
> When he was dead a tractor with a backhoe dug his grave and a great rusty chain was wrapped about him so as to drag his great form to it. He lies there now in the fashion of a hundred other animals of that farm, having returned to the earth. I think of them sometimes, the various spots where they have been buried, spanning all the way back to my childhood, and how some of those places are covered now in saplings and thickets or mown over, or, in a few cases, marked each spring by the emergence of daffodils or tulips. Most farms are like that: landscapes of the dead, from which new things are always growing. But I don't like to dwell on that too much.

Yet when I do think of death—of how I would like to die—it is usually in the prone form of a large animal, yet such an animal as God must have saw when he first envisioned the creatures of the earth before all time. Never in my life have I known a being truer to the nature of itself.

Disconnection functions here through the inevitability of death in the life cycle. The horse and his human admirer are parted by death, although the event also functions as a deepening of love on the human narrator's part. You might think of this example, then, as literal disconnection that contains psychological and emotional overtures of connection.

 **WRITING PROMPT**

A morning trip to school shapes up as power struggle between protagonist child and antagonist mom, resolved with a connecting hug or a parting blast. Decide which you prefer, and portray it in your journal.

The Least You Need to Know

- Most all narratives involve journeys.
- The struggle for power or simple conflict is usually what moves narrative action forward.
- Connections between characters provide mutual understanding and sometimes also levity.
- Disconnection is a tragic element that involves partings and often death.

Short-Form Genres

So far, you've learned about the various tools that come in handy for most any kind of creative writing. Part 4 begins the process of investigating just what kinds of creative writing you can practice and perhaps attempt to get published in. I begin with these shorter genres because beginning writers are going to write a story before a novel, a scene before a play, and so on. However, if you are determined to, say, write a novel, don't skip Part 4. It's still very important because it provides techniques that make composing longer genre forms possible.

We've already explored some of the fundamental differences between nonfiction and fiction writing, and Chapter 10 focuses on a short version of the former, the essay, because I believe getting that right helps with the slightly more complex topic of Chapter 10, the short story. In the last decade or so, a special kind of very short story called *flash fiction* has gained a growing readership, and Chapter 11 examines the challenge of writing the shortest of self-contained prose. Chapter 12 moves into perhaps the most difficult kind of creative writing, the poem, while Chapter 13 explores a genre familiar to many people, thanks to the popularity of movies, the dramatic scene or one-act play.

The Masterful Essay

You might think the writing of a truthful nonfiction piece—an *essay*—would be an undertaking that would appear and remain close to the heart. Not necessarily so. In fact, it has often been said that the key element in any essay is finding a measure of distance from your experience, or learning to stand back, narrow your eyes, and scrutinize your own life with skepticism.

Distance is important because it helps authors separate themselves as living, breathing people from the projection of themselves who narrates the essay. In other words, it makes you less touchy and embarrassed about relating your imperfections in places where your essay calls for that. It's also important to reveal your faults so the reader will believe what you relate. If an entity who has never tasted defeat or rejection is narrating the essay, the reader is going to resent them at worst and reject them as a false and inhuman voice at best.

In This Chapter

- Exposition in nonfiction writing
- Description in nonfiction writing
- Persuasion in nonfiction writing
- The "New Journalism" movement

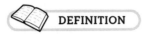 **DEFINITION**

> An **essay** is a short piece of nonfiction prose composed on a particular theme.

In addition to the idea of distance, good nonfiction writers always strive for the interesting ideas or questions that lie beneath the generalities of a subject. True, they might begin with generalities, but very quickly they're going to jump into what makes their experience unique. By way of example, here's the opening of the essay *SCHOOLED: Life Lessons of a College Professor:*

> I count myself among the luckiest of creatures. By nature and profession I have had the good fortune to have been a teacher and a learner for nearly my entire life. It is the best occupation I could ever hope for. I am surrounded by brilliant young people and coworkers who constantly teach me new things, and who also seem to believe there are things I can teach them. Though I have not always been so, I have become grateful in retrospect for the other jobs I've had—farm hand, trail guide, manual laborer, park ranger, bus driver, writer of semi-important speeches and unimportant manuals, among many others—and have come to love them all in different ways for the things they taught me. In the end, however, my collective experience in these employments has only served to make me treasure even more my current occupation, which I happen to consider my true calling.

> When, not long ago, I was threatened with the not unrelated loss of both my eyesight and my brain, together with certain other compromised functions, I experienced the relatively common sufferer's reaction of waxing even more appreciative of my occupation, as well as the little everyday pleasures it is in our preoccupied natures to take for granted: the feather, for example, drifting on the breeze, catching the sun, not a bird in sight. Indeed, being of an artistic disposition, the very slightest variables of existence began to leap out at me with a power and vividness I had never before experienced. I stood in awe of them, stunned, barely even able to function sometimes in the presence of what it was my privilege to witness over the course of a given interval. I would find myself weeping for what an objective onlooker might consider no apparent reason when, in truth, the reason simply lay beyond his faculties to discern. An old writing teacher of mine liked to say that one of the gifts and curses of certain serious writers is that we possess the capacity to see, feel, and suffer more than others—and I have found that to be true. But when one adds to that dynamic the prospect of one's imminent demise—either via outright death or, perhaps worse, the loss of those powers which have enabled one to see and love and know with the deepest and most vivid passion and clarity— then that ability to discern and comprehend is multiplied a thousand-fold.

Essays exploring a one's decline into serious illness are among the most commonly seen by editors of magazines. There's a good reason for this: these events are among the most traumatizing you can experience. Too often, however, when writing about such a malady, the writer focuses on the idea that what has happened isn't fair and that they're entitled to great pity. Are these reactions natural and true? Sure. But are they interesting for a reader? Not very often.

The problem is that there are certain things readers already know, and that includes mortal illness—either involving themselves or someone they know. What seems truly significant, then, when it occurs in your own life, generates a misleading illusion that it will stir powerful feelings for readers.

The opening of *SCHOOLED* throws the reader off-balance. The narrator, although medically compromised, feels fortunate; he values a wide array of occupations from his past as equally valuable; and he marvels at the intensified sense of observation his malady affords him. These dynamics are going to interest readers more than those of a narrator who chooses merely to bemoan his plight.

Always try to imagine an audience made up of real people who do not know you and are not inherently eager to read what you have written. You must invite or hook these readers into your work, or you risk losing them. Only by focusing on these anonymous readers will you find a way to truly reach your audience.

Now let's have a look at some different kinds of essays—expository, descriptive, persuasive, the "New Journalism"—that make this short genre of contemporary writing.

Expository Essays

The *expository essay* requires you to investigate an idea, evaluate evidence, expound on the idea, and set forth an argument concerning that idea in a clear and concise manner. This can be accomplished through comparison and contrast, definition, example, the analysis of cause and effect, etc. Sounds very much like an academic paper, doesn't it? It draws on many of the same elements, only it still allows for personal voice and various manifestations of artfulness.

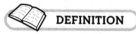 **DEFINITION**

An **expository essay** is a piece of writing in which the writer presents data, opinions, points of view, ideas, concepts, and arguments on a particular topic in an effort to explain it.

Given its similarity to academic research writing, the structure of the expository essay is quite prescriptive and consists of the following:

- A clear, concise, and defined thesis statement that occurs in the first paragraph of the essay.

- Clear and logical transitions between the introduction, body, and conclusion.

- Body paragraphs that include evidential support.

- Evidential support, whether factual, logical, statistical, or anecdotal.

- A conclusion that does not simply restate the thesis, but readdresses it in light of the evidence provided.

As noted, although creativity and artfulness are not always associated with expository essay writing, it is an art form nonetheless. As prescriptive as it might seem, try not to get stuck on the formulaic nature of expository writing at the expense of writing something interesting. Remember, although you might not be crafting the next great novel, you are attempting to leave a lasting impression on the people reading this kind of essay.

It might prove helpful for you to think of an expository essay in terms of a conversation or debate with a friend of equal knowledge and education. If I were to discuss the cause of the Great Depression and its effect on those who lived through the tumultuous time, there likely would be a beginning, middle, and end to the conversation. In fact, if I were to end the exposition in the middle of my second point, questions would arise concerning the current effects on those who lived through the depression. It would be something akin to an interruption in the conversation. Therefore, the expository essay must be complete, and logically so, leaving no doubt as to its intent or argument. However, that doesn't mean it can't be infused with artfulness, wit, and a sense of humor. In fact, one or more of these elements is often its saving grace.

Descriptive Essays

The goal of descriptive writing is for readers to see, hear, smell, taste, or feel (see the importance of those again?) your topic as if it's right in front of them. Descriptive writing has a point, although it isn't always directly stated—in which case it's conveying a dominant impression.

Writing a *descriptive essay* often involves both objective and subjective elements. Objective elements are the plain facts. For example, let's say the temperature is 97 degrees Fahrenheit. In objective description, you would simply state the temperature. But in subjective description, you might refer to the temperature as "stuffy" or "sweltering." That's your assessment of the temperature; another person might disagree. Thus, which details you choose about a topic and the language you use to convey them create the dominant impression.

 **DEFINITION**

> A **descriptive essay** is a piece of writing used to explain something in detail, usually employing the five senses.

How much detail is needed depends on your audience, what you're describing, and the goal of your description. Almost everyone has experienced 97 degrees, so describing it would require just enough details to create the dominant impression. Readers would fill in the rest from their own experience with heat.

On the other hand, almost no one has been on the moon. So if you wanted to describe the lunar landscape, you would have to go into specific detail about what you'd see and how sounds are exceedingly rare. How would it feel to move in that kind of gravity? Readers would need you to try to give them every detail of the scene because they—and probably you as well—have no experience to draw from. In addition, the more you want readers to focus on something, the more description you should give it. This technique lets you control what your readers dwell on and what they pass over quickly.

With these variables in mind, here are the steps to successful descriptive writing:

1. Gather specific details on your topic.

2. Use the most vivid language you can to describe the topic.

3. Decide what dominant impression you want to convey.

4. Present details in spatial order to make your description flow.

It's important to select a natural starting point based on your topic. When describing a person, you might start with their face. With a house, you would start at the front door. In describing a whole scene, it's usually best to work from big to small. Describe the trees in the forest before the insects, for example. Use transition words to move from one detail to the next.

Ideally, your goal is to put your sensory experience into words so powerfully, your reader will feel like they're right there. As much as possible, use concrete words that describe physical objects or sensations.

When you really can't find a word to describe a sensory detail, or if you've run out of words, you can describe one thing by comparing it to another. You might write that the medicine tasted like shampoo, for example. Or the sweater was as soft as your cat's fur.

To choose a dominant impression, ask yourself what you notice most about your subject. What makes this person, place, or object distinctive and unlike others? Focus your description around what stands out. Like expository essays, descriptive pieces can be very dry, so employ as much creativity as you can muster.

WATCH OUT!

Don't confuse describing with making value judgments. Remember that the primary goal is to convey sensory information. You can't describe a town, for example, just by saying it's a nice place. You have to give physical details like the size of the town, its layout, the style of the buildings, and so forth. The best descriptive writing creates a clear image in the audience's mind. Readers can then decide for themselves that it's a nice town.

Persuasive Essays

In persuasive (and argumentative) writing, you try to convince readers to agree with your facts, share your values, accept your argument and conclusions, and essentially adopt your way of thinking. Sounds a little like brainwashing, doesn't it? However, few of your readers will be so mentally amiable when it comes to embracing your concepts in place of their own. Thus, for effective persuasive and argumentative writing, it's very important to establish your facts, clarify relevant values, and have confidence in your beliefs.

The creative writing aspect of the *persuasive essay* is evident in that the writer must arrange words to convince readers to believe their opinion and/or perform an action. Often this is merely a simple structure of arguments persuading the reader to follow the writer's point of view. Persuasive essay writing is one of the most commonly used writing types in the world—just think of all the advertisements urging you to purchase products.

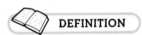

DEFINITION

A **persuasive essay,** also known as an *argument essay,* utilizes logic and reason to show that one idea or position is more legitimate than others.

Argumentative essay writing in particular tends to make its claim and prove it somewhat more aggressively. To be effective, when writing an argumentative essay, you must follow key points:

1. Select a topic you feel strongly and/or passionately about.

2. Make a list of points for both sides of the argument, and pick your side.

3. After you present both sides with an assessment of each, present your own personal perspective with as many verbal fireworks as possible, concluding with a statement that makes your position seem like the obvious one to adopt.

4. Consider strong arguments for the "other" side, and knock them down with passion and fervor, as well as reason.

Think of argumentative writing as a fiery, aggressive, hyperactive version of persuasive writing.

Both persuasive and argumentative writers employ many techniques to develop their argument and show support for their claim and opinions. When you begin writing, you have to come up with a good idea—a foundation upon which you can base the entire paper. It needs to be a topic you know a lot about and/or have researched thoroughly.

When you determine the thesis of your essay, introduce it with an opening sentence that captures the reader's attention. This can be done with a statement that identifies unusual statistics, addresses a controversial question, challenges popular thoughts, or outright shocks the reader.

By way of conclusion, here are some opening lines that would shock many readers. These might not be great sentences, but chances are, they would elicit enough stunned interest for the reader to keep going.

> "For the first month of Ricardo and Felicity's affair, they greeted one another at every stolen rendezvous with a kiss—a lengthy, ravenous kiss, Ricardo lapping and sucking at Felicity's mouth as if she were a giant cage-mounted water bottle and he were the world's thirstiest gerbil."

> "It was such a beautiful night; the bright moonlight illuminated the sky, the thick clouds floated leisurely by just above the silhouette of tall, majestic trees, and I was viewing it all from the front row seat of the bullet hole in my car trunk."

> "She sipped her latte gracefully, unaware of the milk foam droplets building on her mustache, which was not the peachy-fine baby fuzz that Nordic girls might have, but a really dense, dark, hirsute lip-lining row of fur common to southern Mediterranean ladies nearing menopause, and winked at the obviously charmed Spaniard at the next table."

> "The professor looked down at his new young lover, who rested fitfully, lashed as she was with duct tape to the side of his stolen hovercraft, her head lolling gently in the breeze, and as they soared over the buildings of downtown Richmond to his secret lair beside the river he mused that she was much like a sweet ripe juicy peach, except for her not being a fuzzy three-inch sphere produced by a tree with pink blossoms and that she had internal organs and could talk."

> "As the mysterious stranger approached, I bit my lip anxiously, hoping with every nerve, cell, and fiber of my being that this would be the one man who would understand—who could take me away from all this—and who wouldn't just squeeze my boobs and make a loud honking noise like all the others had."

The "New Journalism"

In the mid-1960s, a new form of essay writing materialized in conjunction with a group of journalists who broke away from traditional journalism to a much more free, candid, and creative style of reporting. From the invention of the printing press, this subjective form of journalism existed on the fringes of society, but it wasn't until the emergence of *New Journalism* in the mid-'60s that this form of writing became popular and was considered a new genre of American literature, a rebellion from old journalism, and a critique of the American novel.

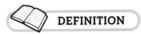 **DEFINITION**

> **New Journalism** is a type of writing that relies on the reporter's subjective interpretations and often features fictional dramatized elements to emphasize personal involvement.

The distinctive difference of New Journalism from traditional journalism is the style the writers attempt by making the story their own, drawn in and artistic in relation to the events that they report and comment upon. This journalism does not intend to be objective, and it exposes the writer's commitment and personality.

New journalists have tested the techniques of subjectivity and still write within the frame of factual testimony. The biggest part of the style is that it has a direct correlation to the drastically new happenings and characters that were determining the American culture in the 1960s. It is an attempt to record and evaluate history by keeping language and attitude in step to the style of the events happening during the current era.

In New Journalism, then, the writer tells an intriguing, occasionally terrifying, occasionally comedic account of their own experience and other events that, normally, would not be reported by regular news outlets. The spirit of the traditional journalistic style is still there; however, there's no filtering, depersonalizing, objectifying style of inoffensive reporting.

The new journalists seem to gravitate toward writing underground, "behind the news" stories rather than writing a more watered-down version that's offered to the general public because it doesn't run the risk of offending or creating thoughtful analysis from the readers. In fact, some people found the writing of New Journalists to be distasteful or confusing.

A new journalist would be interested in the details of the events, such as how the dealings he or she came upon were created or destroyed and how they affected his or her own thoughts and feelings, and the effect on the human experience and the people involved. They would create a thorough account of the event that would be written using all the tools of fiction and creative writing in general.

Here's an example of New Journalism writing from "'Reunification by Bayonet'?" It records the opening of a new Museum of the Confederacy in Virginia:

> The Confederate reenactors largely resembled their Union counterparts in physical appearance—mostly late middle-aged and portly—though a few were very young, perhaps even high schoolers. The uninhabited age gap between these extraordinarily young men and the elder majority struck me as odd.
>
> Trailing just behind the last of the soldiers followed six women dressed in period attire. No one seemed to know who they were supposed to represent: prostitutes following the army? Mourners in search of dead family members? It didn't seem to matter. When all had assumed their places off to the right of Mr. Rawls a generous round of applause ensued, exclamated by an anonymous "Yee-haw!" from somewhere in our midst.
>
> This introductory procession having concluded, Mr. Rawls proceeded to introduce the notable politicians, educators, and benefactors in attendance, which included Virginia Lieutenant Governor William Bolling and renowned Civil War historian Dr. James "Bud" Robertson, both of whom were on the program to speak. Yet before he abdicated the podium Rawls delivered his own thoughts on the war and the museum, ambiguously noting that "Virginia stands alone in its history." He concluded by thanking the museum staff via a quote from the African-American soul singer James Brown: "This is the hardest working group in show business." As Waite beamed in the wake of the remark, no one around me laughed nor nodded. I concluded they either never had heard of James Brown or didn't particularly care for the reference.

In the opening paragraph of the excerpt, the description of the reenactors is accompanied by the author's own commentary on the age gap between the very young men and the middle-aged participants.

In the next paragraph, the author not only remarks that no one knew the purpose of the female reenactors, but offers his own possibilities as well. Near the end of the paragraph, he also offers dialogue when an anonymous person shouts, "Yee-haw!"

In the final paragraph of the excerpt, the author identifies more participants while also remarking upon the coolness with which the James Brown reference is met: an implicit commentary on the cultural makeup of the event's audience.

 WRITING PROMPT

Attend an event of your choice—sports match, concert, religious service—and then document it in the New Journalism style, mixing your own impressions with the facts that transpired.

New Journalists believe good writers take note of the world around them and then describe their own reactions to it, whether that reaction is predominantly objective, personal, or a little of both. Some critics, however, have often doubted the validity of the facts of these pieces. Other critics believe that the facts involved are not meant to be scrutinized because they're the means to an end: to let the reader experience the world they have researched, experienced, and written about.

In any event, New Journalism is fundamentally more artistic than the previous nonfiction essays you've been introduced to. Although mostly nonfiction in form, it utilizes other elements of creative writing to generate greater verisimilitude.

As the 1960s came to an end, the peak of New Journalism started to fade. However, as the excerpt from the preceding essay attests, its influence remains in the present. Its chief practitioners often are identified as Truman Capote, Hunter S. Thompson, and Tom Wolfe. Wolfe is still alive at the time of the of this book's composition, yet it's interesting that his fictional work often has been belittled by contemporary novelists such as Norman Mailer and John Updike as inferior in nature to their own. Although each of the three New Journalist writers penned novels, they remain primarily an influence on journalists as opposed to fiction writers—hence their appearance in this chapter among the various kinds of essay writing.

Yet it remains that, whatever their shortcomings within the realm of fiction, New Journalism writers operate using a genre that possesses the ability to show any era of American culture better than any perhaps other style of writing.

The Least You Need to Know

- Expository essays present data and concepts in an effort to explain something.
- Descriptive essays rely on details and the five senses to capture the essence of something.
- Persuasive or argumentative essays aggressively try to prove one side of an argument while presenting the whole picture.
- The New Journalism was a historical movement that still exists today and allows for the reactions of the author and the use of creative writing techniques not traditionally associated with essays.

CHAPTER 1

The Lifelike Short Story

Short stories are one of the best forms for new writers to hone their craft. However, they're not necessarily the *easiest* option. It takes a great deal of skill to write a good short story that's effective.

For one thing, you have to curtail any tendency to ramble on. Not all fiction writers need to be novelists, but if you have a gift for fictional brevity, the short story is for you. F. Scott Fitzgerald, for example, was quite comfortable (and gifted) as a short story writer and only produced the occasional novel out of pressure from his publisher and his own financial stress. Other gifted short story writers, such as Raymond Carver, never wrote a novel, although it likely would have made more money than any of their short story collections.

Although payment for a single short story published in a magazine hasn't changed much since Fitzgerald's time (the 1920s), they are still written and published at an astonishing rate. And if a book editor or agent admires a short story you have published in a magazine, they might contact you about the possibility of writing a novel. In other words, short stories can function as prose auditions. Of course, if successful, you then face the Fitzgerald/Carver conundrum and have to decide whether to stick with stories or try out the longer fictional form.

In This Chapter

- Story organization
- Individual scenes and summarization
- Story background and the flashback technique
- Word volume

So what is a *short story*? Short stories can be anything from 500 to 6,000 words. Typically, they're shorter in large-circulation commercial magazines and longer in smaller-circulation literary venues. Anything under 500 words tends to be labeled "flash fiction" (a form I address in the next chapter). Anything over 6,000 words is moving into novella territory. I would argue that a short story is something that can be read comfortably in one sitting and doesn't leave you starving or bloated.

 **DEFINITION**

> A **short story** is a brief piece of prose fiction, usually possessing few characters and aiming at unity of effect.

A short story is a slice of life. As such, you should narrow the time frame and geographical location of the piece. One plot, two or three characters, and no more than two locations (one would be better) are the limits for most short stories. If this seems too tight a fit, perhaps you should be writing a novella or a novel.

Start your piece as close to the turning point or climax of the story as possible. Most writers take a paragraph or so to find their feet. On a second reading, they delete the first paragraph as unnecessary exposition or padding.

Your first sentence is crucial; it should be filled with energy, intrigue, and forward momentum. The reader should be stopped in his or her tracks and not able to turn away until they've read the whole thing. The first sentence should raise questions that need to be answered. Take, for example, these openers:

"None of them knew the color of the sky."

—Stephen Crane, "The Open Boat"

"The grandmother didn't want to go to Florida."

—Flannery O'Connor, "A Good Man Is Hard to Find"

"A man stood upon a railroad bridge in northern Alabama, looking down into the swift water twenty feet below."

—Ambrose Bierce, "An Occurrence at Owl Creek Bridge"

Every short story should have an opening that's developed to build tension, that reaches its climax toward the end, after which there is a rapid conclusion. In a short story, you shouldn't spend too much time in the "first act," where development, setting, and exposition take place. Rather, start your narrative as close to the initial crisis as possible.

Your story should follow that arc by allowing your character to face obstacles, setbacks, and minor victories on the way toward reaching the dramatic climax and bringing resolution.

Story Versus Plot

A plot is not a story, nor does every story have a strong plot. Good writers know the importance of both plot and story, especially before they dare to write a story with a "weak" or "thin" plot. Any plot can feature a love story—that illustrates the difference. Plots are events, whereas stories reveal how characters react to those events.

Contrary to many general-purpose dictionaries, a plot is not the main story of a work. Rather, a plot can be summarized without specific names or settings. The search for a murderer is a plot. Surviving a natural disaster is a plot.

DEFINITION

Plot is the series of events providing conflict within a story.

The plot is sometimes called the *spine* of a story. It constitutes the action, while the story is made of the emotions associated with the action. A plot can be caused by the emotions of characters, but the action is *apart* from the story. Plots are the results of choices the characters make; the characters take action (or don't), and events occur as a result.

The beginning of any story ends with the introduction of the primary plotline. The middle ends with a climactic showdown. Many writers map out their plots, like a timeline. This helps them see where choices are made and actions taken, so they can pace the story.

It should be possible to state most good plots in one or two sentences. The primary plot remains simple, although the story may be complex. Almost all of Shakespeare's plots are very simple, but his plays have wonderful depth. Think about some of your favorite stories and how simple the primary plots are.

The plot of a work is the basic conflict, either from which or alongside other conflicts are created. An effective plot contains at least one major conflict. Generally, if you can't state the plot in a 12-word sentence, you have no idea what the primary plot is. If you are the author, that's a bad sign. There are only three or four simple plots used in most books or films:

- Man versus man
- Man versus nature
- Man versus self
- Man versus man's work

Remember, these are the most prevalent conflict models, and highly complex stories do exist that include not only elements of several of these conflicts, but also others.

A man-versus-man plot features a central character and an opposition character as the primary actors. The central character has a goal, and the opposition is going to attempt to stop the central character before he or she obtains that goal. Meanwhile, a man-versus-nature plot features a central character against a natural event or other phenomenon that threatens the character or something important to the character. These stories are about a search for inner strength. Nature is not a "moral" entity; it simply exists. To overcome nature requires something internal; a character must rise to the challenges nature presents.

Generally not the source of a primary plot, internal struggles are commonly story elements that are considered subplots. Because the most interesting character has some manner of internal flaw (an emotional issue to discover and conquer), there's an element of man versus self in many great stories. On the other hand, it's a cliché of sorts, but narratives like *Frankenstein* and most science fiction delve into the risks of technology without morality. When we create, we seldom think of the consequences. In modern stories, the "work" might be pollution or illness. These are morality plays, as the stories aim to caution readers against a complete faith in their creations.

 **WRITING PROMPT**

In your journal, make a list of possible story ideas under each of the four conflict types.

As opposed to plot, a story is built upon the conflicts created by the plot, unless the work is experimental or, in some cases, philosophical. Stories are plot-driven or character-driven. A plot-driven story captivates readers or audiences through the excitement of events. The characters are important, but the action takes precedence. Character-driven stories rely on interesting characters and their responses to situations. The situations arise from the plot, but readers remember the characters.

A story rests upon the foundation of a plot; it is the emotional reactions of and choices made by various characters or groups. The choices move the story to plot points, while each plot point creates yet another choice and the accompanying emotional issues. When you make a choice, some emotion is involved. The choice results in more actions and reactions, leading to yet another choice. That's how both life and a good story work.

Contemporary stories, in all forms, tend to start quickly and end even faster. The middle of the story is two thirds or more of the work. As a result, you have ample opportunity to explore subplots and twists.

With some exceptions, readers and audiences expect stories to start quickly. They don't want to wait for a story to capture their imaginations; they want to interact with the story immediately. Audiences like a challenge. However, they don't want to be guessing what the storyline is.

Dramatic endings don't drag or feature lengthy commentaries. By the climax of action, any social commentaries are out of the way. Only a small number of issues remain unresolved, allowing audiences an opportunity to enjoy the ride.

Scene and Summary

Speaking of enjoying the ride, it's always nice to have some scenery and extra information along the way. However, one of the worst mistakes new writers make, unaccustomed to their craft as they are, is oversummarizing. It's not necessarily the summary that's bad, per se. Some new writers do a very good job summarizing. The problem is that they summarize when they should be writing scenes.

It's the scene that makes your story live and affords it verisimilitude. Summaries are what make short stories what they are. The difference, quite simply, is in their lengths.

When you write a summary, you tell the reader what's before them isn't important enough to slow down and stop on. You're saying to a scrutinizing eye that you don't know how to take your time when you write. And why would you know? No one has told you.

A scene takes place not when the reader is *told* what's happening or what a character thinks or is like, but when a reader is allowed to *experience* it. Scenes take your writing from storytelling to reality in the reader's imagination.

When you write a summary, the reader misses certain key attributes that bring the characters to life. You don't get the interaction between character and surroundings, other characters, and events. The reader misses the senses—the scents, colors, tastes, and sounds of action. The reader also misses out on how the character behaves and reacts. Instead of a 3-D, in-depth being, the reader gets a flat, imageless cutout.

How, then, do you write a scene? First, you must understand what a scene is. Quite simply, a scene is where the action occurs.

📖 **DEFINITION**

> A **scene** is a clearly marked snapshot of a situation that involves one or more characters.

To write a scene (and not a summary), you must capture the nuances of action in your characters and surroundings. You want to draw it out, making use of the five senses.

This might sound simple, but it takes time and imagination—and it'll take a lot of practice to get used to. However, writing scenes well will make you a very good writer. To involve the reader, to allow the reader to experience a story, is something only an experienced writer can do even half-well.

Backstory and Flashback

As noted, when you start a new story, you need to get the reader into the conflict as soon as possible. But you also need to bring them up to speed on what's happened with the characters up to that point. This is usually done through *backstory* or *flashbacks*.

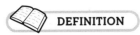 **DEFINITION**

Backstory is a summary of an incident that has happened in the character's past. **Flashbacks** take the reader to the past incident and show it to him through action and dialog.

Backstory is almost always necessary because the reader needs to know where the character is coming from. Flashbacks aren't always necessary, but sometimes the reader needs to be in the moment to truly understand the character's position. The key is to get that history across without interfering with the momentum of the story.

A story needs to have forward momentum, meaning it needs to unfold at a steady pace. Flashbacks (and sometimes backstory) stop or inhibit that momentum. They take the reader somewhere else and get them involved in a different story. Then that stops, too, and we're brought back to the real story. If this happens too much, it can frustrate the reader because he or she is being pulled in too many directions at once and left wondering when it's going to be time to get back to the "real" story.

In general, it's smoother for the reader if backstory can be conveyed in a sentence or two. This is hard to do, but it's worth it because the reader won't be skimming ahead to find the real story again. In this case, less is definitely more because it has a greater impact on the reader.

Flashbacks are trickier because they can't be conveyed in a sentence or two. If a flashback is absolutely necessary, a good way to keep the reader from feeling moved around too much is to start the flashback at the beginning of a story. The catch here is that you'll need to make it clear from the beginning that this is a flashback. Either put all the flashback text in italics, give a date or time frame of when this happened in the past, or change the point of view. This way, the reader will settle in without any confusion and will also be expecting to switch back to the real story later on.

Many writers avoid flashbacks altogether because they're very hard to get right. Likewise, many make a conscious effort to limit backstory to no more than two sentences. This helps keep things from sounding like an info dump. However, as with so many of the techniques I've introduced in this book, you're going to have to discover the best ways for backstory and flashback to work for you—if, in fact, you decide to use them at all.

Patterning with Prosody

Creative writing, like music, is an art of time, or "tempo": it takes time to read or listen to, and it usually presents events, the development of ideas, or the succession of images—or all these together in time.

It can be said that the craft of writing is, in part, the manipulation of a structure in time. So the simplest element of marking time, rhythm, is, therefore, of basic importance in both poetry and prose. *Prosody* is concerned almost entirely with the laws of meter or rhythm in the narrowest sense. It deals with the patterning of sound in time; the number, length, accent, and pitch of syllables; and the modifications of rhythm by vowels and consonants.

 **DEFINITION**

> **Prosody** is the science of versification, either in prose or poetry.

In most poetry and in some prose, certain basic rhythms are repeated with modifications, but not in all. It obviously does neither in the case of the "free forms" of modern poetry, but neither does it in the entire poetry of whole cultures.

Lyric poetry is either the actual text of song or is immediately derived from song, so it is regular in structure nearly everywhere in the world, although the elements of patterning that go into producing its rhythm may vary. The most important of these elements in English poetry, for example, have been accent, grouping of syllables (also called *feet*), number of syllables in the line, and rhyme at the end of a line (and sometimes within it).

The rhythms of prose generally are more complicated, although not necessarily more complex, than those of poetry. The rules of prose patterning are less fixed; patterns evolve and shift indefinitely and are seldom repeated except for special emphasis. Thus, the analysis of prose rhythm is more difficult to establish than the superficial analysis of poetry.

Prosody becomes important in a brief prose form like the short story because the relatively small volume of sentences and words allows for some of the poetic-like conventions it employs. As with backstory and flashback, there's no hard-and-fast rule on using prosody. In fact, it's less a technique and more a dynamic to be aware of in your writing, especially when revising and proofing. If, for example, you discover repetitive sentence structures in your story, you might want to vary them. On the other hand, you might find the repetition pleasing to the ear and perhaps employ it as a method for subtly driving home one of the story's themes. The choice remains yours, but prosody helps determine what readers think of your writing style.

WRITING PROMPT

If you're graphically minded, draw a rough graph or jot down the beginning, middle, and end of your story. Now write the story and fill in the gaps. If you're not so graphically minded, just jot down a few key phrases or events that might carry your story forward to a possible conclusion. Don't worry, this isn't cast in stone, and you can change the beginning, middle, end, and anything in between at any time. Many writers just write to find their voice. That's fine. When you have a first draft, go back and see if it has some kind of structure or arc. If not, you might have to adjust it a little.

To get to the end of writing your story, it's important to know that most stories belong to one of two categories: character-driven or event-driven. Some authors favor memorable characters, while others concentrate on events. Your preference depends both on the genre and style chosen.

A character-driven story relies on the decisions and emotions of characters to advance the plot. The decisions in a character-driven story produce chain reactions and conflict. The events, regardless of how many people they affect, are triggered by characters within the story. Villains tend to drive plots more actively than heroes. Heroes follow rules and tend to fit within traditional types. Villains, meanwhile, are free to do as they (or authors) want.

An event-driven story also relies on external events and circumstances to advance the plot. External events may be natural or human-initiated, as long as the initiator of the events isn't a central character to the story. Natural disasters and wars serve as the foundations for many event-driven stories.

Few current stories begin with a prologue, but it was once a common practice. Today, the first chapter might reveal backstory that serves as a prologue. Wherever it falls, this sets the backstory through quick exposition. Often a paragraph or two provides all the information necessary. Consider any story set in a time of war, for example. Stating the period and location in italics at the beginning sometimes is enough to give readers what they need. Additional backstory, if you have other important information, can always be dispersed throughout the story.

More important is the story's *catalyst*. This is the moment at which the primary character is thrust by circumstance into the action. It serves as the event that indicates your story has started. For some reason, the primary character is starting to lose control, and he or she has to regain power or a balance in life. In a romance story, it's all about finding true love, especially in an unexpected way. In a crime story, the reporting of the crime begins the chase.

A big event related to the catalyst then occurs and concludes the introduction of the story. A big event might be learning the perfect stranger is from the wrong family, as in *Romeo and Juliet*. Whatever it is, it establishes the path of the story. Rare is the story that reaches the main event without knowing the major characters, basic backstory, conflicts, and a bit of the psychology of the primary character. Some stories hold back a character or two for drama but still hint at their existence. However, a reader should be able to predict some events and at least guess at potential solutions to the story's conflicts.

The moment the main character decides there will be a showdown is known as the *pinch*. It might not be as simple as "I'm going to defeat the bad guy," but it can be. More often, it's a decision to continue the quest for a solution while admitting there's a risk. The decision to move ahead, to face conflict, is difficult and results in a point of no return. Ideally, there's more than one possible choice, but all have consequences.

It's common that the true natures of various characters are revealed during the pinch. We see why the hero is heroic and why the villain cannot see that he or she is wrong. It also often contains surprises such as the big, strong man turning out to be a coward. The pinch reveals the psychological underpinnings of the story.

Before the showdown, however, the primary character experiences a crisis of faith embodied by a crisis in the action. He or she experiences doubt, fear, and other troubling emotions. A great story has the reader or audience wondering if the main character will rise to the challenge. If there's not at least some doubt of victory, there is no story.

The showdown, then, is more than a battle between two people. It forces the main character to prove he or she understands any personal weaknesses and has overcome them. The resolution is not about the external victory as much as it is about the internal growth of a character. The end of a story can resemble a kind of dawn after the action concludes. In the last page or two, there's a hint of future actions. This allows readers and audiences an opportunity to imagine what's not written, which often has the effect of making the story stay with them. Maybe you show the criminal planning an escape from prison. Or maybe a new villain seems to have been created by the story's circumstances.

A good writer leaves a question or two unanswered, without undoing the story.

The Least You Need to Know

- Plots are events, whereas stories reveal how characters react to those events.
- Scenes make your story live and afford it verisimilitude; summaries are what make short stories what they are.

- Backstory is almost always necessary because the reader needs to know where the character is coming from. Flashbacks aren't always necessary, but sometimes the reader needs to be in the moment to truly understand the character's position.
- Prosody is concerned almost entirely with the laws of meter or rhythm.

Short and Sweet Flash Fiction

What's flash fiction? It might best be thought of as very short stories of 500 to 2,000 words. You might also see or hear this genre *called blasters, postcard fiction, micro-fiction, sudden fiction,* or *short shorts.* Whatever the name, the essence of the genre is the same: the writer quickly gets into the story and plot and establishes scene and summary. The critical backstory is filled in (often through flashback), and the author speeds toward the climax quickly in terms of prosody.

Almost every instructional writing text stresses the importance of learning to write concisely. Experts advise paring down adjectives and adverbs and shortening lengthy prose by finding the best descriptive words.

As a writer, you hone your skills like a trained athlete, but instead of setting physical tasks for yourself, you exercise daily by writing in your journal. Through these writing exercises, you flesh out characters, try out themes, explore point of view and voice, and sometimes create story drafts—often in just one sitting.

In flash fiction, you create a publishable story in a similar short duration of time. This is ideal for people who want to write during their commutes or lunch breaks or those who face the challenge of frequent interruptions by children.

In This Chapter

- A quick look at flash fiction
- Writing flash fiction well
- Flash fiction authors
- Venues for your work
- What to write about

Excellent writing prompts can trigger ideas for flash fiction in exercises that span as little as 5 minutes. These prompts—such as writing about a will, a death in the family, or a disaster—are terrific journal exercises that can spark your creative juices. What's more, they often lead to publishable works of flash fiction or even longer works such as short stories or novels.

Creating Flash Fiction

To illustrate the process involved in creating a work of flash fiction, let's look at one of my published flash stories, "Reserved Parking," as a guide. Then, we work through the creation steps, from the glimmer of an idea to the plot's resolution through the use of prosody.

Story and Plot

> I have the fortune—good or bad, depending on one's point of view—to reside in the rural county in which I was raised and profess English at a small college in an unremarkable city some twenty miles to the west. My wife and I both have family in the area, and many a Sunday afternoon, I doze in the wake of a generous meal as the idle sounds of gossip or a televised sporting event curl about my lazy ears.

As noted earlier, the first sentences of any piece of writing are critical. I open this flash story with the speaker relating the nature of his life. Like many readers, he lives where he grew up and relates the arrangement as "good or bad" because some readers will embrace this state of affairs whereas others will have endured negative experiences in their lives. The important fact is that the speaker's situation is highly relatable and, thus, helps draw the reader into the story.

The conveyed sleepy quality of everyday life also functions as a form of foreshadowing: even as the reader relates to the speaker's uneventful routine, the reader's subconscious process wonders what's going to come along to interrupt it. In moving the story along, I establish what's referred to as an *indirect hook*.

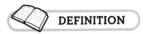 **DEFINITION**

Whereas a *narrative hook* is an inciting incident in which the action of a story literally begins, an **indirect hook** arouses the reader's interest through surface *inaction* that focuses on everyday, highly relatable details.

Remember that whereas a story consists of related chronological events, a plot arranges happenings to accentuate their dramatic effect. The use of an indirect hook in relating the everyday occurrences of a setting suggests plot rather than story. This prompts many readers to wonder why the story is introduced this way—and especially makes them want to know what comes next.

Scene and Summary

Of course, nothing prepared anyone for the house-sized book that appeared one hazy August morning in the parking lot behind the county public library. It was initially reported by a man walking his dog at first light, the otherwise benign creature's hackles rising and a low growl emerging from its throat as its owner, a retired airline pilot, guided them toward the dim, hulking object. Unable to make out the thing in the graying light and suspecting the shape something deposited by the county during the overnight hours, the former airman resolved to pilot his dog in another direction. Civic-minded fellow that he was, though, he did see fit to inform county law enforcement of the indistinct mass he observed.

When my phone rang later that morning it was Ronnie, a county deputy I'd graduated with from high school.

"A book?" I repeated when Ronnie related the appearance of the massive object. "How did it get there?"

"No one knows," he said. "At first we thought it was some kind of joke, but when the highway guys tried to bulldoze it on out of the way, it wouldn't budge."

Following this flash piece's indirect hook, which focuses on the everyday, is a scene and summary that might appear shocking to most readers. Having been lured into the daily practices of a quiet pastoral county resembling that of *The Andy Griffith Show*, the reader receives something of a literary sucker punch with the drastic transition to a massive book that's inexplicably materialized in the library parking lot.

The everyday events in the indirect hook also are related in the form of summary rather than immediate action. Such a technique leads readers to suspect that the action will begin soon. In fact, it must, or you'll lose readers. They'll grow bored if a summary goes on for too long.

By flash fiction standards, this opening summary is quite long, but it gambles with the sucker-punch delivery of the inexplicable massive book into the sleepy country setting. The function of this summary, then, is to heighten the first and final scene—the telephone conversation between the narrator and the deputy—when it finally arrives.

 **WRITING PROMPT**

Review some of the events you've recorded in your journal. How many are best described as summaries? How many as scenes? Now try taking one of the summaries and rendering it as a scene. One possible way to do this is to begin with the dialogue of a conversation.

Backstory and Flashback

"How do you even know it's a book?"

"Hell, Professor, I reckon you've handled enough of 'em: it looks like one. We even tried to pry open the cover with the dozer, but no dice there either. In fact, the machine busted a hydraulic hose tryin'."

"This all sounds crazy, Ronnie, but why are you calling me about it?"

"'Cause we need an expert opinion, Professor—from someone we can trust. Books are your whole deal, right?"

"Sure, but not house-sized ones with no titles."

"That's just it."

"What is?"

"Seems it's got a title and author etched into the cover up where no one can see. We had no idea they were there until we flew a chopper over the thing."

"Well let's have it."

"*Necronomicon,* by some fella named Abdul Alhazred."

"Never heard of it."

"Neither has anyone we've talked to, which is why I'd like for you to look into it for us."

"It sounds like it may have been written in another language, Ronnie. I doubt I'll be much use."

"We'd be obliged if you'd try, Professor."

"Get me out of my next speeding ticket?"

"You bet."

"OK then."

"Thanks … Oh, and Professor: confidential and all, you know."

"Sure Ronnie. Confidential."

Although the story has entered its action via real-time phone dialogue, the conversation itself contains both backstory and flashback through the passing references the narrator and deputy make. Readers learn that Ronnie more or less trusts the professorial narrator (he's both a home-grown good-old-boy and an academic), despite his past episodes of receiving speeding tickets. But the deputy also has concerns about confidentiality—either based on the narrator's past behavior or a more general professional desire for secrecy.

Through the narrator's dialogue, you can glean that he seems at once incredulous about the giant book, doubtful of his ability to help (I wonder how good of an academic he really is), and also something of an opportunistic sort who's less interested in helping out the police and more interested in improving his driving record.

A story like this one, which begins *in medias res* (Latin for "in the midst of things" or in the middle of the action), often is forced to deliver its flashbacks and backstory at various points during its progression. Even in the dialogue near the end, the reader is able to learn things about the deputy, the narrator, and their motivations and past relationship. Yet the possibilities of different interpretations remain at the end: is the narrator being ironic in repeating the word *confidential* because a massive book is difficult to hide, or is he being self-deprecating, exposing his doubts that he can aid the police in their quandary?

 WATCH OUT!

> Conclusions are crucial to all writing. It's important to resolve most of narrative elements, but you need not reveal every little detail. Remember all those horror movies in which there's some vague intimation at the end that the monster may still exist. Explaining away everything can make the reader bored and jeopardize a piece's chances of getting published.

Remember that in all forms of fiction, the best backstory and flashbacks fill in crucial missing information and then quickly bring the reader back to the present action with a bit more knowledge and suspense.

Prosody in Flash Fiction

In fewer than 500 words, readers of "Reserved Parking" have reached their destination, which— as in many interesting stories—answers some questions while leaving plenty for the readers to contemplate as a means of keeping the story working in their minds.

Although I've talked about prosody already, I should note that it's an especially important dynamic in flash fiction. Words are at a premium, so the sound and nuance of each becomes essential, especially as you near the story's climax.

It's no accident that the language in "Reserved Parking" moves from descriptive prose to the short, punchy dialogue that quickens the pacing and ultimately propels the reader to the end. The long sentences and multisyllabic words at the beginning give way to sentences of dialogue— five of which contain three words or fewer. As the sound of the vowels and words becomes shorter, the speed of the narrative increases.

Thus, this flash fiction—although unsatisfying and something of a tease in terms of the information it withholds—concludes sonically with a bang rather than a whimper. The final, one-word sentence ("Confidential.") literally reflects the deputy's request but also symbolically addresses the reader as well: you still don't know why the gigantic book is there.

WRITING PROMPT

While timing yourself or taking a break from work, cleaning, or another task you regularly perform, try writing a short tale based on a story about a child, a story about a secret, or a story about a traumatic event. Let's assume you have 500 words or fewer in which to tell the story.

Choosing Your Topic

Flash fiction presents a special challenge when you set out to write it. Primarily that's because of its length limit. A solution, then, is to focus on small subjects and reduction. For example, play some of your favorite songs and write about how the music and lyrics make you feel. Perhaps one will trigger a brief episode from your life you want to write about.

This approach can also be employed visually: look at some photos that are important to you. What makes one important? What were you doing or thinking at the instant you first saw that picture and were moved by it?

Beyond these personal exercises, you might consider your favorite book or movie and then attempt to write out its narrative in 500 words or less. What you end up with often will bear little resemblance to the original and, in fact, may constitute a unique flash fiction story of its own.

As you continue to experiment with writing flash fiction, you'll discover the techniques that work best for you. As a writer, you now have many of the tools to be successful in both the short story and flash fiction forms.

Reading Other Flash Fiction Writers

Although flash fiction has only recently been identified and labeled as a genre, many celebrated classical writers have produced work that meets all its criteria. Some examples include the very short literary fiction of Anton Chekhov and Ernest Hemingway, or the brief science fiction tales of Ray Bradbury and Arthur C. Clarke.

Writers such as these have withstood the test of time, so for inspiration, begin by reading their flash fiction and then move on to contemporary examples, which you can readily find on the internet or in print anthologies.

Some of the best recent writers and pieces include "Sashimi Cashmere" by Carolyn Forde, "Sleeping" by Katharine Weber, "The Voices in My Head" by Jack Handey, and "Why You Shouldn't Have Gone in the First Place" by Samantha Schoech.

Getting Your Flash Fiction Published

A good way to figure out where to submit your work for publication is to familiarize yourself with the best magazines and venues for flash fiction. The *Vestal Review* (vestalreview.net), for example, is one of the oldest magazines dedicated to flash fiction and insists on publishing work that stays with the reader long after the narrative has been read. Another journal, *Brevity* (brevitymag.com), boasts a number of published writers who have won awards for their work.

Once you read an issue or two of these and other flash fiction magazines, you'll have a better idea which of them favor work that resembles your own. Send your work to those places. In Part 7, you learn more about general practices and approaches for getting your work published.

The Least You Need to Know

- Flash fiction gets into the story and plot as quickly as possible.
- When writing flash fiction, establish scenes and summaries while adding in critical backstory along the way.
- Employ prosody in your flash fiction to speed toward your climax.
- You can use a variety of emotional triggers to help get ideas for flash fiction topics.
- To grasp flash fiction style, familiarize yourself with flash fiction from other writers.

The Arresting Poem

The question of poetry's identity as a form of creative writing used to be easier to answer. If the words rhymed and had a regular *meter* (a type of rhythm), they probably constituted a poem. As cliché goes, "If it walks like a duck, quacks like a duck, and looks like a duck, it must be a duck."

However, these days, not all poems rhyme or fit into standard forms. Moreover, poets and literary theorists alike are fond of offering musings about how important and meaningful poetry is, how it's the true essence of our world, the oxygen that keeps us alive, etc. Some of this is interesting and inspirational, but most of it isn't very helpful if what you're looking for is an actual explanation of what poetry is and how to write it.

One reason why it's so hard to get a straight answer on the subject is because people disagree about what should and shouldn't be considered poetry.

Despite this ambiguity, there are some general differences between poetry and prose you can use as a practical means of identifying the former. In fact, the easiest way to recognize poetry is that it usually *looks* like poetry. (Remember what they say about ducks ….) While prose is organized with sentences and paragraphs, poetry is normally organized into *lines*.

In This Chapter

- Penning formal and free verse
- Images and how you represent them
- Writing depth and urgency
- Using prosody, rhythm, and rhyming

Here's part of a poem by Robert Herrick:

> Gather ye rosebuds while ye may,
> Old Time is still a-flying:
> And this same flower that smiles to-day
> To-morrow will be dying.
> The glorious lamp of heaven, the sun,
> The higher he's a-getting,
> The sooner will his race be run,
> And nearer he's to setting.

See how that kind of looks like poetry? Now here's the same part of the poem, organized in a paragraph as if it were prose:

> Gather ye rosebuds while ye may, Old Time is still a-flying: and this same flower that smiles to-day to-morrow will be dying. The glorious lamp of heaven, the sun, the higher he's a-getting, the sooner will his race be run, and nearer he's to setting.

If you print a page in prose, the ends of the lines depend on where the margin is. With a bigger font size or a bigger margin, the lines are shorter. But in poetry, the poet (and sometimes an editor) decides where the lines end. This choice is an essential part of how you hear and see a poem. It affects how fast or slowly you read and where you pause when you're reading it. It causes certain words to stand out more or less. It affects the way the poem looks to you on the page, too. For example, is there a lot of white space, which affords a feeling of lightness and air, or are the words packed solidly together?

 WRITING PROMPT

Select two of your favorite poems, and render them in prose. Then make a list of how this changes their meanings and your emotional disposition toward them.

Poetry, more than prose, communicates through the way the words sound and way the poem looks on the page. Think of how music can make you feel: angry, irritable, peaceful, sad, triumphant, and so on. Poems work the same way, but instead of sound and rhythm created by instruments, they use the sound and rhythm of words. In songs with good lyrics, the melody joins with the words to create an intense feeling. Similarly, in poetry, the *sound* of the words works together with their *meaning* for more emotional impact.

The look of the poem on the page adds still another dimension. Some poems have smooth shapes; some have delicate shapes; and some have heavy, dense shapes. The breaks in the lines lead your eyes to certain areas. There are even poems with shapes that intentionally imitate what the poem is about. For example, a poem about standing beneath a waterfall could have lines that trickle down the page.

The letters and words in poems do several jobs at once. They do one thing with their meaning and another thing with their sound. Even their meaning may be working on more than one level.

An important characteristic of poetry is compression, or concentrated language. I don't mean *concentrated* in the sense of paying close attention, but rather in the sense of concentrated laundry detergent, or concentrated orange juice. A half-cup of concentrated laundry detergent does the same work as a cup of regular detergent; a poem typically gets across as much meaning as a larger amount of prose. Concentrated orange juice has the water taken out; a good poem has similarly been intensified by removing the nonessential words. This is one reason why poems are often short.

Prose normally talks to the logical part of the reader's mind. It explains and describes things; it makes sense. Poetry does all this, too, but it also tends to work at an emotional or irrational level at the same time. Often, some part of a poem seems to speak directly to the readers' emotions. It gives readers a peaceful feeling or an eerie feeling, or it makes them want to cry, even though they might not be sure why they're reacting that way to it. Sometimes the poet isn't even sure, although usually—like puppet masters—they are.

 WRITING PROMPT

Make a list of what emotions the following opening stanzas of Andrew Marvell's poem, "The Definition of Love" trigger in you and in which directions they seem to travel and intersect.

> My love is of a birth as rare
> As 'tis for object strange and high:
> It was begotten by Despair
> Upon Impossibility.
> Magnanimous Despair alone
> Could show me so divine a thing,
> Where feeble Hope could ne'er have flown
> But vainly flapped its tinsel wing.

One way poems function is through the use of sound. They also tend to suggest things beyond what they actually say. Often what causes the strongest emotions is not what the poem describes, but what it makes the reader *imagine*. Some of the parts of poems come like dreams from deep places in the mind that even the poet might not understand, and they touch something similarly deep in the reader. As ambiguous as that might sound, it's what poets often hope for in their work.

Free Verse and Formal Verse

Free verse and *formal verse*. People who write poetry generally tend to advocate one kind or the other, and tempers sometimes flare over the issue. Robert Frost declared that writing free verse was like playing tennis with the net down and wrote only one free verse poem in his 89-year life. Adrienne Rich, after writing a number of formal poems in her youth, including the memorable, oft-anthologized "Aunt Jennifer's Tigers," moved entirely to free verse as a young adult. William Carlos Williams declared formal verse a thing of the past, unsuited to the complexities of the twentieth century.

 **DEFINITION**

Free verse is poetry open in pattern and recognized as nonconforming and rhymeless verse. Poetry written in **formal verse** follows "rules" regarding stanza length and meter or rhyme patterns.

A poet friend of mine, while in graduate school, mentioned Richard Wilbur (one of the most prominent formalist poets in the United States) to a visiting poet, who responded with great anger, suggesting that a writer of sonnets, ballades, villanelles, etc. should not be considered a poet at all and should never be mentioned in the company of real poets like Williams, Rich, etc.

My friend choked back his answering anger but responded by writing and publishing vast numbers of sonnets, villanelles, sestinas, blank verse narratives, and other formalist poems— rarely producing any of the free verse he was forced to write to placate the visiting poet. He became friends with other formalist poets and went on to edit a journal of great distinction.

Here are some of the more common types of formal verse poetry:

Haiku   A form of Japanese descent, consisting of three lines of five, seven, and five syllables, respectively, and traditionally dealing with natural subjects.

Sonnet   Whether in English or an Italian rhyming scheme, the form constitutes a single- or two-stanza lyric poem containing 14 lines written in iambic pentameter.

Sestina   A six-line stanza followed by a three-line stanza. There is a predetermined pattern in that the same six words are repeated at the end of lines throughout the poem. The last word in the last line of one stanza becomes the last word of the first line in the next stanza. Then, rounding it off with the final three-line stanza, all six end words appear.

Villanelle and the pantoum   Two forms closely related to each other, the villanelle, a nineteen-line poem, is made up of five three-line stanzas and one four-line stanza (or quatrain) at the end of the poem. Alternating between the ends of each tercet (three-line stanza), two refrains eventually end up forming the last two lines of the quatrain. The pantoum, by contrast, is comprised totally of quatrains. In each stanza, the second and fourth lines are repeated in the first and third lines of the following stanza until the final stanza, where the first line is the poem's first and the second line is the poem's third line.

Likewise, although often in flux, here are some of the types of free verse:

Cadence   Common language rhythm is substituted for regular metrical pattern.

Free iambic verse   Verse with an inconstant number of equal feet in a line (as distinguished from the varied feet in free verse). Moreover, verse lines of unequal length are combined freely. See the work of such poets as T. S. Eliot and W. H. Auden.

Free verse proper   A popularly used form in which the inconsistency is at the center of the poem. There's no set metrical rhyme or patterns of meter and rhythm. Unlike traditional verse, free form is not constrained by the rules regulating syllables in stanzas.

Visual poetry   Poetry written in the shape of its subject.

Other various forms of avant-garde poetry related to free verse are surrealism, concrete, and language poetry.

Imagery and Metaphor

Imagery and *metaphor* are two different ways in which things can be described or illuminated upon in poetry (and in all forms of writing).

 **DEFINITION**

> **Imagery** is the description of a person, place, or item using the five senses. As mentioned earlier, a **metaphor** is a comparison between two things, based on resemblance or similarity, without using the words *like* or *as*.

Imagery and metaphor are commonly used in poetry to enhance authors' descriptions. Like many other explicative techniques, the more authors use imagery and metaphor effectively in their writing, the easier it becomes for their readers to form a mental representation of what's being discussed.

Throughout all sorts of writing, imagery is used to describe and illuminate so readers can more easily form mental images about what they're reading. Imagery relies on sensory cues from all five senses to inform readers. A line about a dog as "large, mean-looking and loudly barking" uses the senses of sight and sound, and imagery that refers to nasty ocean water as "cold, salty, and putrid" employs touch, taste, and smell. Metaphors are sometimes a type of imagery when they convey sensory information about a subject. Most importantly, imagery and metaphor can both help enhance an author's poetic descriptions.

Metaphors figuratively describe one thing as actually being another, using a type of comparison to illustrate how two seemingly different things are actually similar in some way. *Similes,* as opposed to metaphors, use the words *like* or *as* to describe and compare.

Sometimes, metaphors can be less straightforward and require more thinking than imagery. For example, if a writer wrote, "American democracy is still in its infancy," you would have to use your powers of reasoning to figure out exactly what this implied.

Metaphors can be powerful ways to describe people. Saying someone is a "wolf in sheep's clothing" implies he or she is mean, untrustworthy, and possibly violent, even though he or she appears to be nice and harmless. (However, you shouldn't use that line in your work because it's a cliché.)

 WRITING PROMPT

Try to write a number of lines of poetry that qualify as both images and metaphors. This is a helpful brainstorming exercise that can result in material suitable for an entire poem.

Density and Intensity

Now for what should read to you as a warning section. Some people try to define poetry based on analysis of the text, often using unquantifiable terms like *density* and *intensity,* or elaborate forms as opposed to spare, energetic types. Sound is frequently mentioned as a quality of difference: a mouthful as opposed to only a few heavily emphasized words. This approach faces several problems.

Such definitions tend to exclude accepted poetic genres—for example, light verse, shaped poetry (poems like "The Red Wheelbarrow"), or language poetry. The definitions also tend to stray into discussing quality rather than category issues, describing what a good poem should have rather than what a poem requires of a writer. Borderline types of poetry (found poetry, prose, narrative poetry, etc.) are difficult to handle.

In addition, readers have certain expectations when told a piece of writing is a poem, and their reading strategy is different for poetry than for prose. There also will be variation among readers, and some readers may change their reading strategy according to the poem's subgenre or form.

Here's a list of some common expectations and assumptions with which readers come to poetry:

Expectations:

- The work is textual.

- The work is a unified whole, with a title.

- The work has a message.

- The work is nonutilitarian.

- The work has an author.

Assumptions:

- Attention to surface structures.

- Freedom to associate, speculate, and consider emotional implications.

- Tolerance of difficulty.

- Readiness to make sense of everything.

Some of these expectations are shared by viewers of works of art in general. None of them, however, is essential.

Some people adopt these strategies readily and in many contexts. More often, something needs to trigger such a response. Most poems are clearly signposted as such (they're in a poetry book, or they have line breaks, for example), so readers generally know when a poetic strategy is being suggested.

A found poem is a piece of text whose context is changed so that readers are encouraged to adopt poetic reading strategies. When, for example, W. B. Yeats added some of Pater's prose to a poetry anthology, he needn't have added a title and line breaks, but doing so reduced the chance of rejection by readers.

Although, watch out. I don't think the preceding description should be deemed controversial. For me, it merely describes how readers behave. After all, readers of math textbooks, detective novels, cookbooks, etc. also have certain expectations and strategies. They, too, will need to contribute to the text, but they'll be faced with fewer borderline cases than what they encounter in poetry.

Furthermore, this idea of reader-centeredness raises some fundamental questions for the writer.

What's to stop people from reading far more into a poem than is really there? Not much. Some poets encourage readers to get more from a poem than the poet consciously put in. Others suppress unintended interpretations. When people discuss their responses to a poem (or when they reread the poem), there may be some consolidation of views.

How (and how much) should a poet foster poetic reader-strategies? This depends on the readership. If it's important that the poem succeeds as a poem, and if the audience doesn't read much poetry, it's a good idea for the text to fulfill the previous expectations and provide rewards for all the listed strategies.

If a reader claims a text isn't a poem despite its claims to be so, how can he or she be convinced otherwise? You can point out some features that a poetic reader strategy might reveal, but the disappointed reader might claim that any text reveals extra features if read with sufficient poetic generosity. The reader still needs to trust the author.

To increase the poetic effect of a text, poets can make the text more "poetic," or they can make the reader adopt a more poetic approach. Context and the author's name are important factors in the reader's choice of strategy and shouldn't be disregarded. It's not so much that rhyme, line breaks, and other conventions identify a text as a poem, but that making a piece of text look like a poem encourages readers to treat it like a poem.

For poetry to exist, there needs to be a text, a reader, and a suitable poetic reading strategy/setting. It's not a stretch to say the once unique poetry habitat is a threatened one, and this metaphor can be extended. When a species' habitat shrinks, a few things are likely to happen:

Populations become isolated: The performance poets, the academics, and the comedians overlap less and less and develop independently.

Evolutionary pressures change: Species survival depends increasingly on its ability to cope with marginal situations and isolation; growth is from the borders rather than the centers. Poets, and artists in general, usually inhabit margins and borders.

Artificial habitats are created: zoos (residencies, grants) help species survive, but also lead to cannibalism (political and personal attacks), incest (political and nepotic alliances), loss of parental skills (bad mentoring and advice), etc. Poetry magazines can suffer side effects, too, and also often contribute to the overall dysfunction.

Prosody, Rhythm, and Rhyme

The preceding "Density and Intensity" section constituted a way of being mindful of reader reactions to a poem, this final section gets you back into the realm of tools you can use.

Poetry is about sound effects at least as much as (and actually, probably more than) it is about meaning, and one of the ways sound effects are created in poetry is through *rhythm*.

 **DEFINITION**

> **Rhythm** is the natural rise and fall of voice when something is being spoken or read aloud.

The rhythmic patterns in poetry are more intense and conspicuous than are the rhythms of prose, although truly effective prose writers are very much aware of the rhythmic dynamics their sentences produce. In fact, you've probably heard praise of a prose writer couched in terms of poetry—as when an admiring critic says that this or that writer's style is so exquisite, it's more like poetry than prose. (By the way, when we want to criticize someone's work as pedestrian and dull, you might call it *prosaic*.)

All poems have rhythm, although some do a better job of using rhythm for poetic effect than others. The word *meter,* which comes from the Greek word for "measure," is used to describe a regular rhythmic pattern that operates throughout a given poem. In English poetry, that regular pattern is usually defined in terms of the recurrence of stressed and unstressed syllables at regular intervals.

To "scan a poem" has a very specific technical meaning. It doesn't mean to glance over a poem. In fact, the word *scansion* is used for the act of determining the meter of a poem by marking the stressed and unstressed syllables in its lines. Accents (stressed syllables) are marked by a slant line (/) above the syllable. Slack (unstressed) syllables are marked in one of two ways—either with an *x* above the syllable, or with a mark that looks like a somewhat flattened *u*.

As noted, not all poems are metrical. Free verse (*vers libre*) poetry does not have an identifiable rhyme scheme or metrical pattern. That doesn't mean there's no rhythm in free verse, or even that the rhythm isn't important and carefully patterned. In a good free verse poem, rhythm is precisely manipulated for effect.

However, if you were to mark the stressed and unstressed syllables in a free verse poem, you wouldn't be able to ascertain a regular pattern. Similarly, a free verse poem might make heavy use of rhymed or partially rhymed words (as well as alliteration, which is akin to rhyme), but you wouldn't be able to mark a rhyme scheme, and the rhymed words might not even occur at the ends of lines. It's the regularity of the pattern of end rhymes (rhymes that occur at the ends of lines) that allow you to label a rhyme scheme, and it's the regularity of the pattern of stressed and unstressed syllables that allows you to identify a metrical pattern in a poem.

Free verse must not be confused with blank verse. Although *blank verse* is unrhymed, it has a very specific metrical pattern—iambic pentameter. In fact, another way to refer to it is "unrhymed iambic pentameter."

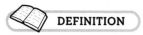 **DEFINITION**

> Poetry written in **blank verse** is similar to free verse. Blank verse poetry does not rhyme but does follow a regular rhythm—iambic pentameter.

Formal verse, on the other hand, makes use of regular metrical patterns and rhyme schemes. Remember that the word *formal* refers to the fact that the rules of relevant forms are strictly followed. Yet the word *formal* as applied to poetry has nothing to do with the level of seriousness, sophistication, or erudition manifested in the poem. Rather, it refers only to the poet's strict adherence to the rules of form he or she has selected for that particular poem.

Just as the word *formal* can be misleading in its meaning, *prosody* does not refer to prose, but rather to the analysis of the technical elements of poetry. Think of the major technical components of poetry as roughly equivalent to the way music is represented on the page, turning something you hear into something you can see. Because it deals with interpretation, it seems worth being mindful of poetic prosody (the technical components of poetry) here at the end of the chapter.

Poetry comes naturally to the human mind. The basic elements of poetry intrigue and delight almost anyone, regardless of age or level of education, and regardless of whether the listener/reader even understands what's being said in the poem. Many people delight in the sounds of poetry in languages they don't comprehend, and oftentimes even infants will quiet when you begin to read or recite poetry to them.

The Least You Need to Know

- Free verse is open in its patterns, while formal verse stringently follows rules.
- Imagery describes using the five senses, and metaphor relies on comparisons.
- *Density* and *intensity* are unreliable terms nevertheless used in interpreting poems.
- Prosody, rhythm, and rhyme are aspects of sound used to construct poems.

The Believable One-Act Play

Full-length plays that have a three-act format can last for more than 2 hours. By contrast, one-act plays are essentially short plays telling a complete story. They are enacted against the backdrop of a single scene and may last for about 30 to 60 minutes.

A budding playwright can get acquainted with the basics of playwriting by learning to write a one-act play. The format and content of the play is largely determined by audience, so it helps to know the target audience in advance. However, if you don't know for sure, you can keep some essential guidelines in mind to help in creating appropriate format and content for a one-act play.

What are the essential features of a one-act play? According to Aristotle, dramas should have a unity of time, location, and action. In conformity with these rules, most traditional plays have a central plot, the action of which unfolds in a single location having a duration of less than a day. These unities of drama can be used effectively in writing one-act plays, which are generally short and have no place for subplots or changes in scenes. The setting of a one-act play is usually restricted to a single scene. Thus, you should take care to generate the setting in such a way that the story line is clear to your audience.

In This Chapter

- Stage matters
- Making the play work
- Spoken audio
- Unspoken audio

One of the important elements in creating the setting is the use of lighting. Be sure to include detailed notes on the use of lighting to create the required setting. Ideally, the setting should engage the five senses to increase the appeal to the audience.

In general, one-act plays possess a lesser number of characters acting against a simple setting. In most cases, the focus is on the main character and his or her goals. Almost every scene of the play features the main character and the dilemmas on hand. The best way to develop the characters is to outline a character sketch and then fill in the details. The characters should be lifelike but also have a basic identifiable purpose in life (and in the play). The problems and situations they face in fulfilling their motives help in further shaping their character.

After the main task of writing a one-act play, you must then test it. The best way would be to enact the play. You can take useful feedback from those connected with the various stages of the play. Additionally, you could seek expert advice in the production of the play. Apart from a number of practice sessions, ideally perform a dress rehearsal in the final practice before a public showing.

Now let's investigate in greater detail the main aspects of a one-act play. They might be organized any number of ways, but I've broken them down into set, action, verbal sound, and nonverbal sound.

Setting the Set

The production maximum for a typical one-act stage play is about 45 pages, but it can be about as short as you like. Most one-act plays are set in the same setting, much like a television sitcom. All the action happens inside the house or in the office (or wherever) because it makes the entire crew's job easier when it comes to performing. If you change the setting every couple pages, and it's only a 10-page script, that's a lot of scene changing in a very short amount of time. You'll run your crew and actors into the ground or watch as they literally break a leg getting the *set* rearranged. Also keep in mind that each page equals about a minute of dialogue, so you don't want to jar the audience out of the story every 10 minutes with a blackout and then have 60 seconds of random people running around onstage.

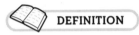 **DEFINITION**

> A **set** is the physical objects that project, sometimes imaginatively, the world of the play.

As you can see already, despite their brevity, one-act plays are not easy genres to write for, and a logical, structured approach will help you.

As for character limits, keep the main characters to a minimum so the audience doesn't have to remember too much about too many people in a short span of time. Television shows with more than one or two main characters usually never number more than five—it simply overpowers the educational level of the average viewer (which is about the eighth grade). Extras and people your audience doesn't really have to pay attention to can be, theoretically, limitless, but I'd try not to use too many of them unless they perform a vitally important function in the play.

Although they have much in common and lend each other to adaptation, plays are different from movies in that in plays, you can use the power of suggestion and the audience will be more willing to play along. If two people walk onstage alone and say, "It's so crowded," the audience will fill in the emptiness with an image of lots of people. In movies and television, however, you'd need the extras, or it would look weird.

Keeping that in mind can help eliminate complications in your playwriting. How many scenes you can put in a one-act play depends on your definition of scene, but as long as there's good flow to the overall action, you can have a handful of scenes or even several dozen. It doesn't really matter as long as you maintain your audience's attention.

The Importance of Action

Of course audience attention often is fostered via *action*. Yet in drama, action cannot be rendered using description. This revelation seems like sacrilege for a creative writer. Writing without description? That can't possibly be correct!

 **DEFINITION**

Action is the manifestation of feelings and thoughts through activity.

Drama, however, is a different art form. Its needs and requirements are different from novels and short stories, especially in terms of visual images and dialogue. In a novel or short story, you might see the phrase, "He wonders if he should have stopped for beer." Or "She's thinking she'll be late for her canasta game." Such sentences are description—narrative prose, to be precise. These are fine in a novel or short story, but they don't work as drama. Why not? Think about it. Can an actor perform them? In a film, can a camera photograph them? No. Therefore, that kind of writing does not belong in a one-act play. Description is a novelist's tool. Dramatists need to write *action*.

Okay, so what is action? And how do you write it? You're probably familiar with the film director's clarion call, "Lights! Camera! Action!" Yet action is one of the most misunderstood terms in the playwright's vocabulary. Often when beginners write a one-act play, their characters scramble about, seemingly very busy. Yet their story sags. It might even be dull. Why? Because, despite all the activity, there's no real action.

In modern English, *action* and *activity* are synonyms for physical movement, and you tend to use the terms interchangeably. In drama, *activity* is indeed physical movement. Beyond mere motion, however, *action* means human behavior, including the underlying emotions and mental processes that trigger behavior.

The real test for action in plays is whether it's behavior that actors can perform. Finally, while narrative prose tends to be written in the past tense and the third person, dramatists write action in the present tense and the first person. Characters are always in a state of "I do," rather than "I did."

Putting this concept into perspective, first you need to explore motivation. Most human behavior begins with a feeling, and the feeling prompts you to want something. Usually (within certain limits), you do something to get it. For example:

1. Jane feels thirsty.

2. She wants merlot.

3. She goes to the kitchen to prepare her drink.

For the most part, this process happens at the subconscious level. Still, the steps exist:

1. Feel.

2. Want.

3. Do.

Whenever you write action, remember that, despite the cliché, a picture really is worth a thousand words. You need to translate the preceding steps into activities that optically reveal feeling and wanting as well as doing. Yes, that's tricky. But the key is to use your imagination and think about the activities people use to express feelings, needs, wants, etc.

 **WRITING PROMPT**

Considering the example of Jane's thirst, what activities can you write that demonstrate how she feels thirsty and wants a drink?

Of course, getting a glass of wine is simple, ordinary behavior. Unless you want the audience to start snoring, you need to charge up the action. But how? What if, when Jane enters her kitchen, she finds a man wearing a ski mask?

1. What will she feel?

2. What will she want?

3. What will she do?

Fear and anger are predictable feelings Jane might have. What kind of behavior could such feelings prompt? As a rule, the stronger the emotion, the greater the desire and the bigger the action. Small, quiet actions are fine because they offer clues about the character's personality. For example, "Jane gasps and stares." This reaction would mean she's not the type to scream and run. For maximum power, however, rely on the strongest emotions: "Teeth clenched, Jane hurls her empty glass at the man and crouches into a defensive posture, fists raised." In this version, Jane is trained in self-defense.

But what if Jane simply stands frozen? What if she screams? Those actions are behavior, too. Sometimes a character doing nothing or acting in a traditional manner has a greater impact than when they do something unique. The writer's greatest priority is to choose behavior that's appropriate for a specific character in a given situation. Who is *your* Jane?

In the preceding examples, we considered Jane's possible actions. But how might her behavior affect the guy in the ski mask? If she screams and runs, what emotions will it spark in him? What will he want? What behavior will he show? In short, what will be his reaction?

Sir Isaac Newton noted, "For every action, there is an equal and opposite reaction." Of course, he was talking about physics. Yet surprisingly, the disciplines of physics and drama have several concepts in common. Whenever you put two or more people together, one person's behavior invariably forces others to react. If you doubt this, walk into a crowded room and start laughing. No warning. No explanation. Just laugh. Most of the people near you will shake their heads, puzzled. Some will be embarrassed and look away. Some people will scowl. Some will get the bug and laugh with you. But they will respond somehow, believe me.

That response will be dramatic action, which simply constitutes people acting upon each other. Dramatic action always comes in two parts: action and reaction. One character's behavior may be interesting, but by itself, it contributes little to plot development. Response from other characters, however, propels the story forward.

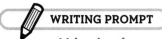 **WRITING PROMPT**

Make a list of actions and reactions you recall from books and movies that involve events and characters. Then see if any of them fit material you could use for a one-act play.

If by now you're thinking in terms of the domino effect (another cliché, but an accurate one), you're quite correct. Dramatic action is a point and counterpoint of behavior, one character playing off against another. Whenever one character wants something, no matter how small, and another character wants something different, they will be in conflict. Their interaction, the give-and-take between them, brings your story to life.

Essential Verbal Sound

The action-propelling interaction between characters discussed in the previous section includes whatever they might say to each other. Speech is an essential part of human behavior, and when one person addresses another, typically it prompts the second person to reply. Indeed, dialogue is our most basic form of dramatic action.

But what if the second person does not speak? What if she turns her back and walks away? That behavior, too, is dramatic action, because it was prompted by the first person's speech.

But now on to verbal sound. There's a myth that the ability to write great dialogue, to make your characters sound real, is a gift that can't be learned and can't be taught. Either you're born with it, or you'll never have it. One version of the myth goes something like this: you have to have an *ear* for dialogue to be able to reproduce realistic, believable, crisp, vocal sound on the page.

Fortunately, writing great dialogue doesn't have to come from having an ear for it. It also doesn't need to come from having some innate gift or talent for writing dialogue. It comes from knowing your characters so well, you know what they'll say and how they'll say it when faced with specific people, situations, or events.

Now that might seem overly simple, and in a way it is; given the same character and same situation, two writers of very different abilities will create greater or lesser dialogue. But I firmly believe that if two writers know their characters equally well, if both writers develop those characters fully, and if both writers know the other characters in a scene equally well, both sets of dialogue will be of a high quality.

Taking this a step further, when you know not only some of the things your characters might say, but the *only* thing they'd say at various times, you're onto something truly special. When a specific piece of dialogue is the only dialogue that could be spoken in a given situation by a given character to another given character, that dialogue can seem brilliant. And it doesn't have to be eloquent dialogue, as long as it's the exactly right dialogue.

"I coulda been a contender," lamented by Marlon Brando's character, Terry, in the 1954 film *On the Waterfront*, resonates through the decades, and even today can be considered brilliant dialogue for its poignancy and for the fact that it was exactly the right thing for Terry to say to Charley in the particular setting and circumstance they were in at that time. What Brando said was so perfect, so believable, given the character he was, where he was, who he was in relationship with, and whom he was saying it to, that it comes across as brilliant. Could anyone write dialogue that brilliant? Perhaps not, but still, the elements that lead up to that scene and that dialogue are all there for us to see, and they are all based on the authors' complete, profound knowledge of who their characters are.

There's another factor in writing great dramatic dialogue. It draws on the fact—echoing the prior section in this chapter—that essentially dialogue is just another event. It's caused by characters and, in turn, causes other events and affects other characters. It's something that happens, that takes place in space and time, and it's both a result and cause, just like an event is.

 WATCH OUT!

> When characters speak, they're doing something, performing an act. But how does that help you improve your dialogue? Think of it this way: what happens when an event in a story occurs that has nothing to do with the rest of the story? It sticks out, doesn't it? That's what happens with dialogue that has nothing to do with the rest of the story.

Remember to make your dialogue relevant to the play. More than just this, however, you have to be aware of the cause and effect of that dialogue just as you're aware of the cause and effect of an incident.

If a guy in your play waves his hands around in an unusual way and nothing comes of it, the audience is left wondering why he did that. However, if they find out that the reason he's waving his hands around oddly is because he's schizophrenic and thinks he has magical powers. If they know he thinks that, with a wave of his hands, he can make his enemy disappear or make a beautiful woman appear, you begin to see the relevance of that odd waving and flailing about.

If you take this a step further and have a beautiful woman witness the odd waving and recognize it as the gesture that accompanies a magical spell, the odd gesture has an effect on another character, and maybe on the story as a whole. Maybe the beautiful woman, believing the delusional guy is a sorcerer, befriends him and takes him on a wild adventure with her because she believes he can actually use his powers to help her.

So now the event works. The audience understands why the event occurs (the guy is schizophrenic with delusions of being a sorcerer), and they understand what effect the event has (it leads to a grand misunderstanding and an even grander adventure). You've connected the event to both the past and the future. You must do the same thing to your dialogue—all of it.

For brilliant dialogue, make what you put on the page the only dialogue your character can possibly say, given who he or she is, where he or she is, and to whom he or she is saying it. Then be sure every event leading up to the dialogue is believable and every event after the dialogues at least partly a result of that dialogue. Finally, make the audience care about the character so they've got a vested interest in what he or she is saying, and in the results of what he or she says. Do these things, and you'll find people responding to your dialogue deeply and excitedly.

 WRITING PROMPT

Take two people you know very well who do not know each other and, based on that intimate knowledge, construct a fictional conversation between them. You might find portions of it useful later for your fictional characters.

Equally Essential Nonverbal Sound

As important as dialogue is, it's not the only variety of sound your one-act play requires. In fact, nonverbal sound can be just as important—and sometimes more.

How something is expressed could carry more significance and weight than *what* is said (the words themselves). Accompanied by a smile or a frown, or said with a loud, scolding voice or a gentle, easy one, the contents of our communications are framed by our perceptions of their context. Those sending the messages may learn to understand themselves better as well as learn to exert some greater consciousness about their manner of speech. Those receiving the messages may learn to better understand their own intuitive responses—sometimes in contrast to what it seems reasonable to think.

Part of our culture involves an unspoken rule that people should ignore these nonverbal elements, as if the injunction were, "Hear what I say, and don't notice the way I say it." These elements are often ignored in school or overridden by parents, so the task of incorporating conscious sensitivity to nonverbal communications is made more difficult for audiences to recognize in plays. In fact, getting it across is often going to come down to the quality of the actor, no matter how well you wrote it. Still, some terms and methods can help you give your character the best shot at conveying a nonverbal message.

Nonverbal communication occurs not only between people, but also internally. People grimace, stand in certain postures, and behave in other ways to reinforce certain positions, attitudes, and implicit beliefs. Unconsciously, they suggest to themselves the role they choose to play, submissive or dominant, trusting or wary, controlled or spontaneous.

Personal Space

Several types of nonverbal sound and communication can help you in your thinking and writing. One is the idea of personal space. This refers to the distance people feel comfortable approaching others or having others approach them.

People from certain countries, such as parts of Latin America or the Middle East, often feel comfortable standing closer to each other, while persons of Northern European descent tend to prefer a relatively greater distance.

Different distances are also intuitively assigned for situations involving intimate relations, ordinary personal relationships (such as friends), social relations (co-workers or salespeople), or in public places (in parks, in restaurants, or on the street).

Eye Contact

Not unrelated to personal space is eye contact. For instance, Spanish women in the nineteenth century combined eye language with the use of a fan to express what wasn't permissible to explicitly say verbally.

In addition, eye contact modifies the meaning of other nonverbal behaviors. For example, people on elevators or crowds can adjust their sense of personal space if they agree to limit eye contact. Modern American business culture values a fair degree of eye contact in interpersonal relations, and looking away is sensed as avoidance or even deviousness. However, some cultures raise children to minimize eye contact, especially with authority figures, lest one be perceived as arrogant or "uppity." When cultures interact, this inhibition of gaze may be misinterpreted as passive aggressive, or worse.

Position and Posture

Position and posture also augment the idea of bodily space. The position one takes in relation to others speaks to the overall interpersonal relationship. A person's bodily stance also communicates a rich variety of messages and carries emotional effects.

Tone of Voice

Moving to the mouth, a playwright should never underestimate the power of tone of voice. Dialect, for example, can suggest class, age, sophistication, etc. How a person uses the language—too snooty, too low-class, too regional—can indicate unconscious associations and possible prejudices.

There's also the problem of understandability, which applies not only to people from other cultures or nations, but also intergenerationally. On some television programs, the characters speak so rapidly and often softly that folks of an older generation can hardly hear or keep up—even with the volume turned up.

Facial Expressions

If you pull back from the mouth to the face, you might be surprised to know that the human face is more highly developed as an organ of expression than in any other animal. In fact, some people's expressions become quite habitual, almost fixed into the chronic muscular structure of the face. Using facial expressions is a great way to identify characters without writing or relating anything else. An example is the squint of people who live in the sun a lot.

More transient expressions often reveal feelings that a person isn't intending to communicate or is even aware of. These also are great tools for revealing how a character is feeling.

Gestures and Movements

Gestures can have many different meanings in different cultures, and what may be friendly in one country or region can be an insult in another. Moreover, how one person touches another communicates a great deal of information: is a grip gentle or firm, and does one hold the other person on the back of the upper arm, on the shoulder, or in the middle of the back? Is the gesture a push or a tug? Is the touch closer to a pat, a rub, or a grabbing?

People have different areas of personal intimacy, and this refers not only to the sexual dimension, but also the dimension of self-control. Even the angle of one's holding another's hand might suggest a hurrying or coercive implicit attitude or, on the other hand, a respectful, gentle, permission-giving approach.

Physical movement in general communicates a great deal, as well as affecting the feelings of the person doing the moving. Does your main character mostly slink or stride? Does he or she pace?

A related variable is the time it takes to react to a stimulus. Some people seem to react to questions, interact in conversations, or are slower or faster on the uptake than others.

 WRITING PROMPT

Again, take two people you know very well who do not know each other, and based on that intimate knowledge, construct communication using only nonverbal sounds and actions between them. Once again, you might find portions of it useful later for your fictional characters.

People react both to the unspoken and nonverbal sound, as much (if not more) to how something is said. Misunderstandings can often be clarified if the people involved have the ability to notice and comment on the nonverbal communications in an interaction. Writers benefit from learning the range of nonverbal behaviors and sounds in order to clarify the often-subtle dynamics of the situations they find themselves portraying. For example, in a marriage, sometimes the other person gets irritated by some mysterious event: exploring what the problem was could lead to an awareness that the way something was said communicated an unintended meaning. By making the nonverbal communication more clear, conflicts can be both portrayed and resolved.

The Least You Need to Know

- When planning and writing your set, be sure it's well organized and well managed.
- Dramatists render action by transmitting feelings and thoughts through activity.
- Verbal sound is essential to dramatic action.
- Nonverbal sound allows for action and communication that dialogue cannot convey.

Long-Form Genres

Now that we've studied the shorter, self-contained genres of creative writing, it's time to get a little more ambitious and consider several of those same genres in their longer manifestations, which is most often a book.

That might sound like an intimidating prospect, but when you break it down and think of a memoir or novel as the best parts of a big story, or a poetry or essay collection as your very best poems and essays, suddenly the task is more about assembling and organizing smaller parts than sitting down a typing a book beginning to end.

In Part 5, we consider the best strategies for putting together different genres in their longer forms, whether that's a novel, a collection, a play, and so on. Likely, the idea of writing your own book is the reason many of you picked up this one.

The Realities of Nonfiction and Memoir

Nonfiction writers and memoirists often take advantage of novel-writing techniques to enhance their prose and develop their books. They create scenes and characters, use dialogue and description, and as much as possible, they try to *show* rather than *tell*.

These are all excellent ways to bring books to life, but in fact, there's more to glean from fiction than scene, description, and dialogue. The strategies behind good storytelling are numerous, and many additional techniques are available for nonfiction writers and memoirists to borrow.

One important method involves setting up the action that's to come in your book. To create the momentum that will keep readers turning the page, setting up future action is vital. This means letting us know in Chapter 3 that in Chapter 4, an important dinner will take place. Tell us not only that this dinner will occur, but why it matters, what's at stake.

I sometimes read manuscripts in which the writer leaps into a high-intensity moment—such as a dinner where she tells her husband she wants a divorce—then inserts a paragraph in the scene to say she's been thinking of taking this step for months. That paragraph is a tipoff. Instead of interrupting a dramatic encounter with explanation, set up the potent conversation in a previous scene so the reader feels the tension and wonders what will happen.

Filmmaker Alfred Hitchcock famously described how to create suspense. In a scene in which a bomb explodes in a football stadium, he said, movie viewers will be frightened for a few moments when the bomb goes off. But if we know the bomb is under a stadium seat and will go off in 10 minutes, we'll be frightened for 10 minutes. When you let the reader know what's coming and why it matters, you increase tension and momentum.

Just as important as creating anticipation for a particular scene is to set up the whole plot trajectory. Elizabeth Gilbert begins her popular memoir *Eat, Pray, Love* with the sentence: "I wish Giovanni would kiss me." We know immediately what she wants (love), we know what's at stake (will she find it? can she be happy without it?), and we're willing to follow her quest. The book, of course, teases us until close to the end.

To get readers to the end of your book, you need to make your scenes have consequences. In real life, after that difficult dinner with your husband, you might have watched the evening news. But if you were writing fiction, there would be a plot consequence to that dinner. The woman initiated divorce. When she did, she flirted with her divorce lawyer, a friend of her husband's. Complications ensued. In creative nonfiction or memoir, as in fiction, you want to develop the result or consequence of the events you portray. What further action did that dinner propel? How did it complicate or feed the larger story?

Emotion and Event

I like to suggest that writers think of the difference between a row of pearls on a string and a row of dominos that can be pushed over with the touch of a finger. The pearls simply sit next to each other, exerting no pressure. The domino, when tipped, will knock over the next, which will knock over the next. Don't let your scenes rest serenely like a string of pearls on debutante no one wants to dance with. Rather, be sure they ripple with the energy and impact of falling dominos, one scene launching another.

 IDEAS AND INSPIRATION

Where you place the plot consequences matters. Sometimes you want to hold off the repercussions for a short time to add tension and keep the reader hanging. But if you drop a particular plot line for too long, tension dissipates.

Limiting the amount of time you cover is one of the most central elements of effective storytelling. Real time progresses in a linear fashion, one day to the next. But dramatic time can leap over inessential events. A skilled storyteller dramatizes only those minutes that have an emotional punch and serve to advance the plot.

In her memoir *Reading Lolita in Tehran*, Azar Nafisi tells the story of a secret reading group of university students who meet weekly at her apartment. She could have easily described the first meeting from beginning to end, described the second meeting, and so on. But Nafisi knew that would be dramatically weak. Instead, she presents only brief slices of the meetings in her book. One day we see the women arriving. In another scene, we see them arguing over a passage in a novel.

These moments reveal crucial conflicts and emotions, and they are so vivid, the reader can easily imagine the whole two years of meetings even though we witness only a scattering of hours. The seasoned creative nonfiction writer or memoirist knows the difference between what the reader needs to witness (what has to be dramatized) and what can be left offstage. Rather than giving a dutiful account of the literary meetings, Nafisi uses the group as an opening to a passionate exploration of oppression, defiance, and identity.

So let emotion and event—not the passage of time—prompt your story. Don't be bound by the calendar. This is another key element of strong dramatic writing. When you use dramatic time (selected, compressed) as a structuring device, you free yourself from the compulsion to follow linear time: June, July; fall, winter. Instead, you let the significant events and the deep emotions they unleash animate your story.

Joan Didion's memoir *The Year of Magical Thinking* ostensibly covers one year, from the evening her husband, John Gregory Dunne, succumbed to a sudden heart attack at the dinner table, to the anniversary of his death a year later. Yet her emotionally driven book is only loosely structured around the calendar year. Mostly it surges and swells with memory, association, and persistent anguish over resonant details from her life with her husband. Didion (or at least her nonfiction projection) surfaces from grief (water is a repeated image, and its fluidity is fitting to the movement of grief) from time to time to let us know it's July or August, but the story immediately veers into another fit of remembered events that rise, like waves, over and over.

Loosening your story from chronological time allows you to follow an emotional logic: a pattern of association and recurring images that goes to the heart of what is significant. In the course of three pages, Didion swerves from a present moment at the Council on Foreign Relations in New York, to a trip to Paris she and John took a month before he died, to his last cardiac procedure eight months before he died, to a taxi ride the night before his death in which he expressed despair. "Real" time is discarded in favor of the inner life of emotion, and the story is driven by memory and pain.

However, before you give yourself over to the driving force of emotion, consider the four elements that constitute important infrastructure for any book-length nonfiction: research, fact/truth, memory, and authorial intrusion.

The Importance of Research

Conducting *research* is the part of the nonfiction aspect of writing creative nonfiction, be it memoir, travel book, or whatever other work. The amount of research required for a writing project depends on a combination of the form of creative nonfiction and the topic at hand.

 **DEFINITION**

> **Research** is the collecting of facts to increase understanding of a person, place, event, idea, experience, or thing.

You carry out research to increase your understanding of a person, topic, or idea. You also do research to see what else has been written on the topic you're going to write about. You don't want to totally duplicate what's already written, even if some of the information bears repeating. You also can do research to become a subject matter expert.

Research also enables you to verify facts. You want to be sure that what you've written is true and accurate.

Research has another purpose as well: to stimulate your memories. Often when you investigate an experience or event, memories associated with the event rise into your mind from the depths of your unconsciousness. In this sense, research acts as a triggering mechanism.

If you intend to write a memoir, you'll be required to complete extensive research into your own life—to recall significant details of people, places, and events from your own past. You also can use facts from research to create metaphors or similes.

As noted, some forms of nonfiction require more research than others. For example, a personal essay about a canoe trip to a lake that resulted in an epiphany requires less research than a memoir. The canoe trip might only require you to consult your writing journal and speak with the friend(s) who accompanied you (if still living), whereas a memoir involves interviewing friends and family, visiting the library and public records offices, revisiting the places you frequented during the period of the memoir, and obtaining details about the popular culture of the time.

There are two drawbacks to doing research. First, the tsunami of facts you collect can overwhelm you, bogging down your narrative. Secondly, research can result in procrastination. In other words, the task of researching a project often prevents you from getting on with the actual writing.

 WATCH OUT!

> Be as sure as you can that your research sources are reliable. If you have doubts about an especially important source, consult an expert or a librarian.

Immersion is one specific method of research you might find useful. With immersion, you acquire an understanding by "living the experience." Suppose you intend to write a narrative about baseball, for example, but you'd never played the game before. You could increase your understanding by playing a few games of rec-league baseball. You could then use what you learned from the experience to write your piece of nonfiction.

Interviewing is another popular approach when it comes to research. Interview a subject matter expert, talk to people who participated in the event or experience, interview those who were witnesses to the event, or interview people who knew the person you're writing about. An interview always requires a list of question to ask. These questions should be open-ended, requiring the person being interviewed to respond with more than a "yes" or "no" answer.

Despite the digital resources available with the click of a button, you'll surprised by the sheer volume of information you discover that does not yet exist on the internet. Print sources that have yet to make their way into cyberspace are available in libraries—be sure to ask a librarian for assistance. The following might especially prove relevant to your topic or area of interest:

- Newspapers

- Magazines

- Books

- Periodicals

- Encyclopedias

- Publications on microfilm, such as old newspapers

Most likely, the internet will be the research aid you're most familiar with. Begin by conducting a Google search, and then read and collect useful facts from websites you can tell are reputable. Many subject matter experts have their own blogs where they post articles, commentaries, and so forth. If you read a fascinating article but still have questions, you might be able to find the expert's blog or email the writer your queries.

Writing a personal essay often requires that you research your own life before writing. This is mandatory when writing a memoir. Research allows you to check the accuracy of memories and enables you to recall details of the popular culture, as well as the social and economic and historical conditions of the life you lived in the past.

Research also enables you to mine your own memory, helping you recall the people, places, events, experiences that might be long forgotten. Why? Because researching a timeline or time period stimulates your memory and helps trigger events that occurred in your life in those times.

IDEAS AND INSPIRATION

Make a timeline of the portion of your life you intend to write about. As you take note of the major events you remember best, you'll be surprised at your ability to fill in the blank spaces you thought you'd forgotten.

Here are some of the ways in which to research your own life:

- What challenges, setbacks, and obstacles have you faced? What is the biggest challenge you have faced, for example? What is the saddest moment in your life?

- Where have you lived? Think about your major moves, leaving home, your first home, the place where you lived after a divorce, etc.

- Consider your calendar—significant birthdays, anniversaries, graduations, marriages, deaths.

- Think about your firsts—first kiss, first new car, first speech, first job, etc.

- What have you achieved? What are your accomplishments?

- What do you want your legacy to be? What do you want to be remembered for?

- Where have you been? Revisit places from your childhood, adolescence, or adulthood.

- Look over old photographs, read old diaries and journals and letters, and leaf through old scrapbooks.

What sort of research will be required? The type of narrative determines what information/facts you need to provide your reader. The key point to remember is that creative nonfiction writers do research to increase their understanding of themselves and the world in which they live. And yet, too much research, a mountain of facts, can blow out the flame of creativity. So only do as much research as required to understand the topic, person, or idea you're writing about.

Writing Truth and Fact

When writing creative nonfiction, you must present facts accurately. You must be honest and truthful. Otherwise, you're writing fiction, a story that's made up. Creative nonfiction involves writing about facts using literary devices, your memories or recollections, and your imagination. You can write about any topic, such as birth, love, sex, death, sports, travel, science, nature, and so forth.

Often you need to remember or recollect the details of what happened, especially if the event or story took place many years ago. Questions will arise from readers about accuracy of your reporting, whether you're telling the truth, and if you're subjectively and objectively presenting the truth. In addition, sometimes you need to check your facts by interviewing friends or relatives who might not want you to write about them, the event, or the story. So you also might be faced with an ethical dilemma.

As noted, to write factually and accurately, you often need to conduct research. For instance, if you're writing a personal essay, you might have to visit the place where the event took place or contact friends and relatives who remember the event.

Sometimes the line between fact and fiction is ambiguous, and in these times, you need to make a judgment call. Some people believe that once a fact is distorted or embellished, it's fictional. Others believe that creative nonfiction that's based on memories or recollections will be distorted, period.

Memories aren't 100 percent accurate, so you'll have to engage in a certain amount of fabrication to present the facts. There's no objective record, only your memories and recollections about an event that happened in the past. So when using dialogue in a memoir, for example, you often have to "invent" the actual dialogue if you don't remember every word that was spoken. The important point to remember is that you must do your best to remember *accurately.* To verify memories or recollections, check your facts to be sure your view is accurate—that your intention is the truth.

When you write creative nonfiction, you're asking your readers to trust you, to believe you. But you must earn that trust. As the reader reads your personal essay, memoir, or travel piece, he or she might think: *Do I trust this writer? Do I believe what this person is saying?*

IDEAS AND INSPIRATION

When writing about past events, you might struggle with memory and accuracy. That's okay. There are no rules here other than you must do your best to present the facts as you know them to be. You might not remember what your exact thoughts were on the day of the event, but you might remember the event, the date it took place, the consequences, and the significance for you. Write about the emotional truth that resulted from the event—what it meant to you, how you felt about the events that took place, your views, etc. To gain your reader's trust, make your account as honest and interesting as you can without fabricating it.

When writing about real people and real events, you will sometimes need to consider ethics, such as the right to privacy and the betrayal of trust. There's a need for full disclosure when interviewing and writing about real people and events. For instance, when interviewing a person, you must make it clear that you're collecting information for a story you intend to write. If you don't disclose your intention to the person you're interviewing, you're being unethical. When writing about events that happened in the past, you often need to obtain oral or written permission to avoid being unethical.

Sometimes a writer won't want to write about a true story because it could hurt or offend people who were participants in the story. For instance, if you're writing about child abuse, you might be reluctant to tell your story. Not only is it embarrassing, but it also could upset or anger others who were aware of the events. On the other hand, if the person is deceased or estranged from you, you might be more willing to disclose this information. Often, ethical decisions are based on your own point of view; to show and tell becomes a matter of considering the costs and benefits.

You might also need to make a decision about point of view (POV). Some writers believe you can write a personal essay or memoir in the first person point of view, using *I*. Obviously, if you're writing a personal essay, you'll write in the first person. It's more intimate, more real, and natural. Moreover, you are the central character in the story.

But there will be times when you aren't the central character. You might be just an observer of the story or events. The question is then whether to narrate your story in the first person or third person. For instance, if you want to tell the story as the events unfolded, you might want to write in the third person using *he* or *she*. It's more objective. Clearly, the decision to place yourself in or out of the story is a personal one.

When writing creative nonfiction, such as a personal essay, memoir, or literary essay, you must remember that your writing needs to be accurate, and you must present the facts to the best of your ability. You also must also ethical in conducting research and revealing personal information about other people. To gain your reader's trust, be honest with yourself and tell the truth. You can include your own perspective or point of view, but you must tell the truth.

Making Use of Memory

Several types of memory are useful for writing memoir and nonfiction: memory for events, for facts, for how to do things, and working memory, which holds ideas in your head just long enough to turn them over. Each of these is malleable, and they're all mysterious, which you don't really realize until they fail you.

When writing creative nonfiction, it's your task to rediscover important memories, make sense of them, and write about them in a way that's interesting to your reader. Memories also help define who we are as human beings and why we are the way we are. It's your memories that define your sense of self. Without memories, you have no past experience. You are continually living in the moment, without any sense of past experience. When writing creative nonfiction, especially a memoir, your job is to rediscover the important memories.

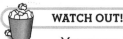 **WATCH OUT!**

Memory can be faulty. Often you won't remember all the details or get the details wrong. In this case, you must rely on emotional truth and fact checking.

You piece together your memories from the fragments of life's events that you've retained to understand who you are. The difficulty is to recapture these memories and make sense of them.

Many personal essay collections and all memoirs are based on the writer's memories. However, because memory can be faulty, you must try to get the facts right to the best of your ability. Other times writing about memories involves writing about the emotional truth. This involves gathering the facts as best as you can, but then filling in the details using your emotional truth, or what seems right to you emotionally.

In other words, if it's true to you on an emotional level, you can write about it as if it is the truth. After all, it's more important to analyze *why* you remember a particular memory than *what* you remember. It's possible to make sense of a memory by describing it in relation to something else.

IDEAS AND INSPIRATION

You can write about memory as a simile. Some memories are vague, like dreams. Others are vivid, like a photograph. Many memories are not understood, like an abstract painting. You can also write about memories as metaphors. A diary is a memory. A photograph is a memory. A personal journal is a memory. Home videos are memories.

Rediscover your memories, make sense of them, and write about them in a creative way. Memories provide the details you need to add to your life story to make it believable and to re-create the experience in your reader's mind. By unlocking one memory, you can discover other memories and sift through them to find useful, interesting, and surprising facts. You can then use your memories to write that collection of personal essays, an autobiography, or a memoir.

What About Authorial Intrusion?

Authorial intrusion, or when an author asserts him- or herself into the story, pulls readers out of the narrative and reminds them that they're reading.

Once upon a time, it was common for writers to insert their own comments or statements into a narrative. In the middle of a romantic scene showing the protagonists finally coming together, for example, the writer might insert a little story about the statue they knocked off the dresser in their exuberance. The readers are left to cool their heels while the author takes this little segue.

Readers today don't tolerate such devices. Writers can intrude on the story in many ways, and sometimes it's unintentional. You might make a comment or observation that isn't what the reader would expect from the point-of-view character, for example. Or perhaps the dialogue seemed to be directed to the reader to explain backstory or as a way to insert the writer's personal view instead of being a natural part of the story. Sometimes the writer includes a detail about the characters or setting that isn't consistent with what was previously written. Factual errors and plot holes are also forms of authorial intrusion.

When you insert or withhold information that isn't consistent with the setting or the character's POV, this is annoying for readers. A more intense scene usually is created without author intrusion to slow things down. Books aren't like movies. The reader can't see or know what's happening off-screen because the characters can't see it. You must show the events as they would be seen through the POV you're using.

Using weak verbs or telling in narrative is another type of authorial intrusion. This is why you *show* rather than *tell*. Telling is one of the most obvious authorial intrusions. It reminds readers that they're reading, pulling them away from the story.

To avoid author intrusion, you must ensure that the narrative adds something to the story, that it moves it forward. Narrative inserted for the sake of filling in a blank spot intrudes on the reader's experience. The reader should only know what the POV character knows and see only what the POV character sees. If you stay out of telling by keep the narrative active, you don't need to annoy the reader by inserting yourself into the book.

The Least You Need to Know

- Research deepens the world of your nonfiction book.
- Facts are important, but the truth of a book can be emotional rather than factual.
- Memory can be misleading, but it also can be reconstructed.
- Avoid authorial intrusion to keep from pulling your readers out of the story.

The Longer Story: The Novel

Writing a novel seems like a big undertaking, and it is. But there are some things you can consider to help demystify it a bit. Like all books, at the most basic level, writing a novel involves just three steps:

1. Planning—this is where you work out what you want to say (in note form).

2. Writing—here, you transform the plan into prose and dialogue.

3. Revising—finally, you polish the words until they shine.

If you're serious about succeeding as a novel writer, you need to take your time and start at very beginning. If you're willing to work as hard as it takes for as long as it takes—without forgetting to enjoy yourself along the way, of course—it's certainly within your power to write a novel. As with so many things in life, success in writing has less to do with talent and more with attitude and discipline.

In This Chapter

- Perfecting novel story and plot
- Writing the scene and summary
- Using backstory and flashback in longer stories
- Working with prosody

First and foremost, you need to decide why you want to write fiction at all. Making money from writing is not a bad motivation, but it involves a fair amount of luck and there are much better ways to ensure you look forward to working on your novel every day. Other tasks here include getting organized (both in terms of paperwork and time) and learning how to harness your inner creativity for the long haul.

An important aspect of learning how to write a novel is adopting a professional attitude. Forget all your romantic ideals of what being a writer is like; selling a novel to a publisher is a business proposition. What does that mean for you? It means that, to stand the best chance of success, you need to know right from the outset where your book will eventually sit in the marketplace.

 IDEAS AND INSPIRATION

In thinking about the marketplace and your novel, look at novels that possess similar content and, if possible, writing styles to what you have in mind for your own.

Before you can plan, of course, you need an idea. Some people will tell you that good novelistic ideas are difficult to come by. I respectfully disagree. In fact, I believe most writers face the opposite problem—not having enough time to turn every idea they have into a novel.

No two people will approach writing a novel the exact same way, so you should feel free to adapt your novel writing process to what works for you. For example, some writers like to plan their fiction in extensive detail before they turn to the business of drafting and revising it. Other writers get by on virtually no planning at all, or even zero planning. They come from the "seat of the pants" school of writing.

Which way is best? There's no absolute right answer. If a particular way of writing fiction that works for you, use it. But if you're unsure what approach to take, I would suggest you plan your novel in as much detail as you can stand before you write the first draft.

Because planning a long work of fiction in detail is such a large task—not to mention a potentially confusing one—the best way to tackle it is to break it down into smaller parts. For the purposes of this chapter, we'll look at story and plot, scene and summary, backstory and flashback, and prosody.

According to writers' agents, most novels are rejected because of weak craftsmanship, and you are far, far more likely to write a well-crafted novel if you take the time and trouble to plan it in some detail first. Knowing where to start and how to keep on going right to the end is something many beginners need to know.

Understanding Novel Story and Plot

People tend to use the words *plot* and *story* interchangeably, and it's easy to think of them as the same thing. It's astonishing how many successful authors don't grasp the difference. Sure, some of them apply one or the other intuitively without knowing they're doing it, but plenty more don't—and their work shows it.

The plot is what happens to your protagonist, and the story is how your protagonist changes inside as a result of the plot. By keeping these two words separate and carefully using them only when you mean the physical (plot) or the emotional (story), you can bring a whole new level of clarity to everything you write.

Another way to think of plot and story is in terms of action and reaction. Some action happens (plot), and your character reacts to it (story). In fact, a novel is nothing more than a repeating series of actions and reactions.

Now that you understand the difference between these two tools, it's easy to see how you can use plot and story continuously throughout your novel. Plot is action, so if things are dragging, add more of plot. But if things are moving too fast, add more story to slow them down. Plot and story work together to keep your novel on pace.

Some novels might be mostly plot—think Clive Cussler adventure stories, for example. Some novels might be mostly story—think Jane Austen. But all novels alternate back and forth, regardless of the emphasis. A successful novel needs plenty of both.

The constant resonance between story and plot creates the dramatic tension you'll need to maintain throughout your story. This is what keeps your readers on the edge of their seats. Without an emotional reaction, a plot development will have no effect on your reader. And without plot developments, your characters—and your reader—will have no motivation.

So when you devise your story, think of it first in emotional terms. What are your characters feeling? What are they thinking? What are their inner struggles? But don't stop there. Story cannot exist without plot to carry it on its way. How will you show what your characters feel? What will express their thoughts? What will reveal their inner struggles?

 IDEAS AND INSPIRATION

As you develop your plot, remember to test every moment of physical action for its emotional value. If an event ends up having little or no emotional value, you should find something better.

The plot you devise depends on the story you want to tell, and the story you want to tell determines your plot options. It's astonishing how much published mainstream fiction lacks a story. This is particularly true of Hollywood movies, but we can easily find the problem in both television and in bookstores.

Every James Bond movie begins with some spectacular stunt. In one—it really doesn't matter which—Bond and Jaws plunge from an airplane with only one parachute between them. After a dramatic midair struggle, Bond ends up with the parachute, and Jaws ends up as tomato soup.

It's an exciting way to start a movie. The problem is, it's completely uninteresting from an emotional standpoint. We haven't even met Bond's character yet in the movie. And if we had, we'd find him shallow (unlike Ian Fleming's books, in which Bond's personality is more fully developed). Unless you have a decent memory and regularly watch Bond films, you might not even recall who Jaws is from a previous movie. This is also why any moderately handsome male actor can play James Bond. Because it's all plot, and you don't really care about Bond the person—although his gadgets, combat decisions, and sex partners might hold your attention ….

On the other hand, when tears stream down the character's face, you are revealing story (emotion) through plot (action). Readers will be moved by the story, not the plot. And they will remember the experience and want to repeat it. Meanwhile, a plot device—no matter how spectacular—is only spectacular the first time we encounter it. That's why each Bond film needs to start with a stunt more spectacular or clever than the last.

Of course, in a novel, you could make the opposite mistake, spending all your time in your character's head, with nothing exciting happening in the physical world. A lot of Stephanie Meyer's *Twilight* books suffer from this problem.

It might surprise you to discover that plot comes second. It's much easier to construct a solid story and then add plot details that make sense than it is to construct a series of events and then try to find rational reasons why people would behave that way. After all, some action we could dream up might have no logical explanation at all and then we'd be stuck!

The difference between plot and story is essential knowledge for successful writing. Once you understand that, it's time to create your main character and send him or her on both a physical and an emotional journey.

Knowing When to Write Scene Versus Summary

It's not unusual for novels to have problems with pacing. This issue pops up in most creative writing, including my own. The trouble is that pacing issues are incredibly difficult to spot when you're in the middle of a piece, just like how I think I'm running at a perfectly normal speed until a fellow runner shows me otherwise.

But these pacing problems can't go unfixed. Have you ever read a book and spent several pages wondering when the author was going to get on with the story? Or has a plot ever moved so quickly, you couldn't keep track of the action? Pacing issues are one of the most common reasons I put down a book and never pick it up again.

One of the biggest contributors to pacing is knowing when to write summaries and when to write scenes. Summaries are responsible for quickening the pace of your story because they usually involve summing up large amounts of time in a quick paragraph. Most authors have heard the caveat "to show, not tell." Summary and telling usually go together, but it's for the good cause of skipping unnecessary parts of your story and keeping your readers engaged.

Here's when you should think about using summary:

- A significant amount of time passes with no major plot points or character developments

- You need to tell readers the character did something mundane that's not worth exploring in depth (going to her dentist appointment, for example)

- A character needs to encounter something that will factor in to the plot later but shouldn't be too obvious right now (the narrator makes a casual reference to a restaurant going out of business, for example)

- An event needs to occur for the purpose of the plot, but the event itself isn't important (Derek's assistant brought Sophie the files she requested at lunch, for example)

 WATCH OUT!

Don't use summaries to avoid sharing details or developing your characters.

Scenes, on the other hand, slow down your story. A scene covering a 15-minute conversation can last for several pages. A good scene involves elements such as character development, monologues and dialogues, and meatier setting descriptions.

Think about using scenes during these instances:

- Conversations that have the potential to reveal new plot points or character developments

- Suspenseful or tense moments, including the book's climax

- Events or conversations that directly relate to your book's theme

- Anything you instinctively know needs room to play out

Yet sometimes even scenes can truck along too quickly for your story, and you might need to deliberately slow them down. When in doubt, ask an honest friend or editor for their opinion.

Employing Backstory and Flashback

When you invent characters for a novel, you need to know all about them, including where they grew up, their childhood fears, their dreams, and more. Where does this information go?

In most cases of backstory, new information is filtered through the main viewpoint character. Specific terminology, even if alien and unfamiliar, is helpful because what's named is no longer so confusing. Implication is essential. Terms can be understood partially in context with the reader (hopefully) waiting for more.

Backstory deepens inner conflict. It can provide motivation for the conflict, deepen the emotional effects, and let the reader empathize with even a villain.

It also increases tension. Hinting at backstory but not telling all makes your readers long to know the secrets, too. They read on to find out what secret is so terrible it provides the motivation for this conflict.

IDEAS AND INSPIRATION

Usually backstory, especially flashbacks, should be put at a point where it enhances the tension and conflict of the story. You can think of a collection of scenes, followed by characters reflecting upon a given scene and deciding what to do next, which leads to the next scene. Scene, reflection, decision, scene. Often the backstory needs to come in that in-between stage where the character is reacting emotionally to the events of the scene that just happened.

For example, Gloria slaps Joe. So what? What are the readers supposed to make of that? What does it mean? We don't know, so the author must interpret the action in some way. The scene could progress without the explanation until Joe turns around and makes a fast exit. Then, Gloria has the time to react emotionally. That's the point for a flashback that explains that Joe once accused Gloria of embezzling money and let her stand trial, even though it was Joe who had stolen the money.

Now the backstory explains and deepens the tension. But an early chapter that goes into a long story of how Gloria and Joe worked together for many years and Joe was Gloria's mentor and they even had a brief affair that Gloria's husband still doesn't know about—that's boring stuff. It doesn't help Gloria make a decision about what to do next. It doesn't add to the present conflict, even if it does explain it somewhat.

Remember, backstory is there for its emotional weight. The story's current situation is emotional, but for some reason, you want to raise the stakes. By adding backstory, you can strengthen the character's motivations and make events mean more. Backstory should add irony, poignancy, regret, hope, or other strong emotions.

That means you put backstory at the point where it most directly impacts the emotions of the characters and/or the reader and impacts the emotional weight of the story. For example, can you interrupt a scene with backstory? Yes. But you'd better have a strong emotional reason to slow down the story at that point.

Here are some ways backstory can impact a novel's emotional weight:

Interpret actions/dialogue/events   Some scenes, such as action scenes, are better left intact with any flashbacks or backstory coming later as the character reflects on the events. Then, the flashback helps the character interpret the scene's importance or outcome.

Help make a decision   Sometimes, though, a scene leads up to a character making a decision. Flashbacks provide needed information and emotion to help the character make the best (or worst) decision.

Change relationships   If the backstory comes in dialogue, instead of as a flashback, it can change relationships.

Provide a story twist   If your plot is too straight-line, a good bit of backstory can add an interesting twist on events.

Flashbacks, scenes or partial scenes of something that happened before this moment in the story timeline, are the best way to insert backstory. In other words, a flashback is a scene that's presented out of chronological order. The flashback relates to the current scene, deepens character motivations, or otherwise illuminates the current action of the novel.

When working with backstory and flashbacks, first write the scene with the current action, and make it as fully developed as possible. If you're going to interrupt the ongoing action of the novel to insert this backstory, then at least give the reader a full scene that will keep their interest.

Then, write the flashback as a fully developed scene. Again, if you're messing with the timeline or chronology of the novel, do it in such a way that you keep the reader's interest. This doesn't mean it has to take up pages; a paragraph of a mini-scene might be perfectly reasonable. On the other hand, the flashback might need to be several pages long in this particular novel. Do what works.

Next, integrate the two scenes. Figure out where exactly in the novel the reader needs this bit of backstory in order to understand the story's action or to create a deeper emotional response. Put the flashback as close to that point as you can. Then smooth out the transitions.

 IDEAS AND INSPIRATION

The trickiest part of a flashback is getting into in and out of it. Try to do it with a single sentence both times. One transition opening sentence should signal a time shift and then go straight into past tense like you would in any scene of a novel.

Remember, a flashback scene needs to be a high point or a low point in a character's life, something worthy of a dedicated flashback. There also needs to be some emotional hook.

Implementing Prosodic Features

Prosodic features are pitch, stress, and length.

Most languages in the world are pitch languages. (English, believe it or not, is in the minority.) What, exactly, is a pitch language? Any language that uses the pitch of a phoneme to differentiate it from other phonemes is a pitch language. The classic example is Chinese, which uses five tones. Pitch allows a language to conserve syllables. Why indulge, like Japanese or Quechua, and create monstrously long words when the same phoneme can express the four concepts of mother, horse, hemp, and swearing?

In the case of pitch, the frequency at which the vocal cords vibrate is not described. Rather only whether they're vibrating (voiced consonants and vowels) or letting air through (stops). Because pitch is a major feature of a language, it must be included under prosodics. This becomes important in revision when reading your novel—and especially your dialogue—aloud.

Another aspect of pitch must be mentioned: the pitch contour. English may not differentiate between different syllables by pitch, but speakers use the overall pitch of a sentence to imply meaning. What do you get when you raise the pitch of your voice at the end of a statement? A question. The challenge then becomes what's the best way to convey that in your novel's dialogue?

Next is stress. Stress is an overlooked feature of English; it doesn't play as large a role as in other languages, but placing emphasis on the wrong syllable can get you some strange looks. Stress is a very simple device. It's basically pronouncing a segment of a word more loudly and, usually, lengthening the vowel. Russian changes regularly depending on where the stress is placed in a word, but English is much more complex. Try pronouncing several words with the stress in different places to see what I mean. Most often in novel writing, stress is indicated by the use of italics or capitalization in the places where you want stress to function on words.

Related to stress is length, which refers to how long to keep the airstream flowing through your mouth and nose as you speak. Many writers mistake the difference between vowels of short and long length as the same between tense and lax, but these are not the same. The difference between the vowel sounds of *foot* and *boot* is not length, but how tense the muscles in your throat are. I cannot think of any examples of varying vowel length in English, but I do know that Estonian, Japanese, and Finnish have different lengths of vowels. In Japanese, *Tsuuji* is a proper name whereas *tsuji* means to move one's bowels. This mistake in pronunciation has been made repeatedly, obviously with much embarrassment to the novelist.

This has been a short, technical subsection, so let's conclude by saying that prosody is most helpful to novelists in terms of determining and thinking about how certain combinations of words sound. It's among the most important reasons for reading your manuscript aloud while revising and especially arranging any dialogue sections.

WRITING PROMPT

Write out a section of dialogue between two characters who use different dialects. Then read the conversation aloud—preferably with a friend reading one of the character parts if possible. You'll be surprised how many words and phrases will need to be revised after you've heard the dialogue read aloud.

Remember that prosody alone won't make or break your novel. However, used in conjunction with other dynamics such as story and characterization, it will deepen the overall effect of your book.

The Least You Need to Know

- Story and plot follow your protagonist's physical and emotional journey.
- Scenes typically slow down a novel's pacing while summary speeds it up.
- Backstory and flashback provide essential history on a novel's characters and places.
- Prosody—including pitch, stress, and length—aids your novel in the sound of your characters and your overall writing.

The Play and Screenplay People Want to Watch

Plays, screenplays, and screenwriting draw on many of the same tools. If you love films and would like to write for the stage or the movies, this is the chapter for you.

Plays—the traditional form that has led to the others— primarily are driven by language and dialogue. Characters often speak in monologue for minutes at a time to express their inner lives, and these speeches are often the high point of the play. Great playwrights are eloquent wordsmiths. One need only invoke the name of Shakespeare to prove that.

Movies, on the other hand, are driven by images. A scene with a long monologue is often considered expository and in need of paring down or cutting. "Find a way to *show* us this instead," is usually the note the screenwriter gets in such instances—especially if the film is a mainstream Hollywood type.

Movies often have long sequences of no dialogue where story is told through action and editing. Great screenwriters are visionary story architects. However, this really only applies to screenplays written after about the late 1950s or so and especially after the mid-1970s. Prior to that, dramatic and narrative principles for both forms were considered almost the same.

In This Chapter

- Where the play happens
- The action during the play
- Play dialogue and other sounds
- Screenwriting in particular

As opposed to plays, contemporary screenplay formatting is very regimented and uses a lot of standardized jargon. Stage plays, on the other hand, have a few rules but they're much looser. In 10 years, my professional drama writing friends have encountered and written scripts with all manner of formatting: some looked almost like screenplays while others were blocked almost like a business letter or a novel. If you have no template from a publisher or production company, the main thing is to stay consistent and readable.

Actors generally prefer it when the play script is not formatted like a screenplay. It reassures them that the writer knows there's a difference. They also appreciate having room in the margins to jot down their thoughts and rehearsal notes.

 WATCH OUT!

There are a few differences between plays and screenplays that fall into the two main categories of aesthetic and stylistic characteristics. The aesthetic differences (you might also think of them as "cosmetic differences") describe the look of the script. Both forms have conventions for tab stops and/or capitalization for dialogue, parentheticals, transitions, and scene headers. While screenplays are largely harmonized, the stage play format is further differentiated between American and international formats.

The stylistic differences recognize the media being depicted. Stage plays tend to be more dialogue-heavy because that's what the audience in the cheap seats needs to make sense of in the scene. The screenplay, however, acknowledges the contribution of both the camera and other members of the cast & crew. As a rule of thumb, a good screenplay only describes what will be seen or heard. A character's internal motivation has no place in most screenplays, nor should the screenwriter tell the actor how to read a line or tell a director where to put the camera.

In this chapter, we stay more or less focused on the writer's duties when it comes to plays and screenplays through the topics of set, action, verbal sound, nonverbal sound, and notes on screenwriting. Now let's allow your mind's-eye camera to roll!

Establishing Setting

It's important to establish the time and place of your story in the opening scene of your play or screenplay. Doing so gives the audience the geographic location and era in which the story takes place right at the start.

By clearly describing the time and place early on, your audience will be immediately engaged in the plot and won't wonder where and when the story takes place. You've probably seen films that fail to do this, and you've probably looked for clues about the setting and the year as you tried to follow the story. It's a distraction. Good plays and films use what's known as an *establishing shot* to identify time and place.

Although screenwriters shouldn't use camera directions in a script and playwrights shouldn't tell a director what to do, it's the writer's job to provide clues for the audience that pinpoint the time period. For example, the story might take place in present day or many years or decades in the past. It can also be set hundreds or thousands of years in the future.

When establishing the setting, or place, you need to give the audience hints about the geographic location of the story. For example, a story can be set in a U.S. city like New York, and we might see the New York City skyline or a Broadway street sign in the opening scene. The story can also be set in Kansas, and we might see a road sign that reads, "Kansas City." It could be set in ancient Rome, in India in 1836, in Los Angeles in the year 2095, or on a distant planet in the year 3000.

Another technique for establishing time and place is the use of a subtitle onscreen or a placard in a play that gives the place and the date. Here's an example:

> EXT. JUNGLE–DAY
>
> Heavy rain falls on dense forest, thick with tangled vines. Mist rises from the forest floor. We HEAR monkeys SCREECHING and birds CALLING.
>
> SUBTITLE FADES IN: BORNEO, INDONESIA–1980

In this example, the scene is described, but it could be a forest anywhere in the world. However, when the subtitle flashes on screen, it tells the audience that this forest is in Borneo, Indonesia, and the year is 1980.

You must establish the time and place of your story at the beginning of your play or screenplay. To do this in your opening scene, ask yourself these two questions:

When does the story take place? Does it take place now, in the past, in the future? When possible, use visual clues to pinpoint the time period. For example, car models, clothing styles, and other elements can identify the time.

Where does the story take place? Describe the geographic location. Include specific details that identify the location such as road signs, skylines, titles on buildings, historic landmarks, etc.

 **WRITING PROMPT**

What other dramatic or cinematic devices can you use to give the audience specific information about the geographic location and year? Would subtitles provide this information?

Writing Action

Action is the most deceptively challenging element both on the stage and in Hollywood. What might seem simple and straightforward on the stage or movie screen actually requires careful planning and extremely creative solutions from the screenwriter.

Many people believe action works against character, plot, and theme, but that's not the case. The best action sequences in plays or films possess deep stories, reveal the complexity of characters, and have a profound effect on the audience.

The challenge for the writer is to maintain compelling characters, surprising plots, and important themes within the limiting structure of an action sequence. Speed is the enemy of the action writer, despite the ongoing trend to increase the pacing of Hollywood films. Ironically, pure speed is not what thrills an audience, which is why good action writers actually try to slow down their play or film to make the action appear faster when it occurs.

The faster the pace of a story, the less chance you have for surprise, and surprise is the fundamental requirement of plot. As a writer, you take on the role of a magician. The audience looks to you for events they can't predict, but thinking back, realize they should have seen coming. When you move characters down a single path at top speed, turns become difficult. The audience can see everything down the path, all the way to the obvious conclusion. If you slow the pacing, you give yourself the luxury of putting a few more twists and turns to work, so the audience can still be surprised and will continue to pay attention.

You can start your play or script with a big action scene if you want (some hit action films do and some don't) but then back off. Give the character a personal problem he or she must solve simultaneously with overcoming the problem that came from the action earlier. You don't need to take a lot of time with it, but do it. You have now set up the all-important double-track line, contrasting the personal with the action problem. The key then becomes making those two lines appear as one to the audience.

Action, by its very nature, pushes the envelope of believability, so you have to convince the audience early that your protagonist is quite capable of what he or she later performs. After all, in most cases, you're showing someone whose ability to act is significantly above normal. It's rare to see a successful action script where the hero learns to be good at physical action over the course of the story. (Films like *Rocky* constitute important exceptions.)

It's a surprise when the chunky-bodied protagonist of *Rocky* is able to develop enough agility to finish his fight with boxing's world heavyweight champion. By "surprise," I mean surprise to the hero as well as to the audience. And that means you have to hide as much about your opposition as you can. In *Rocky,* the audience assumes the champ is great even though no one sees him fight up until the end of the movie, in his contest with the protagonist. The best action plays and scripts deal with deception and hidden information, especially about the true nature and identity of the opponent. Great action scripts are really a battle of wits—it's about who can deceive best and who can think the best.

It's often a good idea to make the protagonist strong but the opponent stronger (or at least appear stronger). Take the necessary time to figure out some special talents and tricks your opponent has that will give your hero fits. But don't show them right away. Hold them back. When you do bring them on, bring them fast and furious. You want the hero reeling so he has to dip into all his skills and perhaps utilize toughness and resourcefulness even he didn't know he had.

WATCH OUT!

Don't make the opponent so strong that realistic victory is an impossibility for the protagonist. If there's not enough evidence for a victory, the audience will reject it as implausible.

Writing Dialogue for the Stage

Many people believe that among writers, there are two camps: those who write excellent description/action, and those who write excellent dialogue. Putting these skills together is what separates the paid from the unpaid.

The next time you're out in a restaurant, open your journal and eavesdrop. Note how people talk over each other constantly and rarely ever finish a complete thought. Don't transcribe conversations verbatim, but jot down interesting phrases, notes regarding the flow of dialogue, and how the flow shifts (or how the dialogue volleys and interesting turns of phrases).

WRITING PROMPT

Write a scene in which a couple is buying a mattress. They're only allowed to speak about the mattress, but through the subtext, we learn of their marital problems. The woman says, "I've always wanted a firm mattress, what with my back problems and all. Plus, we could spend a little more time in bed, couldn't we John?"

Good dialogue both in plays and screenwriting takes short, simple sentences—one thought at a time. If possible, include tension and purpose in every word or sentence. Generally, no more than three uninterrupted sentences of dialogue are acceptable—the occasional lengthy monologue is fine but should be absolutely warranted. If you can, always break up dialogue with action.

Be sure you engage your audience. Viewers are usually engaged by what the writer *doesn't* tell them, not by what the writer does tell. Thus, join scenes late and leave them early. Allow characters to exist offstage. In other words, reference their background lives or acts, at least those aspects worthy of mention, in their dialogue and/or character interactions. Have your characters actually listen to, engage with, interrupt, and react to things other characters say, instead of each character just speaking because it's their turn.

Then, when you're finally done and happy with your scene, go back and cut the dialogue even shorter.

WATCH OUT!

Avoid the following in your play or screenplay: people saying directly what they mean, big speeches, and stating the obvious (particularly in respect to things the audience can see or hear).

When functioning properly, dialogue and other verbal sound reveals character, advances the plot, expresses subtext, and entertains. Every line should resonate with who says it. The flavor of each character's background should be captured in his or her word choices. The syntax (arrangement of words) should be uniquely theirs. Focus on background, attitudes, personality quirks, education, mannerisms—and most importantly—wants and needs when writing dialogue. Remember that strong characters have needs that should come into conflict with the needs of other characters.

Well-written dialogue imperceptibly moves the story forward by having the characters say something that leads to something happening—a decision is made, a question is asked, and information is revealed. As a result, momentum or tension is built. At times, even silence can be moving.

Establish a cause-and-effect relationship between what's spoken and what happens next. Try to instill conflict in your character interactions. In real life, inner conflict often gets externalized, or dumped onto friends or family, but in drama, it helps to be subtle. So let visuals, sounds, tension, and so on drive the meaning behind your characters' words.

Above all, entertain the audience. Dialogue needs to evoke a visceral response and engage the audience. Whether it's a funny line, poignant line, mysterious line, frightening line, emotion-filled line, or so on, the audience should be moved emotionally. Think about what the audience expects from your play or screenplay: is it a horror? Drama? Comedy? Some combination?

Creating Nonverbal Communication

Nonverbal communication involves those nonverbal stimuli in a communication setting that are generated by both the source (the speaker) and his or her use of the environment, and have potential message value. Basically, it's sending and receiving messages in a variety of ways without the use of verbal codes (words).

Nonverbal sound can be both intentional and unintentional. It includes but is not limited to touch, gaze, volume, vocal nuance, proximity, gestures, facial expressions, intonation, dress, posture, smell, and word choice. Broadly speaking, there are two basic categories of nonverbal language: nonverbal messages produced by the body and those produced by the broad setting (time, space, silence).

Nonverbal sound is important because of its multiple functions, which include the following:

- Repeating a verbal message (pointing in a direction while speaking, for example)

- Accenting a verbal message (a verbal tone indicates the actual meaning of the specific words)

- Regulating interactions (nonverbal cues convey when the other person should speak or not speak)

- Substituting for the verbal message, especially if it's blocked by noise, interruption, etc. (gestures—finger to the lips to indicate need for quiet, or facial expressions—a nod instead of a yes)

IDEAS AND INSPIRATION

Note the implications of the cliché "actions speak louder than words." In essence, this underscores the importance of nonverbal communication and why you must not overlook it when writing your play or screenplay.

Plays and films are going to have their set coordinators and costume people, but you can still suggest these elements in what you write to help fuel nonverbal communication. For example, you should note ways dress is used as a sign of status. Body movements between characters can speak volumes as well. One's posture can define a character's mood or even their worldview. Do they slouch or stride erectly? Are they prone to keep their hands in their pockets? Do they sit with their legs crossed?

Gestures and facial expressions affect you every day. Just think of those gestures employed by aggressive drivers on your commute to work. And let's not forget eye contact that indicates one's degree of attention or interest, influences attitude change or persuasion, regulates interaction, communicates emotion, defines power and status, and has a central role in managing impressions of others.

Then there's the all-important and sometimes-controversial matter of touching. Why do you touch, where do you touch, and what meanings do you assign when someone else touches you? Handshakes are common (even for strangers), but hugs and kisses for those of opposite sex occur on an increasingly more intimate basis.

Finally—and not unrelated—is *paralanguage,* which sounds complex but really just refers to vocal characterizers (laugh, cry, yell, moan, whine, belch, yawn, etc.) and vocal qualifiers (volume, pitch, rhythm, tempo, and tone). Obviously, the circumstances and characters involved will dictate how these actions are perceived by your audience.

Tips for Screenwriters

Have you ever viewed a film that had famous, skilled actors and a great director, but the movie wasn't very good? I have—many times. Often the reason for this is that the essence of the film— its story or the way the story was conveyed—was fundamentally wanting. In fact, many film people believe the real magic of a good movie is in the screenwriting or script. If the characters aren't developed well, if the story lags or doesn't keep your interest, then million-dollar stars and directors aren't going to be able to make it work.

Writing for the Big Screen

With all this in mind, here are some notes to ponder when preparing to write your screenplay:

Watch movies, especially the classics. They're called "classics" for a reason, and you can find lists of them on the internet if you don't know where to start. Enjoy them if you can, but more importantly, note how the scenes are put together, characterization is performed, etc. Take notes in your journal if you're compelled to do so.

When working on your own screenplay, keep the main plot simple. If there's too much going on, the general population won't get it. Think accessibility, not complexity—especially since you're new to this kind of writing.

Have a strong beginning. You want to capture and hold your audience's attention.

Play with the setup. The structure of a play is usually beginning, middle, and end, but that doesn't mean they have to be revealed in that order. Flashbacks and flash forwards can help keep the audience surprised and engaged.

Be sure you have an overall goal or point to your story. After all, you need to have a compelling reason for telling it.

A movie should last at least 90 minutes. (If a film is over 100 minutes, the theaters lose one showing of it every day or have to sacrifice money by running two showings on different screens.) As a rule of thumb, 1 page of script equals 1 minute on the screen. It has to be *very* good to warrant being longer.

You must have a protagonist, a fully developed main character. That can be one or more people, a thing, or even a place. The protagonist doesn't always have to be extremely likeable, but he does have to be interesting. In fact, character flaws can add a touch more reality and make audiences empathize.

A workable premise is important. Even if the whole idea is unbelievable, parts of the movie still need to be logical and believable. With all the talking cars and toys of late, you can see this point. However, the toys basically behave in human ways and possess human personalities, which allows the audience to accept both them and the premise.

Be true to yourself, and don't just mimic others. If you do something that's never been done, that could really make your screenplay stand out. At the same time, draw on what you learn from watching other films. Many science fiction films, for example, have both far-out elements and conventions drawn from ancient mythology.

As in so many other pursuits, it helps to have a talent for screenwriting, although the more important elements are willpower and practice. Any aptitude will need refining, and skills need to be strengthened. Keep at it, and you might surprise yourself.

Writing for the Small Screen

In addition to the tips on writing a good movie screenplay, here are some tips on writing television scripts:

Become something of a couch potato at times. Watch a lot of different shows, especially the award-winning ones. Pay attention to your reactions, and make note of them, especially what you liked and didn't like, and what happened right before a commercial. Get a script online and follow along, noticing how the script translates to the screen.

When you decide what kind of show you want to write, research it. If you want to write shows about the police, study police procedures and perhaps even request to ride with a patrolman. Watch shows in the same genre, and figure out a ways for yours to be different.

Outline your plot. Then outline the story and write down the basic action. Next, figure out where the commercial breaks will be, and be sure you leave the audience wanting to keep watching.

Develop your characters. This is crucial to a good show. You'll need main characters who are present most of the time plus supporting characters who show up occasionally. Develop backgrounds for each character, and keep track of mannerisms and catch phrases for each.

Write on a schedule because television shows run on a schedule. Most writers write most days anyway. If you get writer's block, go to another scene and come back to where you got stuck later.

IDEAS AND INSPIRATION

For both film and television screenplays, you need to revise, revise, and revise. This is key to improving your work, regardless of the medium. Rewrite and proofread, ensuring every word counts. You might even want to join a writer's group that proofreads and critiques each other's work.

The Least You Need to Know

- Your set needs to reveal the time and place of your story.
- Action should always advance the plot.
- Verbal sound, or dialogue, is essential to characterization.
- Nonverbal communication often defines people and places.
- Writing for the big or small screen is more visually oriented than writing a play.

The Seamless Book of Poetry

To start this chapter, let's assume you've written a number of poems, sent them out to poetry journals, read them in public, and even had some of them published. Now it's time to assemble those poems a book manuscript—along with some new ones you might feel necessary to complete your collection—you can submit to publishers or publication contests.

Because most of your poems are already written, you might think you just need to patch them together to form your book and fill in with new ones as necessary. Wrong. The process of publishing a poetry collection is difficult and time-consuming.

In This Chapter

- Commonalities in poetry
- Shared images and metaphors
- Identifying density and intensity
- Similarities in prosody, rhythm, and rhyme

Culling Your Existing Poems

Begin by assembling all the poems you want to consider putting into your book, printing one poem per page (unless of course, the poem is longer than a single page) if they're on your computer, or consider photocopying them one per page if they're in your journal. Getting them all out in front of you like this helps you see what you have. And it's a chance for you to make any small revisions you want to make to individual poems so you can then concentrate on the shape of the book as a whole.

Next, decide what size book of poems you want to create. A typical chapbook (a small book of poetry) is 20 to 30 pages, while a full-length collection runs about 50 or more pages. You might well change your mind about the length when you're actually selecting and ordering your poems, which is fine.

With the length of your book in mind, sift through all your printed or copied poems, and put them into piles you feel belong together in some way—a series of poems on related themes, or a group of poems written using a particular form, or a chronological sequence of poems written in the voice of a single character.

Let your piles sit at least overnight without thinking about them. Then come back to them, pick up each pile, and read through the poems, trying to see them as a reader and not as their author. If you know your poems well and find your eyes skipping ahead, read them out loud to yourself to be sure you take the time to really listen to them.

After you've read through a stack of poems, pull out any that no longer seem to fit in that particular pile, and put the poems you want to keep together in the order you want your readers to experience them. You might find yourself doing lots of reshuffling over time, moving poems from one stack into another, melding whole groups of poems together by combining stacks, or discovering new groupings that need to be separate and on their own. That's part of the process. You'll likely come across new ideas for books or chapbooks and also change your mind about decisions you've made earlier in the process a number of times before the poems settle into the shape of a book or chapbook.

IDEAS AND INSPIRATION

After you've pared down and reordered each pile of poems, let them sit again at least overnight. You can use this time to mull over your reading, listening for the poems that stand out in each stack and how they sound together. Pay attention to other poems that might have come to mind when you were reading a certain stack. Should you add them to the stack, or replace similar poems you've already chosen with the ones that now come to mind?

Think again about the length of book you want to create. You might decide that one stack of related poems would make a good short chapbook. Or you might have a really large pile of poems that would all go together into a long collection. Or you might want to combine several of your piles as sections within a full-length book.

If you feel you're endlessly sifting and shuffling among the piles and the poems aren't settling into the shape of a book, try actually making them into a book you can live with and then leaf through it. Make multiple copies of the poems and staple or tape them together, punch holes in the pages and put them into a three-ring notebook, or use your computer to print them out in book format (most word processing programs will do this fairly easily). Don't think too much about typography or design; at this point, you simply want to put the poems in order with facing left and right pages so you can read through the book and see how they interact in that order.

After you've decided on the length and general shape of your book manuscript, choose a title for your book. A title might have suggested itself during your sifting and ordering of the poems, or you might want to read through them again to find one—perhaps the title of a central poem, or a phrase taken from one of the poems, or something completely different.

After you've put together your manuscript, carefully proofread it from beginning to end. If you've spent a lot of time with the book already, you might be tempted to give it only a cursory read-through. I caution you against this, but if this is the route you take, first set it aside for a few days or weeks so that when you come back to it, you can pay close attention to each poem, each title, each line, each punctuation mark. You'll likely find yourself making additional revisions to the poems at this point. Don't hold back because this final reading might be the last chance you have to make changes before you send the book out into the world.

 IDEAS AND INSPIRATION

> Proofreading your own work is difficult, so feel free to ask a friend, or two, to proofread the manuscript for you. Then go through all their notes carefully. Fresh eyes will likely spot some errors that slid right by you, but don't feel that you must accept every editorial change they suggest. When in doubt about punctuation or line breaks, read the poem aloud and see how it sounds.

Now it's time to take a closer look at the main elements that will help you assemble your book, including identifying commonalities in verse; common images and metaphors; tracing density and intensity; and creating commonalities in prosody, rhythm, and rhyme.

Identifying Commonalities in Verse

A fundamental challenge in writing a book of poetry is figuring out how to organize it, whether you arrange it by theme, motif, etc.—in a phrase, identifying commonalities in verse.

For example, readers of my first collection in draft form pointed out the often visceral quality of my poems. As many as *half* of them dealt with a literal death, and a third of the remaining contained some sort of violence (emotional, physical, psychological, etc.). Although I was already aware of this fact, it was nice to have it confirmed by others.

There are *countless* ways to organize a draft of poems or any other type of work. The fact that I've done it in other book genres—novel, memoir, biography, scholarly, textbook, anthology—makes the identification of themes out of hundreds of pages less difficult for me than for a beginning writer. A great deal of the work is intuitive, determining location, harmonies, and pieces that ring or build on each other. The important overall thing for a poetry collection is getting the poems to build off each other in such a way that it drives at something bigger.

One thing to keep in mind is that just because something got published doesn't mean it definitively has more worth than something that appeared in a lesser venue or met with repeated rejection. Things that have nothing to do with your poems can figure into that, such as a given journal's politics/focus and the familiarity of your name—or lack thereof—to the editor. In fact, these elements are so pervasive in the poetry world, I have chosen to publish all my poems under pseudonyms. In addition, tastes constantly change, so trust your instincts. If a poem feels weak to you, leave it out.

Be sure the poems that begin your collection establish the voice and strength of your manuscript. Even those you feel best about should undergo revision, and the very first poems in the book should introduce the issues, images, and sources of conflict or tension that will be revisited throughout.

Because many of my own poems deal with nature, science, and humanism as they affect one being, more than one reader of my manuscript supported the title "Entity." While playing with the order, I put one of my poems in which a child is injected with experimental proteins, followed by a sex poem in which the sex is great but the woman nonetheless feels it's not quite natural in some way. These two poems capture the book's themes while also offering a hint that the male sexual participant is, in fact, the medically victimized boy. Although I did not retain this beginning, at the time I thought it quite promising.

When you have a promising order, think about dividing the book into separate sections. Dividing your work further forces you to not only make the poems interact at a more personal level, but also makes you see how they might be revised to inform the greater trajectory of the work.

As it happened, my own collection settled on subsection organized by theme: the humanism of one character, followed by science, nature, and then a return to humanism, albeit in the form of another character.

WRITING PROMPT

Establish a tentative organization for your collection of poems.

If you think you need to write a few more poems to round out your collection, that's okay. The following sections offer some further advice, beyond what was presented in Chapter 13, that can help you create new poems to fill the caps in your current body of work.

Identifying Common Images and Metaphors

I established earlier in this book that people experience the world through their senses: what they see, hear, smell, etc. Poets seek to re-create the world with words. One way to do this is through the use of metaphor, which allows writers to make comparisons that leave lasting impressions with the reader. Metaphor poems become even more memorable when you create a vivid image appealing to the senses.

As defined in previous chapters, metaphor is a literary device in which the author makes a comparison. She states, for example, that hope is a bird, as Emily Dickinson does. Metaphors have the ability to make an abstract concept seem more concrete. With Dickinson's, she uses the image of the bird to draw readers' attention to abstract qualities of the abstract emotion, hope.

Metaphors also have the power to stir emotions, as Sylvia Plath does in describing her pregnant self as a "melon on two tendrils." Clearly she felt the discomfort of pregnancy.

IDEAS AND INSPIRATION

Use metaphor to show readers the similarities between two seemingly disparate things.

The first step to writing poetry—or almost anything else that's creative in nature—is brainstorming. Start with an idea, whether an emotion or another abstract noun such as identity, as Julio Noboa Polanco does in his poem "Identity." Brainstorm ideas about the topic, writing descriptions and especially comparisons. Take any adjectives from the brainstorming activity, and think of other things that have those qualities. Consider, for instance, Polanco's desire to be strong and free, thus, "I'd rather be a tall, ugly weed." Come up with as many images as possible to describe your idea and then circle one that seems the most representative.

When imagery is employed, it makes your words more powerful. It not only creates a picture in the reader's mind, but the description also seeks to invoke as many senses as possible. For example, in "Seashell," James Berry talks about the "whispers" and "sighs" of the ocean, putting those sounds in the reader's ear. Take the image that serves as the metaphor of your topic, and brainstorm sensory words to describe it. Think of as many descriptors as possible—not just adjectives, but whole phrases that describe your image. Polanco uses phrasing in describing a weed "wind-wavering above high, jagged rocks."

While you're brainstorming, your poem already begins to take shape. At the start, introduce the central metaphor, as Dickinson does with the bird as hope. Build on the image you introduce, adding the sensory words from your brainstorming.

When you've described your image fully, go back and evaluate your writing for poetics. Think about line breaks, ensuring the poem ends in a meaningful spot that reinforces the comparison. Consider every word and whether you can make the image more vivid with a different word choice. Read the poem aloud. Remember that ultimately you want your words to create an image for the metaphorical comparison in your poem.

Tracing Density and Intensity

Wallace Stevens once intimated that poems help us live our lives. (I wonder if he felt that way after breaking his own hand hitting Ernest Hemingway on the jaw, only to have the younger writer give him a thorough pounding and leave him lying on his back in a puddle?) I don't happen to think people's lives are determined by art. I think there are much more powerful determining forces (and I don't mean Hemingway's jaw).

For me, it would be extremely hard to go through life as if for the first time, as though nobody had been there before me. Poetry reconciles us to ourselves, as Stevens says, in that it can't be peculiar to you if someone else has had it before. It's kind of a prophecy of what's to come, so if you're reading something about being 50 or being 70 when you're 30, it doesn't come as quite such a shock when you get to that later age. I don't want to imagine a life without any sense of being companied by other voices that have been along the same road.

It's been maintained that most literary people have an episode in their lives, often in late adolescence, when they write. In my case, I believe this time helped me understand what a different activity creative writing is from criticism, engaging wholly different spheres of the soul, mind, and personal essence.

Sometimes when I write about particularly complex poems, I write them out longhand rather than typing them on my computer. This act makes me feel what it's like to have viscerally formed that poem—what it was like to put down a line and make it connect with the next one. That seems to me to be the single most helpful way to feel them through. You'll also find that because you wrote them, so to speak, you know them by heart. Something goes through the muscles that comes back to the brain, and you know those words in a different way than if you'd just read them.

After you've written out poems (yours or others'), they tend to come up in your mind frequently when you don't have the book around, as a line might rise in the mind of a poet, unbidden and against your will. That experience helps feed into a sense of how the poem gathers itself together. After all, it's only a device like any other.

Does meeting the poets you write about change anything at all–your feeling about their work, for example? I believe it's better not to meet them, but often it's quite helpful to hear them read. I like having heard the voice attach itself to the poems, although it's not indispensable. It's true that some poets are more performative than others—think of the incantatory style W. B. Yeats used in which poets want to chant their poetry.

The opposite approach is the deadpan or restrained reading. Stevens is one of these musing readers rather than a performing reader. Yet the very flatness of it can be revealing when the voice suddenly reads a line in a way that is not flat. That emphasis of the voice—whether hyperbolic, like Robert Bly, or understated, like Stevens—can alert you to elements you haven't quite realized from reading the page.

Experiencing a reading by a poet like Bly or Dylan Thomas is going to be more entertaining than one by Stevens or Charles Wright. Yet that doesn't make Bly or Thomas better poets, nor does it make their poems fundamentally more intense.

Regardless of the skill in its delivery, some poetry is going to be aesthetically uninteresting, conventional, and derivative. And other literature, poorly or ordinarily delivered, is going to be original and unusual and beautiful. Some poems have an enormous density of observed detail so you learn much about what people are wearing, what time the carriage draws up, or how many people were at a party.

There's the density of social detail, a density of population, in some types of poetry, while in others, only one voice speaks. This density of a chorus of voices—polyphonic density—is unusual for lyric poetry, but it's nonetheless possible. More often, there's a single voice—at least in lyric poetry—and a barely sketched scene, if you have any scene at all. There's no plot as such; that is to say there are no events. The poem becomes the event, as Robert Lowell intimated, rather than a record of an event.

With your poems, you're probably going to be enacting an event in the mind of someone else with a single voice. That admission to a single other mind is comparable to a soliloquy in drama: the moment where the mind stops and thinks. That idea suits most poets. They like the single voice. There's something to be said for the power of its private intensity. The intensity of narrative poems, in which the feeling usually is diffused through several characters, generally is viewed as far less gripping than the single intensity of the single voice.

 **WRITING PROMPT**

What kind of poet are you? Make a list of images, and assign each a poetic line of description. Do you find you tend toward density or intensity?

Commonalities in Prosody, Rhythm, and Rhyme

First and foremost, poetry—like any other kind of creative writing—should be entertainment. Sadly, over the years, it has become virtually the preserve of an academically affiliated elite, a handful of whom control the decisions of many publishers and major award committees (at least in the United States). Indeed, the average college-educated American and even many college English professors struggle to relate to or even make sense of much of the poetry being published today.

There was a time, not terribly long ago, when almost all poetry was written in proper verse that rhymed and often appeared in newspapers for the pleasure of the public—it was still something of a democratic art form. Despite the slow swing toward an obscure and still-shrinking readership, poetry benefits even now from clever deployments of rhyme and scansion in making it memorable. The rhythmic form of the poem can even add value to the words used. Clearly, Shakespeare thought there was some merit in writing all his plays in iambic pentameter (*de-dum, de-dum, de-dum, de-dum, de-dum*) while a metric form such as anapest adds the galloping *tiddy-dum, tiddy-dum* rhythm that puts pace and spirit into a narrative unlike any other writing form.

Almost all my fellow poets in academia would be chagrined that much of my own book of poems, albeit written in a language other than English and bearing a name other than Casey Clabough, possesses a fair amount of rhyme and scan. I have been informed these devices are now unnecessary in English and can restrict and shape what's said. I argue that it makes things more difficult, challenging, and risky and, therefore, serves a purpose. Just finishing isn't enough—it's how you get there that matters. Surely there are times when more difficult is more enjoyable and making things easier—as in so-called free verse—serves only to take away the best of the challenge.

The Rhythm of Poetry

I introduced rhythm in Chapter 13, but let's go into a bit more detail here. Sticking to matters of structure, *rhythm,* or *meter,* refers to the accented and unaccented syllables in verse, and so the foot is also known as a *metric foot.* The analysis of the composition of a verse is known as *scanning* or *scansion.* The following table offers a quick rundown of the most common types of meter.

Foot	Syllables	Stress Pattern
Amphibrach (amphibrachic)	3	Unstressed, stressed, unstressed
Anapest (anapestic)	3	Unstressed, unstressed, stressed
Dactyl (dactylic)	3	Stressed, unstressed, unstressed
Iamb (iambic)	2	Unstressed, stressed
Pyrrhic (pyrrhic)	2	Unstressed, unstressed
Spondee (spondaic)	2	Stressed, stressed
Trochee (trochaic)	2	Stressed, unstressed

It's important to remember, however, that meter is not a template or pattern to be followed slavishly when producing a poem, but rather used as a means of describing what you've written. It's easy to think the former because so much is written about the subject and it appears, on the face of it, to be so prescriptive. The most important thing is to write what feels and sounds natural and comfortable to you. Others might disagree, and that's their right, but it's perfectly acceptable to mix feet lengths and metric forms, as long as it sounds and reads naturally and is, of course, executed consistently.

 IDEAS AND INSPIRATION

The Bard himself (in his iambic pentameters) regularly used accentless feet and ended lines with an extra unaccented syllable, making the last foot an amphibrach rather than an iamb (and sometimes known as feminine iambic pentameter). It's also perfectly acceptable, in moderation, to vary a word's natural stress to make it fit a verse's accent pattern. If a reader criticizes part of a poem because it doesn't "conform" in some way, as long as it sounds okay, be sure that if the depths of the theory of prosody are delved into, an exception could be found to justify being criticized. Use the rules of prosody to justify what you write, rather than as a mold into which you fit your poem.

It is possible, and perfectly correct, to mix certain metric forms in a single verse. An example of this can be achieved in an iamb plus an appropriate number of anapests (plus a spare unaccented or feminine syllable—more on masculine and feminine symbols in a few paragraphs):

Amphibrach amphibrachic trimeter:

>   -   ¬ -/   -   ¬ -/   -   ¬   -
> There WAS a / young LAD-y / from BROOK-lyn

Iamb + two anapests:

>   -   ¬ /- -   ¬ /- -   ¬   /-
> There WAS / a young LAD- / y from BROOK- /lyn

Robert Browning's poem "How They Brought the Good News from Ghent to Aix" uses a nice mixture of three amphibrachs and one final iamb, or one initial iamb and three anapests:

Three amphibrachs and an iamb:

> I SPRANG to / the STIRrup, / and JORis, / and HE:
> I GALLoped, / Dirck GALLoped, / we GALLoped / all THREE;

One iamb and three anapests:

> I SPRANG / to the STIR / rup, and JOR / is, and HE:
> I GALL / oped, Dirck GALL / oped, we GALL / oped all THREE;

It doesn't matter how it's described; the effect is the same—and this further illustrates the point that scansion *describes* rather than *prescribes* what's written. It's impossible to imagine Browning sitting tapping out the beat to see what he could write to conform to his meter. On the other hand, it's absolutely easy to see him with this wonderful galloping rhythm beating in his head and the words flowing easily in response.

The Rhyming of Poetry

Rhyme is the repetition of the sound of one word or the last syllable(s) of one word in a second word or the last syllable(s) of a second word. What's important is the sound and not the spelling. Thus, *rough* rhymes with *buff* but not with *through*. The rhyme is constituted by the vowel sound(s), and each part of the rhyme (the two words or syllables) must begin with a different consonant. Two words with totally different spellings and meanings but identical pronunciation cannot be rhymed. While *rough* can be rhymed with *buff*, it cannot be rhymed with *ruff* because the two words have identical sounds.

 WATCH OUT!

In poetry, rhyming words would normally occur at the end of two lines, which may or may not be adjacent to each other. How the rhyming lines are arranged within the poem is unimportant, but whatever the pattern used, it must be consistent. So lines can quite properly rhyme a-a-b-b, or a-b-a-b or a-b-a-c or a-b-c-b where α represents the first rhyme sound; *b*, the second; and so on. (More on rhyme scheme in the following paragraphs.)

The word *rhyme* is sometimes seen spelled *rime*. If anything, this is the more correct spelling, although little used, because the word derives from the Provençal word *rim*. At some point in its history, the word was falsely identified with the Greek word *rhythmos* (from which the word *rhythm*, for "comes"), yet the Greeks had no concept of rhyme.

Rhyme is optional in many forms of verse, but there are many other forms in which a pattern of rhyming is fundamental to the structure. Where used, rhyme adds much to a group of words, enriching both the sound and the sense.

Where a line ends with an accented syllable, it is deemed to have a strong ending and is thus described as *masculine* rhyme. This is either achieved with monosyllabic words like *mind, kind,* or *blind,* or with polysyllabic words ending on an accented syllable like *today, delay,* or *defray.* Iambic or anapestic lines normally end in this way. Trochaic or dactylic lines can also end on an accented syllable but only if one or two unaccented syllables are truncated.

Rhyme ending on an unaccented syllable is said to be weak and, thus, described as feminine. However, although feminine rhyme ends on an unaccented syllable, it must also include a preceding accented one, and both syllables must sound the same to achieve perfect rhyme. *Grammar* rhymes with *hammer,* for example, but not with *simmer* or *dumber,* even though all end in the same unaccented sound. Feminine rhyme is also known as *trochaic rhyme* because it follows the pattern of a trochee, and a perfect trochaic line must have this type of rhyme.

There are many other rhyme schemes you can look up and study. Some of the more common ones include dactylic, near, imperfect, unaccented, half, spelling, identity, dissonance, assonance, alliteration, constant, and grotesque.

Usually, you apply rhyme in a fixed pattern. It requires two lines to create a rhyme, but these don't have to be adjacent to each other. Where two successive lines do, in fact, rhyme, this is known as a *rhyming couplet.* This is the simplest and arguably the most common form of rhyme.

When denoting a rhyme scheme, the convention is to use a letter of the alphabet (starting with *a*) to denote each successive rhyme. Thus, the rhyme scheme of a rhyming couplet would be denoted as a-a, b-b, c-c, d-d, etc. Alternately rhyming lines would be represented as a-b, a-b. Typically, certain verse forms use established rhyme patterns such as these:

> **Couplet:** a-a, b-b. etc.
>
> **Triplet (tercet):** a-b-a, b-c-b, c-d-c, d-e-d. etc.
>
> **Quatrain:** a-a-b-b, or a-b-a-b
>
> **Quintet (cinquain):** x-a-b-b-a

In addition, certain stanza forms have fixed-rhyme patterns. For example, a four-line ballad stanza would rhyme x-a, y-a, where *x* and *y* are random.

IDEAS AND INSPIRATION

Rhyme can be used in poetry other than at the end of a line. Rhyme at the beginning or in the middle of a line is used to achieve effect much in the same way as alliteration. No pattern is necessary, and it can be quite random.

Having examined poems and their construction in greater depth, you now have some working tools and techniques for arranging your own into something book-length that constitutes more than the sum of its poems.

The culture of poetry in the United States may have grown obscure and not a little decadent in the grand scheme of art, but the craft itself remains the most powerful avenue for utilizing words to convey human experience.

The Least You Need to Know

- Identifying commonalities in your poems is essential to organizing your collection.
- Common images and metaphors strengthen your bond with your readership.
- Tracing density and intensity is important in identifying and grouping your poems.
- Commonalities in prosody, rhythm, and rhyme conspire more than anything else to make you the kind of poet you are and place a signature of sorts on your collection.

The Collective Book of Essays/Stories

Whether you're organizing a collection of fiction (stories) or nonfiction (essays) content for a book, you face many of the same challenges. What's more, because every writer is unique in his or her knowledge, experience level, personality, writing ability, and the way they approach a project, there's no one-size-fits-all approach that might work for you.

However, as with poetry collections (see Chapter 18), you can consider a few similarities in your prose pieces to help decide on an organization. Plot, scenes and summaries, use of back-story and flashback, and prosody are all elements you can work with when arranging your work into a larger collection.

Although there's no one hard-and-fast rules, the following paragraphs outline a relatively loose strategy that works for many writers and may be of value to you as well.

First, gather your essays and stories. Write down the titles so you can have them recorded for future reference and also so you can better visualize how they might work in different combinations to fit a topic or theme.

In This Chapter

* Shared plot elements
* Scene and summarization similarities
* Shared use of background information and flashback
* Similarities in prosody

As for themes and topics, avoid a topic that will tempt you to summarize rather than discuss or analyze. Don't choose the plot of *Macbeth* but how the final scene of the play illustrates its theme. The second topic is narrower and less likely to lead to summary. When considering a topic, ask yourself if it can lead to a reasonable thesis.

Also choose a topic that interests you. If you don't care about limiting cigarette advertising, don't select it as a topic for a persuasive essay. You'll have more to say, and you'll write better, on something you care about. Generally, if you choose a topic that's interesting to you, your readers will find it interesting, too.

If your topic requires research, try to choose one on which you can find material. Be sure you select a subject you can develop with sufficient details. And finally, after you've picked a topic, don't be afraid to change it if it isn't working out.

Next, research competitive publications to see what other books are in print on the topic(s) or theme(s) you've chosen for your work. Check out the approach each author has taken in organizing their content. This can help you get ideas on how to make your own collection both competitive and unique.

Start brainstorming what content you want to include in your book, and create another list of these potential areas. After you've these written down, you can play with their organization, create a working table of contents, and again compare your list to other publications on similar topics. Use this table of contents as a working document, and modify it as necessary and appropriate as you write, and as any new ideas come to you.

I typically create a paragraph or so about what content will go into each chapter to help refocus my thinking as I get into the actual organization and revision of a book's content. This helps me stay on track as I write and also gives me a head start on having a synopsis ready for a potential agent or editor.

 IDEAS AND INSPIRATION

When you start organizing your book's content, don't worry about how pretty the language is at this point, and don't get involved in endless edits as you write (small revisions are fine as they come to mind). Just capture the major ideas you already have in print. You can always edit and change things later.

Given the time it takes to generate and work with prose—its sheer bulk as opposed to that of poetry—I suggest you have a tentative schedule or timeline for yourself (for example, you write *X* hours a day, or whatever works for your style and schedule). You shouldn't have to strictly stay with your schedule or feel guilty when you forsake it, but many beginning writers do. If something comes up or you don't feel well one day, take time off to deal with it or recharge your brain.

As you read and reread your essays and stories, stay on track with your vision for the final product while allowing yourself opportunities to restructure as needed along the way. You might even ask a friend or colleague to read through the material to see if it flows, if it's written in an interesting manner, and to offer any suggestions for improvement they might see.

Again, don't worry too much about spelling, punctuation errors, and small details at this point unless they're so severe they impact reader comprehension. When you do finish your manuscript, you'll need to correct grammar, syntax, and punctuation and also evaluate whether you need to do any restructuring. For example, your colleague might point out that you repeat information in several different chapters and suggest you rewrite portions for clarity and effectiveness.

The key to effectively writing any book of collected prose is to have a solid plan at the beginning, make sound adjustments as you go, and make the final product the most professional and effective publication that it can possibly be.

Commonalities in Plot

Many writers believe there's only one essential characteristic of collections, whether it's prose, novels, or nonfiction: the various prose pieces are both self-sufficient and interrelated. On one hand, the pieces work independently of one another: the reader can read and understand each one of them without reading anything else in the book. On the other hand, a common theme extends to all the pieces in the work, similar to a full-length book.

Unlike the story, essay, or novel, however, this form appears under a variety of names. Many works of fiction and nonfiction carry the subtitle "a collection," which likely means these books are assortments of linked prose. And to needlessly complicate things further, the jacket copy, like that of Tim Powers' *Last Call*, often refers to a book as being made up of "linked stories," while other recent books, such as Adam Braver's *Mr. Lincoln's Wars*, carry the subtitle "a novel-in-stories." Some novels, such as Amy Tan's *The Joy Luck Club*, are really collections of linked stories but were published before the term became widely used. Scholars, for their part, often refer to the form as the "short story cycle" or "essay cycle."

 **WRITING PROMPT**

What are some of your favorite linked collections? Make a list in your journal of those that come to mind and then jot down a line or two as to why you like them. This information could be useful if you decide to assemble your own collection.

In any event, most collections of linked stories or essays do not have a consistent voice nor a central plot. They tend to be unified in at least one (and most often a combination) way, the most common of which are sense of place, central protagonist, time period, and writing style. I'll provide a description of each of these in the following paragraphs, along with a note on how they might apply to my memoir *SCHOOLED,* which consists of several essays, many of which were published independently in magazines. (*SCHOOLED* might have easily had a "linked" subtitle, although I chose for it not to.)

Place

James Joyce's *Dubliners* often is singled out as the sterling example of a book in which the author focuses on place as a unifying characteristic. There's no central protagonist in the book, and the characters in the different stories do not significantly interact with each other, yet the feel of Dublin in Joyce's time permeates the book and, as some scholars have argued, functions as a character itself.

Place functions similarly in *SCHOOLED,* although the geography is a bit looser: much of the state of Virginia, rather than one of its cities. Because I was writing nonfiction, this was merely the fact of the matter rather than a conscious decision, although I might have limited its scope to events that occurred only in the city of Richmond or solely in the rural Blue Ridge foothills. In the end, however, it seemed more interesting to mix those environments due to their rather drastic differences.

Central Protagonist

Another kind of linked collection is one in which a central protagonist dominates most, if not all, of the stories or essays. Such collections often are named after the protagonist, such as Katherine Anne Porter's *Miranda Stories,* Sir Arthur Conan Doyle's *Sherlock Holmes* mysteries, and even Ernest Hemingway's posthumous *The Nick Adams Stories.* As with places, there are novels—and even series of novels—that do the same thing with a central protagonist (Nancy Drew, Conan, etc.).

There also exist story or essay cycles that focus on family or group protagonists. These tend to focus on people whose lives intersect across pieces. *SCHOOLED* happens to be a combination of the central and group protagonist approach. Because it's a memoir, a younger projected version of myself is the central character. However, other figures also make appearances across the various essays. I didn't think of this dynamic as a way of connecting the book's sections when I was writing it, even though in essence that's precisely what it does.

Time Period

It's not uncommon to think of F. Scott Fitzgerald and his book *The Jazz Age* when you think of authors and works defined by eras or epochs. My own novel, *Confederado,* although not a linked collection, takes place during the American Civil War and Reconstruction.

Time plays a more nuanced role in my memoir because it reaches back as far as the mid-1970s, but it's also contemporary. However, this is a natural time frame for a memoir written by someone my age because it contains some of my first memories from the mid-1970s, yet also has me functioning in the present. It's true I might have focused it on just the last few years of my life or limited it to a childhood memoir, and either would have been fine. In this kind of writing, you have to figure out what portions of your life are the most significant to you and your readership.

WRITING PROMPT

In your journal, make a list of episodes from your life that might prove interesting to readers as well as yourself. This might turn out useful later if you decide to compose a memoir essay or book-length collection.

Writing Style

Finally, some story and essay collections are unified by a consistent writing style or approach across their various pieces. John Barth's *Lost in the Funhouse,* consisting of meta-fiction exploring the nature of storytelling, qualifies as an example.

This also seems like a good place to insert a personal publishing anecdote, since it involves writing style. As I noted, my memoir takes place in Virginia and possesses a great many rural southern and Appalachian qualities. In terms of subject matter, you might think of the rough American regional content of writers like Erskine Caldwell, Dorothy Allison, and Harry Crews (who wrote a blurb for my book manuscript not long before he passed away).

However, the writing style I chose for my memoir was quite formal, especially in its descriptions. So much so, in fact, that American publishers traditionally dealing with such content were not interested in taking the manuscript. Yet it was the book's very style that eventually proved its salvation in the form of a British editor much enamored of the work of a now-rarely-read modernist novelist named Elizabeth Bowen. This editor felt—whether really accurate or not—my writing in the memoir strongly resembled Bowen's and, thus, enthusiastically offered me a contract, despite the subject matter, which appeared to her generally foreign and crass.

I offer this anecdote not only to underscore the importance of writing style, but also to emphasize the vagaries of the publishing world. If someone had suggested to me years ago that my southern/Appalachian memoir would be published in Britain by an Elizabeth Bowen enthusiast, I likely would have laughed in their face.

IDEAS AND INSPIRATION

Like the world at large, the publishing world is a strange, unpredictable one. Never give up on your manuscript or close your mind to various avenues, however unlikely they might seem. Opportunity eventually may arrive from one of them.

Similarities in Scenes and Summaries

What becomes germane in terms of collections is how they correspond across different stories or essays. As in a single piece, you really don't want too much of one or the other throughout an entire book. So I'll provide some examples from my memoir to show how they can play off one another in different parts of your book.

Summary

Let's start with the easier of the two: summary. Most people use it in every story because it takes a large event or series of events and condenses it to a short description of what happened. For example:

> "B— died alone one spring mid-morning in a single vehicle highway wreck two weeks after I kissed her, running off the road without any cause or reason anyone could determine. Several months later, A— dove head first through an upper floor dormitory window, was withdrawn from school by her parents, and sent away, circumstances equally unfathomable, causes unknown."

In two sentences, you've been given the basic particulars of two peoples' deaths. It glosses over what happened, giving you the bare minimum of details to understand what's been happening. It's telling, not showing. You know these young women died, but you don't know what caused their deaths or the activities they engaged in during the days and hours before their respective demises. You know exactly what happened but none of the sensory details that fill in the gaps of the events or even any dialogue.

Here's an even vaguer example from later in the memoir:

> "I had sex for the first time not long after the events at Sweet Briar. It was with a girl who would never have any opportunity to attend an exclusive private woman's institution, or any other college for that matter. Perhaps she never even finished high school. I can't remember; I don't know what happened to her. Guilt rises in me on those rare occasions I recall her—guilt at not wondering about her more than I do."

In this summary, you learn about the narrator's relation to the young woman at hand but also of his ignorance regarding the rest of her life. She filled an important function in his development, and you know what that function is, albeit very little else. Too many of these kinds of passages would have ruined the memoir, but as it happens, you learn later what this young woman looked like, hear her speak, and even receive part of a sex scene.

Scene

You might think of scene as the complete opposite of summary. Scene takes a relatively short occurrence and expands it, filling it with details. Everyone uses scenes in their work, of course, but not everyone realizes that's what they're doing.

The concept is a little hard to completely understand for some people, so I'll provide an example involving the young woman I summarized in the "Summary" section:

> "Her face, childlike and round, had a certain immobile quality to it regardless of what happened to be going on around her, yet this dynamic was offset by her highly attentive, almost astonished, blue eyes which usually looked as though they had just witnessed something highly unexpected. Her full little mouth not only never smiled, but seemed altogether incapable of forming that expression. Lusterless mousy hair hung in clusters on either side of her head as if its intention was to appear as lifeless and flaccid as the expression on her face. Her shapely bosom breathed calmly like that of a wild animal lying at rest yet alert. Most any girl would have been something of an enigma to me in those inexperienced teenage years, but this one came across especially so. My initial response to her was neither one of attraction nor disinterest, but rather a kind of inquisitiveness I did not understand. Many girls might have possessed such qualities as hers without being remembered for them, but I remember on account of the part she played in my life."

See the difference? Just telling you what she looked like takes several sentences—there are concrete details (the girl's mousy hair, etc.), internal monologue, and sensory perceptions. I chose to take the duration of a glance—a few seconds—and cover it in an entire paragraph. I saw both her description and function in the memoir as important, so I tried to make my presentation of her detailed and unique, increasing the chances that the reader might remember it and her. Hence, a short, significant event and a long description.

I would urge you, as a beginning writer, to find the intuitive balance between summary and scene that will allow your collection to move forward in the way you believe it will best hold your readers' attention.

WATCH OUT!

The main drawback of scenes and their details in books is the effect they have on overall pacing. Henry James, in many of his novels, is a famous example of bogged-down pacing, even though his scenes and descriptions are technically very good. In long, flowing sentences, he often will tell you many of the things something is *not* before finally delivering its key details and significance. However, much of this kind of writing occurred in his mid- and late-career works, when he had already established a sizeable readership. Most writers cannot afford the risk of slowing their pacing to a snail's pace.

Common Use of Backstory and Flashback

As you've learned earlier, when you start a new story, you need to get readers into the conflict as soon as possible. But you also need to bring them up to speed on what's happened with the characters up to that point. This is usually done through backstory or flashbacks.

One nice aspect of collections is that you can use separate pieces or sections to accomplish what backstory and flashback typically do in something like a novel. A narrative needs to have forward momentum, meaning it needs to unfold at a steady pace. Flashbacks (and sometimes backstory) stop that momentum. However, if one story in a short story collection constitutes something from before the book's main time period, then you have a self-contained narrative that also offers information on the more current events the other stories relate.

Flashbacks and backstories that are pieces of story or essay collections take the readers somewhere else and get them involved in a different narrative that hopefully will help the other stories make more sense. Given this dynamic, their use in collections is less likely to frustrate readers who sometimes feel they're being pulled in too many directions at once when flashbacks and backstories are employed in novels or memoirs.

In general, it's still smoother for the readers if backstory can be conveyed in a shorter manner than a flashback. This means if you have a piece that goes back in time in your collection, you should try to make it shorter than the others unless you have a compelling reason not to. Especially impatient readers might still skip ahead to the next present-day piece in a collection, but they'll do so at their peril, as you've chosen to place that earlier time period piece where you have for a reason.

If it's not especially important to the narrative flow, flashbacks and backstories can fall in various pieces without the readers even noticing. I would say this is true in my memoir because I believe its various themes take precedence over issue of different time periods. By way of example, I include the book's table of contents. I've added dates to show when the different nonfiction pieces actually took place:

Part I: Beginnings and Vestiges of Lessons Learned

Prologue, or Lesson Plan for the Self (2011)

My Two High School Dream Girls (1992 and present)

The Skeleton Woman (1982)

Part II: Players, Coaches, and the Empowerment of Others

Home Court Advantage (1987)

The Men Beyond the Fields (1988)

Coaches (varies)

Part III: Passion, Folly, and Coming of Age

Satyr (1988)

Wrath of Achilles (1991 and present)

Willy Mann's Uncle's House (1991)

Use Your Illusion (Girls of Spring) (1992)

Part IV: Mortality and How We Choose to Keep on Going

Eyes Like Mountains (2011)

Epilogue, or Reviewing for the Final Exam (2012)

 WRITING PROMPT

Earlier I asked you to identify significant events from your life and record them in your journal. Now go back to that section and try ordering the incidents from your life into a table of contents that's thematically based rather than chronological.

Commonalities in Prosody

As with backstory and flashback, I've discussed prosody in other places in the book. However, how it functions across pieces of a collection is worth considering here.

Earlier I mentioned the editor who published my memoir and thought the narration resembled that of Elizabeth Bowen, a British novelist of the early twentieth century. The book certainly doesn't read that way to me or anyone else I've spoken with, but it was the intonation the editor heard as she perused the manuscript. In other words, to her ear, my prosodic narrative qualities resembled Bowen's.

Collections of stories and essays face a fundamental prosodic question of either including similar narrative pieces or utilizing variant ones. The advantage of the former is that it provides the book with an overall narrative flow, regardless of what the different pieces cover. On the other hand, because collections contain different free-standing pieces, as the author, you're at liberty to make each one prosodically different if you wish.

Of course, I've been describing prosody in terms of the narrator. It's going to be much more variable throughout a collection in terms of dialogue. Indeed, the functions of prosody are many and truly fascinating. Where speech sounds such as vowels and consonants function mainly to provide an indication of the identity of words and the regional variety of the speaker, prosody can indicate syntax, turn-taking in conversational interactions, types of utterance such as questions and statements, and character's attitudes and feelings.

The forms (or elements) of prosody—pitch or frequency, the length or duration, and the loudness or intensity—are derived from the acoustic characteristics of speech. All are present in varying quantities in every spoken utterance. The varying quantities help determine the function to which listeners orient themselves in interpreting what the characters say.

So if you decide to have lots of disconnected character dialects in your collection's dialogue, it could easily function as a destabilizing force to the book's organization. On the other hand, if you have several dialects, but they recur periodically across different pieces in the collection, the overall language of the book is going to seem much more balanced.

Also, don't forget that the narrator's voice can be a powerful force and can counteract whatever is going on with the dialogue. To return again to the example of my memoir, the editor found the narrative formal and eloquent because it reminded her of Bowen. However, the crassness of the content was at least in part due to the dialects, many of which were those of poor rural Virginians. It's hardly surprising, then, that to her cultivated British ear, these voices seemed grating, strange, and often crude.

 WRITING PROMPT

As a way of exploring the prosodic dichotomy between narrative and dialogue, write out a narrative description in your journal. Then go back and convey the same information through dialogue that uses different dialects and also varies from the narrative voice.

Essay and short story collections present their own sets of challenges. Pragmatically, however, they constitute wonderful ways to group together single pieces and make a book out of them. Unfortunately, it's not as easy as simply throwing together the different pieces, but with revision, patience, and proper organization, the prose collection is still a viable book publication.

The Least You Need to Know

- Commonalities in plot help unite a book of short stories or essays.
- Likewise, similarities in scenes and summaries allow your collection to have better flow.
- The use of backstory and flashback in collections basically takes the form of different pieces in the book.
- Prosody can be an important connective or destabilizing force in a prose collection.

Drafting, Researching, and Editing

When penning any creative writing document, you must ensure the content is appropriate for your audience, your voice is appropriate for the content, your word choice is effective, you use transitions, and the document is formatted properly. Knowing how to draft, research, and edit can make the task of creating an effective work of creative writing much easier.

After taking notes, mining your journal, and outlining, a first draft is constructed. It doesn't have to be perfect because it's a work in progress. Developing a catchy, interesting beginning pulls the reader in and makes him or her want to read more. The body of the work will follow, using a theme or concept as a rough guide.

You can enrich your initial draft by reading period material similar to your own project and taking notes on what's relevant to your work. If possible, travel to some of the unfamiliar places that appear in your manuscript and note their details. Lastly, interview scholars and everyday people who pertain to your subject to vastly enrich the verisimilitude of your work.

When it comes time to revise and edit, you must carefully read each word with new eyes. Word choice is a crucial factor. Do not use the same words over and over. Mix up sentence styles to give your work variety. Readers will appreciate your effort.

Drafting and Structuring

Whether you feel it or not, there's a process to writing that many writers follow naturally. If you're just getting started as a writer, though, or if you always find it a struggle to get going, following a writing process might help.

In this chapter, I offer some tips for getting your writing on track whenever you're feeling stuck.

Getting Unstuck

Have you ever sat staring at a blank piece of paper or a blank document on your computer screen, unable to find words to populate it? Writers traditionally call this the "terror of the blank page." When you feel this, it means you might have skipped the vital first stage of the writing process, prewriting. Prewriting is everything you do before starting your rough draft.

Ideas are all around you. If you want to write but feel you don't have any ideas, try the following:

- Read through your journal.

- Use a writing prompt to get started.

- Write about incidents from your daily life.

- Create a vivid character and then write about him/her.

Then you can build on your idea and add flesh to its bones. Luckily, you have a couple ways to do this. One I've talked about before is called *freewriting*. Open a new document or start a new page, and write everything that comes into your head about your chosen topic. Don't stop to edit, even if you make mistakes. Another is *brainstorming*, in which you write the idea or topic in the center of your page and then jot down ideas that arise from it—the subtopics or directions you could take with the article.

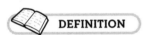 **DEFINITION**

Brainstorming is a prewriting method in which you record ideas stemming from a single central topic or concept.

Once you've done one or both of these prewriting exercises, you need to select what's going into your first draft. Some pieces of writing require more planning than others. Typically, longer pieces, such as novels, need a lot of thought at this stage.

First, decide which ideas you'll use. During your freewriting and brainstorming, you'll have come up with lots of thoughts. Some belong in this piece of writing; others can be kept for another time or project. Then, decide how to order those ideas. Try to have a logical progression. Sometimes, your topic will make this easy: in this section, for instance, it made sense for me to take each step of the writing process in order.

Sit down with your plan beside you, and start your first draft (also known as the rough draft). At this stage, don't think about word count, grammar, spelling, and punctuation. Don't worry if you've gone off topic, or if some sections of your plan don't fit together. If you're a new writer, you might be surprised to learn that professional authors usually go through multiple drafts before they're happy with their work. This is a normal part of the writing process.

As another aid, some writers find setting aside specific time to work on their rough draft helpful. You even could go somewhere you won't be interrupted or have to deal with distractions.

IDEAS AND INSPIRATION

Writing requires concentration and energy. If you're a new writer, don't try to write for hours without stopping. Instead, give yourself a time limit (such as 30 minutes) to really focus. And no checking your phone or email during that time!

Now that you've gotten to the actual writing, let's backtrack and take a closer look at some the most helpful prewriting techniques.

Mining Your Journal

Spend some time rereading old journal entries. You'll notice self-growth, recalling where you were and what you were doing a year ago; discover progress you've made toward your dreams; and find patterns in your life. Reviewing your journal can also serve as a means of research into past events for scene details, characters, and emotions in a creative writing piece you're working on.

In addition, you can review your journal entries to look for metaphors you incorporated into your writing. Metaphors are, essentially, the use of concrete, tangible objects and their characteristics to describe intangible, abstract ideas. Another way of explaining metaphor is the use of images to represent concepts. For example, if you say "time is money," you're using the image of the tangible, concrete object of money to help others understand the abstract concept of time. When you apply the characteristics of money to time, readers understand that time is something we can spend, waste, save, trade for something else, and so on.

Your journal also is an outstanding tool for examining how your background, upbringing, family, and life experiences influence your world views and, ultimately, our shared and individual metaphors. Your journal entries are one place your unique way of understanding life presents itself in the form of metaphor. You can then pull out this material and use it in other forms of creative writing.

WRITING PROMPT

Read 10 to 20 previous journal entries, highlighting images you used to describe feelings or concepts. It's important to do this in a nonjudgmental way. Don't ask yourself whether the metaphor is "good" or not; the merits of your metaphors are not important. Then, once you've identified some images, spend time exploring the nature of the images and their meaning(s) to you both then and today.

Here are some additional journaling prompts that could help you utilize the material you've written in your journal:

- Freewrite for 10 minutes about the image(s) in your journal entries and their possible meanings and/or connections to the way you see the world.

- Choose an image or object and ask yourself what characteristics it has and it applies to the emotion or concept(s) you're trying to express in the passage.

- Think about where and/or when you first associated this object with this concept. Let your mind wander into the past. Think about what parents or other family members may have told you, other influential people, books you've read, and past experiences.

- Perform a word association exercise with the image(s).

- Identify a metaphor and then look for ways can you extend it.

For example, while reading my through my journal pages from several years ago, I found two startling entries that described how I was feeling before I set out to perform the several hundred miles of hiking that would allow me to write my book *The Warrior's Path:*

> *Andrew Sinclair on Jack London:* "He was the archetype of the American hero who tried to live what he wrote."

> *Ambrose Bierce letter to Nellie Sickler:* "[I]t is possible—even probable—that I shall not return. These be 'strange countries,' in which things happen; that is why I am going."

These quotes from important American writers illustrate my thinking about my upcoming hike in at least two different ways. The line about Jack London captures my hope for the book—that I could embody the work through my journey. On the other hand, the Bierce lines reflect my reservations about walking great distances along the sides of roads by myself, but also the exhilaration that accompanies such danger "things happen, that is why I am going."

I have at least two other potential travel books in mind that would require throwing myself out into the world under perilous circumstances. If I undertake them, I surely will return to my journal entries prior to writing *The Warrior's Path* to remind myself of both the aspirations and trepidation that accompany the prospect of dangerous lone travel.

 WRITING PROMPT

What's your current writing project? Even if you haven't been keeping your journal very long, go back through it and look for the images, anecdotes, observations, etc. that might prove useful for your project at hand. Make a list as you go, and order them later.

If the useful materials you discover and explore come from your own journal entries surrounding events you've written about, you (like me) might find that you have a direct use for them in whatever it is you are working on. If not, keep them in your writing journal—perhaps marked by sticky notes—and review them from time to time. The material that comes from your journal is highly personal; it resonates with you at a core level and will, most likely, surface again as you continue to write.

Letting Go: Freewriting

Freewriting is a simple process that's the basis for other discovery techniques. Basic freewriting follows these guidelines:

- You write nonstop for a set period of time (10 to 20 minutes, for example).

- Do not make corrections as you write.

- Keep writing, even if you have to write something like, "I don't know what to write."

- Write whatever comes into your mind.

- Do not judge or censor what you're writing.

Keep in mind that if your freewriting is neat and coherent, you probably haven't loosened up enough. However, remember that you can't fail in freewriting. The point of doing freewriting is the process, not the end result. If you follow the guidelines, your freewriting is successful.

As an example, here's a freewriting example from my journal:

> A character who is obsessed with his DNA halo type and goes around apologizing to anyone he meets whose ancestors may have been subject to his ancestors' inexcusable behavior. He is descended from the Kurgan culture and therefore believes he is at least partially responsible for the Kurgan hordes that overran Europe and Asia in the fifth millennium and thereafter, pillaging, enslaving, and raping all along the way, and were also responsible for the Indo-Europeanization of Europe which undoubtedly—at least to his mind—paved the way for African slavery. He winds up giving away nearly all his material wealth—much of it to conmen who have no relation to the cultures the protagonist's ancestors conquered thousands of years ago.

I should admit right off that this is a pretty clean piece of writing by freewriting standards. Yet that's merely due to the fact that I've been writing professionally for years. Don't hesitate to write out "Uh" or "this is a silly exercise" or "my mind's a blank." Much of the end purpose, after all, is to use the physical act of writing—regardless of what you actually write—to jar your mind toward more articulate ideas.

WRITING PROMPT

Clear your mind, relax, and try freewriting for yourself.

Freewriting has several major benefits:

- It makes you more comfortable with the act of writing.

- It helps you bypass your inner critic who might tell you you can't write.

- It can be a valve to release inner tensions.

- It can help you discover things to write about.

- It can indirectly improve your formal writing.

- It can even be pretty fun.

A few final suggestions for freewriting:

- Be sure to use the writing tool you're most comfortable with—pencil, computer, or whatever.

- Don't cross out anything. Write down the new idea and leave the old one. You never know what might eventually prove useful.

- Don't worry about things like punctuation and run-on sentences. Writing naturally makes your freewriting faster and more fluent.

- Remember that one of the benefits of freewriting is that it's like having a direct connection to your unconscious.

Outlining Your Work

Even today I don't like writing outlines because I feel that they stifle my creativity with their Roman numerals, chapter titles, and the like. Not only have I never tried to summarize scenes in my books, but I've found that deciphering what should be detailed and what could be omitted was almost as difficult as creating the dreaded *synopsis*.

DEFINITION

A **synopsis** is a brief condensation, outline, or summary of the main points of an article, book, or plan.

Yet with direction—with the upcoming events in your work detailed in an outline or synopsis—you'll find you have the ability to conceive of and write the scenes that had previously eluded you. This can work wonders, particularly for a work you have nearly completed.

I typically go at my books with only a few ideas in mind and very little else; the traditional outline stumps me. How can I decide what needs to go into which chapter if the story is still largely a mystery even to me? Every outline attempt of mine was convoluted and difficult to follow. So I gave up.

For the purposes of this chapter, I polled other writers and published authors for what they do. One author explained that before she begins to write, she creates a synopsis and uses it as both an outline and a tool to sell the unwritten book to her publisher.

Yet how can you combine the two into a format you can follow? How can you brainstorm all the "what ifs" and avoid the constant rearranging and renumbering of chapters?

By combining the two—a traditional outline and a synopsis—you can detail a narrative with very little structure but maintain a workable format. What I'm describing, in essence, is a scene outline. Without Roman numerals or chapter headings, you have the freedom to maneuver plot points and swap scenes. New ideas are easy to add without confusing the format. This technique gives you the freedom to write an entire novel, or another lengthy work, in a few short pages.

Like most writers, I picture a rough narrative in my head. Sometimes I know the whole story; at other times, I only know the low and high points. Brainstorming is an integral part of shaping a work. For any writer who's fallen in love with the inherent creativity in freewriting, this is the perfect outlining technique.

IDEAS AND INSPIRATION

> Aspiring writers sometimes forget they are the masters of their universe. Creative outlines are written for your eyes only. The sheer flexibility of this technique lets you go back and insert as much as you'd like, wherever you'd like. The purpose is to breathe life into your outstanding inspiration. Don't edit, don't to stop to research. Use asterisks to make it easy to find areas that require more research later on.

Getting down to particulars, here are some steps that should lead to a promising creative outline:

1. Begin by describing any information that occurs before the opening scene. Use quick, memory-cementing sentences.

2. Write the opening scene the same way, with quick, strident, labeled sentences.

3. Freewrite the rest, conducting research when necessary.

The beauty of such an outline is the ability to be totally creative without stopping to find facts, except when you want to. When you begin the actual work, you'll find that your creativity is stimulated by the research and the development of your characters.

Feel free to play with the structure, rearranging or adding ideas as they occur to you. Making changes is much easier when you're dealing with paragraphs instead of whole chapters or scenes. With very little adjustments to make, adding the results of your brainstorming—even during the actual writing phase—is less daunting and easier to assimilate into the original outline. As you progress through your writing career, the actual outline you make will likely become sketchier and less detailed, but for aspiring writers, this can greatly increase your focus and keep your work in progress on course.

In my experience, too many otherwise-excellent stories are lost in the confusion between where the beginning, middle, and ending scenes should lead the characters and how the plot should develop. With a map to follow, you'll increase your chances of completing those first works.

Another benefit of creative outlining is that once you're familiar with this technique, it will become easier to create, even before it's needed. If you use the outline feature in your word processing software, you usually have options that give you greater freedom to implement the creative outlining technique. When inspiration hits, write the creative outline and save it for your next project. Over the course of a year, you will have developed several such outlines.

Creative outlining provides the benefits of an outline but lets you maintain a higher level of creativity. As master of your writing universe, you can decide to add as much or as little as you need. This simple tool will prompt you during those dark moments when your organization falters and help keep your narrative on course. Have fun playing with "what if," and follow your instincts.

Assembling the Pieces with Quilting

There will be times when disorganization in your writing will discourage you to the point you don't feel like continuing. You'll feel like you can't find a way to order your writing that makes sense, and everything you've written seems chaotic. But when it comes to writing, sometimes a little disorganization can lead to a wonderful unforeseen sequence of events.

Often when people start writing books, they have a complete idea for the plot. However, they don't have a beginning, middle, or an end. In *quilting,* you take whatever you do have—miniature scenes, bits of dialogue, scenery you think will be great for the setting—and patch them together to form a book. Patchwork writing is like sewing a patchwork quilt. In the following paragraphs, I share some manifestations it might take along with some examples from my novel *Confederado.*

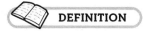 **DEFINITION**

Quilting is a writing technique in which the author forms a patchwork whole from many isolated pieces of writing.

You might try to write dissimilar scenes or ideas for a book and then piece them together at a later time:

No one in the family who had served in a war—the French-Indian, the Revolution, or the 1812—had ever died while serving, which made father's death all the more grievous and dismaying.

Meets old veteran from Bedford County whose home had been destroyed during Hunter's advance on Lynchburg. Says of Bedford: "It is a pretty little place at the foot of the mountains."

Robert E. Lee, the newspaper read, was against migration, asserting that "the South requires the presence of her sons in order to sustain and restore her."

The first of these notes, I will have you know, I simply lost track of. I'm still not certain where I would have inserted it in the finished novel. It seems significant the protagonist's father is the only person in the history of the family to die in a war. However, I include it here to underscore that it's okay to not know here to quilt information and that accidents like losing shreds of information occur in most every book's composition.

I didn't use the Bedford County anecdote either, but it was more a matter of pragmatics. My interest in Hunter's campaign had to do with the fact it was the closest real fighting near the protagonist's home prior to Lee's surrender. However, including it would have involved several pages of description and new characters. Working it in would have meant the pacing of the book would have been compromised. Reluctantly, I had to let it go, just as you likely will find yourself doing on occasion.

The last note I found attractive was Robert E. Lee's only commentary on the Confederado migration. However, he was against it, so I had the problem of trying to reconcile the protagonist's flight with the judgment of a man venerated by many southerners and northerners alike. In the end, my quilting could not accommodate it without potentially diminishing sympathy for the people in the book's title.

I include these aborted shreds of quilt from *Confederado* to show you how much thought and difficulty can go into them. However, another strategy that can help you out and keep a scene in mind is saving it alone on your computer, apart from other sections of manuscript. Then, later, you might read it again and decide where it fits best. Because my novel contains several flashbacks to the Civil War, I found myself doing that with the protagonist's war sequences—often moving them around to feel what different effects they created.

What I've just described is part and parcel of the much more general technique of linking scenes into chapters or breaking down ideas for further plot development. I include the following table of contents for *Confederado,* but really it's less that and more a list of the events and ideas in the book. Only this is how they ended up in terms of organization:

> Prologue: The Fugitive
>
> I. Virginia
>
>> Homecomings: Appomattox
>>
>> Departures: Land and Sea
>
> II. Brazil
>
>> Arrival: Espírito Santo
>>
>> Departure and Arrival: Espírito Santo and Linhares
>>
>> Love and Departure: War of the Triple Alliance
>>
>> Homecoming: Brazil

Although the contents is actually chronological, flashbacks and backstories appear throughout the forward-moving sections, hopefully without bogging down the narrative too much.

Ultimately, this will be your challenge as well: quilting together your own narrative in the manner that makes the most sense to you and, hopefully, to your readers as well.

The Least You Need to Know

- Mining your journal can mean finding potential topics and information to include in your formal writing projects.
- Freewriting is a good way to get your ideas flowing.
- Outlining can help organize the vast stores of information you generate while working on your project.
- Quilting is a good way to assemble information that otherwise might not seem useful or relevant.

Empowering Research

Writers who engage in research for their creative writing are active writers, producing creative works as key parts of their research explorations. In addition, creative writing researchers often consider critical questions concerning the creative writing practice as well as the results of this practice—structural or stylistic questions, questions of form and function, or questions of authorship, for example.

Creative writing research might be driven by thematic or subject-based ideas, concerns with cultural conditions, the psychology or emotive context of creative writing, or explorations of creative writing aesthetics. Some such researchers might be interested in the types of knowledge creative writing entails and offers; others might have an interest in the audiences for creative writing, its distribution, or its reception. These are just a few examples.

Since the 1970s in North America, and from the beginning of the 1990s in Britain and Australia, universities have been offering creative writers the opportunity to study for a doctoral degree in their subject. This has been in addition to a considerable number of Master's-level degree programs that have a research element–practice-led research and/or critical research–at their core.

In This Chapter

- Reading through time
- Note-taking tips
- The importance of travel
- Interviewing info

At present, thousands of creative writers worldwide are writing not only with the aim of perhaps publishing their work, or seeing it performed or produced, but also with the aim of exploring some particular topic or idea through creative and critical research in creative writing.

There are many similarities and a deal of shared territory in both the creative practices and in the critical explorations undertaken. In essence, a wide variety of "sites of knowledge" are being mined. Sometimes there are meeting points, and sometimes, shared experiences. There are unique, but sometimes connected, discoveries being made. Finally, a lively variety of creative and critical works is being produced. All of this is to be celebrated.

Given the vast range of subjects academia supports, and has supported, for those who engage in the writing arts as a way of investigating the world, it's pleasing that creative writing is one of academia's oldest partners. That is, even a "university" as old as Plato's Academy (circa 387 B.C.E.) could be seen to form the first point of contact between the act of writing creatively and formal higher education.

In this chapter, we consider the more pragmatic aspects of creative writing. That is, those that can serve you the best as you generate your writing projects. We look closely at the value of reading period material, taking notes (when and how to do it), traveling to research sites, and interviewing to increase your knowledge of whatever you happen to be writing about.

Reading Period Material

Creative writing and time travel have a lot in common. Both have the goal of whisking the participant through time and space to visit unknown realms of a particular point in the past—or the future if we're talking science fiction. Because you as an author haven't actually lived in many of these times or places, you need to find your own version of the proverbial time travel device to help you write your book. To this end, there are a few things you should think about to help you along your path.

One is the concept of *world building,* which I touched on in Chapter 8. World building is more often associated with writing fantasy or science fiction than literary work, but the principles are the same. You haven't necessarily lived when and where your narrative is set, so before you plunge in, you need to take time to design your world. Readers want to smell, taste, feel, and hear that world. What do the houses look like? What do your characters eat? What do they wear? Don't rely on Hollywood's version of the past; accuracy counts. The authenticity of your work depends on your knowledge of the time period and the historical details you weave into it.

 **DEFINITION**

World building is the concept of creating your narrative's setting through historical research.

Readers want and deserve accurate information from you. They read in part because they already have a love affair with history or contemporary culture. Some of them might know as much or more than you do about the period you choose to write about. And they will be quick to point out your mistakes.

I find that keeping a simple notebook helps. I photocopy important information from print sources; print out internet info; and cut out pictures, maps, and diagrams and place them in the appropriately labeled section. This notebook stays by my side as I write, so I can flip it open to find the exact date of an event or refresh my memory on manners or the correct name for the coin my character is using in the market. Look to experts for help. This isn't as difficult as it might seem. Many teach in local colleges and universities or work at your local historical society.

My writer friends agree you'll do about five times the amount of research than you'll actually use in your book. Be careful not to get caught in the trap of over-researching. Stop as soon as you've gathered enough information on all the basic workings of your time period that are necessary to support your narrative. You can, and most likely will, have to go back from time to time to check a fact or to answer a new question that has cropped up.

When you begin writing, beware of the temptation to share all your newfound knowledge with your readers. It's easy to throw off your novel's pacing by getting lost in the minutiae and putting too much history into the story. Fascinating as you may find it, some of those lengthy paragraphs about doing laundry in ancient Greece will have to go. Be ruthless. Keep only what's important to advance the story or provide your readers with the information they absolutely need to know about your characters and their world. Everything else must go.

Short of using that time machine I mentioned, there's no way of producing an entirely accurate portrayal of historical personages who might crop up in your narrative. Be faithful to the historical record if what that person did during a particular event, or is quoted as having said, is germane to your work. Feel free to fill in the gaps with reasonable actions and dialogue.

Unless the historical person is an important character, keep his or her characterization simple. Focus on a generalized physical description and then try to find one or two personal habits, quirks, or well-known attitudes (Stonewall Jackson's fondness for lemons, for example), and use them to personify the person.

 WATCH OUT!

The ancient Egyptians didn't use zippers. Tiffany was not a popular name in the 1100s. Email was not available during the American Civil War. It's highly unlikely that Henry VIII ever addressed his six wives as "those chicks." You might smile, but these and similar anachronisms have turned up in manuscripts and, worse yet, published novels. While in the throes of writing, with everything else you're trying to keep straight, sometimes contemporary references or modern slang creep into the story. Keep an eye out for these anachronisms.

Having a trusted reader who can proof your narrative before you submit it can be helpful in weeding out these inaccurate slips. In addition, plenty of online dictionaries are available for you to use to check a word's etymology. Be sure whatever source you use to select character names gives not only the origin but also the time period when the name came into usage. Readers and reviewers will have no problem pointing out your mistakes, so take the time to be sure every aspect of your story accurately reflects the period of time you're writing about.

Remember that beliefs and attitudes about the world—and men's and women's proper place in it—have vastly altered since the beginning of recorded history. Prejudices, traditions, and values we no longer approve of were the norm in other times and places. Be objective and respect the people and the time you've chosen to write about. Avoid projecting twenty-first-century values into the story. Make your characters genuine people of the time period they inhabit. There's no need to apologize for their ideas or actions or, worse, try to change them into the only right-thinking person of their time to make them and the story more palatable.

Before you begin, decide which point of view (POV) will best suit your story. Third person, multiple POV is standard, for example, in commercial fiction. Limit the number of POV characters to those who are the key players in your book. Using more than four or five POV character can confuse your readers. Except in the case of letters and journals, using first person might make your main character come across as self-absorbed. Sometimes readers find it off-putting to have a character discuss what they look like, what they're wearing, how their voice sounds, etc. On the other hand, first person is often very popular in young adult (YA) books. Be aware of the challenges presented in using this POV, and be sure it's the best way of presenting your story.

With all the period research you perform, you likely will have a complicated story with lots of fascinating characters. Although it's important for you as the writer to know each character's backstory, the reader doesn't want to be bogged down with all the detail. Avoid lengthy paragraphs about a character's past or an overabundance of flashbacks. Introduce the facts absolutely needed to progress the story in dribs and drabs. As much as possible, characters should reveal backstory through dialogue. Or weave it into short passages of description or exposition broken up by actions. Keep in mind that you're writing creatively, not crafting a history textbook.

In my experience, the best writers are also voracious readers. Don't let your current work in progress chain you to your computer. Take time out to read. Keep a pile of books on your nightstand, and read a little each night. Read in your genre, and read out of it. You'll find yourself reading differently, of course. As writers, we can't help but mentally note how the opening hook is set up, when the goal is brought in, or how the author handles the turning points and a big moment. Still, getting lost in a good book is still possible and also keeps you educated and tuned in to the world of publishing.

Readers of period books are a discriminating lot. Just make a mistake about word usage, manners, or the correct length of evening gloves in a Regency romance, and watch the hate-emails fly and the book sales diminish. Authors need to keep the relationship of the main characters in the forefront while also providing the right dosage of period material and ensuring it's all accurate. This is no easy feat, but the more intimately you know your time period and characters, the better your chances of pulling it off.

The Importance of Taking Notes

Note-taking might seem antithetical to creative writing, but you'll find that "how" you take down an idea can have a lot to do with how much of it you can recall later.

The most basic layout for creative writing note-taking is to divide an 8.5×11 sheet of paper into three sections: two columns with a horizontal section at the bottom. The left column is reserved for keywords or questions that arise while you're writing; the right-hand column is for note-taking or, in the case of prose writers, the bulk of your manuscript; while the bottom horizontal section is used to summarize your work. For prose writers, this is a great place to make note of key players in the scene or any ideas you want to remember or improve upon later.

This method provides an easy way to condense and organize your notes. It can benefit writing projects of all types and can be easily adapted to the format of your journal.

 WRITING PROMPT

> In your journal, try out the three-column method for a narrative concept you have in mind. Take note of how well it works for you. (This may involve ignoring the page for a few days and then going back to it and determining how much of the information you recorded triggers in your mind.)

If you're more computer-focused when you write, try writing software such as *Liquid Story Binder*. With it, you can separate any notes from the rest of your writing using the Line Notes tool. By putting two periods in front of any paragraphs you want to separate, you can view them all separately later using the Line Notes Viewer, or print them independently of your manuscript. You also can specify different formatting so the notes stand out from any hard copies of your manuscript. Any paragraph beginning with two periods is designated as a line note and is excluded from Printing and Word Count Statistics.

Or if low tech is more your speed, you could simply enclose your notes inside two brackets to distinguish them from the rest of your writing.

How you take notes likely is more important than you thought it was. If you're looking for a way to continually brainstorm ideas or focus on potential problem spots in you writing, try some of these methods. Hopefully, one or more of them will be the tool you've been looking for to help you become a more efficient writer.

Pack Your Bags

Many writers hate research. They don't want to spend hours, days, months, and sometimes even years researching a topic for their work. They just want to *write*.

When it comes to research, creative writers usually should only write what they know. Exclusive topics written in your field of experience not only makes you sound like an expert on your topic to your readers, but also helps you avoid lengthy research sessions. Yet if you want to write about Somali pirates, then prepare to do some research. Even if you only watch a few pirate documentaries and read a few books, you have to know what you're talking about.

If you want to write about Thailand, the best research you can do is to go there for yourself and experience things as closely to how your character would experience them. Taste the food, mingle with the locals, and get firsthand experience of life there. Moreover, part of Thailand's fascination is that it's a very corrupt country. Drugs, sex trafficking, and STDs are everyday elements of the culture. You need to learn about them, too, but be smart about it. Travel in a group or with a couple armed government officials.

Of course, if you're writing a historical novel or a futuristic novel, a writer can't actually travel through time. However, museums and space camps and meeting with university professors is a great place to start.

To be a successful creative writer, you must absorb information as naturally as possible. Doing your research, visiting your setting in person, and experiencing a new perspective will add realism and detail to your novel that would otherwise escape your awareness. If you have the opportunity to experience the location of your story in person, do what it takes to get there.

The internet is an excellent resource for beginning your travel research. If you're writing a book that takes place in Libya, get online and check out the many websites where you can interact with expatriates who speak English. Skype, email, and Facebook can help you keep in touch with them.

 WATCH OUT!

Although the internet can be helpful in your research, be careful about the personal information you provide about yourself, especially if some of your contacts are from a war-ravaged country and are desperate for cash (Libya, for example) or involved in activity that would be criminal in the United States (Thailand).

If you're writing about wildlife in Africa, some nature-protection websites have posted cameras throughout national parks to monitor wildlife and protect them from poachers and offer the feed on their site. So although you might not be able to afford that trip your character makes in real life, you can still use the internet to get as close as you possibly can without having to worry about poachers, rebel massacres, or predatory jungle creatures.

Another travel resource is reading other books. Writers who are on a tight budget and unable to travel can get snapshots of the country they're interested in just by readings books about it published in or about the years that interest them. Travel books can take you to faraway places. Nonfiction memoirs in particular can give you a good detailed idea of what life was really like at a given time. Fiction and poetry can provide you with that extra bit of creativity.

If all that doesn't seem like enough, consider meeting with local specialists. A local expert, such as a college professor, is usually all too happy to talk about his or her favorite place and perhaps has even recently returned from an exciting expedition.

Just remember that however you choose to do your research, always add those bit of details of the senses (touch, taste, sound, sight, smell) to give your creative writing the extra edge that makes it seem like the reader is being transported to the place your book wants to go.

Making the Most of Interviews

Interviewing can serve as an integral aspect of research. Although you might assume you can depend on your memory when you write life-based stories, memory isn't always as reliable as you want it to be. Interviews with relevant family members and friends can supplement your memory and broaden your memoir's perspective.

The first step is to select who to interview. If your time is limited, or if your family is large and offers many choices, it's all the more important to identify a manageable number of knowledge-able relatives and friends to interview. For example, Aunt Quanita tends to talk endlessly—all afternoon if you let her. Her conversation seems to have little content as she meanders from one topic to another. Aunt Coco, on the other hand, is an incisive person whose intuition is always informing her (and you) about what things mean. Her many observations and reminiscences are usually interestingly told. Furthermore, they're consonant with your other research. Can there be any doubt who you should interview first? Show Aunt Quanita some love, but when it's time to go to work, sit down with Aunt Coco.

Next, ascertain who else is likely to want to participate in the interview, and decide whether that person may or may not sit in. An unexpected, or inappropriate, person can blur the focus of your interview. For instance, your aunt by marriage, sitting in on the interview, might find what you're doing so interesting she begins to talk about her own life experiences and, in doing so, may not allow your uncle (your mother's brother) much time to talk about his childhood relationship with your grandparents and your mother. Your aunt's experience, however interesting, won't provide the information you need to understand your grandparents and parents. A clever way to get around this is to present your aunt with a gift while taking your uncle out for dinner.

Conversely, don't dismiss other people's input too quickly. Their experiences can be valid for your family, too. By listening carefully to an articulate person talk about a general experience, you might learn a lot about your own family. For example, you're interviewing your mother's brother, and his wife (your aunt by marriage) begins talking about her family. It's likely you didn't know these people she's talking about, and their lives don't fit into your story.

As your aunt shares her stories, however, you realize how many of them are about work in and life around the mining towns of southwestern Virginia and southern West Virginia in the 1930s. Your family's experiences in similar mining communities across the state line in Virginia are not likely to differ widely from her family's. Use some of the information provided by your aunt-in-law to flesh out your family's narrative. But don't get sidetracked on her niece's love story. At that point, the conversation is slipping into gossip, and you risk losing the focus of your interview.

Sometimes an observer at an interview can provide important coaching. For example, a third party might suggest, "John, why don't you tell about the time your mother confronted the company store manager?" Or perhaps the other person will offer, "But, wasn't that before 1937? We were still living on Maple Street then. It wasn't until a month after Edward was born in January of 1938 that we moved to Elm Street!"

In fact, if you know of a person who might be good at prodding a significant but reluctant interviewee, ask that person to be present. But again, be clear about what you're asking this person to do: "I'll be interviewing Uncle Alec about his childhood. Would you come along to encourage him to share his information with me? You might remind him of parts of the story you know when you notice he's overlooking them."

Clear communication and thoughtful preparation of your goals for each interview will heighten your chances of success while interviewing.

By way of example, I include here an interview involving three people. Note how the primary writer, Emma Bolden, interacts with the two people with whom she's lunching:

Regionalism, Fashion, Editing, and Writing: A Lunch Discussion

EMMA BOLDEN, CASEY CLABOUGH, & ALLISON WILIKNS

Writer/editor Emma Bolden sat down for lunch with two of the *James Dickey Review* editors prior to her Owen lecture at Lynchburg College in Spring 2011. What followed was a wide-ranging discussion of regional identity, fashion, editing, and writing which nonetheless managed to capture some commonalities relevant to the themes of both the JDR and the contemporary literary scene.

EB: Kentucky has been really weird. Since it was a border state there's such a bizarre conflict—the thing I've noticed is how many people are obsessed with the South, particularly Alabama, since Alabama is emblematic of the South, and it's just really strange since I had grown up being taught to be ashamed about being from Alabama.

CC: I feel bad for some of the Alabamans, Mississippians, and South Carolinians I know because they get a certain Deep South label what with being in the heart of the old Confederacy and all. It seems a little unfair.

EB: I remember my roommate at Sarah Lawrence was from New York, and she told me at some point that when she got the letter that said her roommate was from Alabama, she cried because she couldn't believe she would have to live with someone from Alabama. *[laughs]* Most of my heritage isn't that southern anyway, it's Sicilian. It's southern, just Southern Italian. But that whole cultural thing is so strong it just seems to keep on surviving.

CC: Were your people even down there during the Civil War?

EB: No, they were in Italy. God knows what my dad—we have no idea … my dad's family is like a big, double-sided-tree-question mark. But they weren't there during the war. What about you?

CC: Well, I seem to get labeled a so-called southern Appalachian writer on account of my people living in the Smokey Mountains for a couple centuries.

EB: Dollywood! I've been there!

CC: Yeah, they've done pretty well I guess, largely on account of caricaturing themselves.

EB: Do they have Civil War history?

CC: Sure, I have an ancestor out of Gatlinburg who was a cavalry Captain, albeit for the North. It's funny. Most people tend to think of Tennessee as the South and that everyone there was Confederate, but most of the mountain people weren't. They were poor, they didn't have slaves or a lot of land. They were unlettered, but they weren't dumb.

EB: Yeah, that sounds similar to the fact nobody believes there is a Sicilian community in Alabama. What happened was, they came over, went to Ellis Island, and the New Yorkers were like, "We've got way too many Italians already so you have to find someplace else to go." They got sent down to New Orleans. And so now there are steel mills and a huge Sicilian-American community in Alabama, and people just don't believe it. "Sorry, New York is full. You'll have to go somewhere else: Alabama!"

[laughter all around; the conversation turns to attire in the academic workplace]

EB: I was told you have to have a suit, you have to have a suit. Is this going to be on record, because this is very important? I went to Banana Republic with my parents to buy a suit. I put it on and opened the dressing room door already crying, and my mom was like, "Oh god! Oh god!" *[laughs]* My mom told my dad, "You need to go to the bookstore or something because this is going to take a while. She looks like a damn drag king." So we ended up just getting dress pants and a jacket, and I thought I wasn't going to get the job I was interviewing for since I didn't have a whole suit.

AW: Maaaaaan.

EB: Actually, another one of my friends had a campus visit, and asked all her professors for advice, and got told the last thing you should do is wear a suit. So maybe I just lucked in with my job deal.

[talk turns to the topic of literary magazines]

CC: We have two associate editors, including Allison, but I tend to feel pretty guilty asking them to look at stuff because of their heavy teaching loads. Any release time for you or is it a labor of love?

EB: It is absolutely a labor of love. The head editor gets a release, but I don't get one. I read every single poetry submission, so everything that comes in under poetry comes over to me. They have a manuscript contest now, but I don't have anything to do with it. When it comes to the journal itself, I read every submission because I feel it's important to honor everything, so I do read every submission and then sort of cull it down and decide what we are going to publish. I'm also the one who does all the proofreading.

AW: Lucky you.

EB: Yeah. We've had two student editors who are absolutely incredible. They did the job better than I could have; they're really good. So they did the proofing and a lot of the work too. Then we have a really great compositor I work with. I tend to accept poems that are crazy on the page, and so the most interesting work has been me working with the compositor and talking about how to get things to fit on the page: the combination between the publishing aspect and what the poet wants. And I mean, I'm guilty of this, but I hit that tab key sometimes and think everything's ok. Apparently, though, it's not something that works in publishing.

CC: I know what you mean. Our operation has a gifted graduate assistant who taught herself InDesign software. Without her, I'd continually be lost messing around with that stuff. It seems very time-consuming.

EB: Yeah. I feel like if we didn't have the student editors, or the compositor, there would be no *Georgetown Review*.

AW: How much stuff do you read?

EB: The *Georgetown Review* doesn't have a page limit, right, so sometimes she's got 20–30 pages of poetry. It's a little different from 25 pages of short story—it's a little different than 25 separate pages. A good thing about that though is that we do get quite a few serious longer poems, which is a form I think is really interesting.

AW: It's hard to get those published most places because they take up so many pages.

EB: Yes, very.

[talk turns briefly to The Love Boat *television show, before shifting to future journal plans]*

CC: Since you're leaving the *Georgetown Review,* do you think you might start a journal at your new university?

EB: I've been talking to a couple of friends about starting a journal for a while. It's something that's been in the back of my mind. I've been thinking about making something a little smaller and handmade.

AW: Nice!

CC: That sounds lovely, but then there's those problems of carving out some release time and still getting your own work done.

EB: Well, I think one of the best things about an M.F.A. degree is that it gives you time to write your first book. Yet one of the worst things is that you are expected to publish that first book, and I think that first book usually has to just die. It's your growing experience—it's where you learn how to put a book together—but you hope maybe a backlog of good poems will come out of it. I do manage to find time to write, but I've also got some older material that may turn out useful eventually.

AW: Yeah, you're learning a lot while you're in a program so you need time for your brain to process what you've gained, and it takes time before you can apply that to the writing you're working on.

EB: Right. And your writing changes directions when you get out of workshop too. I mean, even as much as I want to fight it, there is the workshop poem. There is that signature poem—and it's different from program to program and faculty to faculty— that's obvious to everyone and easy to teach in workshop. And no matter how much of a rebel you are, you're going to write that poem at some point.

AW: Casey didn't do an M.F.A. You didn't take any workshops either, did you?

CC: No. I decided to stay on at South Carolina after Dickey's death and do a lit PhD. So yes: no workshops, no AWP for me. Just learned the old way, which I've found is very unpopular.

EB: You're so unpopular.

CC: I know.

[laughter all around]

EB: Most of the way I learned was through apprenticeship. I didn't take a workshop at Sarah Lawrence and with the mentoring you get to see how writers' minds work. I can't really say I wrote like crazy, but I learned like crazy: from people, about people and their poems.

AW: Which is a healthy attitude.

CC: It's strange. I feel like I got more from Dickey just speaking with him in his office, sick as he was. Many of the people I've talked to who had him multiple times in class didn't seem to get as much.

EB: Some of the most important things I learned came from talking with Kate Johnson(?) in her office. She started going to the Westchester Psychoanalysis Institute when I was a junior, and she eventually became a union analyst. That gave her some unique expertise that proved useful for her poetry. Another important lesson—maybe "the most important"—I had was one the time when I brought in a poem and the teacher read the first line and then just looked at me. I looked back at him and he held out the poem over his trashcan and dropped it in. And then he said, "Doesn't that feel good?" and I was like, "You know what? It does. It totally does. It does feel good."

[closing laughter]

The Least You Need to Know

- Reading period material affords your work historical legitimacy.
- Notes provide resources you can return to for verisimilitude.
- Travel gives you a powerful sense of setting.
- Interviews provide other voices to enrich the story you want to convey.

Revising and Editing

Whatever sort of creative writing you do, it's important to revise and edit your work, especially if you write essays, poems, or short stories you plan on submitting to editors. No matter how much time you took to craft the first draft, you'll always find a few mistakes to correct or wording to revise when you read through your work again.

I've found it's best to set aside your first draft for a few days after you've written it. You need time to get the piece you've been slaving over out of your system. Don't just hit Save on the first draft and start again straight away on the second pass. You'll come to the work fresh if you leave it alone for a while. What you've written might make more sense if you sleep on it or go engage in some activities completely unrelated to writing.

For essays, try to allow at least a day. Fiction and poetry can sometimes take longer. Your mind will carry on, mulling over ideas, while you're doing other things. For example, many novelists I know recommend putting your novel aside for at least a month before starting the revision process, even if you work on another novel in the interim.

In This Chapter

- Utilizing your doubt
- Reading out loud—or not
- Choosing your words
- The size and scope of your work
- When development lags

When you pick up your work again, print it out and read over it quite quickly. Circle any typos and mistakes you spot, but concentrate more on the overall flow. If it's an essay, check for any gaps in logic or any sides of the argument you might have missed. If it's prose, look to see if any passages drag or move too fast.

This is the stage to sort out any big problems. Some writers even rewrite the whole thing (especially when working on fiction), starting afresh with a blank document on the computer. If you're better at getting it right first time, you might not need to do that. However, you might still find yourself cutting out whole paragraphs, adding new material, and changing the direction of the piece.

After you've done this, you might want to ask a friend and/or fellow writer to read the piece. Tell them not to look for tiny errors like typos or clumsy sentences at this stage. Instead, ask whether they think it's broadly okay, or if they have any reservations about the overall direction of the article or story.

When you've sorted out the big picture, you can start fixing any individual sentences and words. Again, it's a good idea to print out the document and do this on paper. I find I miss errors onscreen, especially typos that are valid words, such as *they're* for *their*.

Here are some common things writers miss:

- Typos and misspellings. A good tip is to read backward. You'll go much more slowly, focusing on every individual word instead of getting caught up in reading.

- Clumsy sentences and confusing or misleading phrasing—try reading your work aloud.

- Unnecessary words.

- Commonly misused or confused words.

If you're not 100 percent sure about a spelling, double-check it in a dictionary. The *Oxford English Dictionary* is the authority, but you often can get a convincing consensus by running a word search online. When you can't quite find the right word, using a thesaurus—electronic or print—can help.

Now it's time to explore the factors that will help your revising and editing go even more effectively: using your misgivings, reading aloud, paying attention to language and length, and developing underdeveloped areas.

Using Your Misgivings

Self-doubt is something that plagues most creative souls at one time or another. You might be going along, feeling great about your creations, and then something happens that shakes your confidence. Perhaps you get a rejection letter, or someone makes a nasty comment about your work. Perhaps you unfavorably compare your work to someone else's or your inner critic gets really loud. Or perhaps self-doubt just sneaks up on you out of nowhere, whispers in your ear, and suddenly you'd rather do anything but write. Self-doubt feels awful, but it comes up, so how do you move through it and return to your creativity?

For one thing, be gentle. Don't beat yourself up over your self-doubt. Yelling at yourself might work in the short term, but with most writers I've observed, this turns into a vicious cycle of beating yourself up, avoiding writing, more beating yourself up, followed by procrastinating writing, a final beating of yourself, and finally feeling like dirt.

Instead of going to your drill sergeant voice, try going to a gentle, parental voice instead. Try telling yourself something like, Hey, it's okay that you're doubting yourself right now. It happens. What small step could you take to feel a bit better?

It helps to be reminded of how fabulous you are, so to that end, I recommend keeping a kindness folder. In this appreciation folder, collect kind emails, letters, notes, tweets, etc. When you begin to doubt yourself, go to your kindness folder, read a few of the notes you've saved, and soak up all the collective love that's been directed at you.

Feeling appreciation and love from others is wonderful, but don't forget to give yourself love and appreciation, too. As the late pop singer Whitney Houston used to sing, "Learning to love yourself is the greatest love of all." I've witnessed how helpful it can be to writers when they write letters to themselves. It has been described to me as writing to your artist self from your wiser self. The idea is that your kind, wise self will know just what to say to lift you up. Then you print it out and put in the kindness folder.

It's also important to begin your treatment of self-doubt with baby steps. One of the best remedies for self-doubt is action. Most writers I know prefer to begin with gentle action—action that is full of kindness and permission and playfulness. And the best way to move into action when you're in self-doubt mode is to start small. Start with a doodle on a piece of junk mail, write a silly haiku, dance around your living room, sing in the shower, or play with crayons. Let go of the need to make a masterpiece and for then, for that moment, start with something that brings you delight—one teeny, tiny thing.

IDEAS AND INSPIRATION

Remind yourself of your accomplishments. It's easy to forget all you've accomplished. Take some time to make a list of how much you've already achieved. Looking back over old journal entries can sometimes help remind me how far I've come. On a smaller scale, you can keep an "already done" list each day to keep track of all the things you've accomplished instead of focusing on what you *didn't* do.

Finally, don't lose your sense of adventure; keep taking risks. It's amazing to me how despite self-doubts, writers can courageously keep putting themselves out there. And I want to simply encourage you to keep taking those risks, big and small, in your life and in your art. Taking risks helps squash those pesky self-doubts in a powerful way. Your risks might include trying out a new color, learning a new style, reaching out to a fellow writer, submitting your work to a magazine, posting your work online, or even opening a book shop. Not all your risks will have the results you want, but every risk gives you the inner knowing that you are capable of more than you realize. Be ambitious; go for it!

Reading Aloud or Not at All

Voice is one of those concepts in writing that can mean any number of things—so many that it often dissolves into something so vague it might cease to seem useful. Voice can be variably invested with meaning, mapped onto or found to underlie so many other aspects of writing; it plays a part in every point of the rhetorical triangle and acts as a sort of cognate for tone, style, point of view, personality, and purpose.

In creative writing, one of your long-term goals should be to find your own voice. In red pen in the margins of one of your essays, you might see its various incarnations. It's not something to be rushed.

The abstract notion of voice leads into the act of reading aloud. But personal conviction, active participation in communication, and that hodgepodge of ways voice factors into any piece of writing are all implicated in reading aloud as a standard practice.

As a writing teacher, I continue to take satisfaction in what writing students discover on their own simply by reading their work aloud. Although a student might find reading aloud to be somewhat intimidating, it greatly reduces the awkwardness for both writer and teacher, as reading through the draft can be done together with an active reader and active listener, rather than the teacher reading silently, and perhaps making marks with a pen, while the student sits nearby and sweats it out.

The practical benefits don't end there. In addition, this simple practice manages to catch more mechanical errors, and in a more efficient and shared way, than reading silently by either writer or teacher will. Mechanical concerns that escape the eye are caught by the ear and can be quickly corrected by the writer as he or she reads, or they can simply be noted and then discussed if the student has a specific question about a technical rule. Additionally, sentences that might be technically correct might still sound awkward or unwieldy when heard them out loud, leading the writer to reconsider phrasing and syntax, and often even logic and overall meaning as well.

IDEAS AND INSPIRATION

Pragmatically, reading aloud is a great way to get through the draft before the discussion really starts. But this simple practice can play a dramatic role in transforming the writer's relationship to the writing. Reading your work aloud gives voice to your writing in a way that puts you in a position to own your words, to connect the words on the page to your speaking, thinking, arguing self. Because of the discomfort involved in this process, it's paradoxically empowering and disempowering—which is precisely why it's so useful. When you read aloud, you're forced to take ownership of your words at the same time you're giving them away by sharing them with an audience. It's a confidence-builder.

Reading to a one-person audience in a tutorial session offers more to the writer than an increased awareness of a more abstract audience, although that shouldn't be discounted. Adding a listener into the chain of exchange between student and instructor reminds the student that the instructor is a listener, too. Even the silent reader hears writing, I would argue, more than we as writers often hear our words as we write them. Reading aloud can then lead to heightened investment in not only the meaning of the writing, but also the style.

So to sum up, reading aloud does wonders for proofreading. It can cause a writer to connect the writing task to their sense of self, and, thus, bolster their commitment to its improvement. But there's another sort of paradox at work in reading aloud, which is my favorite: at the same time you're asked to own your words and, thus, become potentially more invested in your work and conscious of how this writing task can represent yourself, you're let off the hook. You can change those words. You can, through dialogue, decide you really want to say something else. There's something about the way reading aloud demands commitment and starts the process of revision in a way that's quite unique.

Word Choice and Language

Some of us are both writers and editors, and some of us are not. Some of us can edit just about anything … except our own written language.

Editing can be much more difficult when it comes to your own writing. Part of the problem is that you've spent so much time with it. Whether you simply can't see your own mistakes, or you're being protective of your work, you can use the following techniques to help you polish your language and improve your writing.

An important thing to remember about editing is that it's not just a one-and-done process. Most work can stand one or two (or even more) polishes. Another thing to keep in mind is that you can perform edits in whatever order you're most comfortable with. You even can do some twice (with a great benefit, even), and you can skip some entirely. A lot of this depends on you—your tone, your style, your voice, and your most common mistakes. As you write more, you'll begin to identify the slipups you typically are prone to.

One of the first things you should check for in your written language is your use of synonyms and repetitions. If you're finding a lot of repetition, it's time to break out your thesaurus (print or online). Don't get too caught up with the thesaurus, though. The two most important things to consider when choosing alternative language are your voice, and your target audience's preferred reading level.

 WATCH OUT!

Don't choose offbeat synonyms for no good reason; they can become distracting to your reader. Along with synonyms, I want to address flashy or overconstrued writing—the so-called purple prose—all writers should watch out for. One hint that your writing might be a bit too flashy is that you secretly pat yourself on the back when it comes to language you deem clever ideas or interesting turns of phrase. Be careful of this.

Also, you're not a dictionary, so using one will aid your language immeasurably during your edit. I've misused words by complete mistake, but I've also done enough reading to see quite a bit of it in other writers. I think we tend to embed the meaning of a word based on where we first hear it, and a lot of times its totally incorrect.

Another aspect of language to be aware of in your edit is active versus passive voice. Most of the time passive voice comes across as weak. However, this isn't true 100 percent of the time. When you find a passive construction, see if it can fit and work, and still flow, as an active construction. Then trust your gut and go with what looks and sounds best.

Speaking of passive voice, also take note of too much weak language. By this, I mean passages that use "I think," "maybe," or "seems." Sometimes it's completely appropriate, but often your language will benefit from getting rid of it and instead presenting a firm statement or idea.

Lastly, and maybe even least, go ahead and use whatever other tools you have to finish your edit. Grammar suggestions, spelling suggestions, and other software tools do indeed have a place and can be useful.

Document Length

When editing for length, most often you'll be looking to refine and cut, unless an editor tells you your needs to have more of something such as dialogue or description. In prose, this process of hacking away at words takes place sentence by sentence.

Adding sentence variety to prose can give it life and rhythm. Too many sentences with the same structure and lengthiness can grow monotonous for readers. Varying sentence style and structure can also reduce repetition and add emphasis. Long sentences work well for incorporating a lot of information, and short sentences can often maximize crucial points. Observing this general rule can help add variety to similar sentences.

As for paragraphs, they can be as long or as short as you want them to be. They can unfold for countless pages or consist of one word—even one letter. An example of the latter would be as follows:

> "W—!"

(Here, someone attempted to shout wait "Wait!" but was cut off by a sudden blow to the head from behind.)

The determination to make in composing a given paragraph is not the number of sentences or words or letters, but the number of ideas. The rule of thumb—in nonfiction, at least—is that each paragraph should focus on one idea or concept. When you shift to a new idea, shift to a new paragraph, too. In fiction, its function is more nebulous because a paragraph functions as a unit of writing that further develops the story through exposition.

However, ideas, as we all know, are slippery things—difficult to package and unlikely to remain in their allotted places. How big or small is an idea? What about an idea within an idea (like a dream within a dream)?

Ultimately, a paragraph is complete when you decide it is. Any rules about them you might have picked up have descended from the well-intentioned but misguided efforts of educators to help students learn the fundamentals of writing. The topic-support-conclusion model is valid in that it helps developing writers discipline themselves to craft effective persuasive arguments.

 WATCH OUT!

> Opinions easily dissipate if they're not backed up by facts or reasoning. But the form is only that—a mold that can—and should—be broken once you learn how to use it. And dictating that a paragraph consist of a given number of sentences is an understandable but lazy approach that ensures that student writers provide details before moving on to the next idea. Yet it doesn't teach them *why* they must hit the given number—much like requiring a word count for an essay or report ensures that most students will grasp for quantity rather than strive for quality and resort to silly tricks like margin and font manipulation.

There are, of course, practical considerations in determining paragraph length. Readers of newspapers and other publications with narrow columns of text are more likely to read paragraphs that don't extend vertically more than a couple inches. Similarly, websites are easier to read when paragraphs are brief.

Take care to avoid paragraphs that extend for more than half a page in book manuscripts. When working in a Microsoft Word file, I break up paragraphs of more than 10 lines in 12-point type with a 6-inch column width for print publications and limit online copy to 5 lines, although results will vary depending on the point size and column width of the particular text you use. And to tell you truth, I regularly break my own rules.

Don't hesitate to adhere to or promote specific models of paragraph construction, but don't hesitate to break them either. Most importantly, pay attention to what the overall pacing of your narrative demands at all times, and be sure your paragraphs provide the required flow.

As for length in poetry, the poetic foot (remember that from Chapters 13 and 18?) shows the placement of accented and unaccented syllables, while pentameter shows the number of feet per line. In the case of pentameter, there are basically five feet per line.

The types of line lengths are as follows:

>One foot: monometer
>
>Two feet: dimeter
>
>Three feet: trimeter
>
>Four feet: tetrameter
>
>Five feet: pentameter
>
>Six feet: hexameter
>
>Seven feet: heptameter
>
>Eight feet: octameter

Rarely is a line of a poem longer than eight feet seen in English language poetry, although the poet C. K. Williams is a relatively well-known exception if you want to see how it works.

As with paragraphs and prose pacing, poetic lines and the overall poem should work in concert—doing what's asked of each other to generate the best overall work.

Developing the Underdeveloped

Underdeveloped aspects of a project can mean way too many things. You really have to look at the preliminary notes as a whole to see what's driving the problem. It also might not be easy to fix.

Here are some of the things that might be behind an underdevelopment issue:

- The characters might not have unique voices.

- They might not have character arcs.

- They might not have emotional journeys.

- They could be inactive and are simply moving from scene to scene.

- They might not have their own wants and needs.

- They might not have their own unique mix of traits.

- The names might sound too generic or too much alike.

I think when editors say "underdeveloped," what they're really saying is your writing is not real enough. They don't know who a person or place really is. I don't think you can fix that by adding a couple names. Instead, you have to delve into details.

For example, screenplay readers look for characters who are realistic and, in the case of the protagonist, relatable. Are they believable? Do they say and do things that could and should be expected of them in their circumstances within the parameters of the story world? Is the protagonist someone people can root for?

The trick to writing believable and relatable characters and narratives is emotion. If you can make people feel what the character feels and what's transpiring in a scene, the people become involved. They subconsciously transfer empathy to the page and want to see the characters succeed. Equally, a great antagonist makes people dislike him/her intensely.

If your characters are busy doing (that is, engaging in action) you might want to give them some opportunity to show their internal workings (i.e., feelings). A successful protagonist has to undergo emotional growth. You don't need big, melodramatic moments for that, but you also don't want a narrative that's underdeveloped. Instead, to enliven and develop your story, provide windows for the characters to show what goes on inside them in relation to the plot. Let the reader participate in their journey.

 **WRITING PROMPT**

Take an underdeveloped character from your journal or from a book or film you admire. Then add fictional qualities that would make the figure developed enough to serve as a protagonist in a given narrative.

The Least You Need to Know

- Pay attention to your misgivings to improve your narrative rather than allowing them to discourage you.
- Reading aloud is a great way to catch mistakes and improve your writing.
- Language is important in reflecting characters, the narrator, and the overall narrative.
- Length plays an important role in establishing pacing for a narrative.
- Watch out for underdevelopment, especially with characters and settings.

Getting Published

We've spent most of this book looking at the techniques and forms of creative writing. However, beyond the joy of writing, most writers want to have their work published for others to read.

There's no sure-fire formula for having your work published. It's mostly a matter of talent, persistence, and luck. First, you have to write very well—well enough to stand out from the competition—and you have to send your material until it reaches someone who appreciates it as much as you do. And no matter how well you write, you're sure to encounter plenty of agents and editors who, for various reasons, do not like your work. Getting published takes drive, determination, and toughness. It can also take years of dedication to the craft of writing.

Part 7 examines how to negotiate the gate-keepers of publishing—agents and editors—by looking at research, cover letters, the synopsis, and the intangibles of rejection and persistence. While I cannot guarantee the publication of your work, I can share the ways of going about it that are better than others.

Finding Agents and Publishers

When you've finalized a piece of creative writing, your next step is figuring out how you can share your work with others. If you want to project it beyond your immediate circle of friends and family, you'll want to publish it. To do so, you need to know whether you need an agent or can submit your material to publishers directly and also how you can most efficiently and cost-effectively go about this.

The first consideration in manuscript submission is whether or not you need a *literary agent* to seek and represent the sale of your work. This can be a tricky issue. Agents aren't required for all approaches to publishers. They only become involved when there's enough money in a publication deal to make their time and effort worthwhile. This means they operate almost exclusively in the realm of major trade publishing houses. It also means that although a short work of yours might lead an agent to have interest in something book-length, they typically have little interest in books that sell few copies. Even very well-known poets, for example, fail to sell half as many books as most any novelist.

In This Chapter

- Planning, planning, planning
- Writing good query letters
- Writing a winning synopsis
- Getting turned down and hanging in there

 **DEFINITION**

A **literary agent** is someone whose job it is to sell a writer's work to a publishing entity, negotiate advances and contracts, and manage royalties and copyright.

You probably don't need to bother with an agent if one or more of the following applies to your work—you can submit directly to the publisher:

- You are self-publishing.

- Your work is an article, short story, or poetry.

- You have a book that's more appropriately published by a small, medium, or academic press.

On the other hand, if you believe your book is commercial enough to interest an agent, here are some of the things a good one can do for you:

- Target the search for a publisher on publishers that are the best fit for you

- Fully understand the provisions of the contract offered by a publisher and be able to explain the terms of the contract to you

- Negotiate the best possible terms and advance for you

- Potentially edit the manuscript (not all of them do this) to make it more marketable

- Run interference for you during the publication process and the marketing phase

- Help you take the best-possible advantage of your publishing rights

- Handle the business matters for the book, including the collection and disbursement of royalties

Like many business people, literary agents work through networking. They mingle with publishers and other agents to determine what's on demand and at what general price. They usually make their offers of representation based on this knowledge. They also network to determine what publishers fit best with the clients they represent.

Reputable agents charge a standard commission on the advance and royalties from all uses of rights. All agent fees and commission should be collected out of book sale proceeds as they come in from the publisher. Publishing receipts generally come through the agent to you, so the agent usually takes out his or her cut as it passes through their hands.

WATCH OUT!

A significant number of businesses pose as serious literary agents. They use the publishing hopes of inexperienced book authors to prey on them. Thoroughly check out prospective agents and, in particular, watch out for agents who request money up front, ask for a reading fee, and recommend someone to improve your book for a fee.

The rest of this chapter is dedicated to helping you save time and money as you search for the right agent and publisher. I will tell you upfront that in my twelve-year professional writing career, I've already been through three agents and eight publishers. It's highly unusual to stay with the same publisher for your entire career anymore, and the book industry has been further destabilized by corporate buyouts and electronic media. However, it remains that a combination of research, effective correspondence, attractive project marketing, and old-fashioned persistence give you the best chance.

Do Your Research

The first step in finding a literary agent or publisher right for you and your work is to put together a list of recent books that you admire or that you think are similar to your work. Then, take note of the publisher and/or who represents the authors of those books. Many authors list their agents on the acknowledgments page in the front or back of their books. If you can't find the agents this way, visit authors' websites.

You can actually use the same basic research methods to find both reputable agents and publishers. Do careful research up front, and target only those agents and publishers who can help you produce a high-quality book. Publishers and agents you target should possess previous success in profitably selling books similar to yours. This means you need to zero in on agents and publishers who would represent your work in the best light, give you the best benefits, and appear as the most reputable. Unfortunately, unless you don't mind making no money or taking a loss on a book you've spent considerable time writing, the ability to sell books like yours should be the bottom line in your evaluation of your agent and publisher options.

You can find out what agents and publishers are available and narrow down the best fits for your book in several ways. First, go to your local big-box bookstore and find the section of books most similar to the genre you want to publish. Note the publishers of these books, and check out the acknowledgment sections to see if specific agents are identified and praised by their client author. Then, when you're home, look up those books online. At some library sites and online bookstores (like amazon.com or barnesandnoble.com), you'll get a list of "similar books" like the one you looked up.

Back at the big-box bookstore, go to the writers' reference section, and write down the titles of some of the books that list agents and publishers. The most useful of these are the annual *Writer's Market* series published by *Writer's Digest* (also sign up for its constantly updating annual subscription online at writersdigest.com) and Jeff Herman's annual *Writer's Guide to Book Editors, Publishers, and Literary Agents.* These books are often available at public libraries for you to review in depth.

Also at the library, ask for the latest edition of the *Literary Marketplace,* known as the *LMP,* which will probably be in the reference section. This guide, printed in two volumes roughly the size of big-city telephone directories, is the bible for the publishing industry listing who does what and how to get in touch with them. The *LMP* contains a pretty comprehensive list of publishers, along with the genres they represent, the number of books they published the previous year, and contact names and addresses.

In addition, you can look for a subsidiary rights section on agent and publisher websites and note agents listed there (and elsewhere) who frequently place books with target publishers.

On the *Publishers Weekly* website (publishersweekly.com), the discussions on what's selling and to whom can be of interest. Especially check out "Hot Deal" section.

I'd recommend you subscribe to *Publishers Lunch,* an email newsletter covering what's being published and publishing deals being made. Find out more at publishersmarketplace.com.

For a fee, *Literary Agent Research and Evaluation* (agentresearch.com) will review a summary of your work and provide you with the names of agents who have sold similar work. The Writer's Digest University (writersonlineworkshops.com) also offers this service.

Finally, search online for agent lists. Two places to start include *Bloomsbury Review* (bloomsburyreview.com), which offers listings of agents, and WritersServices (writersservices. com), which gives listings, from *The Writers Handbook,* of agents in both the United States and the United Kingdom.

When you have a list of appropriate agents or publishers, you can start focusing on the most desirable of these.

Making the Most of Query Letters

Once you have a list of agents you think will be good for your work, send a *query letter* to each one. A good practice is to send five letters at a time, with each letter tailored to the specific agent you're querying. A query letter to an agent should be extremely well written and very brief— only three paragraphs that take up less than one page.

 **DEFINITION**

A **query letter** is an inquiry to an editor that contains a description of your writing and is designed to facilitate the editor's interest in your work.

In the first paragraph of the letter, explain why you are contacting the agent and why him or her specifically. In the second paragraph, give a three- or four-sentence synopsis of your book. Avoid going into detail about the twists and turns of the plot. In the third paragraph, include a short bio, offering information about yourself that pertains to your work or your writing skills. Close the letter with a direct statement of your ultimate purpose, expressing that you'd like to send the agent your manuscript.

Queries sent directly to publishers are somewhat more involved because you need to cover much of the territory that an agent would.

Open your publisher letter with a compelling statement of fact, an interesting anecdote, or another hook that will grab the editor's attention and separate your letter from the many others he or she receives every day. As a writer, you might prove skilled at this challenge, but remember that the editor knows absolutely nothing about your manuscript, so your opening sentences must adequately and accurately capture the essence of your work.

 IDEAS AND INSPIRATION

Editors who are honest sometimes boast about not reading past the third line of a query letter, so the ability to grab their attention right away is paramount. If you don't, the rest of your letter doesn't matter.

After the opening hook, segue into the title of your manuscript and a very short description of what it's about. Basically, you must condense your entire manuscript into two paragraphs so the entire letter fits on one page. Hit the high, unique points while revealing the purpose and tone of the manuscript, and choose accurate and vibrant words. If you don't convey enthusiasm for your manuscript, the editor might wonder why he or she should.

Then explain—again, briefly—why your manuscript would be of interest to the publisher's readers. This is your chance to demonstrate that you've done your research and impress the editor with your knowledge of the publisher. It's all about selling to readers, so be sure to cite parallel demographics, such as age and gender, and other factors that might apply. Your manuscript should come across as a perfect match for the publisher's needs. Not only should it seem promising but also necessary and profitable for the publisher to take your book.

Next, turn to your credentials, focusing first on any previous publishing credits you have. However, be careful about this. If your other books haven't sold well, consider listing relevant magazine publication instead. And if this is your first manuscript, include your educational credentials instead.

Other than a prior strong book-selling record, the most important factor is establishing your credibility about the subject matter, including any on-the-job, public-speaking, or teaching experience. Stay focused, and don't include any information that's not relevant to your manuscript.

Assure the editor that you're happy to answer any questions about your manuscript. This is a small but important point because it conveys your willingness to entertain and discuss changes. Most all manuscripts undergo changes of some sort, and some writers are more willing to perform them than others. Editors sometimes can be reluctant to work with stiff curmudgeons, regardless of how promising the manuscript might seem.

At the end of your letter, thank the editor for his or her time and consideration, and state that you look forward to hearing from them.

Before you send anything, spend at least a couple days proofreading and editing your letter *ruthlessly.* Editors have been known to discard entire manuscripts because a cover letter contains one misspelling. This response might seem severe, but there's some truth in an editor's fear that a writer who submits a sloppy cover letter will also submit a sloppy manuscript.

Drafting a Good Synopsis

Remember the synopsis from Chapter 20? You'll need it here, too. In this case, the purpose of your synopsis is to inform a literary agent or publisher about your book in a concise, appealing fashion, conveying that you're in command of your subject matter. If you want your manuscript to be given serious consideration, a good synopsis is a crucial part of your submission.

The Writers' and Artists' Yearbook can tell you that most publishing houses no longer accept direct submissions, but those that do (usually the smaller houses), usually ask for a cover letter, synopsis, and sample chapters rather than a whole manuscript in the first instance. The same applies to literary agents.

To put it simply, the sample chapters are to show how you write, and the synopsis is to explain what happens when they've finished reading them. This helps the publisher/agent whether decide if it's worth their time to read more. If they do want to read more, they'll ask you.

So if you want to have your manuscript read in its entirety, you must invest time in getting your query letter and book synopsis right.

Before You Start Your Synopsis

Many writers can get disconcerted and nervous by having to produce a synopsis, and there are usually two reasons why.

First, a writer might have an unwieldy story they themselves are not 100 percent convinced by, or a nonfiction project they don't really know enough about. If this is so, summarizing can be difficult because the writer hasn't put in the necessary level of thinking and planning for the project.

> **WATCH OUT!**
>
> If the summary process seems difficult for you, I urge you to ask yourself why. If it's because the story is insufficiently clear, persuasive, or gripping, you need to put in more work to get your manuscript into the kind of shape that would persuade an agent or editor to consider it further.

Second, you genuinely might be able to write a good book but not be experienced in the art of summarizing a work in an effective manner. Maybe you even consider the act of doing so demeaning. If this is the case, I urge you to think not of yourself, but of your future reader, and treat the project as a literary exercise that you should try to enjoy. Make it a challenge and opportunity to show off your work in its essential form. It might help to refer to book blurbs, or plot summaries in reference books such as *The Oxford Companion to Literature*.

Do You Know Your Market?

In addition to letting a publisher or agent know what happens in your manuscript, the synopsis also tells them at a glance if you've thought about how your work fits into the market. This is critical in nonfiction and less so with fiction, although with fiction, awareness of what genre your work fits in is vital.

Also, if what you're writing coincides with any major anniversaries, for example, or if it might have a marketing hook of any other kind, this is important to mention, if not within the synopsis itself then within your query letter.

Do You Know Your Genre?

There are fundamental differences between different kinds of synopses. A fiction synopsis, for example, should comprise a brief summary followed by a more detailed synopsis. But before writing either of these, you must clarify which genre your work fits into.

The most important thing to realize about fiction in respect to how you present it to publishers or agents is that it breaks down into different types. Broadly speaking, here are the most popular genres today:

- Chic lit
- Crime
- Detective
- Erotic
- Fantasy
- Graphic
- Historical saga
- Horror
- Psychological thriller
- Romantic
- Sci-fi
- Thriller
- Young adult (YA)

Classifying your novel within a genre can be a challenge. This is largely because when most people start to write a novel, they do so without having really studied the genre they're writing for. Although, when you start to write, you feel free to explore, practice, and experiment without thinking in terms of the defining limits of a genre. Then, when you begin submitting your work to publishers, it's very important to know which genre your work fits into. In all art forms, there are rule breakers, but almost inevitably—as in the cases of, say, Picasso and Virginia Woolf—even the greatest artists have studied the traditional forms and genres before taking any risks.

Writing Your Synopsis

Having made it your top priority to identify what type of novel you've written, you can make a start on your all-important synopsis. All good synopses should begin with a brief summary of 30 to 75 words. Think of what appears on a book's back cover.

Following the brief summary, write a more detailed synopsis of 350 to 450 words. Literary agents typically don't want a detailed chapter-by-chapter breakdown (if they do, they'll ask for one) because reading them can be tiresome and difficult to follow.

Your main goal in the longer synopsis is to give a detailed overview that clearly and concisely conveys how the story flows and unfolds and what's interesting about it. It also should reconfirm when the story is set, establish the setting or background, introduce the central character, and give a brief reference to other characters who are directly pivotal to the plot. It also should highlight the dramatic turning points and tell the reader of any other salient information that will help convey what kind of work it is, how well imagined the characters are, and how well thought through and alluring the plot is.

As opposed to a fiction synopsis, one tailored for a work of nonfiction performs a different function. The consideration of whether a nonfiction book has a potential market is generally more straightforward than for new fiction. In the case of nonfiction, you certainly should have carefully researched your market before submission and ideally list the competitors in the field, outlining why your project is different and why you're the writer best positioned to write the book you have.

> **IDEAS AND INSPIRATION**
>
> You should be able to list any marketing opportunities you believe your nonfiction book might have, such as identifiable, or even guaranteed, readers such as students if you teach a course, anniversary tie-ins, and so on.

Synopses, Agents, Editor, and Publishers

A literary agent is often prepared to sell a nonfiction work on synopsis and chapters only—an extreme rarity in the case of fiction. This is because it's easier for people to see if there's a market gap that can be filled by the project before the work is finished.

You might not need an agent for more niche types of nonfiction books. In these cases, publishers may well be prepared to take direct submissions from you. Again, this is because in the area of self-help or business books, for example, a publisher will know clearly where the gaps in its list are. In addition, a publisher might have a standard format it publishes books (such as this *Idiot's Guides* series). Research these formats and series, and contact editors' and publishers' specialized lists to find out if they have space for your idea. You also can request guidelines on how they like manuscripts to be presented.

In general, I think it's best for the nonfiction writer to prepare two different types of synopses. The first forms an initial pitch, and the second serves as a follow up if the editor or literary agent asks to see more. Both documents need to be thoroughly persuasive because these might go directly toward securing a book deal.

The initial synopsis should be no more than one or two pages. Include a brief summary and a description of the contents of the book, with an argument for why it should be published now and why you are qualified to write it. Ideally, you should also include an overview of other work in the field and argue why yours fills an important gap. In addition, include a chapter breakdown, giving a provisional title for each chapter with a brief summary, of about 30 to 60 words, of the contents of each chapter to show how the book is structured.

Here also, spell out any ideas you have about how the book might be marketed. Nonfiction markets are more specific than fiction markets, so it's beneficial for you to help the agent or editor know what hooks might help sell copies. As I've said, if you're lucky enough to have any guaranteed markets, such as students in a course you teach, inform the industry of this.

If you can estimate a word count for the length of your manuscript, do so. For some preformatted nonfiction titles, you'll be expected to hit a word length.

The more in-depth synopsis with sample chapter should include the initial pitch, but also include any additional material to defend your position as author or the book's market chances. Most importantly, in the longer pitch, you need to show that you can write the book. Provide more in-depth chapter breakdowns (100 to 150 words each) and critically 5,000 to 10,000 words of polished, irresistibly clear, and well-written text to show that you're capable of executing your intentions in a winning manner. I advise writing the introduction and the opening chapter if possible to really show you mean business. Those two together usually take you to between 5,000 and 10,000 words.

While it's worth spending time ensuring you have a good, short, confident synopsis, there's nothing as important to an editor as the quality of your writing and your ability to sustain the interest of a reader in the main body of the text. A synopsis isn't a magic wand that will influence the real standard of a work. I've seen perfectly polished synopses followed by poor writing. With this combination, you get an editor excited, only to be let down.

If you have the skill to write a gripping synopsis, ensure that you've used your energies wisely in advance of submitting and be sure your manuscript is as good as it possibly can be.

Dealing with Rejection and Staying Persistent

All creative writers have received rejection letters from publishers, editors, and agents. It just goes with the territory. These rejections can be crushing, especially to young writers. However, the more you submit material and the more you write, the less these passes on your work will bother you; your skin will thicken. Also, when you get past any disappointment, it's important to note there are levels of rejection, and you might find that you progress up these levels as you work toward getting published.

Types of Rejections

The most common type of rejections is a form letter. You might receive something boilerplate like: "Thank you for submitting your manuscript, but it is not right for us." There also might be a scribbled illegible squiggle of a signature, with no real name printed.

You then progress to personalized rejections. You might get something like: "Thank you for submitting your manuscript to us. While I enjoyed reading it, I felt that it was not strong enough a story for us to be able to publish it." This one will have a real person's name and signature on it.

A personalized rejection is a success of a kind, even if it's negative. (I once received a postcard that simply read "No.") Why? Because your manuscript was good enough to merit a personal reaction that could not be captured by their form letter. Such letters sometimes can prove to be (although not always) very valuable information.

Before you send your manuscript out again, have another person read it and see how you can make it stronger. I know that's difficult, but the more informed people who read your work, the better your chances of making your manuscript stronger in all its aspects: story, characterization, writing, and so on.

IDEAS AND INSPIRATION

The more specific feedback you get in a personal rejection, the better. This is for two reasons: more specific feedback helps you fix what's wrong, and also it means you're near to having something publishable.

If you get a rejection that says something like: "I really enjoyed reading it and got very caught up in the story. However, I couldn't relate to Marjorie and somehow didn't understand her motivation. I also found the ending to be somewhat weak," then you're really near success. In fact, the next place you send your manuscript might take it with virtually no changes. You don't necessarily have to make Marjorie easier to relate to, make her motivation crystal clear, and give a stronger ending before sending it out again. But if nothing else, you should consider the editor's points.

What you will find frustrating, in addition to rejection, is that not all rejection letters agree. Another might say, "I loved Marjorie! What a great character," and have issues with the manuscript that were lauded by other editors. What do you do then? That's a judgment call. There's no harm in making sure Marjorie is very easy to relate to, and that you make her motivation strong without being patronizing to the reader. But on the other hand, you can't please all the people all the time and maybe you should go with the consensus of opinions. Ultimately, you have to decide.

If you find that you're not progressing beyond the form rejection letters, I recommend you revisit your story completely or perhaps even abandon it in favor of another. I know this is difficult, but those form letters have their own message to you, and it's that your story is far from publishable in its current state.

Keeping the Faith

Even though you should know published writers always generate some material that will never be published (myself included), having your manuscript repeatedly rejected is hard. It just is. However, your success in continually sending it out or moving on to another one is what makes the difference between failure and setback.

Here are a few tips for coping with rejection:

- Laugh at your rejections. I've known writers who have made collages out of their rejection letters, burned them in their fireplaces, and even used them as toilet paper.

- Learn from your rejections. I've talked about this one.

- Always have a new project underway—something that will give you hope no matter how many rejections come your way for the previous project. If a rejection does arrive, it helps to know you have four other pieces in the hands of editors.

Finally, you might take some consolation in knowing the rejection history of these notable writers and works:

- *Dune:* 13 rejections

- *Harry Potter and the Philosopher's Stone:* 14 rejections

- *Jonathan Livingston Seagull:* 18 rejections

- *A Wrinkle in Time:* 29 rejections

- *Carrie* by Stephen King: 52 rejections

- *Gone with the Wind:* 38 rejections

- *A Time to Kill* by John Grisham: 45 rejections

- Louis L'Amour, author of more than 100 western novels: 300+ rejections before publishing his first book

- Ray Bradbury, author of more than 100 science fiction novels and stories: 800 rejections before selling his first story

- *The Tale of Peter Rabbit* by Beatrix Potter: rejected so universally the author decided to self-publish the book

And now for a few specific rejection letter excerpts:

- George Orwell's *Animal Farm:* "It is impossible to sell animal stories in the U.S.A."

- Norman MacLean's *A River Runs Through It:* "These stories have too many trees in them."

- For an article sent to the *San Francisco Examiner* by Rudyard Kipling: "I'm sorry, Mr. Kipling, but you just don't know how to use the English language."

- For *The Diary of Anne Frank:* "The girl doesn't, it seems to me, have a special perception or feeling which would lift that book above the curiosity level."

I hope reading of others' rejections makes you feel better about your own, if you've received some. Simply writing this section has gotten me energized to write and submit new work. Maybe you should return to it if a particular rejection letter gets you down. In the meantime, take heart and get to work. Remember, you are the sole arbiter of your imagination.

The Least You Need to Know

- Research is important for finding the right agent and publisher match for your work.
- Query letters are crucial extensions of your manuscript.
- A synopsis should hold a reader's attention as well as your manuscript.
- Rejection is inevitable; persistence is what makes successful writers successful.

Publishing Your Work

In Chapter 23, we looked at finding the best agents and publishers for your work. In this chapter, I expand on the publishing part a bit more.

Everyone's experiences with publishing are different. There's no magic formula to getting your creative writing published, but some basic guidelines should help you along the way.

In This Chapter

- Doing more research
- Writing more queries
- Getting turned down
- Don't give up!

Submitting to Publishers

Before you approach a publisher, you usually need to have written at least part of the book or the entire story/poem/essay you'd like to get published. Most publishers have certain requirements for submitted work, which you probably can find on their websites. For example, some fiction publishers want to receive a sample chapter and a brief synopsis of the plot; others prefer a full manuscript. Before you send a manuscript, it's a good idea to find out what's required. Also, look up the name of the person you should send your submission to.

IDEAS AND INSPIRATION

Many book publishers, especially publishers of fiction and poetry, publish a book only after a writer has proven him- or herself by publishing work in magazines and journals. Another good way to establish yourself is to enter competitions. Even if you don't win, an honorable mention is still good for your writing résumé. Thus, the usual path to having a book published involves at least some publications in magazines.

Always prepare your submission according to the publisher's requirements. Details are important, so be sure your work is professionally presented and has been carefully proofread. The manuscript should be double-spaced, with generous margins, and printed on one side of the paper only. The pages should be numbered, too. It's usually best not to bind or staple the manuscript: use a fastening that will allow the publisher to photocopy the manuscript easily if they want to.

Accompany your manuscript with a brief cover letter. The main purpose of this letter is not to sell your manuscript, but simply to touch base with the publisher and provide your contact details. You might want to give a little bit of background about yourself and maybe a short description of the manuscript. It might be worthwhile mentioning your publishing history as well. For example, if you have won a short story competition or had short stories published in magazines, this information will be relevant if you're submitting a novel or short story collection.

Send your manuscript by post or internet—whatever the publisher prefers. If it's conventional mail, be sure to include a stamped self-addressed envelope for the publisher's response.

Most publishers receive countless unsolicited manuscripts, so it shouldn't be surprising that it can take some time to get a response on your work. Some publishers send you a brief note—often a preprinted card or email—to say they have received your manuscript and give you an indication of how long it will be before you hear from them. It's common not to hear back for at least a month or two, and some take much longer. Be patient, and use the time to work on other writing projects, as mentioned in Chapter 23. The worst thing you can do is sit around fretting about a process you can't control.

Now let's take a look at the major elements that lead to getting published. Although they are similar to the topic of the preceding chapter, that material was aimed at agents and editors, whereas this chapter is solely about getting your work into print. Between the two chapters, you'll have a solid approach for handling the often enigmatic publishing industry.

More Research

If you want to be a writer, it's important to do your own research to educate yourself about the profession. Don't expect everything to be handed to you. For another thing, the internet is forever reflecting changes in publishing changes, and you should keep abreast of these. New publishers come along all the time; others fold all the time. Thus, any list of publishers I provide here will be outdated by the time this book hits stores.

Instead, I can tell you what to look for and how to do the research so you can figure out what publishers are right for you. Ideally, you'd do all this research before you submit anything. Before you send a query letter or a manuscript, you should do some legwork to come up with your submission list.

As in Chapter 23, one of your first stops should be a bookstore, preferably at least one outpost of each major chain operating in your area: a major general retailer that sells books (Target, Walmart, etc.) and any independent stores in your area that sell the kind of book you write. Go to the section where you think your book would fit, and look at who publishes those books. Those are most likely to be your potential publishers.

If you don't find books from a publisher in any of the stores you check, that's a bad sign. It's harder to judge electronic-only publishers this way because many of them only sell through their own websites and don't have books in stores. That's where you'll have to do more research.

Next, check the organizations representing your genre. Most professional writing organizations list publishers. Membership in the Science Fiction and Fantasy Writers of America (sfwa.org), for example, gives you access to science fiction and fantasy publishers. Romance Writers of America (rwa.org) maintains a list of publishers as well, although you have to join the organization to access it. (If you're writing romance, you owe it to yourself to join this organization to learn about the industry.) Mystery Writers of America (mysterywriters.org) also maintains a list of approved publishers. The Horror Writers Association (horror.org) has a list of recognized publishers, too.

 WATCH OUT!

Check sites like Preditors and Editors (pred-ed.com) and Writer Beware (sfwa.org/other-resources/for-authors/writer-beware) for alerts about possible scams. While you're at it, search for the name of the publisher and see what comes up beyond its own site. One or two complaints might mean embittered writers stinging from rejection. A pattern of complaints or complaints from writing organizations is a big red flag. Agents often discuss real publishers that have engaged in questionable business practices on their blogs, and that should come up in searches, too.

You'll also want to perform an Amazon search for the publisher's titles. Look at the reviews, and note the ones that mention bad editing or lots of typos. You can't judge by just one book, so look for a pattern from that publisher. If most of their books are criticized for bad editing or a lot of typos, that's a bad sign.

Also be wary if most of the titles that come up in your Amazon publisher search aren't actually sold through Amazon but rather through outside sellers. Amazon sells so many books; if it doesn't carry something, there could be a reason why.

Remember, too, that a legitimate publisher makes money by selling books to readers, not by selling books, publishing services, or marketing services to authors. I'd be concerned with any publisher whose acceptance letter contains a menu of optional services like editing, enhanced cover treatment, publicity services, etc. An acceptance letter should only talk about what the publisher will pay you, editing, and publicity. (You might do a lot of your own publicity, but you make your own decision about who to hire and what to pay. You don't pay your publisher for publicity or sending books to Hollywood.)

In summary, don't submit to a publisher without at least checking the alert sites and performing a thorough internet search. Moreover, take the time to determine which publishers produce books that resemble your manuscript. You'll save a lot of paper, stress, and time if you do so.

More Cover Letters

The first thing a publisher sees when your submission package is opened is your cover letter. Your creative writing might be stellar, but this letter can make or break your submission depending, on the editor. After all, this is your first point of contact with someone who, potentially, has part of your creative writing future in their hands, so make the right impression the first time.

For one thing, the letter should be beautifully presented—typed on good quality paper and clean. The person opening your submission package is someone with whom you hope to build a professional relationship. Think of your letter as a job application.

Personally address your letter to the right person. Find out if the agent or editor you're approaching is a Mr. or a Ms., and be sure this is the right person within the organization to handle your genre. Mistakes here show you haven't done your research, which in turn throws a question over how serious you are about getting into the publishing business. Why should an editor spend time reading your submission if you haven't spent time finding out how they spell their surname?

Clearly include all your contact information. Add it in the header or footer of your manuscript, too, just in case the cover letter becomes detached from your submission as it's passed around an editorial office.

Include your book's title, genre, and word count. (The word count immediately tells an editor whether your book is of a commercial length.) Make your letter succinct—a maximum of one page. Try to summarize your book in one or two killer lines. You might need to practice this to get it right, but these will be lines you use continuously.

IDEAS AND INSPIRATION

Don't start your letter with a question the editor might answer "no" to. For a fiction submission, ensure the letter is more about the book than you. Your Himalayan adventures can go into the author profile. For nonfiction, platform and qualifications are very important, so your query should be roughly 60 percent about your book and 40 percent about your platform. (If your book is about surviving in the Himalayas, your adventures are relevant and important.) If you're submitting nonfiction, make it clear why you are the best person to write this book. What are your qualifications/ experience?

Never say you're the next J. K. Rowling or Dan Brown, but do mention other authors whose style your own is similar to. This can give the publisher an idea where you see your book falling in the market.

Also be sure to show you actually can write. Proofread your letter to eliminate typos, tangled sentences, and waffling.

Only pitch one book in this letter. Your book might be part of a trilogy, but that's not the most important thing about it, and if you can't sell one book, you won't be able to sell the other two. Mention in the closing line that you see this book as part of a series if it's really important.

Follow the publisher's submission guidelines assiduously—it's not difficult. Try not to irritate the editor you're submitting to by including the whole book when they've asked for three pages. If they like your book, they'll ask for more. If they only ask for three chapters and you feel your book starts taking off at chapter five, don't send the five chapters. Instead it's on you rewrite those first three chapters if that editor's consideration is really important to you.

Remember that writing for an editor is simply writing for another readership. It's a tough, knowledgeable readership, but you can find all kinds of things about what they prefer (such as what books they've published in the past). It's a balancing act of playing to their preferences and them being the appropriate publisher to begin with. If they're not, move on to the next most likely one.

More Rejection

The final sentence in the last section sounds easier to do than it really is. Rejection is never easy, especially when it comes from someone you respect and hoped to work with.

As a creative writer and teacher of creative writing, I always want to comfort a discouraged student with a line like, "I view rejections as evidence of growth." But to the novice, such advice might sound like, "Eat your spinach; it's good for you." Well, spinach *is* good for you, but if you really hate the taste of it, you're not going to eat it. Similarly, getting rejections might be good for you, but only if they don't cause you to give up submitting material to editors. As noted in Chapter 23, I dutifully eat my spinach—that is, I still get rejected.

It's a healthy fact worth keeping in mind: all successful authors get rejections. When I learned that an award-winning writer I respect named George Garrett had seen all of his 40+ books rejected at least once, I couldn't believe it. Yet successful writers grow as a result of rejection; they learn from the experience. Some aggressive novices even ask editors for advice. They query editors of referred journals for copies of the reviewers' evaluations of their manuscript. With this kind of feedback in hand, rejections can become painful blessings.

Perhaps the best advice for dealing with rejections is to study the rejections immediately, make the necessary improvements, and promptly send the manuscript to another publisher. If you received no feedback, either ask for it or quickly examine your returned manuscript for editorial marks. Then make the needed corrections, put the manuscript and a self-addressed, stamped envelope within another envelope, and send it to another publisher. Remember, often as not, the reasons behind rejections are unrelated to the quality of the manuscript. Rather, it's the subjective tastes of the editor running the show.

I believe there are two reasons for handling rejections hastily. If you leave the rejection on your desk, you'll dwell on them—even if only in your subconscious—and the slight will begin to loom and grow. Second, by promptly sending out the manuscript again, you decrease the time between acceptances, and this increases your number of publications. If your manuscript has any value at all, there's likely to be some correlation between your number of acceptances and the time your manuscript spends on an editor's—any editor's—desk.

Having been rejected many times, I can tell you—at least in my experience—there's no apparent reason or pattern to what gets turned down. I've had some of my best work turned down by good magazines and then had those same magazines accept material I deemed—and still deem—vastly inferior in quality. I've even had an editor of a magazine who was just starting ask me for material and then reject it when I turned in my piece. Subsequently, it ended up in a better venue, and I attributed the novice editor's action to his lack of experience in publishing. However, I should warn you: both editors and writers can hold grudges for years over such scenarios. Obviously, you have to deal with rejection in the way that works best for you, but I hope you at least keep the focus on the work.

Editor and writers come and go, rise and fall, flourish and die; but the things you publish will reside in various libraries far into the future—when most all our names are forgotten and the paper the work is printed on finally is thrown out and/or crumbles to pieces.

IDEAS AND INSPIRATION

I've heard many successful writers remark, "If you haven't been rejected lately, it might mean you simply aren't trying hard enough."

Rejection shouldn't be the most difficult part of writing, but it is. I suspect potential authors don't write for publication because they don't want to deal with rejection. I learned early in my writing career that I would need to develop my own mechanism for addressing it. After a few rejections, I sat down and developed a process:

1. I always attempt to develop quality manuscripts. Usually, when I have a manuscript rejected, it's not because it's poorly written or poorly put together. Nor is it because my idea wasn't well thought out.

2. I target the manuscript for at least two specific journals. If one rejects it, I send it to the other.

3. When I receive a rejection, I read the cover letter and file the manuscript for a week.

4. I return to the manuscript and read the cover letter and the constructive criticism provided on a rating sheet or on the manuscript. (If no constructive comments are provided, I send the manuscript to the second journal).

5. When constructive criticism is provided, I weigh the comments and make those changes I feel are warranted. (Sometimes I don't make any changes.) I then send the manuscript to the second journal.

I don't suggest you copy my approach but rather develop a mechanism that's reflective of your own personality and psychological coping mechanisms.

Now, as a way of preparing you for what you might see in a rejection letter, I've gathered some particularly harsh and/or funny lines from rejection letters. I hope they demonstrate that in addition to being very intelligent and discerning in their tastes, editors can also be flawed and flat-out mean. No doubt you'll recognize the names of some of these rejected writers:

- On Jack Kerouac: "His frenetic and scrambled prose perfectly express the feverish travels of the Beat Generation. But is that enough? I don't think so."

- To D. H. Lawrence on *Lady Chatterley's Lover:* "for your own sake do not publish this book."

- On *Lord of the Flies* by William Golding: "an absurd and uninteresting fantasy which was rubbish and dull."

- On Sylvia Plath: "There certainly isn't enough genuine talent for us to take notice."

- On *Crash* by J. G. Ballard: "The author of this book is beyond psychiatric help."

- On *The Deer Park* by Norman Mailer: "This will set publishing back 25 years."

- On *Catch-22* by Joseph Heller: "I haven't really the foggiest idea about what the man is trying to say … Apparently the author intends it to be funny—possibly even satire—but it is really not funny on any intellectual level … From your long publishing experience you will know that it is less disastrous to turn down a work of genius than to turn down talented mediocrities."

- On *Lolita* by Vladimir Nabokov: "… overwhelmingly nauseating, even to an enlightened Freudian … the whole thing is an unsure cross between hideous reality and improbable fantasy. It often becomes a wild neurotic daydream … I recommend that it be buried under a stone for a thousand years."

Staying at It

If you read all those rejections, this is a good time to take up the topic of writerly persistence. It's more important than all the talent in the world.

In Chapter 23, I included a list of well-known books with the number of times they were rejected by editors and/or agent. How many "no" letters will you take before you call it a day? One? Ten? A hundred? It's an important question to ask yourself.

Everyone has different resources to draw upon to persist and keep at it. For me, I'd say the two things that helped the most were growing up on a farm and playing football. In that agricultural environment, I had to perform work when I didn't feel like it—if it was hot, tough, the garden needed weeding; if it was cold, tough, the stove required firewood. Later, when I played football, I happened to be on losing teams for several years. Almost every week, I'd go into the game knowing that even if I scored a couple touchdowns and made a bunch of tackles, my team wasn't good enough to win the game. Given those circumstances, do you loaf, quit, or somehow make yourself give your best regardless? The last option is what I'm talking about here: persistence.

Don't expect to be an overnight success in your writing because the chances are massively great that you won't be—although it will be a nice surprise for you if you are! Know that you have to put in hours and hours of work into this project—hours when you could otherwise have been watching television, socializing with friends and family, building a business, pursuing another hobby, or—my favorite—sleeping.

Unless you're lucky enough to be independently wealthy, you'll be writing as well as performing your day job—certainly for your first book and probably for your others as well. Know, too, that your book won't get written overnight. Even short stories take an investment of time. If you can accept all this happily (or at least, contentedly), it's easier. Putting in all these hours and resenting it seems too high a price to pay. Why put yourself through that?

IDEAS AND INSPIRATION

In truth, you should be enjoying the process for its own sake—because you love to write. The time spent writing should seem like a gift, not a burden. If it feels like a chore, question why you're doing it, and maybe consider calling it quits.

Having made these statements, even with the most formidable willpower in the world and the absolute certainty that writing is your life path, you still might have days you despair. At such times, you might take solace from the writers' cliché that the difference between a bad writer and a good writers is the ability to work on a bad day.

So there's one approach to the low times: acknowledging that there will be tough days and just accepting them. Having those days and feeling that you shouldn't have them is too high a burden. They will happen and they will pass, and that's all okay.

A positive attitude is one huge way in which you can put the odds of being published more on your side. Keep going when it seems impossible—both with writing your manuscript, and looking for agents/publishers—and you're already ahead of the many, many people who give up too easily.

Don't get me wrong. Not everybody's going to make it, and a stubborn refusal to realize if that means you, isn't doing you any favors. However, there's a huge spectrum between giving up too early and giving up too late—and most people give up too early.

Make up your mind now that you're not going to be one of those people, and your odds of success have just been dramatically boosted.

The Least You Need to Know

- Researching publishers helps find the right home for your book.
- Cover letters can make or break your chance with an editor/publisher, so do them right.
- Rejection is inevitable and part of being a professional writer.
- Persistence is perhaps the most important ingredient for successful writers.

Glossary

abstraction   A condensed, general idea or concept in a piece of writing.

action   The manifestation of feelings and thoughts through activity.

antagonist   A representation of the obstacles to the protagonist's, or the central character's, desires. It might be another human being or some other force. *See also* protagonist.

archetype   A recurring pattern or model from which similar patterns or models are drawn. Characters, action—even writing itself—can be archetypal.

atmosphere   The impression or vibe a given setting gives off to other characters and the reader.

authorial distance   How much the narrator intrudes on the story and the character's point of view.

authorial interpretation   The act of the author writing with an intent that can be identified within his or her work.

autobiographical   A piece of writing that is written by the writer and is about her or his own life.

backstory   A summary of an incident that has happened in the character's past. *See also* flashback.

blank verse   Poetry written in a style similar to free verse but blank verse poetry does not rhyme and does follow a regular rhythm—iambic pentameter.

brainstorming   A prewriting method in which you record ideas stemming from a single central topic or concept.

character voice   The primary speech, thought patterns, and attitude of a figure in a piece of creative writing.

characterization   The act of describing the qualities of someone or something in attempt to make them or it seem real.

concrete detail   A specific detail that forms the core of a piece of writing. Synonyms for concrete details include *facts, specifics, examples, descriptions, illustrations, support, proof, evidence, quotations, paraphrasing,* and *plot references.*

conflict   The heart of any narrative, conflict can be between the protagonist and another character, the antagonist; between the protagonist and nature; or the protagonist and society. It can also be internal or psychological.

contrast   The use of opposing elements, such as colors, forms, or lines, in proximity to produce an intensified effect in a work of creative writing.

cover letter   *See* query letter.

craft   A proficient skill in the art of making something—in this book, creative writing.

descriptive essay   A piece of writing used to explain something in detail, usually employing the five senses.

dialogue   A conversation between characters in a narrative. *See also* direct dialogue; indirect dialogue.

direct dialogue   Speech that addresses a character or reader, often by name.

distance   How far the reader is taken, by the narrator, inside the character's head.

dramatic irony   A difference between what a character says or does and what the reader knows to be true.

epiphany   A sudden realization in which someone or something is seen in a new light.

essay   A short nonfiction prose composition on a particular theme. *See also* descriptive essay; expository essay; persuasive essay.

existential   Dealing with or affirming human existence.

expository essay   A piece of writing in which the writer presents data, opinions, points of view, ideas, concepts, and arguments on a particular topic in an effort to explain it.

figure of speech   The opposite of a literal expression; a word or phrase that means something more or something other than it seems to say and departs from conventional order or significance.

first person   A point of view in which an *I* or *we* serves as the narrator of a piece of fiction.

flashback   A literary device that takes the reader to a past incident and shows it to him through action and dialog. *See also* backstory.

foreshadowing   A usually subtle advance hint of an action that will occur later in a narrative.

formal verse   Poetry following "rules" regarding stanza length and meter or rhyme patterns.

free verse   Poetry open in pattern and recognized as nonconforming and rhymeless verse.

free writing   The practice of writing nonstop about whatever enters your mind for a set period of time without making corrections or censoring anything. Benefits of free writing include making you more comfortable with the act of writing, making you aware of unconscious writing ideas and potential self-censorship, and improving your formal writing.

generalization   A broad statement that applies to many examples.

hyperbolic   A variation of *hyperbole*, in which something has been exaggerated or enlarged beyond what's reasonable.

imagery   The description of a person, place, or item using the five senses.

in medias res   The act of beginning a narrative in the midst of its action.

indirect dialogue   The act of summarizing dialogue.

indirect hook   A technique that arouses the reader's interest through surface inaction that focuses on everyday, highly relatable details. *See also* narrative hook.

irony   A literary device that presents a conflict between appearance and reality.

judgment   The act of evaluating if your writing is achieving its potential.

literary agent   Someone whose job it is to sell a writer's work to a publishing entity, negotiate advances and contracts, and manage royalties and copyright.

memoir   A record of events written by a person having intimate knowledge of them and based on personal observation.

metaphor   A comparison between two things, based on resemblance or similarity, without using the words *like* or *as*.

metonymy   The act of substituting something's meaning and/or attribute for its common name.

mimicry   The activity or art of copying the thoughts and speech of other character voices in creative writing.

narrative hook   An inciting incident in which the action of a story literally begins. *See also* indirect hook.

New Journalism   A type of writing that relies on the reporter's subjective interpretations and often features fictional dramatized elements to emphasize personal involvement.

oxymoron   When seemingly contradictory terms appear side by side.

pacing   The speed at which action takes place in writing.

personification   A figure of speech in which human characteristics are attributed to an abstract quality, animal, or inanimate object.

persuasive essay   Also known as the argument essay, this kind of writing utilizes logic and reason to show that one idea or position is more legitimate than others.

point of view (POV)   A way the events of a story are conveyed to the reader. It's the vantage point from which the narrative is passed from the author to the reader.

plot   The series of events providing conflict within a story.

prosody   The science of versification either in prose or poetry.

protagonist   The central character of a narrative. *See also* antagonist.

plagiarism   To use the words or ideas of another person as if they were your own words or ideas.

plot   Your protagonist's physical journey. *See also* story.

query letter   An inquiry to an editor that contains a description of your writing and is designed to facilitate the editor's interest in your work.

quilting   A writing technique in which the author forms a patchwork whole from many isolated pieces of writing.

research   The collecting of facts to increase understanding of a person, place, event, idea, experience, or thing.

rhythm   The natural rise and fall of voice when something is being spoken or read aloud.

scene   A clearly marked snapshot of a situation that involves one or more characters.

second person   A point of view in which the narrator tells the story to another character using *you*. The story is told through the addressee's point of view.

set   The physical objects that project, sometimes imaginatively, the world of a play.

setting   The location or locations in which a narrative takes place.

short story   A brief piece of prose fiction, usually possessing few characters and aiming at unity of effect.

significant detail   A detail that suggests something greater about a character or setting, making a narrative more plausible.

simile   A figure of speech that uses the words *like* or *as* when comparing two things—often two quite different things—in a way that helps the reader form a mental picture.

situational irony   The difference between how things look and how they really are. The difference between what happens and what should have happened.

stock character   A figure drawn from widely acknowledged cultural types for their characteristics and mannerisms.

story   Your protagonist's emotional journey within the plot. *See also* plot.

synecdoche   A type of metonymy in which the name of a part is substituted for that of a whole or vice versa.

synopsis   A brief condensation, outline, or summary of the main points of an article, book, or plan.

third person   A point of view in which the narrator relates all action using pronouns such as *he* or *she*.

verbal irony   What is said is the opposite of what is meant.

verisimilitude   The degree of lifelike reality present in a creative work.

world building   The concept of creating your narrative's setting through historical research.

Resources

Books About Creative Writing

Bernays, Anne, and Pamela Painter. *What If?: Writing Exercises for Fiction Writers, Third Edition.* New York: HarperCollins, 2009.

Gardner, John. *The Art of Fiction: Notes on Craft for Young Writers.* New York: Vintage Books, 1991.

Goldberg, Natalie. *Wild Mind: Living the Writer's Life.* New York: Bantam, 1990.

———. *Writing Down the Bones: Freeing the Writer Within, Second Edition.* Boston: Shambhala, 2005.

Hughes, Elaine Farris. *Writing from the Inner Self: Writing and Meditation Exercises That Free Your Creativity, Inspire Your Imagination, and Help You Overcome Writer's Block.* New York: HarperCollins, 1991.

Klauser, Henriette Anne. *Writing on Both Sides of the Brain: Breakthrough Techniques for People Who Write.* New York: Harper & Row, 1987.

Kowit, Steve. *In the Palm of Your Hand: The Poet's Portable Workshop.* Gardiner, ME: Tilbury House Publishers, 2003.

Lamott, Anne. *Bird by Bird: Some Instructions on Writing and Live.* New York: Pantheon, 1994.

Lerner, Betsy. *The Forest for the Trees: An Editor's Advice to Writers, Revised and Updated.* New York: Riverhead Books, 2010.

Masello, Robert. *Writer Tells All: Insider Secrets to Getting Your Book Published.* New York: Henry Holt, 2001.

McDowell, Robert. *Poetry as Spiritual Practice: Reading, Writing, and Using Poetry in Your Daily Rituals, Aspirations, and Intentions.* New York: Simon & Schuster, 2008.

Nelson, Victoria. *On Writer's Block: A New Approach to Creativity.* New York: Houghton Mifflin, 1993.

Rico, Gabriele, PhD. *Writing the Natural Way, Fifteenth Anniversary Expanded Edition.* New York: Tarcher/Putnam, 2000.

Saltzman, Joel. *If You Can Talk, You Can Write.* New York: Warner Books, 1993.

Shaughnessy, Susan. *Walking on Alligators: A Book of Meditations for Writers.* San Francisco: HarperSanFrancisco, 1993.

Books About Creativity

Briggs, John. *Fire in the Crucible: The Alchemy of Creative Genius*. New York: St. Martin's Press, 1988.

Cameron, Julia. *The Artist's Way: A Spiritual Path to Higher Creativity, Tenth Anniversary Edition*. New York: Tracer/Putnam, 2002.

Csikszentmihalyi, Mihaly. *Flow: The Psychology of Optimal Experience*. New York: Harper & Row, 1990.

Fritz, Robert. *The Path of Least Resistance: Learning to Become the Creative Force in Your Own Life*. New York: Fawcett, 1989.

Heckler, Richard Strozzi. *The Anatomy of Change: A Way to Move Through Life's Transitions, Second Edition*. Berkley, CA: North Atlantic Books, 1993.

Koestler, Arthur. *The Act of Creation: A Study of the Conscious and Unconscious in Science and Art*. New York: Dell, 1967.

May, Rollo. *The Courage to Create*. New York: Bantam Books, 1975.

Sinetar, Marsha. *Elegant Choices, Healing Choices: Finding Grace and Wholeness in Everything We Choose*. Mawhah, NJ: Paulist Press, 1988.

Ueland, Brenda. *If You Want to Write: A Book About Art, Independence and Spirit*. Thousand Oaks, CA: BN Publishing, 2008.

Organizations

Association of Writers and Writing Programs (AWP)
awpwriter.org
A range of useful information available for free, including a searchable directory of writers' conferences and centers.

Horror Writers Association
horror.org
Offers a list of recognized horror-genre publishers.

Mystery Writers of America
mysterywriters.org
Maintains a list of approved publishers.

Romance Writers of America
rwa.org
Maintains a list of romance publishers as well. (You have to join the organization to access it.)

Science Fiction and Fantasy Writers of America
sfwa.org
Membership gives you access to science fiction and fantasy publishers.

Writer's Guild of America (WGA)
wga.org
Aimed at screen and video writers for animation and new media. Useful links for aspiring film and television writers.

Trade Publications

Poets & Writers
pw.org
This magazine bills itself as the "nation's largest nonprofit organization serving creative writers."

Publishers Weekly
publishersweekly.com
Check here for all things publishing, plus a discussion on what's selling and to whom can be of interest. Especially check out "Hot Deal" section.

Script Magazine
scripmag.com
A wealth of resources for screenwriters is available online. This publication's website is a good place to start.

Writer's Digest
writersdigest.com
This trade publication covers practically every form and genre of writing imaginable.

Submissions

Duotrope's Digest free writer's resource
duotrope.com
Lists more than 3,475 current fiction and poetry publications.

"Top 50 Literary Magazines"
everywritersresource.com/topliterarymagazines.html
From the online reference source Every Writer's Resource comes this annotated list with links to some of the United States' best literary magazines.

Other Helpful Resources

Bloomsbury Review
bloomsburyreview.com
Offers listings of agents.

Literary Agent Research and Evaluation
agentresearch.com
A resource that will, for a fee, review a summary of your work and give you the names of agents who have sold similar work.

Literary Marketplace
literarymarketplace.com
This is the bible for the publishing industry listing who does what and how to get in touch with them.

Preditors and Editors
pred-ed.com
Offers many resources including potential scam alerts.

Publishers Lunch
publishersmarketplace.com
This email newsletter covers what's being published and publishing deals being made.

Writer Bewares
fwa.org/other-resources/for-authors/writer-beware
Check here for alerts about possible scams.

Writer's Digest University
writersonlineworkshops.com
Similar to Literary Agent Research and Evaluation, also matches you up with potential agents.

Writer's Guide to Book Editors, Publishers, and Literary Agents
jeffherman.com
Jeff Herman's annual guide to those in the publishing business.

Writer's Market
writersmarket.com
An annual series published by *Writer's Digest*.

The Writers' and Artists' Yearbook
bloomsbury.com/us/writers-artists-yearbook-2014-9781408192191
A comprehensive guide to "navigating the world of publishing."

WritersServices
writersservices.com
Gives listings, from *The Writers Handbook*, of agents in both the United States and the United Kingdom.

Prose Examples

Throughout the book, I've shared excerpts of my writing. In this appendix, I've culled the full versions of those works.

The Skeleton Woman
(creative nonfiction)

"Tell them I am going to show them what they are." This from my mother while dropping me off at primary school.

She'd agreed to come to Parent Show and Tell Day but we had to report to the teacher what our visiting parent would be talking about. I leaned forward to hug her and she kissed me on the forehead. I always looked up at her, reluctant to go.

"Go on now," she'd say after a moment.

But once I was out of the car I'd always turn around and wave, as if the hug and the kiss hadn't been enough. She would smile a warm, slow smile and then shoo me on with a flick of her wrist.

I'd walk away slowly so long as I could feel her eyes on my back. But when I sensed them move and heard the car pull away, I would stop and walk back, watching as she pulled out onto the road in front of the school. Her car was very loud and rumbled like a faraway storm. Unless a teacher made me move, I would wait listening until it reached the place half a mile away where the speed changed from 25 to 55. Then I would hear the sudden burst of sound that came when Mama stomped the floor. She didn't know it, but that was her real daily goodbye to me.

"Go Mama!" I would say in my mind and wonder if she heard me.

Her car was an old Mercury Cougar she'd bought years ago, before she quit her job. It had an engine called a V8, like the drink I liked.

"It's getting old, like me," she'd say sometimes, "but it's still got plenty of power. More than three hundred horses worth."

*

"My dad's going to bring his axe," announced a boy to our circle of boys. "He's a pulpwood cutter."

"Cool," said one of the other boys. "Mine works on cars. He's going to tell about an engine he helped build for a race car driver named Ward Burton."

The first one looked at me. "What's your dad gonna show?"

Me. "My dad can't make it, so my mom's coming."

"What does your mom do?"

Me, shrugging. "She stays at home a lot."

First boy. "Ha! That means she's a housewife."

"They don't even have jobs," another boy said. "What could she tell about? They just stay at home and do what dads say."

"Yeah," said the first one. "Think of how dumb that would be for show and tell."

Suddenly they seemed to remember me, then looked at each other and laughed.

"Housewife! Housewife!" they sang, laughing.

*

After lunch, the teacher went around the room, having inquired of the class who had a parent coming and what they would be showing or telling.

"My mom's a secretary," said the girl sitting next to me. "She's going to show how fast she can type and then give us our words to take home."

Then it was my turn. "My mom is going to show you what you are."

The teacher, frowning. "What does that mean?"

"I don't know. It's what she told me to say."

Class snickering, slow blush filling my face.

Teacher again. "What does your mother do?"

"She can do a lot of things, but she almost always stays at home."

"So your mother is a homemaker."

"Maybe. I don't know what that word means. I've never heard it before."

Low sing-song whispers from a corner of the room. "Housewife, housewife."

"Shhhh! Shhhh!" said the teacher, growing irritated. Then to me. "There's nothing wrong with being a homemaker, but you should ask your mother if there is anything special about what she does before she shows and tells. A lot of what homemakers do is unremarkable and the same. We don't want all the visiting mothers to say the same things."

*

I cried sometimes during naptime because I missed Mama so much. To help with this she had given me a toy version of her car that was exactly like it in every way. I would lie on my mat and run the car over my chest and up and down my arms making a soft low sound like faraway thunder.

But then in my mind I could see her face at home and tell she was unhappy. My head began to throb and I would cry, softly and quietly, hot tears running over my temples and curving round my ears. It hurt my heart to know she was all by herself and unhappy. I wished I could be there with her. When the teacher grew angry and told me to stop crying, I always felt bad and apologized to her.

I wanted to stop crying, but I couldn't.

*

By the time my mother completed her doctorate at the Medical College of Virginia in the late 1960s, her research had made her one of the world's experts on the pineal gland, and so she received the rare professional privilege of a job offer from the school that had granted her terminal degree. She had been the only woman in her graduating class and, when she accepted the job, the only woman faculty member.

The first course she ever taught was in a large, sloping, concrete-floored lecture hall. One entered at the back and made a long descent to the stage, where stood two long chalkboards and a lab table.

Mama nearly always ran late so that on the first day of class, when she entered the auditorium at the rear, arms full of books and lecture notes, the students, over a hundred of them, all men, were assembled and waiting for her. Her lab coat distinguished her as a professor, but the expressions on their faces as they turned to consider her—disappointment, anxiety, dismissal—told the tale of their collective shock.

Whispers as she begins the slow descent to the stage, heels clicking steadily on the concrete. About halfway down someone launches a brief, piercing whistle—ancient trumpet sound of male admiration—applauded by sporadic laughs from his fellows.

Mama keeps walking.

At the bottom she mounts the two steps to the stage and walks to the lab table, where she sets down her books before looking up around the lecture hall, squinting slightly in the lights, taking in the vague sea of male faces.

She takes off her coat.

"That's right! Take it off!" cries an anonymous voice somewhere off to the left.

"Take it all off!" exclaims another on the opposite side of the room.

Burst of laughter from all sides.

Hands trembling slightly, Mama takes hold of her lecture notes and turns to write on one of the chalkboards.

"Nice ass!" a voice calls.

Then a hollow, slightly grating sound of motion and muffled laughter. Turning from the board Mama spies an empty jar rolling down the central aisle, students seated to the far sides of the auditorium half-rising from their seats so as to follow it with their heads. Picking up speed, the jar hits against the bottom stage step and careens to one side. More muffled laughter.

Mama turns back to the board and keeps writing, listing her key terms for the day.

A minute passes, etched sound of idea transformed into symbol.

Then, again, the rolling sound—closer, louder, varied in texture—as the jar rolls over the boards of the lecture stage. Mama turning just as it glances off her shoe. Loud laughter this time.

As the sound dies, Mama walks to the lab table and sets her chalk down. Then she takes off her glasses and sets them down too. As she looks back up and out over the indistinct audience a slow, warm smile forms on her face—the easy natural smile of a cheerleader or prom court princess, both of which she had been. She looks to one side of the auditorium and then to the other, hands on hips, smiling.

"Cutie!" calls a voice.

"Hottie!" says another.

Smile still intact, unwavering, Mama strides across the stage to where the jar lies resting. Hands still on hips, attitude of sensual affectation, she lifts her right foot, arches an eyebrow at her audience, then brings it down suddenly, heavily, air of the room pierced as glass shatters, echoes, jagged irregular pieces sliding across the stage in various directions.

Silence, pause, then the lonely sound of Mama's heels as she walks back to the table, puts on her glasses, and looks up around the lecture hall.

"Let's get to work, gentlemen."

Another time, lab, students about to begin dissecting cadavers, and Mama circulating about the room, prepping the class, heavy merged smell of chemical preservatives and disinfectant.

A tall student raising his hand, beckoning her toward his group's examination table. "Professor, our specimen here seems to have a problem."

Smirks from the others in the group and the nearby tables as Mama peers down at the cadaver to discover that on his forever limp penis someone has placed a condom.

She glances up at the student who has announced the anomaly, then looks around the table, noting the clenched jaws of his fellows, inner cheek linings held in check by clenched teeth. Then she smiles at them, her slow, warm, cheerleader smile, as if she too shares in the jest.

Leaning forward, she reaches across the table to take hold of the cadaver's penis, tugging it out to its sad, unerect fullness.

"Hell yeah!" exclaims a student in another part of the room.

Then Mama's other hand in motion, bearing her scalpel. Sudden, deft flash of metal in the fluorescent light and her hand comes away with the leaden member.

Sharp, collective intake of air from multiple mouths and a couple of audible groans.

"This little thing isn't relevant or useful for this lab practical, or even to the semester's curriculum," she announces in her lecture voice, shaking the hand that holds it for emphasis. "It's just not useful."

With that she tosses it in the tableside biowaste container and moves on to inspect the cadaver on the next table, students falling back from her, two of them stumbling over each other, almost falling, as if some new invisible force surrounds this woman's body, emanating outward on all sides.

When she quit she took everything her grant money had purchased: microscopes, vials, petri dishes, burners, hamster cages, protein formulae, a cross-section composite of a fetal pig, even a human skeleton.

"Surely," said the department chair, "you are not taking the skeleton. It will be of little use beyond the academic community."

"He goes with me," my mother said, "And if I were you, I wouldn't be too sure of anything."

*

"There is … a class of monsters who might live, but which would always remain freaks."

—Charles Sumner Bacon, *"A Symposium on Obstetrical Abnormalities" (1916)*

Sitting on a shelf in a little windowless supply room just off one of the dissection labs was the Medical College's collection of genetic mutations: a dozen infants and fetuses afloat in large, clear glass containers of formaldehyde. I used to dream about them when I was younger.

The variations of these beings were obvious and subtle, shocking and secretive. Several were possessed of different degrees of encephaloceles, the meninges protruding from their heads' occipital region in a number of different shapes and geometric designs. What would that feel like? One was visited with holoprosencephaly, its nostril displaced and its optical qualities all fused together into a great single orb. What might such an eye have seen? And an instance of doubling to balance this cyclopean collapse: an infant possessed of one body and two heads, the result of duplication of the neural tube. What would these heads have said to each other? What would they have thought?

Later, in college, reading on my own, I would come across a poem about a baby that was half-child, half-lamb. "In a museum in Atlanta," it reads, "Way back in a corner somewhere/There's this thing that's only half/Sheep like a woolly baby/Pickled in alcohol …." I thought so much of the poem that I resolved to study writing under the man who had created it, hoping perhaps to develop the powers to commit my own real and imagined monsters to paper—to afford them a kind of immortality through my rendering, which might also, in turn—I hoped—provide me with something at last from them. "Are we," asks my old literary master, "Because we remember, remembered/In the terrible dust of museums?"

When I dreamed of them, they would move, but they never left their containers. Their meninges would pulsate, throb, with life. The mouths of the two heads would take turns opening and closing, bubbles emerging into the vat's closed liquid world, traveling upward. And then, very, very slowly, as if awakening even as I slept, the lid of the great single eye would draw back and the enormous orb would regard me—neither warmly nor coldly, but with some vague aspect of feeling—watching.

Little lamb, who made thee?

Dost thou know who made thee?

I suppose they did look monstrous and terrible, but I was never afraid of them. They were my friends.

If they could have smiled at me, they would have. And I would have smiled back.

*

The pineal gland is situated in the very center of the brain, in a tiny little cave-like enclosure beyond and above the pituitary gland, and directly behind the eyes—to which it is attached by the third ventricle.

It controls the biorhythms of the body, and though head injuries may activate it, it typically is triggered by changes in light, working in harmony with the hypothalamus gland to direct our emotions, thirst, hunger, sexual desire, and the biological clock that determines aging.

The Greeks considered the pineal gland our site of connection to The Realms of Thought. Descartes thought it the seat of the soul—the place where the interaction between the intellect and the body takes place. Myth and legend from a time before science? Even now there are those who refer to it as "The Third Eye."

*

Sitting together in a pasture meadow, patched quilt spread out beneath us, Mama's arm resting across my shoulders. Afternoon sun of spring casting long shadows of tree branches upon the ground, where the breeze flutters slightly the new blades of grass.

A blue bird, landing less than a foot from my foot, chirping and turning its tiny head sideways to regard me. Then he hops—three short, plump, quick hops—to the end of my shoe and bends forward, craning his neck to examine it.

I whisper something and he searches my face before hopping onto my shoe, glancing at me again, then launching himself, soaring up and then back behind us, toward the trees that cast shadows.

I turn back from the bird's path to discover Mama watching me intently.

"Why did the bird come so close, Mama?"

"Animals can tell things about other creatures."

"You mean just by looking?"

"More than just looking. We can't really explain what they do because we are not them."

"The little bird could tell about me."

"That's right. He could tell about you. That's why he came so close."

I lean my head against her and as I do she draws back her arm and then lets it fall, trailing her forefinger down my back, tapping each ridge of my spine as if marking a paper. Then the hand comes back up, fingers absently playing about my hair like butterflies.

"You are very nearly perfect," she says. "Just how I imagined you would be."

She draws me to her. "My precious creation."

After a while I pull away and look up at her. "Mama, I can tell about you. You're sad."

"I'm not sad, honey. I was only thinking."

"Does thinking make you sad?"

Short laugh. "It can, I suppose, but I'm not sad. You're here with me and when we're together I can never be sad."

Silence from me and she smiles. "Now, what are you thinking about?"

"I was thinking about the little bird who could tell about me. Do you think he'll be OK when it gets dark? I wish I could help him."

"I think he'll be OK, but it's good you want to help him. You must always help creatures and people if they need help and deserve it."

"Why do I have to help people? Who's going to help me?"

"When you get bigger you aren't going to need help, but because you will have a powerful ability to help people, you must always do so. You needn't help everyone. There are some who won't want it and some who won't deserve it, but you will be able to tell who they are. And remember that when you do help, it's the help they don't realize that helps the most."

"You mean the secret help?"

"That's right. The secret help."

"What if I don't know what to do?"

"It is part of a being's existence to make mistakes, but you have to be brave and try. Even when there are many people against you. That is what is called courage. Do you understand?"

"I think so."

"Then promise me you'll do it."

"I will, Mama. I promise."

*

Mama was always running behind. Usually it was because she had stayed up too late reading or perhaps had lingered too long in bed the following morning with her coffee and books. Sometimes if I was upstairs in my room she would call to me and tell me to go get her a refill to spare her having to get up.

She claimed she hated going anywhere, but she loved to drive. Rushing to town, hopelessly late, well over the speed limit, she was happy.

"Always go into a curve slow and come out of it fast," she would say, stabbing the accelerator as the road broke straight.

And, me, next to her, equally happy, standing on the floorboard, hands on the dashboard, peering out over it, wide-eyed, smiling. "Come out fast, Mama! Come out fast!"

Sometimes, if the road curved to the left, I would fall against the door. And if the curve to the right was a hard one, I would tumble over into her lap and lie there laughing, peering up into her face until she laughed too.

*

She kept the skeleton in a corner of the upstairs cedar closet. It was easy to miss on account of all the various things clinging to different parts of it: winter caps stacked upon its smooth head, heavy old shirts and frayed coats flung over its shoulders, an assortment of Christmas ornaments hanging from its lower ribs, and a child-sized basketball resting in its pelvis. The piled hats leaned slightly to one side, affording the skull a jaunty aspect, while the rough clothing drooping from the shoulders hung irregularly—not unlike rock-hewn prehistoric furs from some distant cold-climate predecessor of us. The basketball resting in the midsection suggested an impossible pregnancy, and the bone-suspended ornaments could not help but appear festive, speaking, it seemed to me, of some secret grisly truth yet to be celebrated. A big steel rod rose out of a metal base resting on rollers and ran upward through the spinal column before terminating in the skull, creating the illusion of a body somehow hovering in air of its volition, feet dangling three or four inches above the floor.

Despite the novelty of the thing's presence, the skeleton really was just another item in storage—something put away, half-forgotten. Sometimes when I was helping Mama in the closet, she would address the occupant with "And how are we today, my good man?" or "Excuse us, sir" or "Don't mind us, old friend." She always seemed happy to see him—an acquaintance from another time; a fondly remembered ally from a war long over.

I would visit him sometimes when I was upstairs alone, rush of cedar as I swung forth the door and flipped on the light. Carefully I would place my little hand against his, studying the contrast, and then pressing each of my fingers against a corresponding fleshless digit.

Even at that age I did not need my mother to tell me this was what I would be some day. That it was what lay in store. Some fundamental cognition knew. And it was comforting in a way, a privilege, to have this visual testament available day or night, close at hand and always the same, which seemed to say, "Beneath all the motion and coating of life, here is what you are."

I have no recollection of the truth of this ever troubling me. Perhaps it had something to do with the fact he did not seem to mind it so much himself. Whenever I opened the door, his expression was the same. He was always smiling.

*

Parent Show and Tell Day and Mama running even later than usual, the time for heading to school coming and going with her propped against her pillows, briskly flipping pages while sipping at her coffee.

"I'll just take you when it gets to be time for my visit," she said when I checked on her. "We'll visit school together. Now go and get me another cup."

Lunchtime passed and I was out in front of the house feeding butterflies, tips of my fingers all sticky with sugar water, when finally I heard her calling me. Upward patchwork flutter as I blew gently on my forefinger to dismiss my guest before turning to run around back of the house.

At first I did not think the woman standing next to the car was Mama, the figure in the sleeveless white spring dress and black heels and sunglasses appearing more like someone out of one of the women's magazines I had seen in doctors' offices. I hesitated, gawking. But then she smiled and waved for me to come on, and I knew it was her.

"Let's go," she called. "We're late!"

Spray of rocks and scattering of panicked chickens as we plowed up the driveway, windows all the way down and Mama humming softly to herself a song I did not know, while behind us, on the back seat, a third passenger lay sprawled.

*

Faster than ever, around the curves and over the straightaways, occasional dry click of bone from the back when the swaying of the car forced an arm or leg to adjust itself. Trio of bodies reacting in unison—dead or alive, no matter— moving as commanded by the physics of motion. Smiles on all our faces.

Then glare of blue lights in the rearview mirror and blast of a siren.

Me, pivoting, knees on the seat, chin atop the headrest, peering backward. "The police, Mama! The police!"

Silently we slow and drift onto the shoulder to the tune of crunched gravel, engine relaxing into a low, steady growl.

Me, staring back at the man in the hat and sunglasses as he considers our car before glancing down. Then, door opening, he rises from his vehicle, sunglasses removed: a tall gangly fellow, polished black belt and holster set in relief against a garb of brown and tan.

And Mama, June sun smiling down into the car upon her, pretty in her sleeveless dress, slender arms rigidly extended, hands on the steering wheel, knuckles white, daring the road ahead with a fixed stare, teeth set to grind, eyes shifting to the rearview mirror as the man approaches.

Me, watching as he comes on, slight sway to his stride, careless gaze resting on the back of Mama's head, ignoring me altogether. Watching still as he reaches the tail end of the car and leans forward, easy look drifting into the back seat— where something catches it, knocks it askew, then empties it of itself. Gaze jerking dumbly from the prone form to the back of Mama's head, before discerning her eyes in the rearview mirror, sunglasses removed, boring into his, fixing him in place. He stands there frozen, as if changed to stone, face slack-jawed, blood drained from it.

"We are late for our school presentation, officer," she calls back to him without turning.

The man, stammering, taking a few tentative steps toward the front of the car.

"It is a matter of vital importance," she goes on, as if lecturing. "We cannot afford further delay. Much is at stake which cannot be made evident to you, and I do not have time to explain."

The officer, a local deputy, draws even with her window, making his best effort to recover himself. "Are you some kind of doctor?"

Mama placing her forearm on the door, smiling up at him her warm, slow smile. "I am indeed a *kind* of doctor," she says, "insofar as I am a woman, concerned with restoring or manipulating human health through the highly detailed study, diagnosis, and treatment of the human body."

She glances over at me and smiles her true smile before turning back to him. "Beneath your clothes and your flesh, you are not very different from that fellow in the back seat. Have you ever thought about that? I mean *really* thought about it? Such is the nature of most all people on this earth: so few come to realize or even bother to think about the fundamental nature of themselves."

Her smile hardens, then lapses into a line and she stares up at him. "We are going to show them what they are."

The deputy, still very pale, nodding slowly and agreeably, wholly acquiescent even as he comprehends nothing. "Mam," he says at last, "I think you know what your business is, and I do believe I am going to let you get about it right now."

With that he turns quickly and walks briskly back to his car, hand slipping slightly on the door handle as he seeks to jerk it open—to get inside, away, anywhere else.

And Mama, back out on the road before the deputy is even in his seat, driving as fast as before, faster even, dials on the dash a confusion of vibrating needles, grinning at the long white highway lines devoured beneath us.

*

Sliding to a stop between two buses in the circular school parking lot, not far from the main entrance. Car doors open, front seats leaned forward, Mama motioning me to climb into the back.

Gesturing at the skeleton's base. "Help me lift him, son."

Me, curiously strong for a child my age, grasping him by the rollers and heaving upward and forward, slipping a bit as I step out onto the gravel, banging a femur against the door.

"Careful now," says Mama, her steady hands clenched about his collarbone.

Then, me, letting down the base and together—me pushing and Mama pulling—bringing him upright. He sways slightly before leveling out between us, blinding white of bone and flashing metal in the end-of-school-year sun.

We roll him slowly, haltingly, over the gravel lot toward the entrance, me pushing while bracing the backs of his legs, and Mama steadying him, arm about his waist in the attitude a nurse will adopt while guiding a frail elderly patient.

Through the heavy school doors to discover emptiness inside, an industrial fan, nearly as tall as our companion, the sole occupant, blowing at the far end of a dim forlorn hallway, caressing our damp foreheads with warm air. Rolling him down the corridor, shut crayoned doors of classrooms passing on either side, the going much easier on the polished smooth floor though a wheel squeaks slightly, piercing occasionally the droning refrain of mechanically pushed air.

As we turn a corner a janitor steps forth from his closet, then, noting us, retreats wide-eyed back into it, drawing the door shut before him, water bucket sloshing—lapsing into a motionless silhouette behind beveled glass.

Arriving at last at the door to my classroom, student roster hanging on it with stars of different colors attending each name. Only a few next to mine, all of a lesser hue.

Mama absorbing this data in a glance, then hand on my shoulder, gentle and firm, moving me out of the way. "Stand aside, son."

Door flung open, swinging inward, and in rolls the skeleton, Mama pushing him from behind, teacher and students frozen in their places, mouths rounded and agape, eyes nearly as large. The skeleton coming forward, passing between the main center rows of desks and up to the very head of the room. He stops before the teacher and Mama steps out from behind, appraising the woman with a frank stare, looking her up and down. The teacher had always seemed to me very big and very frightening, but next to Mama—so tall and pretty and smart in her heels and spring dress—she looked small and old and plain. I felt sorry for her. The teacher's throat moved and she shuddered suddenly—at Mama or the skeleton I couldn't tell which.

When Mama turned to address the class she rolled the skeleton about with her so that they turned together, gracefully, in unison, like dancers or skaters, the teacher falling back away from them, like a lesser actress abandoning the stage.

Then Mama began speaking to the students and as she did a strange glow came over her which I had never seen before. "I am sorry we are late today for show and tell," she says, "but real learning never runs on time and for us I hope you will make an exception."

Quick glance at the teacher, who nods uncertainly, before continuing. "I believe my son informed you that I would show you what you are." Heads swiveling briefly to where I stand at the back of the class.

"Well," she continues, "here you are. Here is what you all are beneath your clothes and your skin. Look at your arm. Look at your hand. Then think about that for a minute. Think about it."

Students extending their arms, holding out their palms before them.

"Your human skeleton, this thing inside you, is very strong and very hard, yet it is relatively light. I bet your mothers weigh you sometimes. We like to know how big you are getting. In a man like this one who weighed maybe 160 pounds the skeleton is only 30 pounds.

"And it is perfectly adapted for locomotion and manipulation," she goes on, lifting the skeleton's forearm so that its elbow joint flexes. "See?"

Widening eyes at this.

"Now, it is our spines that are responsible for our upright posture," she says, running her hand down the skeleton's back. "Because we stand upright, we are able to use our hands in order to manipulate our environment. We reach out and we change things.

"An adult human skeleton consists of 206 bones altogether which are divided into two principal divisions: the axial skeleton and the appendicular skeleton. The axial forms the long axis of the body and it includes the bones of the skull, vertebral column, breastbone, and rib cage. The appendicular consists of the bones of the upper and lower extremities, the shoulder girdle, and the hip girdle."

As Mama points to each bone grouping in succession, naming each again, the students watch her finger, then look down at the corresponding places on their bodies.

"I could show and tell about this forever," Mama says, "but the best showers and tellers care about what other people want to know. I am interested in you all. What do you want to know?"

Stunned silence, then a lethargic stirring as if awakening from the same powerful dream.

"Is it a boy or a girl?" a boy asks.

"He was a man," says Mama, "a very old man. You can tell he was old a lot of different ways, but all of you can see how he's missing some teeth and the ones that are left are all ground down from use."

"Why is that?" another boys asks. "Where did he come from?"

"Southeast Asia," replies Mama. "I can tell because of his bone structure and cranial development."

A girl. "Where is that?"

"On the other side of the world," says Mama. "The people there are much poorer than you and I and don't always get to eat their meals. Think about that for a minute. What if you missed your dinner for a whole week? Just imagine how hungry you would be. This fellow was hungry a lot of the time. His bones say so."

The teacher, off to the side, rigid and frowning.

Another girl. "How did he come all the way here?"

"Sometimes when people die their bodies get sent to scientists so they can be studied. That is what I used to be: a scientist, a *woman* scientist. I studied bodies so that I could learn about how to work on the ones that are alive and make them better."

Students staring at Mama in wonder, a pair of girls peering uncertainly across the aisle at each other, possessed suddenly of new eyes.

"I like talking to you all," she says, smiling a warm, slow smile, and they all smile back at her. "Now for the real fun. Who wants to touch him?"

Eruption of hands and a piping chorus of "Me! Me! Me!" Bodies abandoning their desks, pressing forward as a body. My little classmates, weaving around the skeleton in a frenzy of fascination, quick touches from small forefingers—one girl reaching up to grab a bottom rib, then lifting her shirt to poke at her own.

And me, apart from the others, with eyes only for my mother: towering above the swirl of motion, commanding the classroom, beaming down upon the children, showing them themselves.

Satyr

(creative nonfiction)

"And here it may be randomly suggested, by way of bagatelle, whether some things that men think they do not know, are not for all thoroughly comprehended by them; and yet, so to speak, though contained in themselves, are kept a secret from themselves? The idea of Death seems such a thing."

—Herman Melville, The Ambiguities

"Marvellous!" a character once exclaimed—a British character to be exact, hence the double-L spelling of the word. "The marvellous beauty and fascination of all wild things! The horror of man's unnatural life, his heaped-up civilization!" As it is the magical essence of the former exclamation I wish to get at, I shall say again something of my own relationship with nature, for I have written on it more than once but never seem to get it exactly right. Too often I fear I dwell on its darker, wilder manifestations—the storms, the predation, the humanism—since it is they which have left the deepest marks on body and mind alike, shaping them in the process. Yet in truth I have loved just as well and been molded by a great host of harmless, benign representatives of the natural world, having always possessed, for instance, a pronounced fondness for flowers: whether admiring the uniform arrangements of rare varieties in gardens or watching the wild natural sort sway and bob on a windswept field. Even the manmade manifestations have proven attractive and moving to me on occasion, in particular those which grew beneath Grandmother's needle as I sat at her feet holding the quilt and watching.

Though it was home to three separate fenced-off pastures—the wire of which I had spent many a weekend and summer day running tree to tree or post to post, or some mixture of the two—my family's farm was covered mostly in woods. I am well aware I am not alone in having always felt there is something about a forest, any forest, when considered as an entity of its own, that remains primal, enigmatic, and majestic. It resembles a vast dark sea in the mysteries it conceals and the manner in which it envelops you. One may judge by its sounds how it senses and greets your approach—the scattering and silencing of wildlife, the modulations in bird song, the give of the ground and the old decaying matter beneath your feet. Though I have always found that greeting reassuring, as though returning to a beloved homeland or other scared place, it is a response which nonetheless forces you to sense your insignificance. You do not matter to a forest. Yet the knowledge is comforting to the extent that it also renders your modern trials—paying a bill say, or quarreling with a coworker over some forgettable trifle—into their proper place of insignificance. In a forest the synthetic human communities and accompanying rules which modern life forces us to function within and observe are made to appear ridiculous. Stay there long enough and your concerns give way, consciously or no, to the old animal verities of food, shelter, water. Your shoes and clothes begin to look and feel increasingly out of place, ridiculous even. Our bodies make themselves known to us again and, in doing so, move us a little closer to the stripped down essence of ourselves.

I have found it a great joy and privilege in the woods merely to sit and listen. Doing so over the course of your youth develops within you certain gifts: the ability, for example, to close your eyes and tell what time of year it is solely by the manner in which the leaves rustle. So precious were the woods to me during my own youth that I went through periods during which I loathed to leave them at all and would spend the entire weekend, day and night, within their confines. In preparation for a night's slumber in the forest I would always try to find the thickest bed of bracken to lie down on—often set on the north face of a hillside beneath a dense stand of mountain laurel or rhododendron. If I had heard tell of rain or knew of its coming by other means, I would choose a spot where the leaves on the overhanging branches were thickest so that they might shield me. Otherwise, I slept beneath an opening in the canopy where I might contemplate the moon's cataract or the slow sweep of the stars. Then I would fall into an untroubled yet attuned slumber known only to hunters and other forest folk. Sometimes it seemed to me as though the ragged brittle leaves and sharp pine needles I had heaped about and upon my body were the forest's version of the protective wings of some great loving bird which sought to enclose me in a downy safety. And I loved how the pale white sycamore branches, rising from the low watery places and visible sometimes even in a moonless dark, called to mind bone or silk depending on my mood. They came to be a second home to me, those woods, though a full understanding of them would always evade me. I never felt fearful or restless there, but rather loved that long silence which has been likened to death but in truth was merely the life of the place.

For all their subtle teeming life, it remains forests are places which know death constantly, that rely on it in fact for the ongoing promulgation of their life systems. The most notable human participation in death's function in a wood or grove presents itself nowadays via the mostly lamentable pastimes of logging and hunting. The former most often takes the form of outright annihilation—the severe alteration of the environment into a non-forest: something unrecognizable, or even just "not"—while the latter, though distasteful to many forest lovers, visits a far more negligible impact. Yet the endgame of both actions is "caused death," which is really a form of murder. I continue to count a number of hunters and loggers among my friends, despite the fact I consider them death dealers by virtue of their craft. And I myself— having grown up on a farm and cut short the life of many a tree and creature—would be remiss not to acknowledge my complicity in such actions. But then we might say something similar of undertakers and doctors who specialize in terminal maladies. There is, after all, an art in the way a being chooses to render death; there is too an art of dying. And at least one of those blank canvases will be set before each of us, ready or not, at a certain time, appropriate or not, during the course of one's life.

*

The stallion was my father's great love among all the creatures of the farm. He was, by designation, a rescue horse, delivered from a situation in which his owner could no longer afford to feed him and had grown weary of the expenses, along with the animal's exasperating stubbornness and frequent propensity for loosing the gate hitch with his teeth and liberating himself so as to tear at the rich orchard grass which grew beyond the fence of his own wanting, grassless, dirt pasture. Starved as he was at that time—bones protruding here and there amid the sunken places in his sides—there remained great lumps of muscle about his shoulders, chest, and neck which somehow refused to diminish even after such a prolonged period of wanting care and nutrition.

Malnourished as he was there clung within him a power he refused to abdicate—which he had secreted away somewhere in his soul and translated itself proudly in certain portions of his body. In that condition he had borne the elements beneath leafless trees, without benefit of a barn or even a rough old shed, and yet never known a veterinarian's touch. It was these things, I believe—these manifestations of the spirit of the animal in the face of his privations—which led my father to buy him and, later, love him: just as I would come to in time.

There was something flinty and familiar about the stallion which inaudibly spoke to us: a gaunt, stoic, brutal survivalism harkening back to the nature of my father's Smoky Mountain people, clinging precariously to their hollows and mountainside soil, doing battle with the slope's rock to eke out what crops they could. "Who on the hills," inquires a poem of Robert Penn Warren's, "have seen stand and pass/Stubbornly the taciturn/Lean men that of all things alone/ Were, not as water or the febrile grass,/Figured in kinship to the savage stone." I count it a unique and priceless gift to have known such men early on in my life. The stallion was like them.

When he first came to the farm I took to watching him for long periods of time on account of how different he was from the mares and geldings—even other stallions—I had seen. He cropped the grass in short jerks, shifting his hooves, never leaving his head down long but raising his long neck frequently, ears pricked like daggers, directing the furnace of his gaze out over the world that was his pasture, that he naturally considered his, and every inch of which he would come to learn—more by heart than mind. Even in the confused jumble of dirt, dust, and mud around the stables he would learn to gauge and recognize all the little prints: which people and which of his herd had passed—and when and at what rate of speed, even under what circumstances.

The establishment of his ownership was a natural affair and peaceful as there were no other stallions on the farm, though he would find it necessary to kick an overproud dog or two. When I saw him shake his dark red mane in the snow-covered pasture of his first winter on the farm it was as a flag unfurling, a standard waved to and fro—a banner of sovereignty and challenge. And he guarded what he took to be his with a jealous fury as demonstrated by the carcasses of untold wild dogs, even a beautiful grey fox, he stomped to death beneath those sharp, quick, heavy hooves. Much as a cat will torture its prey so as to convey to it or its owner a meaning, or simply to amuse itself, the stallion did not always kill trespassing animals outright, such as the hunting beagle he left whimpering, dragging its useless hindlegs, every inch a new agony, toward the fence line where I stood waiting with a rifle.

Riding the stallion afforded the impression of a force of nature that seemed not quite animal. He was not overlarge for a horse, but something in the way he assumed command of an outing—the manner in which he adjusted the tack to his liking through a series of powerful shakes, elected where to place his feet, and exhibited a nearly human forethought— made him unlike any others of his kind I had encountered. Sometimes when he ran it felt like clinging to a falling stone, or, at other times, being borne as by a great gust of wind. Even at rest he seemed to emit a dark, invisible fire, the depths of his eyes stretching away into a labyrinth of stern, cruel memories, which—if one stared long enough—collapsed eventually into a wild blur of darkness.

The stallion was the same age as me, my father's favorite, and so I called him brother. Because he was my elder in life experience, I learned far more from him than he from I. For his part, he did not consider me his sibling or equal; he cared about me about as much as the forest did. But he became in time one of my great teachers, whether he wished it or not.

*

For reasons still unclear to me, Mama had at last resolved to go back to teaching. She did so at Sweet Briar, a woman's college not far from where we lived in the foothills of the Blue Ridge Mountains. She took me with her sometimes, partly I think to keep an eye on me but also to keep her company during the drive and perhaps afford me some subtle introduction to the world of higher education which was second-nature to her but an alien realm to my then largely barbarian teenage self.

The college reeked of wealth for reasons I could not immediately discern in their entirety at the time. Part of it was all the nice cars in the parking lots, although a greater portion of the impression seemed to stem from more pervasive, albeit subtler, sources. The architecture, for example, was one such element. It was dominated by the work of Ralph Adams Cram, who had also lent his expertise to the campuses of Princeton and West Point. His signature look whispered an elite understated Gothicism which made for a curious effect amid the bright, rolling pastoral landscape surrounding the college, the holdings of which spanned more than three thousand, mostly wooded, acres and included two or three mountains.

I had read somewhere the institution owned part of Bear Mountain, which I knew was where some of the Monocan lived still. I was excited about hiking to it until Mama told me it was nearly ten miles away and cut off from the rest of the school's land by sizeable chunks of private property. At first I thought she was trying to dissuade me out of concern for my safety by making it sound farther than it really was. But when I looked it up in the college library I discovered what she had said was true, though the mountain lay not quite so distant as she had suggested. I developed an immediate fondness for the names of the other nearby places I discovered on the maps in the library—Fern Woods, Merry Woods, Kentucky Ridge—and resolved to visit them all while Mama taught her classes and held her office hours.

Mama must have sensed in me my plans for exploring, for she took me aside by the arm before departing for her first class and instructed me to stay out of trouble. Then she sighed, which I took to mean she had understood the hopelessness of her imperative even as she had uttered it.
I do not believe I was an especially bad boy, but expecting a heterosexual teenage male to keep from getting underfoot on a campus made up of several hundred mostly well-to-do, mostly attractive, young women must be considered a tall—if not downright unreasonable—order by most any standard.

I did alright for a while, keeping to the trails and paths for which I had discovered maps in the library. Mama had said nothing—purposefully, I believe—of the strong equestrian tradition at Sweet Briar. Probably she feared I would leap on the first horse I saw and gallop it around in the unsubtle, uncouth manner that was mine in those days—that was indicative of my man, or not-quite-man, versus beast mentality. And, of course, that is precisely what I did when I discovered the animals of my own accord, peacefully grazing in a hillside pasture. As manicured and well-groomed as their owners, I thought to myself, when I glimpsed their shiny sleek forms for the first time. I took turns trying out different ones, riding them about the fields bareback as furtively as I might, out of sight of the stables.

Then I became bolder and began letting the ones I liked best out of the pasture through a rear gate so as to gallop them up the Paul Mountain trail. That is how it all came to an end. One early afternoon as I stood trailside behind a stand of dense mountain laurel, one hand hanging on to the halter, the other otherwise occupied, I finished and turned, leaning out of the bushes, abdomen and lower body still obscured, to behold a young jogger, face a mixture of curiosity and fear, as her eyes drifted from the upper part of me protruding—frozen, in fact, at the sight of her—from the privy hedge back along the density of foliage to the place where it terminated and where stood partially obscured equine haunches, tail swishing about them.

Without uttering a word she took off down the mountain at a dead sprint, long ponytail bobbing not unlike a horse's tail. When I regained the pasture perhaps half an hour later, I discovered a buxom woman who must have been the stable master—at least that is what I took her to be—striding toward me across the field, hard face offset by the fact that her body appeared rounded in all directions. I noted, as most any teenage boy would, that she was possessed of a big round bust, and in this description no insult is meant. There was nothing plural about her great curved breast: it loomed in its roundness armpit to armpit, swaying as she came on. When she turned suddenly to look back toward the stables, perhaps for the purpose of signaling a coworker, I discovered the same was true of her bottom—it exhibited the identical lack of pluralness as her bust, only there was much more of it.

When I turned to run back toward the woods, she called after me in a harsh voice, yet I kept on, running easily, knowing she possessed not the means to catch me.

To my knowledge there was never any fallout or publicity from the incident though I assume the campus's security must have been alerted. Of course, I mentioned nothing to Mama, who only became aware of it—or, rather, *will* only become aware of it—when, like you, she read/will read the account I have set down here.

I have found occasion to visit Sweet Briar a few times in recent years and those days of Mama's brief return to teaching and my even shorter pastime of horse-jacking come to mind whenever I do. And when I do think about that curious interval of my life it is the startled jogger, the look on her flushed face, I always end up dwelling upon the most. How I must have appeared to her on that forlorn mountainside: the protruding head and torso of a blemishless golden-haired adolescent boy followed, some yards behind, by the hind end of a horse. I wish I knew if she still thinks about that encounter (if in fact she remembers it at all). I'd like to know if she considered it something frightening or if for her it remains somehow a vision of unqualified wonder unlike anything else she has experienced.

*

I had sex for the first time not long after the events at Sweet Briar. It was with a girl who would never have any opportunity to attend an exclusive private woman's institution, or any other college for that matter. Perhaps she never even finished high school. I can't remember; I don't know what happened to her. Guilt rises in me on those rare occasions I recall her—guilt at not wondering about her more than I do.

Her face, childlike and round, had a certain immobile quality to it regardless of what happened to be going on around her, yet this dynamic was offset by her highly attentive, almost astonished, blue eyes which usually looked as though they had just witnessed something highly unexpected. Her full little mouth not only never smiled, but seemed altogether incapable of forming that expression. Lusterless mousy hair hung in clusters on either side of her head as if its intention was to appear as lifeless and flaccid as the expression on her face. Her shapely bosom breathed calmly like that of a wild animal lying at rest yet alert. Most any girl would have been something of an enigma to me in those inexperienced teenage years, but this one came across especially so. My initial response to her was neither one of attraction nor disinterest, but rather a kind of inquisitiveness I did not understand. Many girls might have possessed such qualities as hers without being remembered for them, but I remember on account of the part she played in my life.

The first time I ever took notice of her was in a class—the subject of which now escapes me—in which the discussion had drifted fancifully off topic toward the question of whether there was more grass covering the planet or more sand. Though I was dozing in the back, as was my custom, I remember one of the serious, scientifically-inclined boys asserting there most certainly was more sand on account of the size of the world's oceans and that most all their deep dark floors were covered with it. But to this Emily—that was the girl's name—responded with something to the effect that those same deep recesses might instead lie covered in a dark waving grass that required almost no light: a grass that no one probably had ever even seen but that likely was as tall as trees and stood in stands that rendered miniscule the earth's greatest prairies. Miles beneath the undulating surface, she maintained, it moved like corn in the wind.

The class had laughed at her when she had finished conveying her deep ocean vision and though I believed their opinions meant almost nothing to her, she had blushed nonetheless. I myself said nothing, did not move even from my drowsy reclining position, but in that moment Emily had won me as a devoted admirer and friend.

And we did become friends, our bond sustained by the most unlikely of variables and exchanges. I admired, for instance, how she smoked in the bathroom between classes, yet was never actually caught doing so even though everyone—teachers, janitors, students—knew her as the culprit. I liked the way in which the rancid tobacco odor would drift across the room to me in the one class I had with her. A student or two sitting close to her occasionally would wrinkle their noses in disgust at the smell, but for me, assigned to a seat on the far side of the room near the back, the wandering smell was a way for her to reach me. When it wafted my way and entered my nostrils it was as though she was sitting beside me so that we might witness the farce of yet another high school class session together.

When not at school we often frequented cemeteries. Why? "Because a lot of them are beautiful and no one's usually around," she said, "and sometimes the tombstones are flat so you can lay down on them and watch the sky." There was more to this, of course, though I did not realize it until much later. Part of what had attracted me to Emily was her fascination with death: with physical being and its lack. Her mother, she said, had bore many children, some of them afflicted or dead on arrival, and one of Emily's favorite and most entertaining pastimes was musing upon alternative scenarios involving these doomed or damaged siblings.

"If that one hadn't died," she'd lament, "I'd have had a playmate almost just my age."

"What if he were right in the head?" she'd say, another time, of a younger brother who wasn't. "Wouldn't all the girls think he was handsome?"

Despite this sad family history, however, or perhaps because of it, Emily was not very sympathetic toward the shortcomings of other people and, in fact, took great pleasure in criticizing their flaws.

"Have you ever noticed how ugly most people are?" she asked me once. "You'd think they'd try to make up for it by being more agreeable."

Her fascination with death and critiques of others had led her to a profound fondness for the carnal aspects of existence: slumber, food, and—especially—sex. Indeed, as if vaulting beyond any ordinary natural impulse, Emily seemed determined to couple with as much frequency as circumstance and her impressive resourcefulness allowed. And so there would be a cold, hard tombstone beneath my back, bouncing breasts and blushing, grunting face above, while a blue sky, stars, or the clouds of night or day wheeled above.

"Emily, I don't want you just for this," I would say, believing I meant it, even as my bobbing cock nodded otherwise.

On one such occasion some lines came to me from the Jove and Europa story translated in my Latin class a week earlier: "Dignity and love are seldom known to go to bed together." I wondered then and know now I did not love her. She was the first girl I had sex with, which for a fourteen-year-old boy seems like love, and we enjoyed some of the offbeat-young-couples-fun that made me think we might could be a couple. But for the most part I found myself shrugging off too much contemplation or misgiving and, as they say, simply enjoying the ride. Walking on jelly legs, surroundings a confusion, head and body reluctant to process them in the wake of what they had just experienced, I would absently consider her in retrospect.

"So this is having your brains f---ed out," I would remark in my mind.

Though it disappointed me at the time, I have grown to be glad that she was the one who ended it. Of course, many of the clichés one expects of a terminating teenage relationship came into play, including the moment when she said, "We can still be friends."

When she said we could still be friends it served as the verbal articulation of an end of sorts, but only what might be termed a preliminary end. Young as I was, I realized it wasn't so much that she wanted to be friends as that she wished to preserve her claim on me. I had learned even then, even in that pre-sexual zone I had been inhabiting and can no longer recall or even imagine, that girls could be like that. So many of them, it seemed, were loath to let a boy go even when they had lost most of their interest in him or sworn devotion to another. I hadn't encountered any boys in my class who seemed cognizant of this quality in girls; indeed, most of them became angry or even abusive when subjected to such conditions. By contrast, I found this quality in girls very precious and endearing when it concerned me—this confused, groping, hanging on which made little sense to either of us. Most often I would treat it with levity or a slow steady vanishing on my part—a firm, gradual disappearance from their lives—as dictated by the circumstances.

Once removed from them, perhaps already nearly forgotten, I could then observe them quickly resigning themselves to the more immediate dynamics of their lives, before rousing myself and moving off toward the next chapter of my own existence, like the spectator who rises last with a yawn, having lingered in the dark of an auditorium long after the falling of the curtain and the departure of the other theatergoers. Upon the arrival of that point at which I sensed I might never even have existed for them, I wasted little time in disappearing from their hearts and minds forever as though sinking into the earth.

I can imagine quite a few readers shaking their heads at such an outlook and its accompanying behavior, but we were a strange people then in those desolate rural parts of the hill-South and there was an old saying among us: that we made good friends but worse enemies. I believed the saying to be true and thus tried to avoid the latter whenever I could help it.

"I believe I'll always have something of a weakness for girls like Emily on account of her," I told my friend S— when it was all said and done.

"It'll pass," she had replied with authority and conviction, tossing aside the whole thing as though it were a gum wrapper. "A lot of the girls in that family are pretty when they're young, but look at their mammas and you'll see they're a fat, unhealthy race of folks on the whole, and I know a fair number of them have like to died young."

*

Things changed in my relationship with the stallion after Emily. He knew I had become sexually active long before anyone else in my family suspected. Something was lost between us. Whereas before I had been his collaborator and fellow adventurer on rides as well as a sibling who moved in another sphere, I now constituted—somewhere in the recesses of his masculine equine sensibility—a potential threat to his herd and livelihood. Likely his sensitive olfactories discerned an alteration in my biochemical processes and perhaps my general manner changed as well. Indeed, though I would have remained unconscious of the fact, I believe the latter probably did occur in the wake of the thrill and pleasure that accompanied my discovery of the new thing of which I was capable.

So it was that he came to watch me warily in the pasture and, if we went for a ride, would wait for my attention to wander before drifting toward the edge of a trail so as to bang one of my kneecaps on a passing tree. And then, one day, when I was turned from him to fetch his halter, he bit me on the shoulder, hard enough almost to draw blood. So shocked was I at this betrayal that when I turned back on him, I hesitated a second before delivering a roundhouse punch to his mouth that sent him snorting and stumbling backward out of his stall. When I held up his halter again and peered into his long face, his eyes—wide and unrelenting—never blinked. It was a sign of obstinacy I understood. I had seen the same expression in the mirror.

The stallion grew more irascible with age, even after I left the farm. Indeed, we both did. Even Mama, who had broken countless horses for Bert Allen in her youth and had learned the art of horsemanship from him and the best of the Meadow Farm and Warwick Stables crowd of the late 1960s, struggled with him, with us, sometimes.

Mr. Allen knew something of the stallion from the pictures Mama sent him along with her greeting cards and read the meaning of his lines, carriage, and disposition without ever having laid eyes on him as only a master trainer like Mr. Allen could.

"Every good horseman," he counseled her, "needs one good horse."

Mr. Allen was not evading the issue in this declaration, but rather underscoring the fact that the stallion's increasing violence and eccentricity remained ultimately of little moment in light of the remarkable thing he continued to constitute to the human who sat atop him—or rather would *allow* to sit atop him.

*

I rode him for the last time on a sunny late-November day, scent of light soot drifting on the air—a remainder of the woodstove's morning fire. The season's last clinging leaves hung flat and colorless.

We were, as I said, the same age, but he had grown old, ancient by equine standards, and I had been warned by Mama not to let him run. Yet when we had trotted out of the pasture and reached the first hill, he strained the reins with his old power and shook the harness. An understanding came to me and I gave him his head so that his great forelegs heaved forward and he sprang away, deep already in the old remembered thing he loved.

I knew I would catch hell if he died, but I knew too he would like nothing better than to die in the wake of one of his dead gallops. Perhaps it was even what he wished, what he was attempting, and so I let him gallop until he had run himself out. When we stopped running wisps of steam were rising from his flanks and I dismounted so as to lead him along and stretch my legs, which had grown cramped clenching the saddle as a result of my being out of riding practice.

As we made our way back toward the farm, a storm blew up suddenly, the wind cutting through my clothes and rending the air with despairing shrieks and groans as it assaulted the forest canopy. Limbs cracked apart from massive trunks and fell here and there like arms torn from sockets.

Through it all the stallion never spooked nor seemed much troubled. Whatever the decline in his physical being, his old spirit and courage were there intact. We reached home safely. That was not his day to die.

In the last few weeks which remained to him of that, his last, season of life, I saw the stallion but little. The trials of my own life kept me away.

When at last the day came when that beautiful strength settled itself to earth, it did so gently as though relaxing into a comfortable state of repose. The expression in his eyes I will never forget. The old labyrinth of stern, cruel memories—the wild blur of darkness—was gone and in its place was something contemplative, yet all its own: like if you threw a stone up in the air and it didn't come down, but rather just stayed there. Perhaps he died marveling at the strange beauty of such a sight.

When he was dead a tractor with a backhoe dug his grave and a great rusty chain was wrapped about him so as to drag his great form to it. He lies there now in the fashion of a hundred other animals of that farm, having returned to the earth. I think of them sometimes, the various spots where they have been buried, spanning all the way back to my childhood, and how some of those places are covered now in saplings and thickets or mown over, or, in a few cases, marked each spring by the emergence of daffodils or tulips. Most farms are like that: landscapes of the dead, from which new things are always growing. But I don't like to dwell on that too much.

Yet when I do think of death—of how I would like to die—it is usually in the prone form of a large animal, yet such an animal as God must have saw when he first envisioned the creatures of the earth before all time. Never in my life have I known a being truer to the nature of itself.

Farm Boy: A Writing and Agricultural Life in the 21st Century
(creative nonfiction)

It is often the case my farm seems to me the only sane place in this country. I take it this is because, other than my wife and some animals, no one else inhabits it. Madman, bore, or perhaps something in between, I am the primary possessor of the human agricultural perspective on a bit of earth American law recognizes as mine, but which, in reality, possesses me as one of its minor living inhabitants. I have tried to do right by it within my significant limits, but, alas, have made enough agricultural mistakes in my life to forget most of them and curse myself in remembrance of those I do recall with a silent condemnation. Since my school days, truth be told, I have not ceased to marvel each year at the fool I have been the year before. Yet, on the extreme other side of these many active mistakes there dwells an attitude of complacency reflected in the way I sometimes idly watch the fields from my rocker, contemplating them all the while—particularly if a jug is handy. The agricultural problems and attributes of the landscape are laid out before me—the solutions to which, if any ever present themselves, destined eventually, in retrospect, to be reckoned ignorant and those of a fool. The former version of me, the doer, is something of an innovator (however meager his rate of success); the latter, the muser, a leisurely pragmatist with a practical, rather than idealistic, penchant for strategizing an approach to something that may never occur. I will be the first to admit my perspicacity often is suspect and misspent, but then trial and error are part of the farmer's (as well as the writer's) trade.

I have chosen to write briefly on my agricultural identity for a number of reasons, not least of which is to combat ongoing negative stereotypes of farms and farmers. In popular culture farm life frequently continues to be characterized as stagnant, dull, parochial, stupid, and backward, largely on account of its hard remitting toil. As with all stereotypes, each of these qualities may prove true depending on a given farm. Yet I also find each one of them problematic with regard to my own agricultural background and observations. As one who has traveled a bit, I would take special exception to the first pejorative word—"stagnant"—by noting simply that all excursions are relative and carry with them their own inherent limitations: life remains life wherever one idealizes and experiences it, even in transit or within the space of a few square miles. Moreover, I would assert the other characterizations primarily arrive from the observations of those who either suffered tragically in their agricultural upbringings or who failed, sometimes willfully, to discern the value of a farm's many underlying nuances.

One simple fact is that the labor farm life demands of an individual usually is to the purpose of the betterment of the self, literal and artistic. "Work is the law," wrote the painter da Vinci. "Like iron that lying idle degenerates into a mass of useless rust, like water that is an unruffled pool sickens into a stagnant and corrupt state, so without action the spirit of men turns to a dead thing, loses its force, ceases prompting us to leave some trace of ourselves on this earth." Work delivers people from evil, or at the least lessens the evil they would do, in most any vocation. In farming, seasonal changes, the almost imperceptible lengthening and shortening of light hours, and variable weather make its undertaking a constant and rigorous exercise in observation, planning, and critical thinking. There is always something different to do, and it may demand to be done very quickly—as during harvest—or at a more leisurely rate (the mending of fences in winter comes to mind).

It was the slow, reflective periods of agricultural life which afforded humans the leisure to develop the arts for hundreds of years until widespread mechanization changed that process in the early twentieth century. Yet everything—the most fundamental and essential qualities of existence (all the elements of art)—may still be found on a farm: strife, peace, love, nature in most all its aspects, ideals, boredom, disgust, inspiration. And they are all diminished or intensified and combined to the degree one wishes or allows. It would be crude (and erroneous) to say these are predominantly surface phenomena. They appear so only until one comes to understand, with time and repetition of experience, their deeper implications. I have found that when possessed of free time, farmers seldom waste it. We may snooze in a rocker or take in the last ten laps of a stock car race, but, to my knowledge, we are least among the professionals when it comes to candidates for sustained outright sloth. We may on occasion appear set in our ways and unwilling to change. I believe this to be a byproduct of our strength, though it is possible for us to waiver and neglect many things for a time—even forget to be ourselves. But that has never much troubled me. At least never for very long. I know such men and am one of them.

*

When I am away too long I miss the qualities of the farm that abide in memory: the crows of the roosters and, yes, even the caws of crows; the gentle roll of the fields; the feel of a heavy maul or lightweight hoe in my hands; the odor of mown hay. In essence, I miss what is pleasing and beautiful about a farm; I pine for what Walt Whitman called "the secluded-beautiful, with young and old trees, and such recesses and vistas!"

There was a time a few years ago when I thought I would be leaving my farm and living in a city, and I actually attempted to do so for a matter of days, securing an apartment in a sprawling early 1900s building which sat alongside a crowded, narrow sloping street. I found myself existing in a dreamlike state whenever I was there, combined with a dreamlike sense of insecurity. When I laid down to try and rest I felt both lost in bliss and ready for any catastrophe. After a time I could feel the greatness of spaces I had known while taking my rest on the farm had disappeared, replaced by labyrinthine darkened walls and other lives pressed close all about me. I found I could not sleep alone in such an environment and would drive out of the city with my camping gear to one of the spots I knew in the national forest. There I would rest in contentment until the morning sun struck my eyelids, turning them red. In truth, I spent not a single full night in the city and when I returned to my farm it was with a powerful sense of relief.

Why was this? For one thing, I know for a fact there is an unbroken line of farmer men on my father's side of the family stretching back to the Bavarian region of the Middle Ages and, I suspect, far beyond. May one simply break that line suddenly? For me, the answer appears to be no. And yet I can hardly remember my feelings toward the farm of my youth other than the vague sensation that somehow I belonged there—that it was where I was supposed to be. Perhaps most all children feel that way about the places they are reared. My memory of my childhood farm still wrestles with itself as if it were an angel or something else fantastic—the clear lights and ugly shadows of those unforgotten days wrapping about themselves in tumult. I do know that with regard to the continuum of agriculture in my life, its earliest recollections have such a peculiar quality that they have become merged into a single sensation of profound emotion containing both careless joy and an invincible sadness. It is this feeling which continues to form me and casts a shadow over the rest of my life, including all I write.

*

In 1953, the Appalachian writer and farmer Byron Herbert Reece remarked to a reporter that his novel writing had been interrupted by the need to plow his potatoes.

The reporter noted, "Anybody can plow potatoes," and urged him to get back to his book.

More than a half-century ago, the reporter's statement was perhaps true, but I would wager in the second decade of the 21st century more people can write novels than plow potatoes.

Indeed, we have lost many of our agricultural ways—even the simplest of them. To know they are something of a rarity is evinced by the fact that when I take my tractor less than a mile up the highway to the gas station I am waved at by numerous anonymous people in passing cars. The children in particular gesture and point in the same manner they might gesticulate at

Indians or buffalo: because of the rarity of the spectacle—something they'd heard of and never expected to encounter on account of the phenomena's fame for near-extinction.

In truth, there are more of us than one might think, though we often pass in disguise. Most all people who farm nowadays, self included, are industrial farmers in the context of Henry Ford's vision: that is, out of economic necessity we work part of the time on the farm and part off. Like writers, farmers are not capable even of subsistence; our farm profits would not be sufficient to pay our property taxes and expenses without the income from our jobs.

Why, then, do we keep on doing it?

*

Here I should say something of my other vocation, which is responsible for the thing you find yourself perusing, and its relationship to farming. When it comes to farming most authors I know who write on the need for agricultural responsibility wouldn't know which end of a horse to feed sugar to. They mean well, but I know for a fact the reality of day-to-day living would not agree with them. For one thing, it would quite simply kick their asses. Unless possessed of exceptional constitutions, at the end of a farm day they would be too spent to write, or do much of anything else for that matter. This was a fact the literary southern agrarians of the 1930s quickly discovered while trying to translate their principles into action, Allen Tate's lazy incompetence at Ben Folly serving perhaps as the best example. A couple of them backed up their pens with pitchforks capably enough—Andrew Lytle, Madison Jones—but for the most part folks writing about agrarianism maintained a safe distance from actually practicing it. There is good sense in this since farming can actually kill you, as it did Byron Herbert Reece, who suffered and perished before his time.

The most famous of us, Wendell Berry, has remarked the only real time his farm chores allow him to write is winter. I generally agree with this assertion, though to an extent that season, too, is interrupted by my teaching duties. Yet it does afford more time than the others because one is not cultivating earth, planting, gathering wood, tending bees, and performing other tasks the remaining three seasons demand. Regardless, it is important to plan both one's farming and writing endeavors with a minimum expenditure of time in mind. Though I occasionally experience impatience with a perceived slowness in others, I count it a great advantage to possess as one of my few gifts a penchant for efficient, streamlined thought.

As I have been seeking to establish, farming and writing are more alike than one might think. They are concerned with the essences of things. It has been remarked neither one's fellows, nor one's god(s), nor one's passions will leave one alone, yet the work of farming and writing constitute realms in which one may find meaning and good during one's fleeting significance in life. Writing affords the writer the privilege of relating all the manifestations of existence, great and little, superficial and profound. The successful writer independently creates through imaginative effort and against all difficulty of expression. And in order to achieve the best creation the writer must sacrifice something—give up some essential shred of the self forever. Writing, then, like farming, is at once painful and taxing and rewarding—only in different ways.

*

And so we reach the time of harvest for this essay. With some reservations, there are a few particulars I feel tentatively certain about. For one thing, this piece has led me to a recognition of the relationship between my occupations of writing and farming—that, in many ways, the latter anchors the former. Farming provides diversion, protection, consolation, the mental relief that comes from grappling with material problems, the wisdom of dealing with other forms of life in all their cycles, and the feeling of well-being that accompanies "riding"—note I refrain from using the word "harnessing"—the elemental powers of nature to a respectable harvest. Nature's power often is hidden, sometimes overcome, though never extinguished. So powerful is its hold on me that I can not give it and its cultivation up. I know because I have tried.

Invariably, farmers and writers answer that call to do our work which comes from within us—which is a way of coming from nature—and has made us who and what we are. We make our farms and writings even as we are made by them. Noticed or unnoticed, ignored or commended, we meet, as best we can, the demands of our special and specialized work and lives. Somewhere within the sincere endeavor to accomplish, to go as far as strength will carry us, to continue undeterred by reproach, lies that integrity which is ours. And if we deign to add to that integrity charity toward our fellow writers and farmers, especially those not so fortunate nor so far along as ourselves, then we approach an even greater good, and one in which there can exist no measure of excess.

Only in our imagination and in nature does every truth of existence find its existence. Imagination and nature, I believe, are the supreme masters of life. The tending of fields, like the rendering of memories, is as much a rendering of fields as a tending of memories. My first great adventures—at least those that were so to my mind—occurred on farms and so, I suspect, will my last. The localities of those early places had definite importance. Yet in the recounting of such a life a certain amount of naïveté, sentimentality, and even flat out error is unavoidable. I remain unapologetic for them as they are natural and probably impossible to overcome. And this fact is as true in farming as it is in writing. Indeed, I have witnessed the wisest and most venerable of farmers and writers betrayed by the hardest of their earned knowledge as they struggled to practice some new task. Some observers, such as myself, are supportive under these circumstances—even admiring of the courage necessary to risk failure in attempting something genuinely new—while others will exhibit only scorn at a person stumbling while seeking to break out of their established mold and identity. Which kind of reader are you?

*

If I could identify the attitude in which I approach writing and farming, and the writing of farming, I would articulate it as the spirit of love. It is a love that springs forth from the fragility of the human species; that—as was not the case three quarters of a century ago—the species possesses the means to destroy itself. What a weak, fragile thing it has transformed itself into—not unlike some delicate, endangered heirloom variety of vegetable. I think we have an obligation to care for it as best we can.

Though much of this essay has been concerned with farming as investigated through the medium of writing, I refrain from laying serious claim to the titles "writer" and "farmer" myself. After all, can one truly know the nature of even one aspect of life? How can we when we don't know even our own thoughts? One may love writing and farming without that fact making one a legitimate participant in those vocations. True, I have loved them and practiced them for decades, but it is not for me to gauge the measure of my failures or successes. Nevertheless, right or no, I have found myself bold enough here to speak of them with a certain measure of authority.

I like to think that when I grow too old to be trusted with a pen or set of tractor keys, I shall lay down my books, quit my fields, and contemplate a place to be buried or, in the old northern European tradition, burned atop a pyre. Perhaps I shall have my books and tractor burned with me, which no doubt would make for an entertaining spectacle among the mourners as well as a source of much gossip in my little rural county. Why not? Who says one cannot both fade away and burn out?

We all have noted how things have changed—the sky, the atmosphere, the light of judgment which falls on our labors, renowned or obscure. No one succeeds in everything they do, and in that sense we are all failures. Yet there are farmers and writers still planning, planting, gathering, even now—reaping the honest harvest of a duty faithfully if imperfectly performed.

Willy Mann's Uncle's House
(creative nonfiction)

"It is a place where one's instinct is to give a reason for being there."

—*F. Scott Fitzgerald, "The Hotel Child"*

The lot of us recently had ventured just beyond that age at which boys learn how to kiss and fondle girls in the back seats and truck beds of remotely parked vehicles while also waxing prodigious in their capacities to render mischief falling on the wrong side of the law. That we found ourselves on that particular Friday night speeding down dark country roads in a Chevy Blazer which sent up cascading fountains of gravel whenever it slid to a stop so that one or two of us might disembark at a dead sprint, bent upon swiping a Christmas lawn ornament or two from someone's yard, constitutes perhaps as sorry a delinquent pastime as ever there was. True, it was not so violent nor federally prosecutable as, say, blowing up mailboxes with dynamite or demolishing them with aluminum bats or cinder blocks flung, drive-by style, from a window or truck bed; nor was it so tame as the more nuanced and, dare I say, graceful (even at times intellectual) art of shoplifting. It must, I reckon, have resided someplace in between.

"I'm so drunk," complained Guy, the driver of the Blazer, which—I have neglected to recount thus far—was given to weave as well as speed along those narrow familiar dirt back roads of our beloved country county.

"Where'd my gloves go?" angrily demanded Brent, the boy riding shotgun, his query apparently aimed at no one in particular and ignoring entirely Guy's lament, probably on account of the fact he was equally drunk.

I watched the erratic jolting and jerking of the backs of their heads—the byproduct of unrelenting torque, poor roads, bad shocks, and equally bad liquor—from my place behind them.

"Gloves or not, here's the last stop," slurred Guy, mashing the brakes so that we slid to a stop yard's edge—a little into the ditch, in fact—of a long brick ranch house horrendously decorated, flooded and mired by the season's yuletide, its rectangular form outlined, bound, by a sea of blinking, multi-colored orbs.

"Go! Go! Go! Go! Go!" screamed Guy into Brent's ear like a Sergeant Airborne directing a jump in a combat zone.

And, door flung open, go Brent did, stumbling out onto the frigid slippery grass, then losing his footing and falling to a knee in the ditch, before rising with an oath and sprinting toward the elaborate manger scene perhaps thirty yards distant in the center of the yard—scores of plastic desert people, robes ostensibly meant to appear soiled by the *Khamaseen* dust winds of Arabia; elaborate two-storey manger diademed by a bright flashing purple Christmas tree; and most all the animals of Noah's Ark milling about below it in various three-dimensional still lifes of locomotion or repose—all of it illuminated in a bright spectacular criss-cross of spotlights no doubt employed for very different purposes during deer seasons of Christmas's past.

On ran Brent, bowling over a zebra and striking a glancing blow to an antelope as he approached, not unlike the manner in which he had flattened and shed would-be tacklers during football season, before ducking into the bright manger aperture and lifting from the raised golden crib—really more a diminutive gaudy throne than a crib—the likeness of that peculiar infant folks even now tend to get mighty worked up about, especially in remote counties such as ours, during that particular time of year.

Deft scoop, smooth swivel, and Brent was sprinting back toward us, deified infant likeness tucked under his arm like a misshapen football. Yet even as he approached porch lights ignited behind him and the front door of the house swung inward, vague male form emerging, waving its arms and shouting something incoherent.

"Woooooooh!" Brent hollered, redoubling his pace, stoked by this new element of peril.

I cheered him on, identical yawp answering his, half my torso protruding from the Blazer's rear passenger window, before shifting my attention to the house.

"Merry Christmas!" I bellowed at the newly dispossessed homeowner.

"God dammit!" screamed the man-form shrilly, voice suddenly coherent on account of its having ascended an outraged octave, "I'll shoot every last one a'yall sons a b----es!"

Turning, he scurried back through the door in a crouched loping manner reminiscent of a hunchback or some half-crippled simian beast, blubbering, apparently incoherent with rage, probably in search of his shotgun.

But already we all were beginning to laugh, for Brent, though winded by the cold air and his drunkenness, had reached the Blazer, Guy flooring the accelerator before the passenger door was even shut, jerking us into the next curve, forcing me to bang my head on the window as I withdrew it back inside. Yet I barely even felt the blow on account of all the liquor and laughter. And indeed the whole Blazer seemed full of it at that moment—alcohol and chortling, that is—in addition to its small new divine occupant.

"Haha," gasped Brent when he could breathe again and give voice to his mirth once more, hefting the faux infant one-handed like some newly won athletic trophy. "What do those fuckers have to celebrate now?"

Then, cradling the baby Jesus in the crook of his arm, he leaned forward and punched it hard in the face twice, grunting as he did so, before tossing the doll over his shoulder into the backseat.

It landed face-up in my lap, sullenly peering up at me with its paint-chipped black eyes: weather-faded, misshapen likeness of some disillusioned deified offspring—swaddling gold towel bleached by the elements to a urine-colored yellow, head dented slightly from Brent's formidable punches. I lifted it before me, grinning into its face.

"Mm, mm, mm," I chided Brent. "Beatin on little Baby Jesus."

"Shit, Clabough," he sneered, head half-turning back toward me, profile a silhouette against the green glow of the dash lights. "You got no room to talk. I heard one of the old ladies in my church call you a demon a couple Sundays back. You believe that? A *demon* from hell. Said she'd never let *her* granddaughter go out with a hellion like you."

"Yeah?" I said, mildly interested on account of the fact I could sense Brent wasn't lying. "What's the girl's name?"

"Missy Robinson. That sophomore with the nice rack."

Then me, smiling, trying not to crack up. "Too late."

And then we were all laughing again as the Blazer sped and wove onward through the night, bearing us toward a place which required none of us to utter its name—where we wouldn't need the services of the Chevy and might restock our stores; reload, as it were—while mingling with friends and strangers alike. A place to serve as harbor and haven for our wasted crew of teen land pirates—that had done so more than once before. That understood destination where all the county's young revelers, partygoers, no-good-doers, and ne'er-do-wells eventually assembled on a Friday night. A place known to them—to us all—as Willy Mann's Uncle's House.

*

Obvious as the nature of such a place might seem to discerning readers such as yourselves—and already I can perceive it forming, with reluctance or anticipation as the case may be, in a number of your minds—it is perhaps best to err on the side of caution here and remark that Willy Mann's Uncle's House was in fact a house: one of those newer structures of perhaps six thousand square feet and three stories (if one counted the basement) that seemed to be cropping up in little clumps during those years on the western edge of the county which lay closest to the city (some fifteen miles distant) and thus proved attractive to upwardly mobile professionals and people of like financial resources who desired vaguely pastoral and ostensibly safe, albeit largely sterile and uniform, communities and neighbors.

The particular domicile in question stood in candid relief—a little more to itself than the others, perhaps forty yards from the road—and probably appearing altogether unremarkable if one glimpsed it in daylight, which none of us ever had. However, though the outside of the house was conventional enough for new homes built during that first half-decade of the 1990s, the interior was highly irregular, even downright bizarre. It was said that Willy Mann's Uncle's wife or mistress or housemate—the enigma of her status was consistent with everything else about the place—had been given free rein to design the interior to her fancy. For one conversant in the art of home decoration it quickly would become apparent this mysterious woman had possessed a fine eye for space and color but, for one reason or another, either had lost hold of her gifts so that they had run amok or purposefully set them loose as a dogfighter releases his pit bull when the last bet is made and the final bit of money changes hands. Indeed, it appeared almost as if the limitless freedom Willy's Mann's Uncle had imparted to his beloved architectural muse had driven her decisions to the maximum of hyperbole in nearly every regard. There were rooms possessed of odd shapes, painted in overpowering colors; sliding doors and hollow panels which often as not led nowhere in particular; ceilings of erratic height which seemed meant either to crowd the occupant or make them feel tiny to the point of insignificance; and long thick rugs dyed in blunt primary colors which matched neither the walls nor the trim of the room or hallway at hand.

As a result of these features the whole physics of the place seemed askew or even reversed and, as if this eclecticism wanted yet another variable, it was rumored that upon the completion of the home the mysterious woman had taken up residence on the side of the structure she had designed especially for her own habitation only to make the tardy revelation that it faced north and, what's more, stood almost next to a thick stand of full grown bushy cedars and stately Virginia pines, so that it remained perpetually darker and colder than the rest of the domicile. Her solution, it was recounted, rather than having the trees cut or moving her effects into the opposite end of the house and forsaking her most favored colors, secret panels, and oddly shaped rooms, was to quit the place entirely—and apparently forever—leaving Willy Mann's Uncle with a freakish alien home that afforded him neither joy nor comfort and, indeed, became a place he was reputed to visit but rarely, though apparently he had made no attempt to sell it.

Here it should be pointed out that of Willy Mann's Uncle no one knew a thing either—not even his name. He was as mysterious as that departed female we referred to, not without a certain measure of awe and reverence, as Willy Mann's Uncle's Woman. Though we frequented his house weekend after alcohol-soaked weekend, no one of our acquaintance had ever laid eyes on him. Willy Mann himself we did know as a peripheral athlete, partier, and classmate—fast to laugh and even faster to take up whatever mischief might offer itself to his twinkling eyes and ready smile. Purposefully vague in his answers and apparently viewing the ritual of these parties as a delightful whimsical game, he was of little assistance to those few who bothered asking him about the man whose house they regularly occupied and occasionally trashed. Indeed, Willy Mann lived at that time what must have been a fascinating existence, at once poor and extravagant: electing to act out a meager sort of social role himself, yet flinging open the doors of his uncle's abandoned house to any and all comers.

And come they did, the rowdiest youth of all central Virginia and points beyond, to this place where the routes of very disparate sorts of people crossed paths and conspired both to create and witness together a remarkable, weird, voluptuous scene. As no one ever wished to be the first to arrive at Willy Mann's Uncle's House on a given weekend night, vehicles customarily would cruise back and forth in front of it once nightfall came on, slowing as they passed, before one eventually committed and turned into the driveway at a slow, respectful speed and at last tentatively rolled to a stop in some discreet, remote location on the lawn in anticipation of the scores of vehicles destined eventually to follow. Usually it was the younger kids who arrived earliest, boys newly possessed of their learners' licenses, younger friends piled in with them, eager to witness for the first time the incredible mythology of the place that had been recounted to them by their slightly older siblings and acquaintances.

If an observer were to attempt to track types, or perhaps stereotypes, one might safely say it was most often the rednecks who were next to appear after the newly mobile youths, truck engines rumbling to a halt wherever they pleased, often belligerently taking up significantly more space than they needed. Then the occupants of cab and bed alike would gather on flung-down tailgates, waiting—boots dangling, drinking cheap beer, muttering jokes and oaths—until enough other people arrived for them to make their collective move toward the house. Following these rednecks there would appear the socially ambitious preppy kids, mostly of white middle-upper class stock and overanxious in their desire to exhibit their studied potentials to appear cool. The Sports Utility Vehicles and occasional sports cars of the parents of such youths would be followed by the heavily-stickered, more rundown vehicles of the alternative crowd, who cared almost nothing for the scene and merely desired a place to get high, listen to their music, and converse quietly among themselves. Often the alternative kids lapsed immediately into critiquing and laughing at those who had arrived before them, for knowing themselves to be different—in appearance, if nothing else—they proudly claimed and reveled in the deviant license of the counterculture minority status they had staked as their own. At last came what was commonly referred to as "high tide": the big push or surge of jumbled people, not all of them high schoolers, representing all manner of identities and walks of life. There were, of course, the athletes and a couple carloads of the least socially-inept and more self-possessed geeks from school, but also there were those we labeled "has-beens," the recently graduated young people who had not departed for college and still awkwardly sought to run with the high school crowd. A certain strain or unease accompanied the presence of these ghosts of classes past. Yet more peculiar than them were the full-fledged adult participants: the falling-down middle-aged alcoholic man everyone laughed at, the thirtyish blonde whore who had done the better part of the football team in pairs or in groups ("Yall are at yall's sexual peak," she had said to us more than once), and a nondescript fatherly man we initially had taken for a narc, but who eventually had earned our trust, functioning as a kind of unofficial vendor of liquor and cigarettes, and never hesitating to transport the younger kids on their maiden beer runs.

Throw these people together, deep in a collective state of social confusion and chemical inebriation, and one might imagine the shifting tide of crazily happy faces that rose and receded each weekend in the various rooms, hallways, and dim stairwells of Willy Mann's Uncle's House. True, it was, by turns, a beautiful, terrible, wrong, and lovely thing, but the force of its existence proved both undeniable and overpowering to us all, for within that house, though we could not articulate or even fully grasp it, all of us heard and felt, however vaguely, that feverish, short-lived heartbeat of teenage wildlife which called to each of us, stoking every youthful heart to dreams, possibility, and action.

*

I doubt my own experience of Willy Mann's Uncle's House was much at variance with that of my companions and fellow revelers, though I did have my own regular way of going about the place. I made it my habit, for instance, to first investigate the kitchen every time I arrived, always noting how there hardly ever was any food inside the stained and smeared refrigerator, while some form of alcohol seemed to lie behind the door of nearly every cabinet and closet, waiting to take part in the unceasing flow.

I have described the peculiar quality of the interior's appearance and indeed one could perpetually *feel* that strangeness, even when the house was packed to capacity and the music turned up to a level at which you could feel it in your chest and barely make out the mouthed scream of the person at your side. Long departed was Willy Mann's Uncle's Woman, but the aura of her—of her peculiar architectural imagination—remained a powerful—at times, overpowering—presence: the indelible remnant of her eccentric yet august taste.

I was then going through a phase of my youth in which I generally disliked meeting new people but enjoyed the feeling of encountering familiar faces without ever having to make their acquaintance, allowing them to disappear from memory until the next occasion their appearance produced some flicker of recognition.

Inevitably, it seemed, I would encounter "that guy" or "that girl" from the last party at Willy Mann's Uncle's House, but they remained only that. And it reassured me to come across them, early or late in the evening's revelry, standing as they always did, saying the same things, dressed not much different from the last time, signature drink in hand. I was always happy to see them and they me.

"Hey girl," or "What's up, man," I would say, and they would offer something in kind as we floated past each other like soul ships in the night bound for separate, far off ports. Then it would be over between us; nothing more ever was said. Seldom did we cross paths more than once per party, unless pure coincidence conspired to have us briefly glimpse one another emerging from a bathroom or straightening from an open cooler, shaking ice and water from a free hand. Such secondary chance meetings might elicit a smile or a wave but nothing more. Words were out of the question. Indeed, even so much as uttering each other's names—if in fact we knew them—would ruin the precious magic we enjoyed in being "that guy" or "that girl" to one another and destroy the comfort each afforded the other by way of that curious near-anonymity on a more or less weekly basis.

On the particular Friday night we had kidnapped Baby Jesus prior to our arrival at Willy Mann's Uncle's House (on the later side of things, as it happened), I found myself, having performed my customary survey of the kitchen, standing with two couples the girls of which I knew vaguely—neither too well, nor too little—and the boys not at all, which was just as I preferred. I had slept with the girls within a few weeks of each other the previous summer, but each of the trysts had been more or less understood as frivolous even at the times of their unfoldings which allowed us all to remain on more or less comfortable speaking terms, albeit a little guarded if a current love interest or two happened to be on hand.

The looks, names, even the personalities, of these two girls I took to be more or less interchangeable and when I smiled at each of them I enjoyed no luck at all in recalling which I had slept with first.

Their boyfriends, both of whom were from the city, had never visited Willy Mann's Uncle's House before and were chattering about sports cars—a little self-consciously, I thought—probably on account of the fact they knew hardly anyone in the place. Yet during a lull in their automotive conversation the novelty of their surroundings appeared suddenly to dawn on them, slicing through the confused haze of their social unease, significant egos, and shared automotive jargon.

"What's this guy's name again?" one of them asked me. "This guy's uncle?"

"Yeah," the other, taller, drunker one said. "Where exactly are we?"

"Don't know, guys," I said, shrugging. "No one's ever really seen him, except maybe Willy Mann, I guess. He's got a pretty cool house, though."

To this they could not help but offer up their assent and they looked about them—a little more comfortably, it seemed—before taking up their previous conversation. Turning my back on them, I winked at their dates before moving away across the room in search of a refill.

One of the great wonders of Willy Mann's Uncle's House lay in the menagerie of new faces it offered up week in week out. Some never-before-glimpsed set of features would drift in on a tide, as it were, only to find itself borne away by some invisible current, never to be seen again.

So it was that when I returned with a new drink the couples of my vague acquaintance were gone but in their place stood a girl of ripe and abundant charms who appeared lost, or, in any event, separated from anyone she knew. From the way she carried herself, it was obvious she was proud, as she had reason to be, of her breasts. She was shapely, dark, good-looking, yet it was not so much her prettiness that captivated me as the pronounced naturalness—the comfort with herself—which made her stand out, despite the uncertainty she was experiencing at that particular instant, among the more affected fellow party goers in her midst.

As I zigzagged toward her, evading swaying bodies and disarrayed furniture, I became aware of the familiar electric tremors moving within me and a slight pressure deep in my head. When she discerned my approach she appraised me flatly and as I arrived at her side, said nothing, waiting instead for me to speak.

"Lost your people?" I inquired.

She nodded coolly but offered no comment.

"It happens," I said. "This house has a tendency to swallow people. They go down a hallway or disappear into a room and you just don't see them again."

She smiled at this, glanced around, and then spoke for the first time—a breathy voice with a slight twang. "I've never seen the like of it."

I asked her where she was from.

"Nellysford. Born and raised."

"That's in the mountains."

She nodded. "You?"

"This very county. Raised but not born."

"Doesn't count then," she said. "Where are you from?"

"Richmond."

She smiled. "Ah, city boy."

I ignored the insult. "I was made there," I explained. "A long time ago."

"That's an odd way to put it."

I smiled at her, then nodded in agreement. "Best I can do, I'm afraid. Football. All those knocks on the head. Makes the slow ones like me even slower."

She laughed at this but shook her pretty head, a little reproachfully. "That's no excuse. All my brothers played and they're still sharp guys."

The conversation moved on from there to her interests and comparisons of our respective schools and upbringings. I studied her when she spoke, noting how hers was a vacant yet categorical sort of beauty that might have been a projection of her mind. She knew she was beautiful yet this knowledge seemed to make her sad. Despite my odd wariness toward dark-haired girls in those days, I decided I liked her—more than liked her really, under the circumstances, and suddenly—pressure in my head deepening—I felt as though I knew everything about her: her religious conviction (or lack thereof), her sexual history (adventurous within certain bounds), and her great life aspiration (to be envied and adored by great hordes of her peers).

I saw in my mind too in that moment—by way of a certain form of foreseeing, right or wrong, accurate or not—that she probably never would be truly satisfied; that she would serve as bridesmaid more than a dozen times before she reached thirty; that she would have affairs only with married men; that she would frequently be gossiped about and despised by lesser females. All this revealed itself to me as one glimpses an expanse of rugged terrain in a flash of lightning. But being a fatalistic loner I knew I would never get to know her better. "There is this night," I thought. "There is this night only." I grinned and, bending to swipe a can from a lonely unattended cooler at my feet, offered her a beer.

Just then a heavily hair-sprayed blonde ran past us, Guy in close pursuit, casting a sleazy drunken smile my way as he pressed past.

"Stop it, Guy! Stop it!" we heard in another part of the house a couple moments later.

The girl I'd been talking to looked troubled, but I smiled, retrieved the beer I had given her, and popped it open for her before handing it back.

"That happens most every time those two come here," I said with a bemused shake of the head—lying, smiling, vaguely worried about Guy's girl on account of what I knew of him.

But when the girl at my side smiled I knew the comment had done its work and saved the awkward moment, much to my relief and satisfaction. It humored me to believe I was something more than the meaty, insipid stud-males like Guy the stupid randy girls seemed to fall for so often, but then, at other times, I wasn't so certain.

And this girl was no fool, for suddenly her smile had disappeared, replaced, it seemed, by some wondrous intuition that if she came to know me better I would needlessly complicate her life. It was as if in that moment she saw directly into the shallow portion of my mind possessed of that simplicity which could not realize there were certain perfectly obvious things you could not do without involving yourself in more trouble than they are worth.

An awkward silence ensued and we averted our eyes from one another, glancing around, taking in the magnificent revel. I tried absently to gauge how drunk I was, yet this proved impossible since everyone around us was drunk too.

Just then something struck me near the top of the back, forcing me to take an involuntary step forward. I turned to discover an inebriated boy, much larger than me, laughing in the wake of the shove he had just delivered, though his eyes remained hard and refrained from participating in his guffaws. I noted too the girl I had been talking to had vanished into the crowd.

"That's my cooler, asshole," he said, pointing to the open igloo at my feet.

"Cool," I said, bending to retrieve another beer from it and handing it to him. "Have a cold one."

Drunk as he was, his face already was red, but it grew redder still as he swiped the beverage from my hand.

I waited, watching him. He was a couple inches taller than me and probably sixty or seventy pounds heavier, but he was fleshy and soft. Probably he was an offensive lineman, second string if the team was any good, or a starter if he happened to play for one of the sorry private school, rich-kid teams in the city.

He threw his beer down and took a step toward me, not realizing the mistake he was making. In those days I weighed probably a hundred and eighty pounds but could bench-press nearly twice my body weight and run fast and forever. I crouched, dropping my own drink and edging backward as he came on unsteadily.

"P----," he said in a low, slurred voice.

Then he lunged at me, or lurched rather, and began pummeling me clumsily with his fleshy fists. My raised right forearm took the ill-begotten blows readily enough and I noted between them how he was breathing hard already.

He was a fool. I knew all it would take was a slight shift in my footing and then the uncoiling upward.

Voices around us hooted. "Fight!"

"Hit him!" a part of my mind implored me seductively. "Destroy his face!"

But another part spoke too. "He's winded and played out," it murmured reassuringly. "He can't hurt you anyway."

Bad as I wanted to, I didn't hit him. Something in my head wouldn't let me. Perhaps it was the fact that he was a fool: a fat, drunken, f---ed-out fool possessing no inkling of the nature of his opponent or even where he was. All he knew in that dim-minded moment was his beer stash had dwindled by two and that it was worth fighting over.

But just then our own ungraceful drama gave way to another in the form of cries of alarm and the sounds of confused motion in other parts of the house.

"Cops! Cops!" someone yelled shrilly and suddenly all was a tumult—previously coveted coolers kicked over; drinks hurled down; illegal stashes hastily swallowed, shoved beneath cushions, or cast through open windows; stylish coats and pocket books stomped on—as indecision took hold of the partygoers and each contemplated somewhere in their minds whether to flee, affect innocence, or embrace the presence of the law and tearfully confess all their crimes and those of their friends.

My assailant having vanished—or rather lumbered away, pressing his own path through the confusion—I retreated slowly until my back brushed up against a wall next to one of the windows which had been flung open. I took a quick peek through it, noting the manageable distance to the barely discernible lawn, feeling the frigid refreshing December night air wash over my face. I could have jumped then, but I didn't. My curiosity held me in check. I knew I was clean and enough in control of myself to pass any drunk test, save a breathalyzer, and I wasn't driving. I wanted to see what the cops would do.

So I waited and soon there came the sound of authoritative adult male voices and the filing into the room—which, it so happened, was the largest in the house—of glum apprehended revelers, heads and shoulders drooped in dejection, fatigue, or perhaps the prospect of some indeterminate punishment.

The last of them were followed by two county deputies—a skinny, harried-looking man possessed of an angular, tight-lipped countenance, and a taller portly fellow whose expression was not unfriendly though his left hand never strayed from the top of the night stick dangling from his shiny black belt. When they had us all lined up along the walls and facing where they stood in tandem in the middle of the disheveled room, the friendly-looking one spoke in a voice many a country preacher would have envied for its affected warmth and goodwill.

"Now, friends," he said, "We're sorry to break in on your little assembly here, but it seems that in addition to the underage drinking goin on in here, there's been a most heinous theft performed by one in yall's number tonight."

As he let these words sink in on us the skinny deputy seemed about to speak, but instead bit his lip, face troubled and sour.

"Now it may be," continued the round, oily-voiced deputy, hand casually shifting from night stick to belt buckle, "that there don't got to be no arrests tonight. It may be everybody can just drive on home from this crazy-lookin place that we've known about for some time."

"For some time," he repeated for emphasis, nodding as he did so, eyes sweeping back and forth over us.

"But all that can cease to matter right here and now if one of yall tells us who's driving that green Blazer out there—the one with all the dents and the Farm Use plates."

I felt my body involuntarily tighten when these words were uttered, but then relax when I realized Guy wasn't in the room and that we had arrived late enough not to be observed getting out of his vehicle, which, in truth, was largely unknown even to our friends on account of the fact it seldom strayed from the pastures of Guy's family's farm, where he was fond of taking it down creeks and ramming it into terrified cattle.

A silence set in, which at last wrenched from the thin-lipped skinny deputy the words he could keep under wraps in his throat no longer.

"Where's that Jesus yall stole?" he asked in a short, clipped voice—a manner of speaking meant to throttle back the significant outrage which lay behind it.

Everyone looked around the room at each other, some in our number too drunk even to follow what was being asked of them.

"Looky here now," said the fat deputy, voice still smooth, "This can be a kindly-solved case or one that might call for a little pain and trouble so that we can get at the truth." He paused for effect. "But it will be solved tonight."

"Oh yes," he said, smiling again and offering another slow nod. "It will be."

It was then, as if the action was one he had rehearsed, the taunt slim officer dramatically drew out his night stick and began circling around the room, eyeing each of us in turn.

"Where's that Jesus?" he asked, clutching the weapon tightly as though he might wring the answer from it. "Don't nobody steal Jesus from a preacher's house in this county and get away with it."

"Just before Christmas too," said the fat one, voice somber, reproachful, seeking to elicit guilt even as the demeanor of his partner threatened. Good cop, bad cop, I could not help thinking.

The angular deputy passed by me, peering searchingly, meaningfully, into my face, and I cast down my eyes with a humble nod so as to appear in full compliance.

"Yall best tell us where that Jesus is at," he repeated, moving on, addressing no one in particular.

It was in that same moment, as if in answer to this incessant line of questioning, that the house itself responded—or seemed to—for all the lights in the place died simultaneously, sentencing everyone en masse to a blind placelessness that rendered us at once equals and strangers to one another.

An anonymous, democratic orchestra of stumbling, crashing, and curses filled the dark as young suspects made for hastily imagined exits while the deputies likely fumbled for their flashlights.

My proximity to the window made my own departure perhaps the most convenient of any in the place. Having located its sill, I stepped up onto it and then hopped out into the external lesser darkness, hitting the ground—some ten feet below, I'd guess—without so much as a stumble.

I landed in back of the house where a dim stretch of yard lay before me, framed on three sides by the deeper darkness of woods. It was the darkest patch of trees off to the left I made for, which, had there been more light, I would have recognized as the thick grove of old Virginia pines and cedars Willy Mann's Uncle's Woman had refused to have cut. Yet I knew it as such when sticky pine resin and cedar burrs greeted my hands and face as I entered the stand, slowing my progress and dissuading me from venturing too far in.

I turned to look back at the house, mist from my mouth floating across my field of vision. Noting that I hadn't been followed and that the structure was still possessed of a yawning blackness, I resolved to have a seat at the base of one of the cedars, head just below its bushy, prickly lower limbs. Hardened as they were from farm labor, my palms nonetheless gathered more burrs when I placed them on the ground so as to scoot to a slightly more suitable position, back against the trunk.

I have to say I was not uncomfortable then, sitting in the cold, dark, venerable grove Willy Mann's Uncle's Woman had found unable to timber—whose solemn silent presence had ushered her away—waiting to see what would happen next.

Eyes having adjusted to the dimness of a post-midnight quarter moon hindered by periodic cloud cover, I watched as thin shafts of light began to dart about inside the house, the deputies, I assumed, having located and ignited their flashlights at last. There was the sound too, from in front of the house, of slammed vehicular doors, awakening engines, and a barely audible fragment of voice here and there as my peers effected their getaways.

At last the irregular light show inside ceased and there occurred a final slamming of doors and starting of engines, before all was abandoned to darkness and silence. I kept as still as I could beneath the cedar, barely breathing, eyes fixed on the hulking blackness of the house. It was very cold—probably in the lower teens—and I had left my jacket inside, but I smiled in the dark, not knowing why I was happy, just knowing that I was. I sat there for a long time beneath those elder evergreen trees which had driven away Willy Mann's Uncle's Woman, alternately studying the house and the sky, enjoying myself in a way that was all mine. I tell you, I could have sat there the whole night and cannot recall anymore what drove me to elect not to. Cold has never much troubled me.

*

It was through the ornate basement entrance that I reentered Willy Mann's Uncle's House, its French doors already open, yawning tragically in the dim moonlight, white floor-length curtains billowing inward like beckoning valets. Between them I passed like a thief in the night, a forefinger barely tracing the outermost flutter of the curtain to my right.

I made my way about the place slowly. Here and there small battery-powered nightlights revealed meager stretches of floor and wall. Above one such illumination on the wall hung a clock which had stopped running, preserving indefinitely the instant at which the house had answered the deputy.

Of course, it was obvious to me that someone had thrown the main power switch in order to plunge the party into darkness and aid the revelers in escaping the police, but I came across no power box in the basement and, looking back now, likely made little effort, if any, to locate it. I much preferred the idea the house itself was responsible—that it had resolved to pause, freezing the downward current of its sands, as if to reflect on the events of that night, strangle the prospect of further action within its walls, and perhaps gather itself anew. Houses, I have learned, in the courses of their histories, witness many sad and happy sights, and some are more apt to forget or recall them than others. I knew even then Willy Mann's Uncle's House was a domicile that did not forget. Its memory was elephantine. It was one of the reasons I loved it.

As my friends were all long departed and the telephone receiver I succeeded in finding proved dead as the rest of the house when I lifted it to my ear, I made my way out as best I could, bumping a corner or chair with my hip here, toppling an empty or half-empty bottle with my foot there. Fond as I was of the place, gaining the front door was a relief, the frigid air of the late watch a blessing—not unlike a greeting from an old friend.

At the terminus of the frost-covered front yard which lay strapped by numerous tire tracks, I turned to take in the house a final time before starting down the road in the direction of a teammate's house I knew lay two or three miles distant. But barely had I mastered a hundred paces, approaching a point where the road curved dramatically, when I became aware of headlights and the roar of an engine coming toward me at an extraordinary speed. Indeed, it seemed sound and light were almost on top of me so fast, I marveled—even amid my alarm as I leapt into the ditch—how the car could master the curve at that speed.

Yet the driver must have been extremely familiar with that stretch of road, for he not only negotiated the curve, but used it as a kind of slingshot to propel the low, sleek shape of his car, brakes wailing, skidding toward the mailbox of Willy Mann's Uncle's House, where it came to a stop, not two feet from it, expertly aligned.

A hand deftly flipped open the door of the box and, joined by its other, withdrew a mountain of printed material. Then the car's engine revved and the machine jerked into the driveway, thin metallic sound of beer cans crunching beneath it, and the hollow roll of a bottle on pavement, to which the car must have struck only a glancing blow. The driver came to a stop precisely where he must have known an automatic outside flood light would switch on, for come on it did, bathing the rumbling dark shape in a stark white light, removing the night's mask to reveal a cherry red Camaro.

Either power had returned to the house since the short interval of my departure or the motion-triggered flood light was solar-powered (a distinct rarity in that region in those days). No matter, the nature of the vehicle was revealed to me, as was the figure now emerging from it with a great mass of mail tucked beneath an arm. He shut the car door gently and then turned to appraise the house, reclining lightly, casually, against his car as if he did not wish to disturb or trouble it too much. He was a slim man probably in his late thirties or early forties. Though not tall he was possessed of that sort of ranging leanness that lends vicarious inches to a man. His mouth and chin were sculpted in profile, and his nose would have been a fine one did it not seem a little askew, as if it once had been broken in such a way that ever after it must incline a little to the side. Though he slouched against his car, making no move to approach the house, there was an air of assurance about him—of ownership. It was difficult to be certain in that light, but it seemed his face was stubbled as though he had not shaved for perhaps the latter half of that week, and his dark hair was swept back, rather cavalierly, I thought. Half-zipped jacket by Members Only.

It was Willy Mann's Uncle. It had to be.

He took a few paces toward the side door of the house, ignoring the litter of beer cans and other trash in the driveway and yard, before turning to look back in my direction.

It was possible he might have glimpsed my moving form on the road as he sped into that curve as only he could, yet it was a distinct impossibility he could see me now where I stood, obscured by the night and trunk of a roadside oak. I say it was impossible and yet he stood there a moment longer, gazing in my direction, with an expression that might have been a smile—that I choose to imagine as such.

Then, turning suddenly, mail tucked beneath his arm—each parcel bearing the name I would never come to know—he flung open the door. He entered his house.

*

I turned it all over, or as much as I could, in my mind while walking down that quiet country rode, its silence and stillness deepened by the intense cold.

It felt to me then, as it does now, that Willy Mann's Uncle's grand, sudden moonlight arrival and my witnessing of it had signaled some kind of final departure for us all.

"We'll be back next weekend," everyone would say as a matter of course at the conclusion of a party.

But it was not true that night, for none of us were ever coming back any more. Time would move on in spite of the stopped clocks of Willie Mann's Uncle's House and reveal the majority of we country folk as retail salespeople and manual laborers living day to day, or—as then—weekend to weekend. Some of us would become alcoholics, several of us already well on our way, and others would do and sell drugs, commit brutal acts of violence, and engage in smalltime crime.

A couple would kill people and a couple others submit to a kind of stupefied despair, culminating in the extinguishing of themselves. How our seemingly inexhaustible springs of freshness and emotion—a bubbling cauldron or torrent when gathered together in that house—would diminish into bare trickles or bone-dry depressions in a matter of years.

Of course we none of us, even the most intuitive of our lot, could foresee with any clarity those sad destinies at that time. Our youth blinded us, as do the youths of all beings in all times. A kind of felt green and growing world surrounded us even in winter, vining about our minds, and we succumbed to it willingly enough, the overpowering brilliance of its intense sun discouraging us from gazing too long or intently at anything far off—any particular horizon.

For this reason and others, I choose to view that period of the 1990s as the time when the people of the generation I am counted among felt themselves most fully alive. And Willy Mann's Uncle's House enjoyed a paramount role in that experience, coming to possess us all after a fashion, though what particular brand of fascination or madness unwound our brains I am still at a loss to say. It almost seemed as though that house, as if conscious of its strange power, had demanded of each of us a conquering despot's fealty, an exorbitant price, that each of us eventually would be obliged to pay—sooner or later. Even me.

It is my belief, too, that Willy Mann's Uncle's House had, through its fueling of our lives, in some way come also to determine them, for when I had looked back at the house that final time, silent and inscrutable in its shroud of darkness, I had felt a connection with it—a vague feeling that my own usefulness was just beginning even as its had only just been used up. But then a deep and powerful yearning had taken hold of me when the house had released me and I struck out down the road again—a hope that in coming to be used up myself I might, in the process, discover some manner by which to recall and memorialize that pulse of savage exhilarating youthful life, of as many passionate lives, as that house had.

The Witching Women at Road's End
(creative nonfiction)

Slightly more than a century ago a Mr. Sherman Clabough was sheriff of Sevier County, Tennessee. One of his now scarce-remembered duties was to see to it that any young man in the section who turned twenty-one work the roads for an indeterminate period so as to pay off his mandatory poll tax. Of course, in theory a young man might satisfy the sum out of pocket, but it was irregular for anyone to have much, if any, money in those times, especially folk who came from families back up in the hollows and hills. So it was that between the young men in the district and whatever convicts happened to be on hand, the roads in the county—some of which spanned and twisted high up onto remote lonely slopes of the Smokies—were tenuously maintained.

The sheriff was a tall, stern man with blonde hair and blue eyes that occasionally were remarked upon for their piercing quality.

"He don't need that six-shooter to put holes in a body," a local man was heard to remark.

The sheriff's pa, dead for nearly a decade, had been a Captain in the 9th Cavalry during the war and Sherman, as his name intimated, had inherited much of his father's martial bearing. Though he was the runt of the family and the youngest of the four boys, it was he who took after his pa the most and so everyone allowed it was natural he should become a lawman or a soldier rather than a farmer or a preacher.

Before he was twenty he married a Dodgen girl, Mary, who gave him one child and died trying to deliver another not long after she turned eighteen. He remarried to an Ogle named Beda inside of two weeks, before Mary and her infant were even settled in the ground, and she filled his house with six children in eight years, the last four all born within a year of each other.

Now entering his fourth decade and with a sizeable family to feed, Sherman did not take unnecessary risks, though in his younger years he had drawn his pistol more readily and even killed a man on one occasion while riding against the White Caps. Sevierville, having cleared its streets of such vigilantes and been purged by fire at the turn of the century, had become a peaceable hamlet and Sherman found his duties not especially perilous. The occasional family feud in the mountains and mean weekend drunk were the only times he ever gave thought to drawing his pistol, and more often than not it was his capable deputies who handled such matters as these.

*

When trouble at last found Sheriff Clabough it was of a particularly woeful variety as it both implicated his official position and involved his extended family. One of his nephews, Columbus Clabough—the fifth child in his eldest brother Isaac's brood—had disappeared high in the mountains while working the roads to pay off his poll tax. Now everyone knew Columbus was no ordinary youngun of twenty-one. For one thing, he was either envied or admired among his male peers for having won the affection of the girl widely considered the prettiest thing around Gatlinburg, Cora Nichols. He was also the prized son of his father Isaac on account of having stayed on to work the family farm rather than taking flight like his older brothers and running off to Knoxville or joining up with the army.

It was a fact, however, that though Columbus was respected in those parts for having remained to help his ma and pa, there were aspects of his personality which were deemed not exactly in his favor. Some thought him mighty queer on account of the fact he always kept to himself so much, never leaving the homeplace up at the head of the hollow unless it was to attend the Banner schoolhouse, which he ceased to do at the age of fourteen, or run an errand for his folks in the Burg, which he always did directly and without any tarrying of his own. Though possessed of a good singing voice, he never attended church—not even revival, which generally was thought the best opportunity for a young man to accomplish any serious courting. Instead it was Columbus's habit when not working the farm to stray across the mountains—hunting, trapping, or gathering big messes of sang or ramps. What he came back with was always of uncommonly good quantity and quality, which drove more than one young man to try to follow him so as to determine where he harvested his bounty. Yet none ever succeeded in doing so. Either in a stream, a thicket, or on a rocky hillside, the boy's trail eventually would fade out and the thwarted tracker would return, not a little agitated and remarking how queer it was for a body to just melt away into the mountains like that.

Given such behavior, it surprised folks all the more that a gal like Cora Nichols had set her head on marrying a fellow like Columbus and done everything she knew to bring it about, from baking him cakes and pies aplenty to delivering them in her best red and yellow dress with neck cut low. She met with no initial success on account of usually finding Columbus out working the fields or away from home altogether on one of his jaunts across the mountains. By and by, however, he began to take notice of her and would bring vittles and furs and other things down the hollow to where Cora lived in a little cabin with her Aunt Azelia. Whenever he came to call the three of them inevitably would end up out on the porch in twisted old hickory limb chairs, perhaps in the wake of a meal, and hunt their heads for words to trade. Often this was a chore since Columbus wasn't the talking type and Cora and her aunt had said about everything two women could to one another on account of having lived together ever since Cora's folks had passed away when she was nigh more than knee-high. Yet they were all comfortable enough in each other's silent company in that way people not much given to talk often are.

There was never any sparking to speak of, nor even what might rightly be named courting, but a day eventually arrived when it may be said an understanding came about.

"How come you quit the Banner school," Cora asked Columbus, leaning forward in her chair so that it creaked, "when you was the best at reading for your age?"

It was the most direct question she had ever asked him and Columbus was silent for a long moment before responding. "I don't rightly know," he said at last, eyes vaguely peering up the hollow. "I reckon I'd about learned what I could and didn't much care for the company no more."

Undeterred by this response, which implicated Cora since she had attended the school as well, she followed it with another question, just as direct: "And why is it you never go to church and never been to revival?"

Columbus shifted a little in his chair in what might have been a slight show of discomfort, though when he answered his voice was the same. "I reckon again I don't much miss the company and most times I'm away across the mountains somewhere come Sunday."

Then Cora asked her most direct question, the one in fact which brought about their understanding. "Do you reckon when your ma and pa are gone you'll live all alone in that house up at the head of the hollow and never go nowhere except across them mountains?"

Columbus was silent for a long time, but when at last he answered he looked Cora directly in the face, with the same blue eyes his Uncle Sherman had. "I've never given any thought to the time when ma and pa are to be laid to rest, and I reckon there'll always be spells when I'm away in the mountains." He paused before continuing. "But whatever others may say, there is folks I like visiting and company I hope to always keep."

Columbus grinned as he uttered these last words even as Cora blushed, and though Aunt Azelia remained silent as a porch post, the words in her mind were "Praise be."

*

Though Sherman Clabough did not know the particulars of his nephew's vague and unconventional engagement, word had reached him of the young man's impending marriage to Cora Nichols. A fair judge of folks on account of the duties of his office, the sheriff was not so surprised as others by the arrangement. Having sporadically taken note of the boy as he grew, he admired rather than took umbrage at Columbus's withdrawn silence, independence, and penchant for hunting up things in the mountains. Moreover, the fact that the boy had stayed on to work brother Isaac's farm was a comfort to his mind and he mused more than once that if the youngun were to become a little more sociable and were so inclined, he might make a decent deputy by and by.

Yet now Sherman feared the worst and suffered a not insignificant burden of guilt as each day passed following Columbus's disappearance. After all, it was he who had allowed the boy to conduct his road work alone, as he had requested, along the most obscure of mountain thoroughfares, many of which constituted little more than trails. At the time it had seemed a natural fit for his nephew's independence and extensive knowledge of the slopes. Yet now all manner of potential dangers haunted his mind: from chance encounters with rattlers or painters to human menaces from the likes of bootleggers or jealous admirers of Cora Nichols.

Columbus's axe, rake, and shovel had been discovered resting against a stunted chestnut tree at the end of a road high on a rocky peak as if they had been set there in no particular hurry, yet in vain Sherman rode the nearby trails and hillsides, putting his deputies and volunteer searchers to shame by staying out the better part of several nights and occasionally even sleeping in the saddle. Still the mountains offered him no clues and with each passing day Sherman's hope waned even as his deputies took to trading uncertain glances among themselves and the volunteers began to straggle away. After all, it was not unusual for a man to be taken by the mountains and the folks who lived among the Smokies had a feeling— not unlike a clock in the head—when it looked as though a body was gone for good. And as much as Sherman Clabough sought to ignore the ticking in his own mind, he had begun to accept, loath as he was to do so, that too much time had elapsed and it was not for him to lay eyes on his nephew again.

*

On the day of his disappearance, Columbus Clabough worked steadily toward the end of the road he knew was about to give out. He had passed the last residence, a dilapidated abandoned cabin said to have been built by a trapper before the war, some two miles back down the mountain and kept on along the switchback curves and crumbling limestone roadbed as the way grew ever narrower. Here and there saplings had sprung up in the road due to its lack of use and these he felled with one-handed blows of the axe, leaving them where they lay as he moved on, rake and shovel gripped together in his other hand. A more challenging task was lifting or rolling to the roadside boulders which had tumbled down into the thoroughfare. Some were the manageable size of cantaloupes or watermelons while others proved more on the order of trunks or chests. It was these latter rocks he struggled with the most, grunting as he awkwardly turned them end over end toward the road's edge.

It was getting on late in the work day. The sky remained overcast. Even though it was only the beginning of October, the air was raw and pointed, propelled by a constant breeze one often encounters when nearing the summit of a mountain. Columbus knew if he lingered much longer he would be hard-pressed to make it home before dark. Yet something within him—pride, stubbornness, the vanity of youth—filled him with a desire to finish off the road: to see both it and his labor on it to their respective ends.

It is not difficult to guess which course of action won out. Toil on he did, hurling or rolling boulders and chopping saplings, until he arrived at what he reckoned must have been the road's terminus. One must say reckoned, for though the imprint of the roadbed continued on, the saplings sprang up in clumps, mere inches from each other, and two great immovable rocks the size of wagons blocked any further potential progress by a wheeled vehicle.

The clouds had thickened, dimming the mountainsides, and casting the hollows into a deeper hue of darkness. Columbus knew it was time to depart and that he'd likely be walking in the moonlight ere he reached the other side of Gatlinburg. Yet he lingered on for a moment considering with some satisfaction first the cleared way behind him and then the wall of rock and wood which dictated the thoroughfare's end. But just as he turned from taking in the sloping mountainside forest which lay beyond the cessation of his efforts, his nose caught a whiff of wood smoke and another odor he could not quite place. Taking note of the shifting breeze, he determined the smell was borne from around the mountainside. He paused only for an instant, realizing that searching out the smoke condemned him to a night's journey or sleeping in the woods, yet he had embraced such privations before and, besides, had made it his life's business to search out the mysteries and forlorn places of the Smokies. Carefully he laid his tools against a chestnut trunk and set off in the direction the wind beckoned.

He walked perhaps a quarter of an hour in the fading dimness before he caught the smell again. It was stronger this time but issued it seemed from a place higher up the mountain. Accordingly, he adjusted his course, making his way patiently, taking short shuffling steps so as to avoid slipping on an invisible loose rock or tumbling over a wayward root.

The mountainside steepened, the quantity of trees lessening and giving way to bushes and outcroppings of rock. Columbus found himself leaning forward, grasping narrow trunks and edges of rock for support, before collapsing to all fours and drawing himself up bodily wherever his hands found something sturdy enough to bear him. It was dark now and he advanced as much by touch as sight.

At last he emerged on a rock plateau of sorts where he could stand straight again, and it was here his search concluded, for some way across the rocks, accompanied by the now-familiar odor, he made out the faint glow of a fire flickering in the breeze and what he took to be the hint of a voice.

It was not difficult to walk quietly over the rock and Columbus advanced slowly in the darkness, taking short steps, ears attuned. Yet silent as he treaded, when he came within perhaps twenty paces of the fire, a voice rang out—feminine, old, raspy.

"Come on over and fool your face, pilgrim!" it exclaimed.

"Yes'm," he replied into the mountain wind for lack of anything else better to say.

As he advanced the unsteady flames revealed two old women clad all in black standing on either side of the fire, on which stood a large dark pot.

The sight of the pot revealed to Columbus the odor he had been unable to name: moonshine. Yet he had never heard tell of woman bootleggers and ancient ones at that. Indeed, their bearing and the whole scene rather suggested his mother's childhood tales of witching women. Lacking in superstition, Columbus felt foolish at the thought but troubled nonetheless.

When he came to stand within the full illumination offered by the firelight, what he saw added to his discomfort. The two female figures might have been twins in their horrid decrepitude. They shared the same deep wrinkles, hooked noses, and toothless mouths, only one of the old women—the one he guessed must have called out to him—possessed twinkling, hard black eyes while the other wore a near-oblivious expression on her hanging yellow cheeks.

The more observant of the pair watched Columbus as her hand stirred the pot with a thick stick.

"Welcome, Columbus Clabough," she said.

"You know my name?" replied the incredulous youth.

"It's long been our habit to know what goes on in these mountains," said the old woman, "and we figure there's less than the number of fingers on a hand, the men who might hunt us out when we're about our business—and Isaac Clabough's wandering boy is one of them."

"But I won't hunting you," said Columbus, growing more uncomfortable.

"Yet here you are," said the old woman, black eyes flashing briefly in the firelight. "Here you are."

To combat his growing anxiety Columbus began to talk, unconscious of the fact his words occasionally stumbled over each other. He was working the old road that ran up the other side of the mountain. He had smelled the smoke. It was nothing to him what the two old ladies were doing up here.

The speaking crone interrupted him. "When there's folks that take an interest in a body's business, even if they don't mean to, well then them's folks a body most likely can do without."

For the first time the other old woman made a sound—a guttural, watery, ascending noise that might have been muffled laughter.

Columbus fought back something akin to fear. He was being threatened. The thought of such feeble creatures doing him any physical harm seemed laughable, yet he wondered if they were alone or if there could be others somewhere out in the darkness. How had these two hags toted a big pot to the summit of the mountain without benefit of any road or trail Columbus knew of? He shivered involuntarily.

"There's a comet a-coming," said the first one.

"What?" asked Columbus, nearly at wits' end. "What's that?"

"A thing that flies from place to place across the heavens. Folks will have never seen the like."

The other hag grinned.

"It'll glow at night," continued the first one, "and the tail that comes out behind it will be near as wide as the sky and black as coal."

She ceased stirring the pot suddenly and, flattening her wrinkled hand, passed it over the pot.

"The tail of that comet will sweep across the earth," she continued, "and when it passes some things will be changed though folks won't know what they are."

Then she lapsed into a raspy fragment of song:

> There was an old woman didn't have but one eye.
> But she had a long tail that she let fly.
> Every time that she went through a gap,
> She left a piece of her tail in a trap.

The crone grinned at Columbus in the wake of the last verse, the gaping blackness where her teeth should have been transforming the expression into a disgusting, mirthless gesture.

"What's the tune about, boy? It's a riddle."

Columbus shook his head, no longer capable of thinking clearly.

"Why, a needle, of course," said the old woman, as if instructing a child.

"Now looky here," she continued, "you do something for us—you make like that needle and go where we say go for a spell—and you needn't pay no mind to comets and ailments and the like. You'll live a long life to boot, though its writ on you you'll never have any younguns to call your own."

"Elect to do otherwise and you'll have worries aplenty, now and on up till the time of your dying."

Columbus looked from one hag to the other, taking in again their dreadful physical degradation which nonetheless afforded them a power he lacked the capacity to fathom. He realized suddenly he had been sweating heavily, his shirt well-nigh drenched. The breeze shifted suddenly and the smoke of the fire washed over him, forcing unbidden tears to form in the corners of his eyes. He coughed softly, lowering his head, and on trembling lips he offered them his response.

*

Columbus Clabough died in December 1973, a few months shy of his ninetieth birthday and just a handful of weeks before I entered the world. True to the prophecy of the witching women he and Cora Nichols never had any children, and true to an oath they exacted of him, he never told anyone the nature of the service he performed for them. His body lies in Lynnhurst Cemetery, Knoxville, the secret buried with him.

The Succubus and I: A True Romance of the Twenty-First Century
(fiction)

Succubus (suhk-yuh-buhs)*: a supernatural female entity who engages in sexual intercourse with a mortal man, feeding on his life force to sustain herself until he is exhausted of all energy and/or perishes.*

—*Professor Nicolas Bourbaki*, Necronomicon Concordia, Volume III

In truth the collective identification and study of the curious entities termed Succubi among English-speaking scholars of the occult has unfolded only as a most gradual process of distillation across time and cultures, so that even now—in this unprecedented era of highly specialized scientific disciplines and technologies—these paranormal females remain but half-believed manifestations of vague legend or rumor, inhabiting precariously only the remotest recesses of the popular mind. Yet it remains they constitute a fundamental phenomenon, a kind of barely discernible archetypal echo, tethered to our very beginnings, and moreover—that is, if we happen to cast an uneasy eye toward the other end of the great divide of existence—one that seems destined to dwell with us: to accompany our sad species, not unlike an attractive date to some dreaded momentous social function, as we approach our impending collective end. Or at least I can here step forward from this introduction's cloud of ruminative abstraction to attest that, in my own circumstances, the being of their kind with whom I became acquainted elected not to abandon me at the threshold of death.

Doubts notwithstanding, it should prove easy enough for even the most skeptical and iconoclastic of readers among you—those whose polite disdain for the supernatural long ago mushroomed into unfeigned ridicule—to envision and appreciate the nature of Succubi since they have come to be—however unconscious the apprehended presence of their being—something most all of us vaguely sense or otherwise know, lurking about, as it were, within the liquid-wall confines of what the mind scientists once termed the collective unconscious with an apparent total disregard for and immunity from such otherwise limiting factors as borders, beliefs, and epochs. In a number of African cultures, for example, the Succubus is known as "the witch riding your back," while the Yoruba people of southwest Nigeria variantly refer to her as "Ogun Oru," which means "nocturnal warfare." An obscure and as yet untranslated article in the *Chirurgical Journal,* that authoritative nineteenth century periodical of parapsychological studies, noted that in the frigid and forlorn island folk culture of Iceland she is called "Mara," and here we must note that our still much-used, perhaps overly-used, word "night*mare*" has drifted down to we speakers of English by way of that name. Other traditional European cultures recognized her in like fashion and named her in kind: the Proto-Germanic "maron"; the Old English "mære"; the German "Mahr"; the Dutch "nachtmerrie"; the Old Norse "Faroese"; the Old Irish "morrigain"; the Polish "mora"; the French "cauchemar"; the Romanian "moroi"; the Czech "mura"; and so on.

By definition and persuasion she is a taker, a conqueror: a powerful being driven nonetheless by great hunger, prodigious needs. In India, where she is called Mohini, she ascends into the world of mortals by way of a remote deep well—the appearance of which, when you peer down into it, is really more akin to an abyss than a well—in search of that particular male lover who might help to provide her with the more-than-human child-being she desires. In New Guinea this process of male-harvesting is called "Suk Ninmyo" and is believed to originate from certain sacred trees which feed nocturnally on the essence of human men in order to sustain themselves.

In Greece and on Cyprus, where the Succubus might take the name of Vrahnas or the more ominous-sounding Varypnas, she is said to abscond with her victim's speech—his fundamental ability to form words—as well as his energy and love, and is known sometimes to sit atop him, pressing down upon his chest with extraordinary force, occasionally to the point of asphyxiating him. Similarly, in Hmong culture there exists a description of an experience called "dab tsog" or "crushing demon," in which the victim becomes aware of a tiny female figure, no larger than a small child really, straddling his torso and squeezing with a power capable of fracturing a strong man's ribs. And as incredible as the fact might seem to the educated contemporary mind, it is nonetheless all too tragic and true that the vast and disturbing number of American Hmong males on record as having died in their sleep for no apparent reason has prompted the Centers for Disease Control to add to its distressing institutional vocabulary the specialized term "Sudden Unexpected Nocturnal Death Syndrome."

Indeed, as the story I am about to convey will attest, men of our own time are far from spared the dire, yet ultimately largely traceless, otherworldly presence of these Succubi. Of special note, in sections of the American South (the states of the old Confederacy), including my own native Virginia, she often is referred to as "Old Hag" despite her alluring appearance of youth and beauty, though in the mountain South of my father's people, the craggy hills and hollows of Appalachia, she is more likely to be labeled a "haint," a visitation from whom usually serves as an omen for some approaching tragedy or mishap. The death of a great uncle, in fact, was foretold in just this manner when a haint of extraordinary beauty and force called upon my great-grandfather as he lay sleeping beneath Heintooga Bald in the midst of a winter journey across the Smoky Mountains to Asheville during the eighth decade of the nineteenth century.

As I was not the first in my family line to encounter a Succubus, what more might be said here of the nature of the visited, for without such men as us there would exist no record of the entity? Does our victimhood, such as it is, derive from some arcane curse or gift? Or might there be more tangible reasons—traceable variables or traits—that lead us to be chosen? In researching these questions parapsychologists have pointed to a link between male sexuality and ultraconsciousness—that is, a communicative association which couples the masculine sex drive with certain paranormal predispositions. The concomitant measure of each, proclaims the data, is determined largely by a combination of a man's psychological attitudes toward sex and a complex array of particular genetic factors as determined and modulated by the pineal gland: a tiny endocrine gland located deep inside the skull which functions both as an eye receptor and a regulator of sexual maturation.

Is it possible, then, that there is something about the victim which dictates the attraction and subsequent conduct of a Succubus? Might it turn out, after all, in the great majority of cases, that he is truly less a victim and more a catalyst— perhaps even a catalyst possessed of some curious degree of agency? Could it be that we victims so-called are as much the haunters of their world as they of ours? Perhaps the successful proof of such a hypothesis would indeed prove something unprecedented and even profound, though I am not at liberty to say what. And whether it ultimately would have, beyond the most restless shadows of doubt, any bearing upon the unlikely events I am about to recount likely will never be known.

I shall tell you what occurred. You can judge for yourself.

*

I had fallen into an existence of cloudy weather, eschewing both the spotlight of stark illumination and the sightless black of darkness deepest. There is many a person whose soul, at one time or another, has gone to sleep like a leg, and such a person then was I. My usually responsive face, perpetually open and receptive to all the four winds, had taken on an abstract look as though posing to the various beings and things it encountered the same unanswerable question.

I had been suffering from a medical condition, an especially debilitating manifestation of a certain peculiar affliction which had haunted me since my earliest days but had grown much worse of late, until at last it had broken me. The effect of this defeat left me not so much a bad man, but, in a very real and unfortunate sense, a ruined man—that is, damaged in such a way that seemed beyond my capacity to self-diagnose or repair. It was as if I had realized very suddenly just how debilitated and exhausted I gradually had become and, as a result of the jolt accompanying that epiphanic knowledge, had subsequently collapsed into a low ebb of existence—a particular, self-styled Slough of Despond—which those conditions prescribed and demanded.

It is true that even before my illness I had been described on occasion by even my fondest of acquaintances as eccentric or mysterious or even sorcerous, but we are not privy here to the requisite space for an investigation of these purported unnatural—what some might even consider "magical"—qualities. I believe you will agree when I suggest these outlandish (and, I dare say, wholly inaccurate) characterizations must necessarily prove of little relevant moment in light of the nature of that otherworldly being who sought me out. This document should be more her story than mine, or, at the very least, the faithful account of my dealings with she who I suppose must be labeled the heroine of this tale.

Here I am strongly tempted to dawdle for a while and indulge in the particulars of how the association between the Succubus and I began and unfolded. Indeed, were I to follow my own wishes, I would assemble a minute and detailed description of our first encounter as well as the ensuing earliest meetings—of our various talks and hastily deepening bond. Fortunately, however, I am aware the great majority of readers in your midst would not share my enjoyment of such an exercise. To combat that risk of readerly superfluousness then and get on to the more crucial events, I shall reluctantly omit the particulars of those initial episodes in favor of summarizing their general flavor and hue. In other words, let's keep a few paces back from the canvas for now, taking in the whole of the painting, rather than drawing out some magnifying glass and craning forward to scrutinize one of its insignificant corners.

I should admit, however, before proceeding further, that the narrative decision I have just settled upon is as much one of literal necessity as it is a carefully weighed preference, for were I to attempt a conveyance of the details of my initial meetings with the Succubus, it likely would neither form in my mind nor leap from the page very readily. Though the precise reasons for this haziness of recollection and expression evade me, I am not especially surprised by the condition, knowing as I do how my great-grandfather's memory of his episode with the haint on the Heintooga mountainside was afflicted by a similar lack of detail: a like degree of impeded clarity, a blurriness with regard to past experience. Attempting to summon up an account of my very first meeting with the Succubus, I am rewarded with almost nothing, though I do recall that it occurred very late into the night, perhaps closer to early morning. I recollect too the unprecedented sensation of becoming aware of a mysterious and powerful sensual essence beyond any state of dream which slowly coalesced into the felt form of a female being. Beyond the intensity of sexual experience which followed, however, I can offer very little. Whether we kissed once or many times I cannot recall. The truth of whether we joined in love once or repeated the oldest human dance twice or more is gone from my mind now as well. And it troubles me to no small degree, as moving as the experiences was—among the most significant of my life, really—that I cannot recollect more.

I can tell you that the nature of the visitations, for she did come again, over the course of the ensuing nights altered slowly so that they seemed less wild physical passion and more the delirious abstract promise of overpowering happiness. In fact, the sensuousness of sensation seemed as much an exchange of minds as of real or imagined bodies. She murmured sympathetically to me about matters concerning myself as well as my closest relations, followed by long meaningful silences of the sort that occur without awkwardness only among the best and most intimate of confidants. I awakened mornings with a sense of undeserved joy hovering about the bed. Despite the fantastic—perhaps even the outrageous—quality of what was transpiring, I have to say that my reaction to her discovery of me was not one of surprise. Rather I felt as though I had been expecting her my entire life.

From my very first acquaintance with the Succubus I realized she possessed a degree of beauty and intuition that living females do not enjoy. Though I could not see her, the image of her form that came to me most often was of a young woman in a long white dress swaying slowly, rhythmically, patiently, in a rocker or porch swing, seemingly at her leisure yet all the while marking intently the world about her. Whenever she appeared to me the nature of existence itself suddenly became a beautiful and enchanting phenomenon, the very air shimmering with her presence and echoing with a high, cascading, sustained sound not unlike wind chimes. I relate these descriptions, mind you, with the full realization that their fanciful quality is likely to deepen those reservations of skepticism harbored by some of you and perhaps lead others in your midst to proceed even further and reckon me mad. Be that as it may, I hope that for the moment you will suspend your judgment of me in favor of focusing on and appreciating the nature of the entity I am describing. For truly she *was* something at which to marvel. And surely any man among you—regardless of time and circumstance, including those of you just becoming young men in this uncertain now of today—would quickly come to adore and treasure a being such as her. I must insist that it would be so, for I cannot imagine otherwise.

Very quickly it seemed to me as though the Succubus became my female counterpart or equivalent in just about every particular. We felt little need for asking each other questions. We seemed to know each other better than anyone else. It was like this: we grew into each other like two winding trees rising from the same bit of earth: pressing, touching, overlapping. And in the midst of this growing, against the backdrop of our shared silence, I became aware of a pleasant low hum as if some expert chorus of molecules had come to inhabit and serenade the air around us. At first I did not know what this meant, but gradually it dawned on me. What I was hearing was the sound which announces that love has begun.

Our happiness was lyrical. "I am the embodiment of all you have ever wanted in a woman," she would say in that husky voice of hers. And in the same voice she informed me of the previous men whose lives she had emptied or otherwise claimed, drawing on them until they were little more than hollow-eyed, lean-jawed shells. There had been a great host of them and they all had wanted her very much. "But you are different," she would say in the voice. "You are the one I will leave yourself so that you might dwell with me."

But then, very suddenly, as is often the case in life, the course of events changed. The meteorological hue of my sunny, almost daily experience with the Succubus, which had smiled upon me warmly up to that point, began to darken and cool, slowly altering its expression to that of a frown. It was if she had come to sense some hesitancy or reluctance on my part toward the overpowering quality and depth of our connection and had not the capacity to process that impression with anything other than fear and resentment. I knew very little about her past at that time, but I was visited by the impression that here was a being whose experience had taught her to fear the worst even as all appears well. It was as if the anxiousness with which she watched me gauged by subtle signs some imminent unpleasant event, the flames of her anxiety fanned by an intimate knowledge of how he or she who has lost and who fears the more remains always the inferior and the sufferer. I would add to this interpretation of the ripples of her thought the simple observation that, in my experience, any gifts added to a beautiful and remarkable woman must be paid for—that is to say, those very qualities which pass as positive characteristics in less attractive and accomplished females too often manifest themselves as dangerous liabilities in their more desirable sisters. Despite her supernatural essence, I believe she was subject to this all-too-human truth.

And so the whimsical sensual nature of the Succubus that had so drawn and compelled me turned brooding and lugubrious. Her voice, theretofore a delicious medley of rare hot spices and rich soothing honey, came forth now with dog-voiced harshness. I am ashamed to admit that my response to her anxiety was wanting, for I made the mistake of attempting to reason with her, recalling too late that a tactic of that sort falls in line with certain forms of magnanimity which function very well among men but are usually misplaced, if not utterly disastrous, in dealings between men and women. There is, as the saying goes, a man's atmosphere and a woman's atmosphere, and it is rare for them to mix very well except in the proper place: beneath the sheets. Thus the Succubus turned and changed, her alteration hastened by fear, while I failed repeatedly in my attempts to soften or placate her. She ceased to visit me altogether and in place of her presence I began to awake in the night with a tightness in my chest as though some invisible force sought to pin me to my bed. I knew nothing then of Hmong culture or "Sudden Unexpected Nocturnal Death Syndrome"—I had yet to embark on the formal study that would contextualize the precise nature of what I was I dealing with—but my dark vivid dreams and occasional near-suffocation constituted sufficient evidence that my nightly discomfort stemmed from something more than coincidence or a sagging mattress. I sensed the imperceptible movements of her graceful hands behind my cloud of discomfort and came almost to be afraid of her.

It was during this period of adversity and uncertainty that I might have made one of those firm and fine moral decisions people make in books and resolved to shun her, quitting the region perhaps and removing to some other part of the country. As I was, by that time, well on the way to recovery from my aforementioned malady—my experience, my romance if you will, with the Succubus having hastened my convalescence—I felt healthy enough to knock about again as I once did and, indeed, the temptation at that time to disappear for a week or so into one of the vast stretches of Virginia's national forests, as I had done on occasion in my younger years, was very great.

Instead, owing to my general state of indecision and perhaps a craving for some limited measure of distraction and fellowship, I resolved to spend an evening with a friend at a favorite café. I had many friends in those days, most of whom owed me a favor or two on account of some secret, unbidden deed I likely had performed on their behalf behind the scenes. It was one of the things I was known for back then. The friend I had selected to share my company and absorb the unburdening of my dilemma was a fellow I knew neither too little nor too well. A steady chap, he might have been called—unimaginative, balanced, conservative—whose discreteness I knew had been favorably put to the test by others of our acquaintance on a number of occasions. Gauging my own mind as a whimsical one, I likely hoped his more sensible outlook might offer a judicious perspective on my circumstances if one was to be had.

Indeed, such was the almost unflappable quality of this fellow's steadfastness that his eyebrows raised but slightly as I completed the account of my association with the Succubus up to its then current state of menacing downward trajectory.

He sipped at his drink, for a long pull would have violated that signature cool steadfastness, and leaned back in his chair before speaking. "Why did you keep on seeing her when it started going all to hell? Why are you still sleeping in the same bed, the same house, now?"

"It's like I'm compelled to. She draws me, I reckon."

"Draws you?"

"Draws me."

His eyes grew more intense as I repeated myself, until they acquired a slightly glazed quality. "If that's the case, then I think its all the more crucial you keep away from the place."

"What if she follows after me?"

"Well, you say she hasn't been visiting you lately. Maybe she won't."

"I was thinking just that thought when I fell asleep last night. It was when I heard her voice in my head."

"Her voice?"

"Yes. She wasn't there. I mean, I didn't feel her presence. But I heard her. I heard that voice."

Phlegmatic as my manner was in those days, I must have looked disturbed when I answered, for his lips were already slightly parted before he asked the inevitable question. "What did she say?"

I hesitated before answering. "What she told me was that when I died I would be hers."

In the ensuing moments both of us were silent, each of us toying with our drinks, our eyes wandering around the other tables of the dark little café, reluctant to meet each other. At last he began holding forth with the long-winded clichéd perspective on life which I had expected to receive beforehand and knew was designed to rally my spirits.

"All of this will pass," my friend said as he neared his conclusion. "People don't live in a state of emergency forever; things work themselves out. I hope you won't take this the wrong way—its kindly meant—but I think maybe you've been spared some of the periodic jolts the rest of us encounter fairly regularly. Perhaps when you do happen to experience a real crisis your friends are slow to recognize it on account of your having been that fellow who has been there so often for them. That and you always seem to have it together—at least outwardly. I believe our mutual friends tend to buy into a certain illusion that your life is settled and easy just because you're clever and good-looking and are rumored to have a fat cock or whatever. It's shallow but understandable, you know?"

He laughed abruptly before allowing the lines of his mouth to lapse into a sympathetic smile. Yes, I did know, but merely returned his smile and said nothing. I had learned it is just as well to let friends tell you things you already know when they wish to. It disposes them kindly toward you if you suffer them to impart information they deem, however erroneously, special and their own. In truth, as cynical as it might sound, I have to say I expected no real wisdom from him or even an intelligent understanding of my trials. My friends in those days were all very charming, and charming friends need not possess much in the way of minds for us to be fond of them. I was of a kind who loved his friends most dearly—would do anything for them—yet I had long ago ceased to confide in them anything of an especially private or significant nature. I was decidedly out of practice then when it came to disclosing the complexities of my inner life and probably had done so poorly on this occasion. When I thanked my friend I did so with heartfelt gratitude and sincerity, but it was accompanied by the sad and helpless abstract feeling that I had come to know too many people and had been much happier when there were not so many in my life.

I dwelled on that somber thought again as I lay in bed that night but made no further progress with it. It was replaced following a period of dozing by the words the Succubus had uttered to me the night before: "When you die you will be mine."

I possessed no inkling then that this statement might eventually confirm itself as nothing short of true, and, indeed, how could I? At that time I was still laboring beneath the misconception that I remained master of my fate. Whatever the limits of my perceptions and devices, however, a collective darkness—what might be labeled, in the vernacular, a "bad feeling"—perpetually inhabited the fringes of all my ruminations, and the essence of it existed in—was articulated by—the words of the Succubus. There was something in their sound and meaning that felt wrong and humiliating, like overhearing one's partner joke with their lover about your most intimate shortcomings and faults. Yes, there was something of that. But worse than hurtful irreverence, worse even than the declaration that all I constituted was destined to become forcibly owned, was the coupling of the two of us—of the Succubus and I, of all that so recently had been beauty and love and freedom—beneath so cruel and black a banner of fate. It felt to me, as though in a nightmare—like thought melted into nightmare—as if some great winding dark sheet were descending from the heavens to envelop us both in a common grave.

*

We arrive now at the big gap of time that stared me in the face when I began this narrative, and though minute actions certainly occurred during the interval we are about to skip over and life went on, I believe it is in the best service of what I wish to convey to pause briefly for the purpose of engaging in a little necessary speculation and reflection. As I have refrained to this point from relating too many tiresome particulars, I hope you will see fit to perform a kindness and indulge me a little here.

Chiefly, I wish to address the important question of why I might have been singled out by the Succubus, for beyond the genetic and parapsychological factors I outlined in my ponderous introduction, there is little really which has established me as being much at variance with other men of my time. Yet it is true that throughout my life I have been something of a wanderer and a wonderer and a taker of risks—far beyond the extent, in fact, of anyone I have known—and I believe that is one of the chief reasons the Succubus was attracted to me so. By any conventional measure, I should have died on a number of occasions, and eventually, of course, I did. For here I must own up that I have been deceased these past two years. I hope you will forgive me for withholding this crucial fact up until now, but it seemed necessary to do so in order to establish between us something resembling a bond. For those readers among you who may feel slighted or cheated or betrayed by the tardiness of the disclosure rest assured the particulars of my demise are directly forthcoming. I trust you realize how truly grateful I am at the privilege of having passionate, discerning readers such as yourselves considering my words at all and my gratitude in light of your generous and enduring patience is especially deep and appreciative. Thank you for bearing with me, for suspending your impatience, that we might soon come to understand one another a little better.

When I graduated from college, there were two things I could do remarkably well: write a passable paper and deliver prodigious amounts of pleasure to those with whom I found myself intimate. Despite having chosen as mine a retiring sort of scribbling academic profession, the second of these abilities—a talent for loving, it might be called—proved far more meaningful and rewarding over the course of my life than the first.

I seem to have been born with an ability, often associated with those possessed of an artistic temperament, to place myself in and experience the lives of others, and, in particular, I have always felt a special affinity for girls—that is, the behaviors and manners that mark them as girls and which conspire to make them appear whimsical and even altogether traceless to most all boys. Even at the very first childhood dances of my youth—the girls huddled at one end of the floor and the boys at the other, unmindful of the urgings of chaperones and parents—it was I who broke the stalemate, drifting across the empty divide and selecting always the girl who seemed to me the most alone, the most apart from the others. She might have been the prettiest girl though most often she was not. Remarking first upon her hair or how her earrings matched her shoes or the way in which the manifold shades of her long dress seemed to flow so fluidly into one another, I would get around at last to requesting that she join me on the dance floor. Though the following statement very well may be construed as a manifestation of pride or vanity, I must offer nonetheless that not on a single occasion was I rejected. And once this groundbreaking action was performed—my chosen partner and I swaying alone in tandem, apart from everyone else, the sole denizens of a dim musical universe—the others gradually would pair off and fall in, helping us to people that curious space we two had been first to discover and explore.

Because I was genuinely interested in the girls that I knew, I always listened to them very closely, and, in turn, they treasured the unusual fact that a boy their age would be interested enough to listen and, moreover, take their concerns seriously. For this reason, on a number of occasions, I often was the only boy in attendance at some birthday party or social function otherwise populated solely by girls and perhaps a few of their mothers. Either out of politeness or genuine acceptance, no one to my knowledge ever commented upon the curiousness of this phenomenon. If anything, the mothers in attendance tended to make over me more than the daughters of their peers, referring to me as a good sport and a little gentleman and so on. As for my own mother who bore me to these functions the mild social oddity of my being the only boy in attendance either passed unnoticed or seemed a subject of relative insignificance to her formidable and otherwise occupied nonconformist intellect.

And so the girls at these parties giggled and squirmed in their chairs, white stockinged feet in shiny black buckled shoes tapping loudly on hardwood floors beneath some white table-clothed dining room table, while I smiled and looked on and joined in when it was time to blow out the candles or sing a song. Afterwards I would dutifully play the games that had been planned—pin-the-tail-on-the-donkey a mainstay among them—performing neither too well nor too shabby, pacing myself alongside those girls who tried but a little or tried hard and failed, so as not to arouse jealousy or call too much attention to myself. And if our play spilled out of doors into some spacious backyard or shady country grove, skirts and ribbons fluttering amid the headlong, I inevitably was assigned the role of fort guardian or prince or king in the imaginary scenario at hand, though I was always careful to remain within the limits of the stage directions given me and not adlib too much. If, however, it happened that one of the younger or less popular girls began to cry on account of being left out, I would then take it upon myself to shape the collective story, lightly sketching along the corners of its canvas you might say, by drawing the sad girl in question aside and informing her that she was in fact the king's daughter or the prince's younger sister, either prospect of which delighted her since it meant she was a princess of some importance.

As we all aged and changed my appearances at such functions and then the very occasions themselves became rarer and rarer until at last they disappeared entirely, passed on like some treasured outgrown hand-me-down to our younger sisters. But though these events melted away the associations that had accompanied them did not, for to a few of these girls I would remain something on the order of the elder brother they never had, brushing away a tear or offering a shoulder to cry on when another of my sex had torn or wrecked their hearts and sometimes their bodies. "You are," I would say at such times, having drawn them aside, "a woman of some importance."

If pressed to speculate upon identifying a reason as to my strong and early connection to girls, the best explanation I likely might offer would come in the form of an additional anecdote involving another and very different peer group of females. I am speaking here of my grandmother's circle of Bridge Club ladies—all of them widows, all of them cultivated and accomplished, all of them well within a decade of their deaths.

These monthly Bridge gatherings were stately occasions for the venerable ladies involved as they constituted the only activities which drew them from their homes save church and the various mundane weekly errands that sustain an elderly woman in her widowhood. Who can blame them for uniting with each other and making the most of such times—for donning their favorite jewelry and sleek antiquated evening dresses: outfits that surely would have been considered scandalous demimonde attire in the matronly eyes of their more severe churchgoing contemporaries? Indeed, it affords me a curious happiness even now to think of the pleasure they must have taken in slipping on and parading for each other those treasured things they had not worn in years, perhaps decades.

I do not recall any other child ever having been in attendance at these Bridge Club gatherings and I find myself struggling, as much from a wanting vocabulary as a hazy memory, to articulate the exact nature of the relationship that existed between that remarkable circle of women and myself. I do remember, however, very clearly my grandmother's pride as the ritual of their making over me ensued at the outset of each gathering, my smile fixed like one in a photograph as I beamed up at them all.

"What a little gentleman he is!" one would exclaim.

"But look at his eyes!" the faded beauty in their midst declared, clasping her ringed hands together. "He is an angel, a little angel sent from God!"

"I shall arrange a marriage between him and my great niece who is about to start St. Catherine's!" another announced with equal enthusiasm.

"They are both blonde," she continued by way of explanation, her gin glass suddenly empty.

Then they would pass me around among them, smell of tobacco and alcohol and mints on their dry stale breaths as their withered lips kissed me and whispered endearments in my ear, before pressing me to their soft drooping bosoms, until it was time for the night's agenda to commence and I was banished to some unoccupied corner of the hostess's home, often the study of her long dead husband—walls lined with war medals, advanced degrees, deer heads, pipes—where I entertained myself as best I could among his musty effects.

It was my favorite of the group, a sassy little woman named Miss Ruby whose husband had owned the Lucky Strike cigarette factory in the state capitol, who usually came in at the conclusion of the evening to wake me, brushing my cheek or fingering a pale strand of my hair, as I lay sprawled on some sofa, rug, or chair.

"You are our little mascot!" one of them would declare as I stood bleary-eyed in their midst, eager to depart, and they would all hug me yet again, squeezing me tighter than before.

"Promise you'll always be a good boy," Miss Ruby would say, "and won't ever forget us."

"I promise," I would reply. But of course I would go on to break both conditions of that promise all too frequently over the course of my life—sometimes outrageously. Yet setting down these words here should serve as proof enough that I never forgot those splendid grand dames and the impression they made upon me. Indeed, I think of them even now on those infrequent occasions when I have managed to be of genuine assistance to a woman who needed me—when I truly have been good.

It was my grandmother, a vivacious personality and master storyteller, who made it possible for me to appreciate the ladies of her Bridge circle. Otherwise, I might have taken a conventional young boy's jaundiced view of the aged and reckoned them all dull crones. But with grandmother everything, even a morning of widow's errands in town, became its own adventure, deepened by its shared quality between us. And when she recounted to me a selection from her rich collection of tales the past would spring to life in vivid colors, smells, and sensations. Again there would arise that element of sharing as she gauged my reaction to each sentence—to each new twist and turn in the narrative.

"They said she lived beneath the ground," grandmother said, rocking in her chair, eyes shining, hands busy with her knitting, "in the muck where it's cold and wet."

She was telling one of the stories I liked best: an old Tidewater tale concerning Grace Sherwood—"the Witch of Gisburne" who had lived in Princess Anne County.

"And they said she had webbing in her armpits like a fish," she continued, dropping a needle and leaning forward to poke my armpit with a bony forefinger. "The better to slide through the mud. It opened like a lady's fan when she raised her arm—so thin you could almost see through it."

I would giggle then and ask the question I always did. "She wasn't like normal people, was she?"

And grandmother, erect in her chair, maintaining an air of mock-severity while suppressing a smile. "She most certainly was not."

"And her fins helped her swim," I would exclaim with increasing enthusiasm, unwilling to wait for her to tell the next part. "She swam with the Devil in the water, didn't she?"

"That's right. They say she would frolic with the Devil out in the Chesapeake Bay on moonlit nights. The witch and the Devil would swim and dive and play like newlyweds on their honeymoon."

"They were happy together."

"Yes," she would say, fingers slowing in their work as she moved her head so as to peer out into the dark woods beyond the porch. "I suppose they were. Boatmen spied them way out among the whitecaps and hunters glimpsed them in lonely tangled inlets when the tide was going out. They rode on the current, you see; it carried them with it. And the winter that Caucus Bay froze over one old fisherman even saw them dancing on the ice in the predawn—just dancing away like a couple of lusty young lovers."

And on it went, the weaving of the tale proceeding between us in this way while grandmother's hands kept busy at their knitting and I sat or lay on the floor before her, gazing up into her face warmly, adoringly, living my entire life inside the world she had summoned forth from her mind and made real for me with her words.

*

I suppose, then, it was impression made upon me by the remarkable females of my acquaintance—those unique personalities I had the good fortune to keep company with and draw lessons from during my earliest years—that figured most prominently into the Succubus's attraction to and selection of me. It is true she never said as much, but the manner in which she responded to certain things I uttered or did led me to strongly believe that it was so—that owing to my encounters with certain particular females she treasured in me something that was perhaps rare in all but the smallest handful of males. The world is a very curious place and it so happens I have discovered that people may become quite valuable, even obsessively coveted, on account of their singularities—their uniqueness, their eccentricity, and, yes, even their madness. Yet it remains that between the sexes, like thoroughfares between provinces, there are certain common roads travelers are expected to take—that lie within our best interests to frequent. To journey along those more tangled and obscure paths is to do so at one's peril.

So it was during that interval when the Succubus had refrained from visiting me a heavy sense of foreboding nonetheless permeated my waking moments, particularly after midnight when single moments develop the capacity to stretch into vast ponderous labyrinths of feeling and meaning. It was an ominous time, uneventful on its surface but possessed of a calm not unlike that before the proverbial coastal gale. The presence of the Succubus kept away but into its place there crept a shadow or echo of her essence—what might be termed a kind of trace element—which I could sense reconnoitering me, gauging my movements, even my thoughts. Discount this intuition, unsubstantiated as it is, if you like. I hope you will believe me when I profess I am loath to engage in too much fanciful speculation or to arouse additional conjecture concerning my mental constitution, but, after all, this *is* a supernatural tale and thus fantastic elements such as these should not be ignored or discounted.

Despite the general disquiet and feeling of imminent adversity that haunted my daily living during this period, I was not idle and, in fact, used my constant anxiety as a catalyst for becoming proactive in responding to the circumstances in which I found myself. For it was during this time that I took it upon myself to master all I could from the spectral body of recorded evidence—half-science, half-myth—concerning Succubi and, what's more, if possible, learn what I could about my particular entity: who she had been when, like you, she traversed the world of the living.

I am not boasting when I contend that what I conveyed to you in this narrative's introduction is but a small sampling of the vast knowledge I managed to attain on the subject of Succubi. The hours I spent in study were both exhausting and exhaustive. I journeyed to a number of distinguished libraries and scholarly holding sites, corresponded with the best minds in the field, and even proposed a collaborative research project to be administered and published by myself and a distinguished German parapsychologist whose state-of-the-art laboratory facility lay on the outskirts of one of those small decaying cities along the Rhine.

My efforts concerning my own Succubus, however, afforded me almost nothing, though the one shred of information I did uncover—the record of a tombstone bearing her name in the oldest cemetery of Virginia's state capitol—proved crucial enough in that it led to our next meeting: the last occasion in fact that I ever would draw breath as a living creature upon the earth.

It so happens the day I sought out her grave exists now not so much as a day of its own, but a date that stands between other days as a kind of divide. It was after the lunch hour when I reached the cemetery and as I passed through its gates a watery sun bashfully showed itself for the first time through densely layered clouds. Her simple marker was not difficult to find. It stood on a sloping hillside where the cemetery's peripheral plots give way to the dense undergrowth which falls away in the direction of the river. The simple moss-flecked stone bearing her name bore no epigraph nor any dates. It was as if that name—which I must reluctantly refuse to record here—captured and defined all there was to know and understand of her.

I stood there mutely, staring down at the marker, thinking of what it must be like to have departed the world of the living yet still retain one's consciousness—some vague alimentation of feeling and thought. Would one still sense the stifling fumes of the damp earth, its soil darkened and enriched by the nearby ancient river, its lower layers inhabited by the alien fossils of distant epochs? Would you be capable of feeling the funeral garments which cling to your former body? And what of the absolute blackness and the silence which I have heard described as a "sea that overwhelms"? What of the unseen but palpable presence of the scavengers of the earth burrowing through the recently disturbed ground around you, relentless in their hunger? Could it be that the atoms of some of the oldest decomposed bodies find their way to life again in the form of the dark bushy holly and tangled ivy covering the damp invisible terrain as it slopes away toward the endlessly-flowing river?

I thought too of the Succubus as a mortal woman drawing breath and wondered what it might have been like to know her as such. It was then the sad thought struck me that so many things in our lives seem to happen out of alignment and sequence, as if all the pages of some voluminous picture book are torn out by invisible hands and thrown into the wind to flutter and land where they will. We had missed each other in time, she and I—missed the living of each other's lives—yet something had brought us together nonetheless. Suddenly I felt very tired, given to a burdened leaden sensation unlike any I ever had experienced. I allowed my body to sink to the ground and seated myself with my back against the stone surety of her gravestone. The cool of its smooth surface penetrated my shirt, causing the skin along my spine to tingle. The sky had grown overcast, its clouds having darkened and drifted lower, paralleling the course of the river in their slow procession eastward. The air was still; not a single note of birdsong or rustle of foliage disturbed it. Slowly my head came forward as though descending into— affording a long slow single nod of agreement to—slumber.

That was how she found me in the twilight of that day: sleeping on the grass at the southern boundary of the city's oldest cemetery. I grew aware of her in my slumber as she drew near, the familiarity of her presence filling my mind in such a way as to make it seem as though we had never been parted all those weeks and that, in truth, my soul had lived side by side with hers throughout that interval like shoots sprung in tandem from the same rare root.

"I have missed you," I heard my voice say in my mind.

And she replied in kind in a soft voice that sounded musical as if singing to itself quietly.

"Sing me a song," I said.

"What kind of song?"

"It doesn't matter. No, wait, make it a sad one."

And she sang to me then a song I did not know, but one so tragic and beautiful as to deepen the gathering darkness that lay beyond my sleep, as if hastening that defining day's journey into night.

"That was wonderful," I murmured when the song was over. "Could you sing another?"

"Of course," the answer a song in itself. "I have forever. I'll sing to you here as long as you like."

Her voice became music once more and as it did I felt my heart sinking into my shoes as my body lay there listening among the old cemetery's assortment of stone angels, little marble lamps, and the occasional granite cross. It seemed that only then did I realize how much I wanted her. It was as if I was glimpsing too late the true nature of things cast against that canvas which showed a tale of the degree to which I cared.

I knew it was weak of me to linger on that way, listening, but the line between thought and action had somehow become severed. It was like being under the fascination of a serpent. I thought to get up, to stir my prone body, but it proved an idle thought only. And in the instant when she stopped singing suddenly I knew that any course of action on my part was too late.

She gave me a look as though she might kill me, and then she did, the essence of my life burning and melting away within the depths of her eyes. I could not see them, mark you—could not see her—but I felt, as much as I ever have felt anything, their absorbing look. Such was the way in which she drew the life out of my being. Life and breath flowed out of me together.

*

Verily what are the things that lie in and behind the taking of a life?

Back during my time as a young runner who seldom lost races I often would look for things to amuse me as the athletic season wore on and my workout routines dwindled into some stale combination of strides and twenty minute runs. One afternoon prior to another such mundane practice I was delighted to find in a dark corner of the school's equipment room an archaic javelin possessed of a rusty iron head and a smooth wooden shaft lined with small jagged cracks. Toting it out to the old football practice field beyond the tennis courts, I amused myself hurling it again and again until my coach yelled at me to fall in with the other runners for stretching.

The casting of the javelin became a daily ritual for me and he could not see the point of it, my coach, on account of the fact that the throwing of javelins did not constitute a sanctioned competitive event.

He viewed my hurling of that antiquated object as a waste of time, though he did afford me the grudging remark, "If javelin were a high school event in this state you'd win it easy."

"I don't care about that, Coach," I had replied with a smile. "I just like doing it."

He had shaken his head as he turned and walked away, but he stopped and looked back at me after a few paces. "You know, son," he said, "if you did really care about winning, if put your heart and soul into practice the way you do tossing that stupid old stick, you'd be one holy terror of a runner."

But the nature of an event—the nature of any action—has always held a greater degree of fascination and satisfaction for me than its prospect of competitive success. Earlier in my life, when I was a boy growing up on a farm, my father had ordered me to use something other than a gun whenever possible to dispatch the predatory nocturnal varmints that plagued our livestock so as to ration his stock of bullets. My implement of choice for this chore became an old pitchfork which had journeyed northward to Virginia with my grandfather from the Smoky Mountains. I liked not only that its many prongs, five all told, increased one's chances of connecting with its target, but also that, if thrust with enough force, it would pass all the way through the animal's body and embed itself in the ground or the old soft wood of the barn floor or whatever happened to lie behind which might give a little. Thus the pierced creature would find itself pinned, squirming, trapped, crucified, until breath and life departed it.

Despite being only a boy I became very good at wielding that pitchfork—expert, you might say. Never have I encountered anyone who handled one so well. It came to fascinate me too how when I withdrew the pitchfork from a pierced animal the prongs would leave five neat little red points where they had penetrated the hide. These small circular crimson blots always created in my mind the fantastic impression that the creature's life might have been extinguished—sucked out, as it were—not by the pitchfork, but rather by the penetrating fingertips of God himself. And, indeed, sometimes I did let go the implement's antiquated chestnut shaft in favor of reaching out my little fingers to touch gently those red holes which welled but slowly or brush ever so slightly the creature's fur so as to feel the fading of its last warmth.

"We are the children of death," said prophet, "and it is death that rescues us from the deceptions of life."

Much later, as a young man living on a farm of my own, at the end of a chore involving a pitchfork—the same one, in fact, for it had been passed on to me—I sometimes would carry that remarkable family heirloom out into the pasture and cast it a few times just for the sheer joy of it, admiring its arc against the sun as it attained and then curved rainbow-like beyond its zenith. Beginning with a slow trot, knees thrusting high, I would hold back, waiting to achieve the proper speed and rhythm, before planting my forefoot and allowing the smooth rotation of the shoulders, the flow of my long muscular arms, to roll forward.

I have always imagined I must have appeared a little ridiculous heaving that old pitchfork clad in my shirtless overalls or torn up farm jeans, but I can tell you that people who witnessed me doing so never laughed. If anything their manner was politely noncommittal though on at least a couple of occasions the onlooker offered a bland compliment, perhaps in a fruitless effort to mask the troubled expression that had formed behind the eyes. And I have to say that though I took great pleasure in the activity, I wasn't playing around when I did it. I mean, I really threw it out there.

*

Queer and inexplicable as the business of my death may seem, I did not hold any of it against the Succubus. I do not regret it, though I would not relish the prospect of going through the experience again. The truth of the matter is that I welcomed my death, realizing even then that its surface misfortune was, in reality, my good fortune. Whatever lingering shortcomings to which my faculties may have been subject at that time, they proved acute enough at least to appreciate that to experience love deeply and romantically in death or in life, regardless of any and all circumstances, is a precious gift and a very rare thing indeed. Its fundamental essence is a sublime and indescribable joy which ultimately makes small or renders moot the nature of a living existence or its lack. She had left it for me to choose and I had.

And when at last I was dead I finally was able to see her. I had felt her, of course—each minute aspect of her form—many times: every curve and contour memorized in the sweet-scented darkness of joy. And I knew from this profound touching, as a blind man might, that she was beautiful—something of a goddess really, with her perfect cheeks and lips, her supple neck and arms, her heavy breasts, her silken skin and hair. But it was only when I was dead, after she had killed me, that I finally was able to see her truly: a radiant being of loveliness, staggering features surpassed by graceful manner—those slow, purposeful motions. She had, in particular, a way of moving her hips and a charming manner of tilting her head which touch alone failed to convey in fullness. When I looked at her face it was impossible for me to remember the faces of other people. Surely, I thought, she was the flower and consummation of her kind, whatever the nature of any others.

What more is there left to tell? Only this. Joining our ghostly hands we drifted east along the serpentine course of that river named for an inept and long-dead king, and then up into the streets of the state capitol—the city, in fact, where, at different times, both of us had entered the world of the living. It was a place I seldom visited in my adulthood, but I discovered its sloping streets, old magnolias, and rocky river were surroundings of happy familiarity for her. Appropriately enough, it is a city where very few things begin but many things end, yet each of us had begun there in our own separate fashions.

Often we watch the people passing down Grace Street or moving along over the crest of Shockoe Hill, meandering to the eye yet all pregnant with some manner of purpose—the eternal life of each of them not so very distant from that instant in which they are glimpsed by us. But my favorite occasions are when we depart the city gliding west, flying just above the surface of the river. Startled geese flap up from their sandbars and shadowlike bass dart beneath rocks at our approach, but not a single human eye ever fixes its sight upon us. When the sun is out during such excursions I wait for the light and time of day to become exactly right, slanting from the west, and when it does I peer down at the bright smooth surface passing beneath us and watch her moving face on the water.

When I was alive people often would remark how deeply I loved rivers and animals and other manifestations of nature. And also how these entities seemed to love me: the cats that sought out my lap, the dogs slumbering curled atop my feet, the butterflies or honeybees that flitted about my head, occasionally lighting upon a finger or shoulder—even the way in which the waters of the river bore me along, buoying me up, or how its breezes played about my brow as if caressing it. But I have to admit that though I was grateful for the love of these things, they were not things I had always loved. For isn't it so that even the best of us tend to take the best of things for granted? Rather the things I make mention of were things that over time I had learned to appreciate—had learned to love. Things I had learned to love, and chief among them the Succubus: who came for me and found me—who entered my life and claimed it—who killed me and made me hers forever.

Gold Thong
(fiction)

"I only put it on when I'm desperate to get out of a big slump ... All of them [Derek Jeter, Bernie Williams, Johnny Damon, Robin Ventura, Robinson Cano] wore it and got hits ... The thong works every time."

—Jason Giambi, #25, formerly of the New York Yankees

My opinion of Shay Garehart changed after he loaned me the Gold Thong. But I'm getting ahead of myself. That's what professors tend to do, mind you: lurching in our generally uncoordinated pompous geeky manner toward our answers and conclusions, usually without the necessary degrees of perspective and lived experience to make them accurate or even relevant.

Not Shay Garehart. Shay the studly writer and campus super scholar—hated and envied by many, some of whom find themselves pining for him nonetheless. I'm not gay, at least not consciously, but I must admit I once counted myself among that latter group, the members of which vehemently curse his name even as many of them find themselves drawn on by a reluctant longing.

As you might imagine, Shay doesn't look or sound like an academic at all, but he negotiates the ponderous mire of a college campus better than any pencil-necked, egg-head lectern-boy or sloppy neurotic feminist I ever saw. He runs rings around us all even as we mumble through our meetings and classes while seeking simultaneously to embrace and problematize the latest discursive fashions on the research front in the hopes of getting ahead, or at least pulling even, in our various fields of inquiry.

Not Shay. Perhaps I felt an initial bond with him on account of flattering myself there might be a little of his manner—a very, very meager portion of his magnetic eccentricity—lurking somewhere inside me. I recall last year how the campus sororities had selected us both as judges for Hopwood College's Miss HC Contest. The third judge, a befuddled elderly dean who did not seem entirely certain why he was there, and myself had waited as the contest's start time came and went, and still no Shay. The mindless pop music blared on from the massive speaker cabinets and the sorority presidents nervously conversed onstage in their evening dresses while the audience grew antsy.

At last he arrived, sauntering down the auditorium aisle with a smile and an easy swagger. Rather than the irritated boos I half-expected to shower him, I was surprised to witness his greeting articulated by a booming chorus of cheers from the undergraduate masses.

He waved at the sorority throngs as he came on toward the judges' table, voice ringing with goodwill: "Hello girls! Hello!"

A particularly buxom lass in the front row squealed excitedly and jumped up and down, gravity accentuating her charms, while holding a large sign over her head which read "I ♥ Gare ♥!"

He slapped me on the back, a little too hard I thought, and sat down next to me, casting a subtle nod and knowing wink in my direction.

"Let's get this meat market going!" he hollered at the stage and the audience applauded again.

The elderly dean scowled, but it didn't matter; Shay had gotten tenure the year before.

A swanky, slightly tipsy MC proceeded to approach us one by one with the request that we rise and introduce ourselves to the clamoring young hordes.

The elderly dean went first, muttering something lengthy and incoherent, and when the mic proceeded to come before me I stuttered slightly but received a generous measure of applause, which caused me to blush despite the overwhelming ridiculousness of setting and circumstance.

Then it was Shay's turn.

"Shay Garehart, writer," he said, leaning toward the MC's offered mic, and the ovation thundered.

Then he grabbed the mic from its complacent faraway-eyed owner. "Good people," he said, the warmth of his slight southern accent filling the auditorium, "I want you to know I got the automatic dial on my cell set to 911, 'cause tonight I'm fully expecting to witness a *talent overdose!*"

Wild cheers ensued as he tossed the mic to the MC and rolled his hips in a little victory dance, which concluded with a smooth foot-slide to the left. Laughter, applause, and high-pitched squeals of delight made up his garland of approval as he resumed his seat.

To say Shay Garehart possessed a strong rapport with the students was a gross understatement, but oh how he grated upon the tender frazzled nerves of his colleagues. Likely he knew too well the extent to which he inhabited our heads: the unspoken measuring stick of academic success. How we hated his good looks and the apparent ease with which he had published the five books before the age of thirty-five. How we despised his strong youthful body and relaxed demeanor, and the fact that visiting writers and scholars had read his work and knew who he was, seeking him out at receptions while ignoring the rest of us. How we hated the awards he received and his natural inborn freedom and creativity—his damn near sorcerous ability to conceive and then subsequently implement new and sometimes lucrative ideas. But more than any of this, we hated the fact that he seemed to evince limited or only playfully half-serious interest in the rest of us—in *our* concerns.

"He never comes to our parties," someone inevitably would say.

"He's stuck up," another would add.

"Maybe he's just got a life," I sometimes would offer. "Look at everything he does. *How* does he do it?"

Indeed, *how* Shay spent his time had become a popular topic of interest and wide-ranging speculation among my own particular circle of campus friends. There were stories of secret trips to beaches and other countries, of affairs with students and faculty wives, of half-crazed pedagogy, of terrible things he had said to and about colleagues. But then there were the equally compelling and numerous tales that balanced and discredited these rumors: the books, the sky-high teaching evaluations, the student publications, the financial loans and ghost writing he performed for hard-pressed colleagues.

Ever did the enigma of Shay Garehart appear to expand and deepen as he strode carelessly across campus, a book or two beneath his arm, a twinkle in his eye, and a ready smile for life, the universe, and everything.

*

It was during the recess following the talent component of the Miss HC Contest that I tentatively hazarded to feel Shay out on the matter of his hazy campus identity. He eyed me with amusement as he professed that such topics were of little moment to him since they hadn't much to do with life's primary concerns.

"Don't get me wrong," he explained. "I think academics are OK people and all, but, come on, they're *academics*. Their lives are boring. Listen to what they talk about off campus: stupid school shit mostly, or how little Rudy crapped her pants but got over her cold. Fuck that, man! That's not how I'm spending my time off the clock!"

Just then a stunning slinky blonde appeared behind him and, bending over his shoulder, whispered in his ear, softball-shaped breasts pressed against his back. I could have sworn I saw tongue as she pulled away. Shay laughed loudly and swiveled in his chair to playfully make cat claws at her as she retreated smiling and melted into the audience.

"Not a student, I gather," I commented dryly, having reluctantly withdrawn my eyes from the back of her departing form.

"No," said Shay with a chuckle. "I got her at church."

"Church?"

"Sure. Think about it, my man. We live in a backward southern city with a large fundamentalist university on the opposite side of town. Odds are most of the attractive chicks are going to be down with J.C. You got to know the kind of game you're playing if you're going to score big."

"So you go to churches to pick up women?"

"Why not?" he shrugged. "Sunday morning's a slow time of day anyhow; beats nursing a hangover. The formula is to tell the Sunday school class or whatever that you're on the fence about coming to J.C. but still have your doubts. Apparently it's some kind of glory to God or something for them to win over new followers. They basically trample each other trying to convince you to join their particular herd. I can tell you, man, it ain't hard at all to pick and choose the phone numbers."

Shay grinned. "Then it's on me, so to speak," he said, "to do the converting: from J.C. to Shay-Gay, that is!"

I laughed uneasily, but even as I did Shay suddenly seemed to turn serious. "You know, every night I fall asleep thinking my life can't get any better …."

He paused, as if for effect, his expression one of baffled marvelment, before adding, "but then it does. It's like I can't help it, man. It must be magic or something."

Oh, how we hated Shay Garehart! How his unconscious grandeur cut us wide and deep!

But this opening has run a little long and, as I say, all of that changed with the Gold Thong, which brings me, at last, to my story proper.

*

I might have departed the Miss HC Contest feeling every bit as bitter, envious, and fascinated toward Shay Garehart as many of my campus friends if, having delivered the contest trophy to a bareback tri-delt and sung her praises over the PA system, he had not pulled me aside confidentially as the auditorium emptied.

"Look," he said when we were alone, the slight drawl in his voice earnest, "this ain't any of my business, but I hear you been told you got to get going with your pubs."

Shay's comment took me off guard and I stammered. "Is that common knowledge?"

"I don't much give a damn what passes for knowledge around this place," Shay said, irritably making a dismissive gesture, "but if you need any help, feel free to call on me. I've been known to scribble a line or two."

Flustered, I thanked him awkwardly as he turned to go.

"Wait," I said. "A question. Writer's block. What do you know about writer's block?"

Shay faced me again, his expression more serious than before and tinged with a slight degree of reproach, as if I had just uttered something offensive and forbidden. "It's the writer's worst bane," he said. "You got all your info ready but the engine won't fire. Many is the time I've tucked tail and turned from the computer screen to the bourbon bottle in despair at not being able to find those precious words."

"Is there a solution for it?" I asked. "A trick or something you know about?"

Shay considered this for a moment with downcast eyes, hand upon his chin, before his gaze rose to meet mine, expression grave. "The Gold Thong," he said at last.

"The Gold *Thong?*" I repeated.

"It's the last line of defense with me and my writer friends," he elaborated. "First, there's the cop mustache. You're not allowed to shave until the words start coming the way they should. It's predicated on pressure, you see. So long as you don't write, the hair above your mouth grows. Eventually you wind up with a stupid fucking mustache that makes you look like a highway cop, especially when you wear sunglasses. It's worked before—for me and others."

"But if that doesn't do it," Shay continued, "or if you're in a rush, then it's time to break out the Gold Thong."

Again my face told a speechless tale of incredulity.

"I know it sounds ridiculous," Shay said quickly, "but it's the bonafide secret weapon—the doomsday motherload—when it comes to writer's block. Now, in point of fact, no one knows where the Gold Thong came from, but it's saved me and my whole circle of writing buddies many a time."

"How does it work?" I asked, helplessly enthralled despite the insanity of what I was hearing.

"You just wear it," Shay said with a shrug. "Wear it and plant your ass in front of the computer until the writing comes."

I must have looked uncertain for he continued. "Look," he said, "I know you read fiction, even though it's not your field. Wil Hickson's book *Grab You a Handful?* Gold Thong. John Towne's novel *Jane Anor, Space Nurse?* Gold Thong. There's even this woman scribbler—a rough old d--- down in Texas who does children's books. Word was she hit the wall when it came time to finish up the last volume of a trilogy about an androgynous cat that does homework for its little-girl-owner by working math problems on this calculator that has those super-sized number pads for old people. Now from what I hear, that old gal wasn't too keen on men—to put it mildly. But when the going got tough and the writing deadline loomed, guess what she had on under them men's jeans?"

"A gold thong?" I answered tentatively.

"You bet your ass she did," Shay said with conviction. "*The* Gold Thong, that is."

"There's only one, you see," he elaborated.

"I see," I muttered weakly, before rallying as best I could. "Look, it's true. I've got to publish some articles or I'm likely done for at this place, but I haven't written hardly anything since graduate school—at least nothing of any value. I just can't seem to get it going at the keyboard. Could you let me try this thing out?"

"There's no try to it!" snapped Shay. "All of us—Hickson, Towne, Van Holmes, that crusty old d--- down in Waco, yours truly—all of us wore it and beat the block to glory. The Gold Thong works every time. But it only works if you're truly hard-up and desperate—I mean really balls to the wall—and from what I'm hearing, you've definitely got that going for you."

"One more thing," he added, "before you commit for sure. The Gold Thong's been worn a lot. It's as dirty a garment as you'll ever see. It's got stuff on it—stains—who knows what all? And it *smells*. I mean it smells *bad*—just godawful. But here's the thing: you can't wash it. It can *never* be washed. In fact, you'll have to fork over to me a security deposit, which I'll be obliged to keep if the Gold Thong is washed or damaged in any way."

"We'll make it a modest amount," he said, placing a hand on my shoulder and softening his voice. "Us teachers don't make a hell of a lot, do we? But believe me buddy, it's better to risk losing a few bucks than have a mob of angry writers track you down to take it out of your ass if something happens to the Gold Thong."

"Alright," I said, troubled and ashamed by my own pliability, yet desperate and helplessly compelled beyond reason. "I promise not to wash it and we get paid at the end of the week."

"Alright," echoed Shay, shaking my hand as if we had just successfully negotiated some momentous life decision—and perhaps we had. "I know you'll be good for the security deposit so I'll have the Gold Thong mailed here priority right away. I'll bill you the postage, of course."

"Mailed?" I asked.

"Sure nuff," said Shay. "It's in the UK right now. Wales. A buddy of mine just used it to finish his creative writing dissertation. He'll be loath to part with it, I can tell you. But I've got news for that limey, which you'd just as soon hear now too. The Gold Thong heeds no master."

"Heeds no master and grants no quarter," he said, smiling, eyebrows raised, before shaking his head. "Wales, England. The Gold Thong does get around, don't it?"

He winked at me again and, turning, sauntered up the aisle toward the exit, whistling "Dixie."

*

The transaction went well enough, I guess. Payday came and I reluctantly handed over the five hundred dollars Shay demanded. It was a far steeper security deposit than I had expected and more or less guaranteed I would be behind on my rent again. A shrug and an easy smile accompanied by a scattering of words of encouragement constituted Shay's brief rejoinder to my lament before he abandoned me to my doubts. Was all this really necessary? Had my writer's block come to this?

Early the next week I arrived home from class to find a small, slightly dented cardboard box stamped with British postage sitting by my doorstep. Pulse quickening, I bent to collect the parcel and remarked its lightness, which in turn made me shake my head in bafflement at why I might have expected it to be heavy. Inside the house I placed the box on my work desk in the back room, a little ill-insulated add-on meant to serve as a guest bedroom. Taking up the letter opener, I began cutting the tape along one of the edges. But then something made me pause. Placing the letter opener on the desk, I stepped back to consider the box: its British postage—the profile of some snotty nobleman—and my own address, wrought with the broad confident strokes of an overseas Sharpie.

What was it I was doing? I blinked, aware suddenly that something like hysteria had crept upward from my bowels to tug subtly yet insistently at the corners of my mind. But then, as if banished by my awareness of it, the panic subsided and I laughed suddenly, my voice loud and harsh amid the stillness of the little room.

"We'll just see about this," I said resolutely, and, seizing my laptop, headed for the sofa, determined to get an article going without any measure of Shay Garehart's support, including his ridiculous imported undergarment.

*

Hours elapsed. Dusk darkened the windows until only the cold pale glow of the empty screen illuminated the room, the blinking cursor mocking me in time. Blip, blip, blip, blip. On it went indefinitely, as it had so often of late, measuring out the tale of my futility like an hour glass possessed of inexhaustible sands. The muscles in my back ached from the uninterrupted hunched position I had assumed hours ago before the despairing screen, not unlike an unwilling attitude of prayer. The burden of my head waxed immense atop my tired shoulders, grown rounded and weak like an old woman's, yet with nothing to show for their fruitless toil and sacrifice. I felt tired and old. Tired and old and *empty*.

As my eyelids drooped a vision of Shay's youthful smiling face loomed, bobbing before the empty screen, the magnificent blonde Christian woman behind him, biting her lip suggestively and tracing the contour of his ear with a forefinger.

His drawl echoed in my mind. "Many is the time," it said, "I've tucked tail and turned from the computer screen to the bourbon bottle in despair at not being able to find those precious words."

With a groan I closed the laptop and staggered to my feet, palms pressed against my eyes. Stumbling blindly into the kitchen, I jerked open the cabinet next to the refrigerator, the hollow sound of heavy glass clinking as my hands rummaged for the right bottle.

I spied the desired decanter, could just make it out, resting undisturbed near the back, its small greeting card secured by a red band about the neck and flapping slightly as I drew the bottle forward. On the label was a black and white illustration of a cavalryman charging, saber drawn, beneath which a caption proclaimed "Especially for the South." This was the unopened fifth of Rebel Yell Shay had presented to me three years ago when I'd moved to Lynchburg.

"Just shut up and drink," prescribed the familiar scrawl inside the little card, "but don't be afraid to holler."

Ripping open the bottle, I cursed Shay's name by way of a toast and took a heavy swig. Never having been a bourbon drinker—fruity rums and vodkas are my typical fare—I immediately wanted to gag at the brown liquid's remorseless overpowering odor and the terrible burning it inflicted upon my nose and throat.

But then, as I brought the bottle down, I could hear Shay's voice again, talking down to me, like a kid brother. "Hey, it's OK," it said. "It's not everyman can drink straight bourbon. Let me just run out and get you a wine cooler or something."

Cursing, I again brought the bourbon to my lips and guzzled. Eyes beginning to tear, I set the bottle down and stumbled to the sink, flipping on the faucet. As I eagerly leaned forward, however, my gut convulsed unannounced and instead of imbibing cool water, I found my parched mouth spewing forth the contents of my stomach. Desperately I gripped the kitchen counter, holding on for life, while the torrent of meals past poured forth, my throaty ejaculations echoing hollowly off the kitchen linoleum as my abdominal muscles writhed in a tangle like a bed of serpents.

At last the eruptions subsided and, emptied and breathing hard, I leaned forward again to partake of the faucet. How cool and comforting was the water as it passed between my lips and embarked upon its journey down my ravaged esophagus.

Then, suddenly, again, the convulsed unexpected agony of the stomach's contents desperately seeking liberation and I violently gagged anew, dry heaved, before collapsing to my knees before the sink, choked with frustration.

"Damn you, Shay Garehart!" I cried, sputtering and shaking my fist at the ceiling, tears rolling down my cheeks, insides all aflame. "Damn you!"

*

I arose late the following morning and passed the day in the company of student papers and multiple pots of coffee. When at last night returned and I felt once more myself, I poured a tall glass of water and headed back to my study.

Upon the desk it sat still, the package from Wales, patiently waiting. With a resigned shrug of inevitability I took up the letter opener, cut away the remaining tape, and tentatively proceeded to raise the top of the box. However instead of the shining gold fabric I had expected to encounter, I was greeted by a dense bed of packing peanuts atop which rested an anonymous note on a small slip of vanilla paper.

"Get ready to write, mate," it read, "and kiss those days of being a word wanker goodbye. God bless the Gold Thong and God bless Shay Garehart!"

Cursing under my breath, I crumpled up the note and tossed it into the waste basket. Then, with sudden resolve, I took up the box in both hands and, flipping it over, shook the contents onto the desk. A larger object tumbled out amid the blizzard of packing material, landing with a light thump. And there it was amid the scattered packing peanuts: a soiled crumpled lamé thong of gold, tastelessly adorned with black tiger stripes and set off by a flame-colored waistband. A heavy stale musky odor arose from it which turned my still-vulnerable stomach and I placed a hand over my mouth and nose as I backed away.

From a safe distance just inside the doorway I considered the garment anew and shook my head, incredulous at the nature of the circumstances surrounding me. My career had come to *this?* To hang in the balance of a *thong?*

"*The Gold Thong!*" Shay's voice thundered suddenly in my head and I started in spite of myself, glancing about wildly, half-expecting him to step forward from a dark corner.

*

For two days I could hardly bear to glance at it, much less consider putting it on. Yet its presence pervaded and dominated the house and my thoughts nevertheless. At odd moments when I was supposed to be folding laundry or making the grocery list I would find myself standing motionless in the doorway of the study contemplating the thong where it rested in a wrinkled mass amid the uncollected litter of packing peanuts.

Then, on the second night, I dreamed of it—a long exhausting affair of flight in which the thong flew after me, literally, for it had taken on the aspect of some predatory reptilian bird of ages past. On went the pursuit, down labyrinthine networks of dark alleyways and across vast paper recycling depots consisting of great hills and valleys of old student essays. Up I would climb, my hands sinking into a hillside of paper and ink, and at the top achieve neither pause nor rest, for the thong threateningly fluttered ever about me. Instead I would hurry down the opposite slope, rolling and sliding, falling, face and naked arms stained with the ink of a million printers.

The chase unfolded endlessly in the manner time may be drawn out or otherwise hindered in the netherworld of slumber, thus forming a seemingly eternal landscape of fear upon which we journey forever and from which there may be no escape save in waking. But then, as I climbed and clawed my way up yet another mountain of undergraduate detritus, hands riddled with paper cuts, the thong continuously diving and wheeling above me, a gold-colored chopper descended from the heavens and drew nigh, causing student documents to fly up into the air all around me, loose pages slapping me about the face and lodging in the folds of my clothes. A helmeted pilot in shades waved and gave me the thumbs up. It was Shay.

"Quit running from the thong!" he hollered, his voice barely audible amid the noise of the engine and whirring blades. He said something else I couldn't make out before nodding and smiling reassuringly.

"You're ruining my life!" I screamed, impotently hurling a handful of papers in the direction of the chopper, two of which immediately flew back and affixed themselves flat against my face, temporarily blinding me.

I peeled off the pages to discover the gorgeous blonde Christian woman had somehow joined Shay in the cockpit, straddling him and showering him with kisses, clad only in a red string bikini.

"Gotta go, champ!" Shay hollered, smiling and giving the thumbs up again.

Then the chopper departed, weaving a little lopsidedly, papers fluttering from the hilltops beneath its irregular path of flight.

*

Next morning, dark eyed and somber, I resolved to email the writers Shay had mentioned by name as having used the thong with favorable results and request information as to how exactly it worked—if in fact it did. It was not long before two of them responded, though the answers were not particularly helpful. Each sung the thong's praises, proclaiming it seemed to function via some untraceable mystery, yet their subsequent speculations as to the nature of its underpinnings struck out along divergent strands of analysis.

"It's because you're not worrying about your hands or the keyboard," Wil Hickson's message hypothesized. "You're only worried about the uncomfortable feeling you're receiving down below."

John Towne entertained a different theory. "It keeps one side of my brain occupied when I'm writing longhand on my legal pad," he explained, "thus keeping the other side slightly off-center and out of balance, which is where it's supposed to be for artists—or at least that's what my shrink says."

I was in the midst of reading the conclusion of Towne's message when the phone rang. It was Freida Bond, a friend and confidant from Hopwood, always in the know and much given to relating the sad minor circumstances that pass for campus intrigue among our humble circle of friends.

"I heard you got that awful thing from Shay," she said, her voice soft with concern, "and wanted to let you know that asshole's likely just playing an elaborate joke on you."

I was surprised to experience relief rather than outrage.

"You know Ted Fabrice?" she inquired. "That short guy over in Econ? Well, his wife's best friend took a ballet class at Virginia Tech with our wonderful Mr. Gay-hart. Apparently that's another way he picks up women, since he's almost always the only guy enrolled. But that's another story. Anyway, she says he found that thing one night on the floor of the men's locker room when he was changing for class. Says he had it on over his tights when he came out and was dancing all around, proclaiming he would let everyone touch it for a quarter. Then he took it off and was waving it over his head like a lasso or something."

I thanked Freida and got off the line as quickly as I could, careful not to reveal anything she might add to her store of tales and pass on to the next listener.

"Well that's that," I thought to myself with a deep breath.

Or was it? Upon further review I found myself wavering. On one side stood the testimonials of two published writers. True, they were friends of Shay's. But what was in it for them to perpetuate the hoax? Also, I doubted seriously I occupied enough space in Shay's mind, if any at all, for him to concoct such an elaborate scheme at my expense. Doubtless he had, as he was often fond of boasting, "Bigger chitlins to fry." Though it had been related by a friend, the account of an idle campus gossip suddenly seemed rather flimsy in light of the alternative evidence from legitimate writers.

But there was only one way to find out and my ensuing long sigh of resignation was heavy enough to have contained oceans of apprehension and house all the despair of the world.

*

Before me I held the Gold Thong at arm's length, employing only the very tips, the very nails, of my thumbs and forefingers, touching it as little as possible. Though its odor had subsided somewhat, its funky scent remained much in evidence and the garment itself hung stretched and filthy, hazy lines of grime lining its seams and the narrow inner strip of its rear enclosure stained with the skid marks of untold literary bottoms.

From it I glanced down to the open laptop on the sofa, its white screen blank, the cursor blinking, waiting with indefatigable patience. Letting go an exhalation, I brought the thong down before me and stepped into it slowly, one leg at a time. So far so good. Then a deep intake of air and I held my breath as I slowly pulled it up around my hips. This limited maneuver accomplished, I exhaled again and glanced down to consider the thing which now formed an aspect of myself. I was embarrassed to note that the silky feel of the lamé afforded a pronounced sensation of sensual comfort, while the elasticity in the waistband allowed the upper part of the thong to hug my midsection thoroughly enough. However the lower reaches, front and back, were loose—a good thing, I thought, in the back, where the narrow rear strip hung slightly below my bottom. On the other hand, the bagginess in the crotch made me feel a little, well, inadequate.

"Don't feel bad," I could hear Shay's voice remarking. "Look who broke it in good."

Shaking my head to dismiss the thought, I inhaled deeply yet again. Slowly, wincing slightly in apprehension, I lowered myself to the sofa and gently lifted the laptop onto that which I hoped would constitute the source of my salvation.

*

I sat there quietly, the shadows of the room lengthening, telling their story of time—of another day passed—the laptop's cursor verifying the tale in its own measured language. Blip, blip, blip, blip. Expectantly I waited, the windows growing dimmer, the light of the world abandoning my house to the pale glow of a small computer and all my future hopes.

Blip, blip, blip, blip. On and on it went and still nothing. I waited and waited, until after a time I became aware of a tightness forming inside my chest—a rising bubble of pressure which I knew intuitively must be home to my long-stowed and ill-dealt-with wrath—the essence of all my frustrations. Again, an image of Shay Garehart. Of his loud laughter as he considered my useless near-naked form on the sofa, clad in the thong and hunched before an empty computer screen. And, of course, at his side, the magnificent blonde Christian woman in her red string bikini, divine body coiled about him, pointing and laughing in complement.

Suddenly the bubble in my chest burst and out poured all my misbegotten hatred into a keyboard-pounding, expletive-laden email to Shay—an account of all my trials and agonies at his hands, concluding with the wild accusation that he was in fact a demon. No! The very devil himself!

"Damn you, Shay Garehart," I muttered under my breath as a final click dispatched the message.

To my surprise it was answered almost immediately. "Don't get your shorts in a bunch over this," Shay's message read. "Give it time. And so what if it doesn't work? This whole academic thing's a swindle anyway: a house of straw or, perhaps more properly, a shanty of flimsy old solar-powered pocket calculators."

"We all got our ideas," it went on, "of how things are supposed to play out in this life. Me? Just give me a fast yacht with its own margarita machine and a nickel-plated Zippo to light my hair on fire. Burn and fly, baby! That's what I say. Maximum overdrive—'til the bottle and tank run empty!"

I deleted the message with yet another curse and, flinging the laptop to the side, began to rise. Then Shay's voice was in my head, louder than it had ever been, hard and irritable at having been summoned from someplace infinitely more interesting and pleasurable.

"Just wear it!" it boomed with authority. "Wear it and plant your ass in front of the computer until the writing comes."

Suddenly the Gold Thong seemed possessed of an immense weight, an impossible heaviness, as if crafted of a substance possessing a density vastly greater than iron. From the half-risen position in which I had paused to heed Shay's words, I began to sink slowly back toward the sofa, midsection guided by a force resembling a pulley or, perhaps more properly, an invisible tractor beam. And as I sunk, the nature of the Gold Thong altered. No longer did it hang baggy and loose but suddenly seemed possessed of an incredible gripping elasticity which it now employed to constrict itself about my thighs and groin. I gasped as my legs went numb and found myself dropping the short remainder of space toward the sofa's cushions. The distance couldn't have been more than a few inches but the fall, as though unfolding in dream, seemed to exact an eternity.

When at last my bottom struck the sofa the concomitant sensations of weight, elasticity, and timelessness vanished suddenly. Woozy and rubbery, I felt as though my body had just been released by an incredible power—something beyond the world—a force that if it were a hand might deign to crush reality itself in the palm of its terrible grasp. There I lay, helpless, breathing hard, uncertain of what had transpired—unable even to think, to order my thoughts. My eyes blinked rapidly, focusing unsteadily on the computer screen—on the cursor that blinked continuously upon its white field of nothingness. Blip, blip, blip, blip.

Then it came. Unannounced. Silent lightning from nowhere. The first sentence.

Index

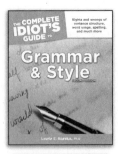

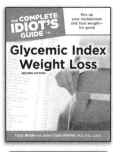

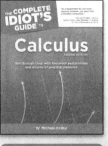

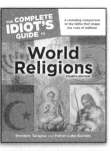

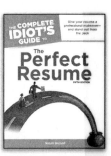